The
Death
Lobby

Books by Kenneth R. Timmerman

The Wren Hunt
Fanning the Flames
Gorbachev's Technology Wars
The Death Lobby

Kenneth R. Timmerman

THE
DEATH
LOBBY

How the West
Armed Iraq

Fourth Estate
London

For Jack Belden
(1910–1989)

Contents

Preface

With great fanfare, President George Bush declared victory over Iraq on February 27, 1991. By all appearances, Operation Desert Storm was an overwhelming success. Saddam Hussein had been forced out of Kuwait, his armies were in a rout, and his dictatorship seemed doomed. America and its allies had once again shown that it was possible to fight a just war and win.

But the fight against Saddam Hussein had little to do with the liberation of Kuwait, no matter how much President Bush and his advisors tried to focus publicly on that goal. It wasn't about jobs, as Secretary of State James Baker once argued, or even about oil. Simply put, the United States went to war to smash the death machine that this country and its Western allies had helped Saddam assemble in the first place. The United States and its allies had no choice but to combat Saddam Hussein on the battlefield because of the greed of Western businesses, misguided analyses by the foreign policy establishment, and the incompetence of regulatory officials.

President Bush acknowledged as much in his Thanksgiving Day address to U.S. troops in Saudi Arabia, before the war against Iraq actually started. With every passing day, Bush warned, Saddam was "one step closer to realizing his goal of a nuclear weapons arsenal." The threat of an Iraqi nuclear weapon, designed and built with the help of Western companies and scientists, gave "a real sense of urgency" to the allied deployment in the Gulf. Bush didn't tell the troops just how close Saddam had come to making the bomb (the Pentagon's Defense Intelligence Agency had informed the president only a few days earlier that Iraq could assemble its first nuclear weapon within three to six months). "This I know for sure," Bush said, "he's never possessed a weapon he did not use."

Over the fifteen years leading up to Saddam's invasion of Kuwait, Western businesses and governments helped Iraq assemble one of the most formidable arsenals ever seen in the Middle East. They sold the Iraqis tanks, supersonic fighters, chemical weapons, ballistic missiles, and the materials to make an atomic bomb. Altogether, the companies, their bankers, and their supporters in government formed a powerful interest group whose principal bond was the creation of a Frankenstein's monster in the Middle East. Each group contributed in its own way to Saddam's death machine and lobbied hard to protect the Iraqi connection. The members of this death lobby may have competed fiercely among themselves, but they banded together when it came to defending Iraq.

Saddam Hussein was quick to take advantage of this solicitude. Fifteen years before the invasion of Kuwait, after the Soviet Union had decided to embargo arms deliveries to Iraq, Saddam set up a master procurement plan with the aim of securing Iraq's independence from its foreign suppliers. At the same time that he was building up his conventional forces, he was dispatching agents around the world to purchase the industrial tools and equipment necessary to manufacture an entire strategic arsenal, so that Iraq could weather economic sanctions and arms embargoes. Throughout this incredible military and industrial buildup, much of which occurred on the open market, never once did a red flag of warning go up in the West. Only four months before the invasion of Kuwait, Assistant Secretary of State John Kelly told Congress that Saddam Hussein was a "force of moderation" in the region, just as his predecessors had been saying for years. A more forthright statement of the truth could be found in the corporate balance sheets: Iraq was a great market for France, Germany, Italy, Britain, Austria, and the United States. Saddam Hussein was our creation, our monster. We built him up and then tried to take him down.

This book is a cautionary tale of what can happen when monumental greed meets boundless ambition. It is the story of the many men, companies, and governments that helped Iraq transform itself from an insignificant oil state into a regional superpower. It shows for the first time how we created Saddam Hussein step by step, piece by piece — through greed, willful blindness, and abysmal error. And it shows what Saddam Hussein intended to do with the enormous arsenal he was assembling. Astonishing as it may seem, Saddam seldom tried to disguise his ambitions, yet the policy makers and the lobbyists always managed not to hear. The confluence of interests fueling the Iraqi arms buildup simply overwhelmed the timid voices of caution that were occasionally raised.

The Death Lobby is the product of six years spent scrutinizing Iraqi weapons programs, most of them at a time when few people were interested in Iraq or in the extraordinary ambitions of Saddam Hussein. As a defense correspondent, I benefited from the experience of dozens of weapons designers, technicians, and military trainers who worked in Iraq and were generous enough to share their knowledge with me over the years. Unless otherwise noted, the information presented in these pages came from firsthand sources. They had access to Iraqi military installations and projects that have never before been exposed to the public eye. In hundreds of interviews they described what the Iraqis were buying and how they were using it. Only on rare occasions can I name them in this book.

Also unnamed are the many intelligence analysts, diplomats, and other government officials in nearly a dozen Western and Middle Eastern capitals who shared their thoughts with me as this work progressed. Some of these people were particularly valuable.

Sometimes I stumbled on new leads almost by chance. During a 1985 tour of South African weapons plants, I happened to wander into the shipping yard of a new ammunitions factory. To my surprise, I saw mountains of artillery shells packed in wooden crates and stamped with their destination: Ministry of Defense, Baghdad, Iraq. Inadvertently, I had discovered the South African connection and the fatal involvement of ballistics wizard Gerald Bull.

Many of the keys to Iraq's long-range weapons programs were supplied by the Iraqis themselves, during interviews they accorded me as a defense correspondent. From 1986 on, I met on several occasions with top officials from what became the Ministry of Industry and Military Industrialization, including the minister, Hussein Kamil al-Majid, and his two top deputies, Amer Hamoudi al-Saadi and Amer Rashid al-Ubeidi. Dozens of other, unnamed Iraqi weapons engineers provided their insights during numerous trips to Baghdad. They were proud of what they had accomplished and sought to share it with someone they considered a defense professional.

I have tried to respect as scrupulously as possible the actual order of the events that contributed to the overarming of Iraq, so that the reader can appreciate what decision makers knew at the time, without the benefit of hindsight. Saddam Hussein did not emerge from obscurity on August 2, 1990, when he invaded Kuwait. The arming of Iraq was a fifteen-year love affair. And it was a world-class enterprise.

Acknowledgments

During the course of this work I traded stories and information with many of my colleagues. Richard Greenberg, Pierre Salinger, and Gordon Platt of ABC News were generous enough to share some of their Iraq files with me, as were Tom Hamburger of the *Minneapolis Star Tribune;* Ken Mate of KCBS Television of Los Angeles; David Lewis of CNN; William Dowell of *Time;* Christopher Dickey of *Newsweek;* Norman Leister of Radio Canada; Jacques Delestapy, Gerard Willing, and Jerome Dumoulin in Paris; and Fabio Signoretti and Giuseppe Mennella in Rome.

Aaron Karp of SIPRI and Seth Carus of the Washington Institute for Near East Policy consistently provided insightful guidance on proliferation issues, as did Leonard Spector of the Carnegie Institution and Dr. Stephen Bryen, a former deputy undersecretary of defense for trade security policy. As the public outcry over Western support of Saddam Hussein's arms industry grew, half a dozen congressional committees began researching issues such as the BNL blunder and the abysmal failure of the Department of Commerce to control the outpouring of American technology to Iraq. Congressional staffers Dennis Kane, Ted Jacobs, William C. Triplett, and Randy Rydell have done excellent work in these areas and were willing to share some of their extensive knowledge with me as I prepared this book.

Finally, I owe a special debt to Caleb Carr, without whom I probably would not have undertaken this project, and to my agent, Suzanne Gluck, of International Creative Management. Henry Ferris of Houghton Mifflin provided excellent guidance in structuring the massive amounts of data I had accumulated during six years of research. If I have succeeded in transforming dozens of notebooks, file boxes, and computer disks into a readable account, it is thanks to Henry's vigilance and to the wisdom of my wife, Christina, who has never accepted second best.

Iraqi Weapons Plants

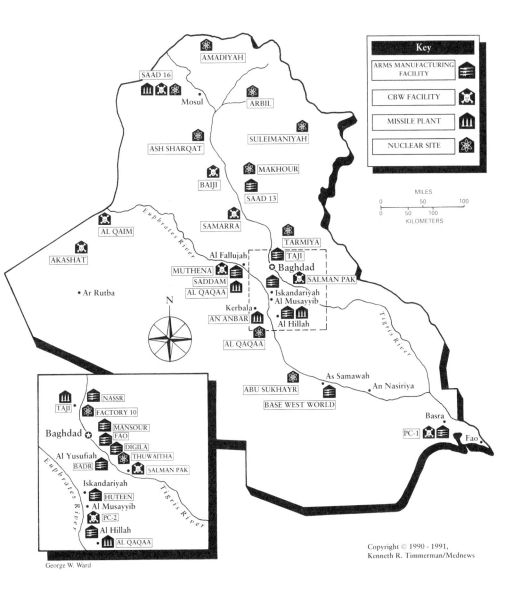

Key

ARMS MANUFACTURING FACILITY	
CBW FACILITY	
MISSILE PLANT	
NUCLEAR SITE	

MILES
0   50   100
0 50 100
KILOMETERS

AMADIYAH

SAAD 16

Mosul

ARBIL

ASH SHARQAT

SULEIMANIYAH

MAKHOUR

BAIJI

SAAD 13

AL QAIM

SAMARRA

Euphrates River

AKASHAT

TARMIYA

Al Fallujah   TAJI

• Ar Rutba

MUTHENA   Baghdad

SADDAM   SALMAN PAK

AL QAQAA   • Iskandariyah
• Al Musayyib

N

Kerbala •

AN ANBAR   • Al Hillah

AL QAQAA   Tigris River

As Samawah

ABU SUKHAYR   • An Nasiriya

BASE WEST WORLD

Basra

PC-1   Fao

Copyright © 1990 - 1991,
Kenneth R. Timmerman/Mednews

TAJI   NASSR

FACTORY 10

Baghdad   MANSOUR
FAO

Al Yusufiah   DIGILA
THUWAITHA

BADR   SALMAN PAK

Iskandariyah
HUTEEN

• Al Musayyib

PC-2

Euphrates River   AL QAQAA
Al Hillah   Tigris River

George W. Ward

Prologue

It was a magnificent early autumn afternoon when Saddam's Hussein's Boeing 707 touched down at Orly airport in Paris, decked out for the occasion with the eagle of Saladin, Iraq's national symbol. The date was Friday, September 5, 1975. Jacques Chirac, the French premier, was on hand to greet his visitor. A long red carpet led into the VIP lounge, where champagne and cocktail sandwiches awaited the Iraqi guests. "I welcome you as my personal friend," Chirac told his visitor. "I assure you of my esteem, my consideration, and my affection."

Touched by this reception, Saddam replied with characteristic modesty. "We hope that the relations France maintains with [other] Arab countries will benefit from the same warmth and cordiality as you have shown today. The relations between our two countries will assuredly improve as a result of my visit, which, I hope, will be beneficial for world peace in general."

What Saddam didn't say was that his notion of world peace was one that many in the West would have shunned. Peace, for him, meant total victory over his enemies, real or imagined; it meant transforming the Middle East, once again, into a killing field. He had come to France to seal a strategic pact that would soon translate into massive sales of French arms and the transfer of critical nuclear technologies to Iraq, dramatically accelerating the Middle East arms race and marking the start of Saddam's ambitious program to acquire nuclear weapons.

Until this fateful trip to France, the Soviet Union had been Iraq's principal arms supplier. But the French were eager to get their foot in the door. In newspaper editorials dedicated to the "philosophy" of technology transfer, they explained their willingness to sell arms and technology to Iraq in grandiloquent terms. Prime Minister Chirac and his advisors made a direct pitch. Buying arms from the French offered Iraq a "third way" out of the superpower embrace and had no political strings attached. This argument struck home with Saddam Hussein, who was eager to wriggle out of the Soviet grip.

Although the thirty-eight-year-old Saddam was nominally only second in command of the Baathist regime, the French accorded him all the honors of a head of state. They lodged him at the sumptuous Marigny Palace in Paris, where visiting kings and state presidents stayed. They threw a gala reception in his honor at Versailles. President Valéry Giscard d'Estaing invited him to state lunches at the Élysée, and Chirac stuck to him like glue. The five-day trip was a succession of champagne panegyrics. The French wanted Saddam as desperately as Saddam wanted them, for the Iraqi had something they needed to keep their economy afloat: oil. French media pundits, taking a tip from the spin doctors at the Élysée, called it "a marriage of reason." Today it has become a cliché to speak of arms-for-oil deals, but this is where it all started, as a love affair between France and Iraq.

That weekend Chirac tapped an old Gaullist party hand, Raymond Thullier, to assist him in wooing oil-rich (and arms-hungry) Saddam. Thullier, one of France's best-known chefs, had served as mayor of Les Baux-de-Provence for more than twenty years and had hosted the mighty many times before. His resort, L'Oustau de Baumanière, was one of the most extravagant weekend hideaways frequented by the French political elite. Nestled in a sheltered ravine in the depths of Provence, not far from the Mediterranean coast, it offered a dramatic view of an abandoned medieval fortress town perched on the cliffs like a Wild West version of the Hanging Gardens of Babylon.

Although he was almost ninety when he recalled Saddam's visit to L'Oustau, Thullier's mind was as lively as ever. He described the menu he had served his distinguished guests and dug up photographs of Chirac sitting with the new master of Babylon, drinking coffee after their meal in the sheltered gardens. "Chirac never left him for a second," Thullier recalled. "They were like bride and bridegroom." In the photograph, Saddam is wearing a white-and-black checkerboard suit with a colored shirt and a clashing tie. "He glowed like a peacock," Thullier said, laughing. Not long after this trip, Iraqi exiles say, Saddam invited a French tailor to take up residence at his palace in Baghdad so he would never be embarrassed by the poor quality of his Egyptian-made suits again.

After lunch Chirac had prepared a surprise for his guest: a bullfight through the ruined streets of the medieval town up on the cliffs. Thullier, who had supervised the restoration work, handled all the arrangements. The site was sealed off from tourists, bleachers were set up, and a large, well-protected bull pen was erected among the crumbling buildings. The village boys trained for days for the *jeu de taurillons,* which is something of a Provençal tradition. Unlike Spanish bullfights, it involves no bloodshed. It is more of a game, pitting young bulls against the local boys, who scamper around the ring trying to pluck a bright flower from behind the ear of the bull.

"Saddam caught on almost immediately," Thullier recalled. "After the first bull, he was jumping up and down and shouting, encouraging the boys. Then one of his retainers came up to me and said he was offering one million francs [around $200,000] to the boy who could beat the next bull. You can imagine what happened after that! Every boy in town tried to get into the ring."

Three times, Thullier said, Saddam bet on the bulls, and each time he promised a prize of one million francs. "After it was all over, the kids who won came up to me and asked if I thought he was serious. 'Of course he is,' I said. 'Just you wait and see.'"

A few weeks later, Thullier recalled, an emissary from the Iraqi embassy in Paris came into his office and delivered three checks, each for one million francs. Saddam had come through for the local boys. Soon he would come through for the big boys as well. Over the next fifteen years he would spend $20 billion on French arms. For Saddam Hussein it was the price of independence from the Soviets. For the French it was a bonanza.

O N E

The Search Is On

Saddam Hussein was born on April 28, 1937, near the town of Tikrit, along the Tigris River north of Baghdad. He grew up to the sound of cannon fire from British soldiers, who were using the country as a bridgehead for their occupation of Iran. Unlike Europe, the Middle East was not transformed into a pile of smoldering rubble by World War II. The Nazi conflagration left Arab dreams and Arab resentments intact.

By the time he was eight, Saddam had already marshaled the boys of his village into a mock militia, that marched up and down the dusty streets of Tikrit with wooden guns. At ten he found a mentor in his maternal uncle, Khairallah al-Tulfah, a recently cashiered army officer whose hatred of British colonial rule was matched only by his admiration for Adolf Hitler and his Nazi ideals.

Saddam turned to his uncle at least in part because of problems at home. His father had deserted the family when Saddam was a young child, and his mother's second husband, an illiterate shepherd named Ibrahim Hassan, beat the boy whenever he refused to tend the sheep. When he was twelve, Saddam took refuge in his uncle Khairallah's house. He learned to read by the light of an oil lamp and fed his spirit on his uncle's tales of exploits with pro-German officers in the Iraqi army. Khairallah al-Tulfah had a dream that Arabs would one day be free of foreign occupation and foreign rule. The Germans, Khairallah said, were the only ones who respected the Arabs as equals. The British were just after their oil.

In the early 1950s Khairallah al-Tulfah decided to pull up stakes. The tiny village of al-Auja, near Tikrit, had become too provincial for his tastes, so he headed for Baghdad, where many Tikritis were settling to become merchants. Saddam, who went with him, soon became known as "al-Tikriti," after his town of origin. Such names were common practice among provincial Arabs, giving them a bond of common heritage.

Saddam grew into manhood with Khairallah's son, Adnan. The two boys were the same age and resembled each other physically in many ways. But because he had started school late and his grades were poor, Saddam could only look on in admiration as his cousin joined the National Military Academy, one of the oldest and most prestigious schools in the Arab world.

Baghdad in the 1950s seethed with political revolt. The Anglo-French invasion of Suez in 1956 had galvanized the Arab world. Moved by his uncle's fierce anti-British sentiments, Saddam joined the newly formed Baath party. Two years later he committed his first political murder, assassinating a distant cousin who had become a police informer. (The Iraqi leader has always been proud of this fact, which is mentioned in all the official hagiographies.) Already Saddam's life was becoming a paradigm of an old Arabic saying: *I and my brother against my cousin, I and my cousin against my neighbor, I and my neighbor against the world.*

The Baath party, or the Party of Arab Renaissance, called for the creation of a single Arab political union that would reach from North Africa to the border of Iran. Formed in 1947 in response to the emerging state of Israel, the party fired the imagination of many young Iraqis like Saddam Hussein al-Tikriti. For the young Baathists, the event that forever fixed their way of looking at the world was "the takeover of Palestine by international Zionism." As one Baathist writer put it, the influx of Jews to Palestine during the Holocaust in Europe "was bound to generate a great deal of bitterness, resentment, hostility. This sort of feeling naturally led certain sectors of Arab public opinion to sympathize with the Axis" powers.[1]

British colonialism bore immense responsibility for the "disaster" of Palestine, the Baathists felt, and in their speeches and ideological writings they consistently identified the two. "It is our unshakable belief," the founder of the Baath party, Michel Aflak, wrote in 1956, "that if the battle takes place sooner or later, it will be to liberate not Palestine alone but the whole of the Arab home-land."[2] The struggle for freedom from British domination and the pro-British regime, then in power throughout the Arab world, was to become, as Saddam would put it later, "the mother of all bat-tles."

One facet of Baathist ideology helps shed some light on the origins of Saddam Hussein's political beliefs. To the Baathists, the Arab world formed a single "nation" united by language, culture, and religion. (That religion was Islam, the Baath founders insisted, even though they themselves were Christians.) Opposed to this Arab "nation," which had been splintered by an imperialist con-spiracy, were the Arab "regions," the nation states that had come into being during the twentieth century, whose borders the Baath-ists considered as artificial relics of the colonial era. When the Baathists talked about the "Regional Command," they meant the Iraqi or the Syrian Baath party, whereas the "National Command" referred to a theoretical body where "regional" leaders from the various Arab states would meet to determine the fate of the larger "nation." Like many prophets before them, the early Baathists believed that their prayers would become flesh in the body of a great leader, a man destined to rule the Arab nation with an iron will. Under his leadership, fifty million Arabs would rise up and expel the Jews and the colonial powers from the Middle East. Until then the Arab world would remain fragmented, weak, and submis-sive.

Hero worship was not the only similarity between the Baathist and Nazi ideologies. Both believed in racial identity, in foreign devils, and in war as purification. As Aflak wrote on the eve of his party's creation, when the ashes of the Nazi dream had not yet gone cold, "Real struggle can never be destruction, negativeness, or inaction. It is creativeness, building, a fruitful and positive action."[3] War was great, the young Baathists surrounding Saddam believed: Long live its purifying fire.

The great event occurred on July 14, 1958, when a group of Free Officers headed by Brigadier General Abdel Karim Qassem and Colonel Abdel Salaam Arif took Baghdad by storm and stamped out the pro-British Hashemite monarchy of King Faisal II. Crowds cheered when the king's death was announced. They leered when his pro-British prime minister, Nuri Said, was captured trying to escape the city disguised as a veiled woman. He, too, was instantly put to death.

The young Baathists saw in the 1958 revolution a historic opportunity to achieve their goal of Arab unity. But their dreams soon turned into bitter disappointment. Iraq's new leader, General Qassem, allied himself with the pro-Soviet Iraqi Communist party, a foreign force that the Baathists considered just as dangerous as British colonialism. Communist and Baathist gangs fought in the streets of Baghdad; in parts of northern Iraq, law and order collapsed entirely. Special "Red Terror" courts were set up by Qassem's Communist allies to hunt down the Baathists and bring them to trial. The small party's very existence was at stake.

Saddam Hussein was at the forefront of the street battles with the Communists. In October 1959 he got wind of an assassination plot against Qassem and begged to be given a part. The Baathists were planning to take over the government by force, and Saddam wanted a piece of the action. The plan was to ambush Qassem on Baghdad's principal thoroughfare, Rasheed Street, as he drove through the narrow shopping district. With the general out of the way, the Baathists intended to do a little bloodletting of their own against the Communists. They would make Qassem's "Red Terror" courts look like models of democratic justice.

According to Saddam's semiofficial biographer, Fouad Matar, the future Iraqi president's assignment was to cover the four-man hit team as it made its escape. But Saddam was "too enthusiastic to control himself" and opened fire on Qassem's motorcade with the others. The would-be assassins fired wildly with their brand-new machine guns but failed to kill the general. In the ensuing melee, as Qassem's bodyguards fired back and the Baathists tried to escape, Saddam was wounded in the left foot. (Some say he shot himself by accident in the excitement.) The legend has it that he extracted the bullet himself with a knife that night, after hobbling to a Baathist safe house. Later the twenty-two-year-old future hero escaped over the border to Syria with help from his family in Tikrit.

In exile in Damascus and later in Cairo, Saddam rose in the ranks of the clandestine apparatus of the Baath party, forming the friendships and alliances that would serve him well in later years. His most powerful ally in the Baath was Ahmed Hassan al-Bakr, a distant cousin from Tikrit. Al-Bakr was one of the Free Officers who had taken part in the 1958 revolution, but he had grown disenchanted with the Qassem regime and had thrown in his lot with the Baathists. An outspoken admirer of the then-popular Egyptian leader, Gamal Abdel Nasser, al-Bakr was a welcome addition to the ranks. More important, he gave the Baathists access to the Iraqi army. Without the army they would never manage to seize power, let alone hold onto it.

While in Cairo, Saddam wrote to his uncle, asking for the hand of his daughter, Sajida, in marriage. In most Arab households it was difficult for young men and women to get acquainted without going through a tedious formal courtship. The sexes were separated, and the girls forbidden from showing their faces to outsiders. Saddam had come to know Sajida without a veil as a teenager, when he had lived in his uncle's house as a member of the family. The two were married in Cairo in 1963. Saddam may also have been counting on the marriage for political support, since Sajida's brother, Adnan Khairallah, was by now a commissioned officer in the Iraqi army, a corps Saddam knew he could not join.

In February 1963 the Baathists joined forces with Qassem's former partner, Army Colonel Abdel Arif, in a successful coup. To make sure the message of the Baathist victory got through to the Iraqi people, the leaders of the coup exhibited Qassem's bullet-ridden body on national television.

When the news of Qassem's death reached Saddam in exile in Cairo, he rushed back to take part in the new regime. His love of conspiracy and talent for psychological manipulation opened up a new vocation for him as a torturer in the Baath party's main prison for political opponents, the Qasr al-Nihayyah, or Palace of the End.[4]

The Baathist regime of 1963 was headed by Arif, who became president, and by al-Bakr as prime minister. But the real power was held by the Baath party leader, Ali Salih as Saadi, who manipulated the government from behind the scenes.[5] The Baath leadership relied on a brutal armed militia to track down, terrorize, and assassinate their enemies. The active membership of the party was estimated at a mere one thousand.

Within months the alliance between the Baathists and the military fell apart. One reason for the split was al-Bakr's bloody war against the Kurds, led by Mustapha Barzani, in the mountains of the north. At night the garrisoned Iraqi troops fell prey to determined guerrilla bands. The Kurds were openly receiving arms and aid from the Soviet Union, where Barzani was living in exile. The Iraqi military bridled at the Baathist policy, which turned them into targets of the guerrillas without giving them the means to fight. In November General Arif ousted the Baathists from his government, and once again Saddam Hussein was forced to flee the country. He took refuge in Damascus and worked his best suit: his blood tie to al-Bakr. In 1965 al-Bakr became the party general secretary of the Baath party in exile. As a reward for his loyalty, Saddam was promoted to the party's number-two spot. His long march to absolute power had begun.

From 1965 on, until the Baathists successfully grabbed power on July 30, 1968, Saddam Hussein was the party's principal organizer. He was the apparatchik who forged the Baath into a powerful subversive tool capable of staging a military coup and holding power. His tactics were a mixture of Trotsky and Goebbels. Returning to Baghdad in secret, he purchased weapons, rented safe houses, and organized clandestine training bases for Baathist fighters. He also set up a Special Security Section called the Jihaz Haneen, or Instrument of Yearning, whose main task was to police the party by weeding out potential dissenters and breeding a fierce personal loyalty based on fear. The Baathists, who had begun their careers as pan-Arabists, now found themselves opposing the planned union of Iraq and Egypt because of differences with Egypt's President Nasser and supporting a war against the Kurds that threatened to break Iraq apart. With the party line in confusion, "the Baath increasingly was pervaded by cliques from the same village, town, or tribe."[6] Primary among these cliques were the Tikritis loyal to al-Bakr and Saddam Hussein. It was the old Arab saying again: *I and my brother against my cousin, I and my cousin against my neighbor, I and my neighbor against the world.*

The experience of working underground would later form the basis of Saddam's political culture, giving him a strong taste for secrecy and a flair for intelligence work. Although Saddam gradually transformed the Baath into a mass movement and successfully used Goebbels's principle of the Big Lie to manipulate public opinion at home and abroad, he never abandoned the Baath's secretive cell structure. If he were forced to go underground again, he could rely on this deep inner core of the party, which was fiercely loyal to him.

After a Baathist plot to overthrow the Arif regime failed, Iraqi police tracked Saddam down to a safe house in Baghdad and jailed him. By all accounts, however, the deputy secretary general of the Baath party was considered a privileged "guest" at the jail. Discontent with the Arif regime was widespread, and Saddam succeeded in converting many of the prison guards to his cause. They allowed friends and family members to visit, bringing him newspapers, food, and coded letters from his cousin and patron, Ahmed Hassan al-Bakr who was following the political situation closely on the outside. One day his wife arrived with a particularly sensitive note. "Feel under the baby's diaper," she whispered as she pinched their firstborn son so he would cry. The concerned father reached inside the baby's clothes and pulled out a folded sheet of paper from al-Bakr. The Baath had learned that disaffected army officers were planning another coup against Arif, the note read. It was an occasion the party should not miss. The note contained a detailed plan for Saddam to escape from jail.

The jail break was the handiwork of Saddoun Shaker, a childhood friend from Tikrit, who recalls the incident well. Baathist agents inside the prison had informed him that Saddam was to be transferred to a high-security prison, but that they had arranged for an escort of Baathist sympathizers during the transfer. Shaker planted himself in a getaway car along the route. As the "jailers" were driving him through the streets of Baghdad, Saddam, as instructed, asked that they stop for lunch at a popular restaurant on Abu Nawas Street. While the guards waited at the table, he excused himself to the lavatory and walked out the back door. Shaker picked him up on a deserted side street, and they were gone. The Baathist intelligence apparatus had scored its first success.

On the morning of July 17, 1968, Saddam Hussein burst into the grounds of the presidential palace on top of a tank, along with an Iraqi armored brigade. Although he was not an army officer, he had donned military garb, and his companions must have thought he was one of them. Other Baathists, posing as soldiers, seized control of the radio, the television, and the gendarmerie. In fact, the coup was the work of two former supporters of Arif, Colonel Abdel

Razzaq an-Nayef, and Ibrahim ad Daud. The Baathists merely piggybacked on their efforts by offering the support of their clandestine apparatus, to position themselves for a power play later on.

Saddam Hussein and al-Bakr were determined not to make the same mistakes they had made five years before. They knew the Baath could never rule in a coalition with the army. So their first task was to get rid of an-Nayef, who headed the revolutionary officers, and bring the unruly Iraqi army to heel.

Many details of the Baathist putsch against the officers have been provided by Saddoun Shaker, who told the story with some pride to Saddam's biographer, Fouad Matar, many years later. With the approval of al-Bakr, Saddam organized a showdown at the presidential palace. When an-Nayef naively agreed to go to al-Bakr's office alone after lunch, Saddoun Shaker and his ten bodyguards sealed off the corridors and neutralized an-Nayef's men. Inside the office, Saddam drew his revolver and began beating an-Nayef in the face until he broke down. "I've got four children," he wailed. "Why are you doing this to me?"

"You and your children will be fine if you leave Iraq and accept an ambassadorship," Saddam said coldly.

After some discussion, an-Nayef accepted an honorary position as ambassador to Morocco. But that was not enough for Saddam; he insisted on driving an-Nayef to the Baghdad airport. "Just act normally," Saddam hissed as they passed through the army checkpoints, many of which were manned by an-Nayef's men. "Don't forget: the pistol is inside my coat."[7]

As Saddam watched the plane prepare for takeoff, Shaker recalls, tears welled in his eyes. They did not come from sympathy for an-Nayef. "I suddenly realized that a single bullet could have killed the entire operation," Saddam said later. "It was fate that decreed it would happen like this." But Saddam Hussein was never one to trust in fate alone. Not long after an-Nayef's departure, Saddam sent agents from the Istikhbarat, or Military Security, to keep tabs on him. They followed him at every step, reminding him that he was a marked man who could never return home. In the end, Saddam's killers gunned down an-Nayef as he was leaving his London apartment in July 1978, ten years to the day after his exile began. Saddam Hussein had learned one lesson well: never give your opponents a second chance.[8]

*   *   *

The second Baathist regime began on a fragile footing. The political climate in Iraq in 1968 was rife with intrigue, rivalries, and corruption. Less than two months after the July 30 putsch, a coalition of Arif supporters and pro-Nasser officers attempted a coup. In October the regime announced that it had broken up a "Zionist" spy ring. On January 7, 1969, a public show trial against eleven Iraqi Jews began. It was a way of galvanizing public support against an "external" enemy, when in fact Iraq was plagued with deep internal divisions.

Al-Bakr and Saddam ruled Iraq through a unique power-sharing arrangement, a dual leadership they maintained for the next eleven years. Al-Bakr, who commanded a certain respect from the public as an army officer and well-known supporter of Arab nationalism, played the good cop as Iraq's president. He signed decrees, received visiting heads of state, and gave rabble-rousing speeches denouncing Jews, Zionists, and foreign "plots." In reality, however, his power was limited. By the time the Baathist putsch elevated him to the presidency, the party was under the control of his younger cousin. Saddam, nominally vice president when the duo began their rule, inherited the most difficult task of all: ensuring the survival of the regime.

Saddam's principal talent, and the one that would keep him in power against tremendous odds, was an uncanny ability to sniff out potential rivals and eliminate them before they could mount a serious challenge to his rule. Like a cancer specialist, he tried to isolate the disease of dissent to keep it from spreading. From the start he relied heavily on a wide range of secret police organizations to enforce his rule. Principal among them was the Jihaz Haneen, which in the days following the 1968 putsch was expanded and given a new name: the Mukhabarat, or General Intelligence Department.[9] The mission of this powerful state organization was to keep an eye on virtually every aspect of Iraqi society, starting with the Communists. Saddam placed his trusted childhood friend, Saddoun Shaker, at the helm of this key institution. And to keep an eye on Shaker, Saddam made his oldest half-brother, Barzan Ibrahim Hassan al-Tikriti, Shaker's deputy.

Al-Bakr ordered Saddam to cut and purge. According to Samir al-Khalil's *Republic of Fear*, a chilling account of the Baathist regime, in 1969 alone public executions of the regime's opponents took place on February 20, April 14 and 30, May 15, August 21 and 25, September 8, and November 26. "The great and immortal squares of Iraq shall be filled up with the corpses of traitors and spies! Just wait!" one Baathist minister told the crowds after the first execution of Iraqi Jews in January.[10] Al-Bakr was no less practiced in the arts of demagoguery. "We shall strike mercilessly with a fist of steel at those exploiters and fifth columnists, the handmaidens of imperialism and Zionism," he told Iraqi television viewers when he unveiled the "Zionist plot."

The Baathists faced threats from several corners. The most dramatic in these early years was the guerrilla war in the three Kurdish provinces of the north, which had raged for more than ten years. By early 1969, when the hangings began in Baghdad, the war with the Kurds threatened to split the nation apart.

The Kurds were a distinct ethnic minority from the Arabs. They spoke a different language and had different habits and customs. During the final years of Ottoman rule the vast majority of Kurds lived in what has today become Turkey and participated in the massacres of their Christian Armenian neighbors, which culminated in the genocide of 1915–16, when half of Turkey's three million Armenians were killed. At the end of World War I, the Kurds were denied statehood by the victorious Allied powers at Versailles. The lands they had occupied for generations were split among Syria, Iraq, Turkey, and Iran.

Iraq's Kurdish minority, which accounted for slightly less than 20 percent of the total population, had been waging a guerrilla war against successive regimes in Baghdad for years. When Saddam Hussein first tackled the problem in early 1969, the principal Kurdish guerrilla force was led by Mustapha Barzani.

From 1968 on, the Soviets used aid to Barzani as a means of putting pressure on Saddam, who had never been their favorite candidate to rule Iraq. When they wanted something from Saddam, such as an exclusive oil concession, they stepped up aid to the Kurdish leader. When Saddam became more pliant, they slacked off. The Soviets never openly opposed Saddam's participation in the Baathist government, but for years they did their best to keep him off balance. The idea was to remind the Baathist leader that he owed his survival to Moscow. Iraq was not the only country where the Soviets were meddling in internal politics, but they did know the Iraqi players exceptionally well. Ever since Qassem's overthrow of the monarchy in 1958, the Soviets had been playing rival groups against one another in an effort to keep Iraq weak and divided.

Saddam's first instinct was to confront the Kurds on the battlefield. In April 1969 he called out garrison troops and the small Iraqi air force. On August 8 the army razed the Kurdish village of Dakan, near the northern city of Mosul. But the rugged terrain of Kurdistan was not well suited to the tanks and heavy armored vehicles of the Iraqi troops. The Kurdish guerrillas, called *peshmergas* ("those who walk before death"), used the high mountain passes and steep valleys to their advantage. When the air force tried to bomb them, they simply dug in or hid in caves. The valleys were so narrow that the Iraqi pilots had difficulty in maneuvering. Sometimes, unable to pull up in time, they crashed their planes into the mountain peaks. To make matters worse, the Iraqi Communist party (with Moscow's blessing) threw in its lot with the Kurds. It was a potentially deadly alliance for Saddam.

After several months of heavy fighting, Saddam realized that he was headed for a humiliating defeat. Instead of continuing, he sought a compromise. In January 1970 he made his first pilgrimage to Moscow, Iraq's principal supplier of arms, hoping to negotiate a deal with President Aleksey Kosygin to withdraw Soviet support from the Kurds. But the Russian was implacable: he wanted no massacre of Iraqi Kurds. As Saddam explained it in a conversation years later with Congressman Stephen Solarz, Moscow's decided lack of sympathy with his difficulties provided a rude awakening. "We were, of course, young Baathists," he told Solarz. "We had conflicts with the Communist party in Iraq, some of which were bloody. Yet we kept thinking the Soviet Union could behave differently."[11]

On March 11, 1970, after returning from Moscow, Saddam announced with great fanfare a new "autonomy plan" for Kurdistan, which promised the Kurds many of the political and cultural rights they had been demanding for years. So much for the provisions Kosygin had insisted on. The hook was in the application. As his condition for relinquishing control over the three oil-rich Kurdish provinces, Saddam insisted that the autonomy agreement not go into effect for another four years, enough time for Saddam to solve the problem his way. Warily and reluctantly, Barzani agreed.

The Kurdish war forced Saddam into a formal allegiance with the Soviets, which took the form of a fifteen-year treaty of friendship and cooperation. In April 1972 Kosygin made a historic trip to Baghdad to sign the treaty documents with al-Bakr and Saddam. As he strolled through the marble hallways of the presidential palace in Baghdad, accompanied by a handsome blonde (provided by Saddam), the Russian strategist savored his victory. By using Barzani and the Kurdish rebellion, he had succeeded in "breaking" Saddam. He had won extensive oil concessions for the USSR and stepped up arms sales to Iraq. And the geopolitical gains were even sweeter. Without firing a shot, Kosygin had gained a new ally, who with a little coaching could be used to counter American influence in the Persian Gulf. The treaty allowed Soviet warships to make port calls at Iraq's small naval base at Oum Qasr at the head of the Gulf, right under the noses of the U.S. Navy in Iran. To Kosygin's mind, this provision brought the Russian empire one step closer to its centuries-old goal of reaching the warm southern seas. The treaty guaranteed Soviet access to Iraqi airbases and called for the training of thousands of Iraqi officers in Soviet military academies. It also referred to the "harmonization" of Soviet and Iraqi foreign policy, a polite way of saying that Saddam would take orders from Moscow on issues such as Iraq's votes at the United Nations. In return for Saddam's allegiance, the Soviets agreed to maintain him in power. They also agreed to help him nationalize Western oil company holdings in Iraq. That was a fatal mistake.

Saddam Hussein was aware of the enormous political strings the treaty entailed, but he had little choice. Without appeasing Moscow, which had already shown it was capable of plunging Iraq into civil war, the Baathists were doomed. "We never expected that the Soviets would support us without guarantees that our friendship would serve their strategic interests," Saddam explained later.[12] The new treaty was an encroachment on Iraqi sovereignty and it was a bitter pill. But it was better than utter defeat at the hands of the Communists and the Kurds. Besides, Saddam Hussein had more than one iron in the fire. At the same time that he was being forced into an alliance with Moscow, he was negotiating his freedom with others. His salvation lay in Iraq's virtually untapped underground wealth. By gaining control over Iraq's oil, he hoped to buy freedom from outside domination. To do so, he needed at least one ally from among the Western owners of the Iraq Petroleum Company (IPC). He chose the French.

French President Georges Pompidou was happy to welcome Saddam Hussein to Paris in June 1972 to discuss helping the Iraqis wriggle out of the Soviet embrace. Like Britain and the United States, the French had been angered by the Iraqi announcement that it intended to complete the nationalization of the IPC that year, consummating three years of delicate negotiations secretly orchestrated by Kosygin's top troubleshooters, Valentin Chachin and Ivan Arkhipov. But Pompidou was willing to forgive and forget — for a price. In return for acquiescing in the nationalization of the French share in the IPC, Pompidou demanded guaranteed oil deliveries from Iraq at concessionary prices. "Already," the French daily *Le Monde* noted, "there was talk of secret negotiations for an arms sale estimated at 6 billion FF." In exchange for the oil, Saddam wanted arms. It was a deal the French simply could not refuse.

For the Iraqi leader, this first barter of arms for oil with a Western nation was a test. The equipment he agreed to purchase — 16 Alouette attack helicopters and 128 Panhard armored cars — would hardly tip the military balance in his favor against his internal enemies and would do even less against Iran, which the Nixon administration was arming at an alarming rate. Saddam wanted to send the Soviets a clear message that Iraq did not intend to become a vassal state and would seek arms and technology wherever it saw fit. Beyond that, he wanted to discover whether the French were valid partners for his long-range scheme.

Saddam Hussein's driving ambition was to build Iraq into the greatest military power the Arab world had ever seen. Bred on the humiliation the Arabs felt at the hands of the British, and on the defeat his Arab brothers had suffered at the hands of the Israelis, Saddam was determined to vindicate Arab honor by the force of arms. Iraq would have to become Israel's equal on the battlefield.

"Our nation has a message," he liked to say. "That is why it can never be an average nation. Throughout history, our nation has either soared to the heights or fallen into the abyss through the envy, conspiracy, and enmity of others."[13] Saddam Hussein was driven by no ordinary vision. Again and again he would refer back to Nebuchadnezzar, the biblical king of Babylon. His favorite episode in the saga was when Nebuchadnezzar brought the Jews into captivity in Babylon. Saddam hoped to repeat that feat.

On October 6, 1973, Egypt and Syria launched a combined attack on Israel. It was Yom Kippur, the Day of Atonement, one of the most holy days for Jews. The attack took the Israeli army by surprise. It also came as a surprise to Saddam Hussein, who was piqued that he had not been informed of his Arab brothers' intentions. That Egyptian President Anwar Sadat, whom he scarcely knew, had kept the attack secret he could accept. But that Syrian President Hafiz al-Assad, a fellow member of the Baath party, should fail to consult with Baghdad was an unforgivable slight.

The Yom Kippur war drove home another point for Saddam. In its dramatic comeback following the surprise attack, Israel made good use of the Mirage fighter planes it had purchased from France. These aircraft, in Saddam's eyes, vastly outperformed the Syrian and Egyptian MiGs provided by the USSR. Israel's American-built M-60 tanks made mincemeat of the Arabs' aging Soviet T-54s. Saddam suspected that the Soviet Union was supplying inferior and outdated equipment to the Arab world. If the Arabs were ever to rise up against Israel, they would have to acquire Western technology and Western arms.

By 1974 the Baathists felt confident of their grasp on the state. The Soviets had agreed to diminish their support for the Kurds, while Saddam secretly prepared his army for the coming battle. As head of Iraq's powerful security apparatus, recently reinforced through a secret intelligence agreement with KGB chief Yuri Andropov, Saddam Hussein had purged the Baath party of his rivals and had virtually succeeded in neutralizing most other threats to the Baath. With Ahmed al-Bakr in failing health, Saddam had become the man to be reckoned with in Iraq.

The quadrupling of OPEC oil prices following the Yom Kippur war convinced Saddam that the time had come to jump-start his economy. He signed contracts with the USSR to expand Iraq's oil industry. He signed contracts with the French to build huge turnkey factory complexes, equipped with everything from machinery and production jigs to pencils on the director's desk. He called on the Brazilians to build railroads, on the Belgians to build a phosphate complex, and on the Yugoslavs, Bulgarians, Germans, and Japanese for high technology, labor, and expertise. He built schools and a powerful radio network capable of broadcasting Baathist propaganda throughout the Arab world. He extended Iraq's electricity grid into the most remote areas of the countryside. Foreign observers began pointing to Iraq as one of the rare success stories of the Third World. Its vast new revenues were not squandered on useless prestige projects, white elephants like those of many African nations. Saddam's projects actually improved the standard of living of the Iraqi people.

Saddam's favorite tactic was to have Soviet and Western companies bid against each other on contracts so that Iraq would get the best deal. The catchword for this policy was "nonalignment." Saddam Hussein wanted above all to preserve his freedom of action, which was why he had worked so hard to nationalize Iraqi oil. He was happy to become a client, but he did not want Iraq to be a client state.

When he called in the foreigners, Saddam kept up his guard. His security services were careful to isolate foreign workers in Iraq, using many of the same tactics on them he had used with success to terrorize his own people. He was determined to maintain his ideological virginity by preventing any contact between "contaminating influences" and ordinary Iraqis. Foreigners were followed, interrogated, warned away from social contacts. Foreign newspapers and magazines were confiscated. Foreign engineers were required to apply for exit visas to leave the country, and these permits were routinely withheld as a means of intimidation. For foreign workers, the money was good. But Iraq was a prison with golden bars.

Saddam explained his vision of cooperation with the West to a group of Arab journalists visiting Baghdad in 1974. The billions of dollars in fresh oil revenues had given him new confidence that Iraq could break the bonds of dependence, the political strings attached to foreign commerce. The West was a gigantic industrial supermarket, and Saddam was a cash-and-carry customer.

> We have no fear of dealing with any state in the world, with the exception of the Zionist entity which we do not consider as a state and with whom we have no intention of cooperating, ever. The severing of diplomatic relations with the United States of America [in the wake of the 1967 Arab–Israeli war] was a political attitude based on principle. . . . But we have no reservations about dealing

with companies anywhere in the world, on a basis that guarantees the respect of our sovereignty and ensures both parties a legitimate profit.

Our country has large-scale projects, prodigious projects, and we have great ambitions. The idea that we might isolate ourselves from the world to live according to our own devices is foreign to us, and we refuse it categorically.

We must therefore cooperate and deal with States and companies who implement for us, here in Iraq, projects that our experience and capabilities cannot handle in their entirety or which are beyond our technical capabilities.

Iraq today has contracts with American and West European companies. We are cooperating with numerous Western states, and with all the Socialist states, without exception. But our dealings with all of them are determined by our national interest. Sometimes we deal with them on the basis of a strategic conception, as is the case with the Socialist countries; other times on the basis of temporary mutual interest, as is the case with some Western, even some American companies. A contractor comes forward and carries out a certain project for us within a specified period. We agree on the price, the timing, and the technical specifications. He carries out his obligations, and we settle ours by paying him. *And then he leaves.* There is therefore no contradiction between our decision to sever diplomatic relations with America and to deal commercially with some American companies on these bases. The presence of these American companies will never open the door to a change in our political program, but neither will our political position toward the United States prevent us from dealing with American companies in the way I have just mentioned.[14]

The last real threat to Baathist rule was the festering revolt in the northern provinces. The autonomy agreement Saddam Hussein had negotiated with Mustapha Barzani four years earlier, in 1970, was now scheduled to go into effect. As the four-year grace period drew to a close, tensions mounted. Saddam had no intention of allowing the Kurds to set up a truly autonomous government, and he was seeking to exclude the oil-rich area around Kirkuk from the future Kurdish region to deprive it of a major financial resource. He felt he was now strong enough to resolve the Kurdish problem once and for all — by force. He was wrong. And the humiliation he suffered during the ensuing military campaign conditioned his behavior for the next fifteen years.

On the morning of March 11, 1974, Saddam Hussein met for the last time with Idriss Barzani, the son of the Kurdish leader. "I know when you leave here, you will set off an uprising," Saddam told him. "But you will regret it, because your calculations are wrong." When Barzani left Baghdad that afternoon, the Kurdish politicians Saddam had invited to join the central government went with him. It was a mass walkout, and Saddam was furious. Some accounts say he ordered the Amn al-Amm (State Internal Security) to assassinate Barzani and his father a few days later, once they were reunited in Kurdistan. Toward the end of March, Saddam called out the army, and his orders were clear. They were to crush what had now become a full-blown Kurdish rebellion, even if it meant devastating the entire region.

Events soon turned against the government troops. Saddam had made two major miscalculations. He had overlooked the depth of Soviet rancor for his repeated purges of the Iraqi Communists (ICP), and the determination of U.S. Secretary of State Henry Kissinger to punish him for signing the friendship and cooperation agreement with Moscow, which had given the USSR a foothold in the Gulf. The results were devastating. The Soviets cut off arms shipments to Baghdad, despite Saddam's temporary alliance with the ICP against the Kurds. Meanwhile, the CIA helped Barzani and his Kurdish fighters by massive arms deliveries through Iran. This combination of American and Soviet policies, one of the weird tacit alliances of the Cold War, nearly brought Saddam down.

Saddam's army, pushed back on every front, incurred large losses in men and equipment. Even the areas nominally under its control were unsafe at night. Foreign engineers were told to remain in Baghdad. If they had to go to Kurdistan, they were to travel only during the day, in convoys escorted by the army. At night the government troops returned to their barracks in fear. The Kurds controlled nearly one-third of the country.

By the end of 1974 the government forces gradually ran out of arms and ammunition. Iraqi ground troops hunkered down in their barracks, Iraqi pilots flew fewer and fewer sorties. What irritated Saddam Hussein the most was that the Soviets simply refused to discuss sending arms. They rejected requests to meet with Saddam's chief of staff, Lieutenant General Abdel Jabbar Shenshall, who had prepared a list of weapons Iraq desperately needed in order to wage the final offensive against the Kurds. It didn't help that Shenshall was a Kurd (in fact, he was doggedly faithful to Saddam). Aleksey Kosygin supported the autonomy plan for Kurdistan since it would keep Iraq weak and manageable. He did not support a war against the Kurds.

The Soviet attitude was debilitating to Saddam, morally and militarily. Ever since they had replaced Great Britain as Iraq's principal arms supplier in 1958, the Soviets had very carefully, like drug pushers, built up Iraq's dependence. Lavish supplies of arms were coupled to strict policies concerning maintenance and training. The Iraqi air force had been the first customer outside the Warsaw Pact to receive the MiG-21 fighter, but for years the Iraqis were not allowed to learn how to service the plane themselves. It was the same with the T-54 tanks, the workhorse of the Iraqi army. Iraq could not wage a military campaign without active Soviet support. The USSR knew that in a matter of months, Saddam would run out of munitions and spare parts. And so with a marked absence of polemic — not even a reproach — Kosygin simply turned a deaf ear to Saddam's pressing requests for more arms. The Soviets never called it an embargo per se. But for Saddam, it was humiliating. It was this bitter experience with the USSR that convinced him to go shopping elsewhere.

Toward the end of 1974, with the approval of his ailing cousin, President al-Bakr, Saddam set up a three-man Strategic Planning Committee, whose aim was to guarantee Iraq's long-term independence. Never again, Saddam vowed, would Iraq depend so heavily on a single arms supplier. If his nation was going to be truly independent, it would have to diversity its sources of weaponry to a far greater extent than ever before. More importantly, it would have to build up a powerful domestic armaments industry in Iraq. Saddam's goal was to make sure that any future embargo attempted by foreign suppliers failed. Iraq was going to be the first Arab country capable of relying on itself.

Saddam turned to two men to help him map out his long-range strategy of military self-reliance: Adnan Khairallah, his cousin and brother-in-law, and Adnan Hamdani, first deputy prime minister. Khairallah, now a general, was in charge of the purely military aspects of their venture. Hamdani, trained as a lawyer, was Saddam's bag man and chief negotiator. Together with Saddam, they worked out a long-range plan that included a massive buildup in conventional weapons and the construction of Iraq's strategic weapons industries.

Hamdani had good commercial contacts and turned almost immediately to a Palestinian consulting group in Beirut, called Arab Projects and Developments (APD). APD was set up as a nonprofit organization aimed at "promoting the economic, social, and cultural progress of Arab countries." It was run by two fabulously successful businessmen, Kamel Abdel Rahman and Hassib Sabbagh, who believed that their fellow Palestinians should pay back their Arab supporters by putting their brains to use for the Arab cause.

Rahman and Sabbagh were close to PLO leader Yasser Arafat, and through him they were plugged into the Palestinian diaspora, the thousands of well-educated engineers and technicians spread across the world. Many had graduated from U.S. technical institutes such as MIT. What APD could offer Iraq was a vast pool of highly qualified engineers. Until it was forced to close in 1976 by the heavy fighting of Lebanon's civil war, APD served as Saddam Hussein's talent scout. It tracked down Palestinian and other Arab researchers, offering them work in Iraq on petrochemical and infrastructure projects. According to an account in London's *Independent,* APD hired as many as 4,000 Arab scientists and researchers to work in Iraq. Egyptians, Moroccans, Palestinians, Algerians, Syrians, and other Arabs left good jobs in the United States, Britain, Canada, Brazil, and dozens of other countries, bringing to Iraq a wealth of technical expertise. Although Hasib Sabbagh denies that he ever advised the Iraqi authorities "about projects for the production of nuclear, chemical, or bacteriological weapons, or participated in the procurement of teams of scientists for such activities," his consulting firm played a key role in Saddam Hussein's plan.[15]

The real service APD provided, Sabbagh revealed in an interview, was the design of Iraq's entire higher education system. "We delivered them an entire system, a turnkey project." Sabbagh says the deal was handled through a team of outside consultants led by APD staffer Dr. Antoine Zahlan, a Lebanese engineer of Palestinian origin. "We saw that Iraq needed an educated elite," Sabbagh said. "We showed them how to train that elite themselves."

"That was the crucial first phase of Saddam's long-range game plan," commented a Pentagon analyst who had studied the development of Iraq's defense industry closely. "Before you can build weapons, and before you can build factories, you need the skilled labor force to make it work."

The APD plan called for the overhaul of the entire education system, with particular emphasis on building technical schools and universities. It provided the blueprint for the only type of development that interested Saddam — the development of a powerful Arab army and war industry. The first tangible result was the opening not long afterward of al-Bakr Military University. Over the next ten years the number of Iraqi students in technical fields would increase by 300 percent, to more than 120,000. A Foundation of Technical Institutes was established, as well as a specialized University of Technology. Graduates paid the state for their education by going to work in top-secret industrial plants and research labs. To build arms, Iraq had to have specialists.

Saddam Hussein was attracted early on to bacteriological weapons. They were cheap, relatively simple to manufacture, and potentially deadly. A single vial of anthrax virus dropped in an urban water system was enough, in certain conditions, to launch a full-scale epidemic. It was a terrorist's weapon if there ever was one.

Iraq's first attempt to acquire biological weapons of this kind seemed innocent enough. The committee turned to a trusted Baathist, Izzat al-Douri, then serving on the ruling Revolutionary Command Council as minister of agriculture. On November 2, 1974, al-Douri signed a contract with the Paris-based Institut Merieux, to set up Iraq's first bacteriological laboratory. The Iraqis explained that they needed to be able to manufacture large quantities of vaccines in order to develop agricultural and animal production. The official Iraqi purchasing agency was called the General Directorate of Veterinary Services. No one in France batted an eye. But for the Iraqis, the vaccine protocol was so important that when the French agricultural minister, Christian Bonnet, visited Iraq, he was invited to meet with the vice president of the Revolutionary Command Council, Saddam Hussein.

Al-Douri's success won him a promotion and made him a de

facto member of the team, the three-man Strategic Planning Committee, along with Saddam, Khairallah, and Adnan Hamdani. By the end of the year he was shifted to the Ministry of the Interior, all the while retaining his responsibilities for "agricultural" development.

When French Prime Minister Jacques Chirac faced the press in Baghdad on December 2, 1974, he had just completed three days of talks with Saddam Hussein. The young French premier was exuberant. Saddam had told him that Iraq intended to turn to France for billions of dollars' worth of civilian and military contracts. It was great news to announce at a time when the quadrupling of oil prices that resulted from the 1973 Arab-Israeli war had plunged the French economy, along with the rest of Europe, into deep recession.

Chirac had another reason to be pleased. His appointment as prime minister a few months before had deeply upset his Gaullist party. The Gaullists had opposed Valéry Giscard d'Estaing in the 1974 presidential elections, but their candidate lost because Chirac refused at the last minute to support him against Giscard. By bringing in new Arab business and being seen as the prime mover behind Iraq's defection from the Soviet Union, Chirac hoped to appease Gaullist heavyweights back in Paris — and, perhaps, to fill the party's coffers.

Chirac met with Saddam and the other two members of the Strategic Planning Committee, Adnan Khairallah and Adnan Hamdani. Civilian contracts were certainly discussed, and when Chirac met the press he spoke of a "veritable bonanza." But two subjects topped the list of Iraqi requests: Mirage fighters, like those of the Israeli air force, and nuclear technology.

With oil revenues suddenly worth billions of dollars, Saddam Hussein now had the means to realize his dream of building Iraq into a modern military power. His search to achieve military superiority over Israel was on. Chirac convinced him that the French were more than willing to help.

Saddam Hussein had always been attracted to General Charles de Gaulle because of the French leader's insistence on national sovereignty and because of the agile dance he had performed between the superpowers. Chirac spoke that same language. Even better, he was Saddam's own age and understood what it was like to work in the shadow of another politician. France could help Iraq break out of the Soviet embrace, Chirac said, without thrusting it into the American camp. The principal means of doing this, of course, was by selling Iraq arms. But because the French never liked to see themselves as salesmen of any sort, let alone purveyors of death, they put it all into a nice little theory. The French policy on exporting arms, one influential scholar wrote at the time, was oriented "toward helping those countries desiring to throw off the yoke of a superpower." What better way of proving this high-minded ideal than by offering billions in high-tech weaponry to Saddam's Iraq?[16]

TWO

Saddam's French Lover

By February 1975, the Kurdish revolt had gotten out of hand. Long convoys of weapons were seen crossing the mountains from Iran, where they loaded up in full view of the Shah's army. By Saddam's own admission, the Kurds were better armed, better trained, and more highly motivated than the Iraqi army that had been sent in to crush the revolt. By early March, Saddam explained, the situation had become "extremely dangerous." The Iraqi army had taken a real beating during the twelve-month campaign (more than 16,000 casualties), while indiscriminate bombing, reprisal raids, and massacres had killed another 40,000 civilians. These were Saddam's own figures. The real ones may have been much higher.

To make matters worse, the Soviet arms embargo was taking its toll. "The goal sought after was to inflict a defeat on our valiant army and to render it incapable of facing the rebellion once its munitions were exhausted and its equipment partially destroyed," Saddam recalled bitterly five years later, when he finally explained the dramatic events of March 1975 to his Baathist colleagues. The unspoken alliance between the United States and the USSR made it possible to "execute an imperialist-Zionist plot, to isolate and weaken Iraq and stifle its Arab role. The situation became extremely dangerous when our materiel and essential munitions cruelly began to run out. We had almost no more heavy artillery shells. Our air force had only three bombs left."[1]

Barzani and the rebels were in control of nearly one-third of Iraq, and the Baathist regime in Baghdad was on the brink of collapse because of the military disaster it had brought on itself. Saddam Hussein decided to swallow his pride and approach the

Shah of Iran, Mohammed Reza Pahlavi, about striking a deal over the Kurds. The Iranian monarch held the key to the Kurdish supply lines.

In 1975 the Shah was at the apogee of his power. He was the de facto head of OPEC, and he commanded a huge arsenal of modern American weaponry, purchased with only a tiny fraction of his oil wealth. By supporting Barzani's Kurdish revolt, the Shah was hoping to wrest sizable territorial concessions from Saddam. He also wanted the Iraqis to agree to halt subversive activities within the Iranian province of Khuzestan, which the Iraqis persisted in calling Arabistan because the majority of the population was Arab, not Persian. Saddam agreed on a date with the Shah to discuss a deal.

Once Saddam had decided to negotiate with the Shah, he could turn to his long-range goal of securing new sources of modern weaponry. In utmost secrecy, Saddam left Baghdad on March 3, 1975, and flew to Paris, where he met with Prime Minister Chirac and President Giscard d'Estaing. Saddam presented a long shopping list of French weapons he wanted to buy. Although the trip was brief, his mood was serious, and Chirac agreed to arrange for a detailed presentation of the equipment Saddam wanted as soon as possible. Chirac suggested that he return to Paris in six months, but the Iraqi insisted on having a French team meet his air force chiefs to discuss the technical details within a week. Chirac gulped. He said he would see what he could do.

From Paris, Saddam flew on to Algiers, where OPEC leaders were holding a summit to discuss oil prices. But Saddam was less interested in oil than he was in his own immediate survival. His real agenda in Algiers revolved around the secret meetings with the Shah, which had been set up by Algerian President Houari Boumédienne.

The encounter went better than either participant had probably dared hope. On March 6, Saddam Hussein and the Shah published a joint statement announcing the resolution of their long-standing border dispute. Iraq made substantial territorial concessions, including relinquishing partial sovereignty over the Shatt-al-Arab waterway, which formed the southern border between the two countries and provided Iraq with its only outlet to the Gulf. In exchange, the Shah agreed to withdraw Iran's support for the Kurds. It was a flawed agreement, and it would provide the *casus belli* for Iraq's invasion of Iran five years later. But as the Iraqi foreign minister, Saddoun Hammadi, put it, "It was either that or lose the north of the country."[2]

The effect of the Iran-Iraq agreement was immediate. Without constant arms supplies from Iran, the Kurds were beaten; within a matter of weeks, their rebellion was over. Not trusting Saddam's offer of amnesty, some 30,000 *peshmerga* guerrillas crossed the mountains into Iran to join the estimated 200,000 civilian refugees who had fled the fighting.

Negotiating with the Shah may have saved Saddam's regime, but it did not fulfill his long-range needs for weapons. Saddam was not in a position to break all ties with the USSR after the Kurdish war unless he wanted to turn his army's vast quantities of Soviet hardware into scrap metal for lack of spare parts and maintenance. So in early April he made a quick jaunt to Moscow with Hammadi and Shenshall, the army chief of staff, to negotiate a new arms agreement and sign a nuclear cooperation pact with Soviets. The USSR was willing to train Iraqi nuclear physicists and provide Iraq with significant nuclear technologies, including a research reactor that could be used to make weapons-grade fuel. But there was a catch. The Soviets also insisted on rigorous safeguards to ensure that Iraq did not use its equipment to develop a nuclear weapon. Saddam hated it, but signed.

Saddam continued to purchase vast quantities of weapons from the Soviets, but in his scramble to diversify Iraq's sources of armaments and to acquire strategic technologies, he dramatically reduced Iraq's *dependence* on the USSR. The Soviet share of Iraqi military supplies plummeted from 95 percent in 1972 to 63 percent by 1979. Saddam was turning elsewhere.

The technical team Saddam had asked Chirac to dispatch within a week of his stopover in Paris arrived in Baghdad on March 12, 1975. Three French companies sent marketing experts: Avions Marcel Dassault-Bréguet Aviation, the only manufacturer of military aircraft in France; Snecma, their partner for military jet engines; and the Office Générale de l'Air, a government-controlled export sales agency, which had permanent representatives throughout the Middle East and coordinated its activities with French defense attachés. A five-page confidential report by one of the engineers who participated in the week-long briefing shows that the sessions were also attended by the French chargé d'affaires in Baghdad, M. Saillard, and the military attaché, Lieutenant Colonel Marchandise. It was one more sign that the French government was treating the Mirage sale as an affair of state. As Jean-François Dubos noted in his doctoral thesis, "Today, the ambassador himself can become a salesman, [while] the consuls and military attachés are left to supervise the operation."

To start with, the French brought good news. Not only could they sell Iraq the same Mirage fighters that Israel had recently flown against the Arabs, they could do better. The French air force was just completing flight tests of a new generation fighter, the Mirage F1, which was far superior to the Mirage 3 the Israelis had received. The new plane was the equivalent of the American F-16, which had just narrowly beaten out the Mirage in the "contract of the century" to reequip a half dozen NATO air forces. The engineers showed films of the new fighter in action and gave an extensive technical briefing. The Iraqis were overjoyed.

The head of the Iraqi air force, General Naama al-Dulaimi, told the French he had been given orders to discuss the purchase of thirty-six fighters and to take an option on thirty-six more. The French team tried to hook the Iraqis on their latest jet trainer, the Alphajet, as well, which was being designed and built with the German aircraft manufacturer Dornier. (According to the terms of the capitulation of Hitler's Reich, the Germans were not yet allowed to export arms, so they went through the French.) They even tabled an offer for forty planes, but the Iraqis shrugged it off. In their confidential report on the marketing mission, the French conceded that the Iraqis had just agreed to purchase the less advanced L-39 Albatross trainer from Czechoslovakia. The four-year lead time for the Alphajet was simply "too long" to meet the Iraqi air force's needs.

However, the air force showed a "marked interest in the option of setting up an engine overhaul facility in Iraq" for the Mirage F1, the report stated, and they "knew the subject well." So eager were the Iraqis to obtain critical military engine technology, the experts wrote, that the sale of a "complete engine overhaul factory . . . should be discussed at length at our next meetings."

What the French didn't realize at the time was that Saddam

wanted more than just weapons; he wanted independence. That meant purchasing the weapons, the means to service them and, eventually, the means to manufacture them as well. As time went on, the French codified the new type of relationship between arms seller and buyer that Saddam was seeking: they called it "technology transfer." Considering the Soviets' refusal to give the Iraqis any information relating to maintenance, let alone manufacture (they insisted that advanced systems such as aircraft engines be shipped back to the USSR for repair), the French approach gave them a crucial marketing advantage. So long as the Iraqis could pay, the French let them buy virtually anything they wanted. This is how France became one of Saddam's first full-fledged partners in the momentous enterprise of building an indigenous armaments industry.

When Vice President Saddam Hussein returned to Paris on September 5, 1975, to utter the marriage vows with Jacques Chirac, he was the virtual ruler of Iraq. Al-Bakr was in ill health and could feel his younger protégé breathing down his neck. Besides the presidency, al-Bakr retained his title as Iraq's minister of defense. But that position was just another sinecure. Real power at the Defense Ministry was exercised by the deputy minister, General Adnan Khairallah.

As in the presidency and the Defense Ministry, power in most of the Iraqi government was concentrated "in the hands of a narrowly based elite, united by close family and tribal ties," the official U.S. government handbook on Iraq reads. "The most powerful men in the Baath thus were all somehow related to the triumvirate of Saddam Hussein, al-Bakr, and General Adnan Khairallah al-Tulfah. All were members of the party, the Revolutionary Command Council, and the cabinet, and all were members of the Tulfah family of Tikrit. Saddam Hussein was married to Adnan Khairallah's sister and Adnan Khairallah was married to Bakr's daughter. Increasingly, the most sensitive military posts were going to the Tikritis." *I and my brother against my cousin, I and my cousin against our neighbor, I and my neighbor against the world.* The Baath Party was becoming a family enterprise, with Saddam Hussein at its head.[3]

If Saddam had gone to France seeking a way out of the Soviet embrace, the French had reasons for wooing Saddam besides the need for a steady supply of cheap oil. One major factor that is often overlooked involved the dynamics of the French arms industry, which used export markets as a means of financing new weapons systems for the French armed forces. Given Iraq's skyrocketing oil revenues in the wake of the 1973–74 Arab oil boycott, and France's need to discover new markets abroad for its weapons, the two countries were a natural fit. The French derived added pleasure from squeezing into the cracks between the superpowers, locked in an intense geopolitical struggle in the region. Both the United States and the USSR had begun pouring vast quantities of modern weaponry into their respective client states, Iran and Iraq. Knowing that they could compete only marginally with the United States, the French saw greater opportunities in stealing markets from the Soviets. "We have always been competing against the USSR," commented Hugues de l'Estoile, marketing director of Dassault International. As far as he was concerned, Iraq was a natural choice.

While touring Provence with Chirac and de l'Estoile, Saddam made a side trip that few people in France paid much attention to at the time. On their way to the bullfights at Les Baux, Saddam's French hosts took him through the Cadarache nuclear research center, one of the most advanced in Europe. In this small Provençal town just north of Marseilles the Commissariat à l'Energie Atomique (CEA) had set up its first experimental fast-breeder reactor. They called it Rapsodie. It certainly enchanted Saddam.

The basic principle of a fast-breeder reactor, also called a super-generator, is to "breed" more nuclear fuel than it consumes. In the process, it transforms significant quantities of uranium into plutonium. While plutonium is a by-product of most nuclear fuel cycles, and can be extracted from spent fuel by chemical reprocessing, it has little utility except for making bombs. Iraq's interest in fast-breeder reactors was motivated by one concern alone: obtaining a sure source of plutonium for use in a nuclear weapons program. This was a central goal set out by the Strategic Planning Committee. Saddam was determined to have a bomb within ten years.

Officials at the Commissariat à l'Energie Atomique categorically deny that France ever intended to sell proliferating technologies to Iraq. Many former officials, including Bernard Goldschmidt, the CEA's international affairs director at the time of Saddam's visit to Cadarache, deny it to the point of absurdity. "I have no recollection whatsoever of that particular visit," Goldschmidt, now retired, says today. He compared the guided tour he presided over to a funeral. "People talk to each other because they are there, but you forget what you spoke about the minute they have left."

Goldschmidt, who had been deeply involved in sales of nuclear technology to Israel in the 1950s and 1960s, is not the only official who prefers to forget France's nuclear adventure with Saddam. One of Saddam's guides for the visit to Cadarache was the head of the CEA, André Giraud, a well-respected technocrat who went on to become President Valéry Giscard d'Estaing's minister of industry ("my oil minister," Giscard used to joke), in part because of his good contacts with Iraq. Like Chirac, Giraud made no effort to hide his pleasure at doing business with Saddam, despite clear warnings that the Iraqi wanted the bomb.

Iraq's nuclear research program began in the 1960s, when the Arif government purchased an experimental nuclear reactor from the USSR. To house the modest-sized IRT 2000 plant, Iraq built its first nuclear research center in the desert at Thuwaitha, some fifteen miles south of Baghdad. Later the Soviets upgraded this light-water research reactor to 5-megawatt capacity. They also delivered three "hot cells" capable of manipulating spent fuel, built a laboratory capable of producing radioisotopes (ostensibly for medical research, in a nation that had fewer doctors per capita than the USSR), and trained at least a hundred Iraqi nuclear physicists. But in April 1975 Brezhnev and Kosygin had refused the Iraqis' pleas to purchase more advanced technology. So once again, Saddam decided to turn to France.

At first the Iraqis said they wanted to develop a nuclear power industry. For a nation sitting on top of the world's second largest oil reserves, that was already an odd desire. Next they inquired into purchasing a 500-megawatt natural uranium/gas-graphite reactor, a French design more remarkable for the amount of plutonium it produced than for the electric power it generated. By the time Saddam toured the Cadarache reactor in September 1975, Electricité de France had already dropped the gas-graphite design in favor of more efficient light water reactors. The French did continue to operate a few gas-graphite plants, however. All served as plutonium breeders for the French nuclear weapons program.

Giraud and Goldschmidt explained to Saddam why they could not sell him the gas-graphite reactor.[4] Instead they could offer him an Osiris research reactor and a scale model called Isis, both of which could breed smaller quantities of bomb-grade material by irradiating natural uranium placed in a "blanket" around the reactor's open core. Saddam agreed to buy them on one condition: that France deliver an extra one-year supply of reactor fuel at start-up. Osiris and Isis were designed to run on weapons-grade uranium enriched to 93 percent. A one-year supply came to 72 kilograms — enough for several bombs the size of the one dropped on Hiroshima.

The Iraqis called the reactor Osirak, but later changed the name, probably at the request of the French when the Parisian press made it rhyme with the prime minister's name ("O'Chirac"). The reactors came to be known as Tammuz I and Tammuz II after the Sumerian corn god, lover of Ishtar, who is brought back to life from the nether world to symbolize the eternity of the harvest. Tammuz also happens to be the name of the month when Saddam's Baath party seized power. The reactors would provide the lightning that would usher in the eternal rule of the Baath — once they had turned the whole region into a nuclear graveyard.

If the French chose to believe that oil-rich Iraq was interested in developing nuclear power for civilian use, Saddam could have enlightened them as to his true intentions. Only days after visiting Cadarache, he gave an interview to a Lebanese weekly, *Al Usbu al-Arabi*, which was published the day he ended his official visit to France. "The agreement with France," Saddam declared, "is the first concrete step toward the production of the Arab atomic weapon." The statement should have sounded alarm bells throughout the French government. But the interview failed to arouse any interest, at least in France.

After the weekend of play with the Provençal bulls, serious business resumed. On September 8, 1975, Chirac and his defense minister accompanied Saddam and Adnan Hamdani on the spectacular fifteen-mile drive through the *garigue* to the French air force testing ground at Istres, just northwest of Marseilles. They were joined by Saddam's military advisor, General Saadoun Ghaidan, and a horde of French arms export officials, both in government and from private industry. No one at the time realized that Saddam Hussein was about to launch the first stage of a long-term strategic plan. Nor did they understand Hamdani's status in the Iraqi government, for Saddam referred to him as his personal secretary.

The Istres base was a must for all important foreign visitors. By no means a Spartan installation, it was dotted with sumptuous chalets belonging to the major French aerospace contractors, where they entertained foreign dignitaries while showing off helicopters, jet fighters, trainers, cluster bombs, runway-busting bombs, air-to-air missiles, and air defense systems — the latest inventions of France's innovative aerospace industry.

But Saddam's mind was set on the Mirage. As he sat on the terrace of the Dassault chalet at Istres, watching the acrobatics of the Mirage, he turned to Ghaidan. "This is the plane that nearly beat the F-16?" he asked, referring to the recent NATO competition. As Ghaidan nodded, Saddam made up his mind. "When can we get it?"

He had Hamdani inquire into delivery lead times, while Ghaidan discussed the type of avionics the French were offering. Iraq would settle for nothing short of the best, Saddam insisted. He wanted the same avionics that Dassault had promised the French air force: the same radar, the same electronic countermeasures (ECM), the same weapons system. He wanted a front-line NATO fighter. It was that, or nothing.

When they returned to Paris, Saddam decided to prepare a surprise for his "personal friend," Jacques Chirac. It had been easier to win over the French than Saddam had dreamed. He wanted to seal their pact on a personal note. Much to the chagrin of the maître d'hôtel at the Marigny Palace, where he was staying, Saddam ordered his personal cook to return to Baghdad on the presidential plane to retrieve a load of victuals for Chirac. Top on the list was one and a half tons of an Iraqi river fish called *masgouf,* which Chirac had enjoyed in Baghdad the year before. With Iraqi security guards patrolling the kitchens of the Marigny Palace with their machine pistols, Saddam's cooks roasted the huge, greasy carp over open fires. Raymond Thullier, who was later told the story by Chirac, said that "the whole place smelled of charred flesh. It was amusing, but a mess."

By the end of Saddam's trip, the French Foreign Ministry, the

Quai d'Orsay, had briefed the press thoroughly on the "objective, historical reasons" for strengthening ties with Baghdad. As *Le Monde* wrote, Iraq saw France "as the most natural ally on the geopolitical scene today to help it escape the hegemony of the superpowers. . . . If Paris is seeking to convert its political capital into economic gains, Baghdad hopes to turn its economic strength into political gains." It was a formula that fulfilled the French need for aesthetic balance.[5]

Chirac waxed eloquent as he bade his guest farewell. French policy, he declared, "is dictated not merely by interest, but also by the heart. France deems it necessary to establish relationships between producers and consumers on terms that best conform to the interests of both parties."

Beyond Iraqi oil and the Mirage deal — which was not signed until Chirac had left the prime minister's job — those interests included petrochemical plants, desalinization plants, gas liquefaction complexes, housing projects, telecommunications systems, broadcasting networks, fertilizer plants, defense electronics factories, car assembly plants, a new airport, a subway system, and a navy yard, not to mention Exocet, Milan, HOT, Magic, Martel, and Armat missiles; Alouette III, Gazelle, and Super-Puma helicopters; AMX 30-GCT howitzers; Tiger-G radar, and a nuclear reactor capable of making the bomb. It was a multibillion-dollar relationship, and it was based on the kind of "balance" that appealed to Saddam Hussein: a balance of terror.

As a token of his esteem for the Iraqi leader, Chirac offered him a special gift before he left: a pair of harlequin costumes, purchased in the ancient Provençal city of Arles (where the clowns were called *arlesiennes*). The costumes had been made to fit Saddam's two young daughters, Raghed and Rana, and the Iraqi leader was touched. On Chirac's next trip to Baghdad, in January 1976, Saddam would honor him by parading the embarrassed girls about his palace, dressed in the particolored frills and dunce caps of the *arlesienne* clowns. Saddam planned to take good care of his "personal friend," for as long as France kept the arms and technology coming.

Soon afterward, President Valéry Giscard d'Estaing dispatched one of his most trusted political allies to Baghdad. In his briefcase was the final text of the Franco-Iraqi Nuclear Cooperation Treaty.

When Michel d'Ordano, then serving as minister of industry and research, initialed the treaty in Baghdad on November 18, 1975, it was billed by the French press as a simple export sale. The deal, worth 1.45 billion French francs (around $3 billion at then-current rates), covered the sale of Osiris / Tammuz I, the breeder reactor, and Isis / Tammuz II, the experimental scale model. Tammuz II was important because it would allow Iraqi nuclear scientists to experiment with different reactor loads without shutting down Tammuz I breeder plant. D'Ordano also announced major contracts for Matra, a French missile manufacturer, and the Franco-American computer company Honeywell.

"France will be training large numbers of Iraqi personnel," d'Ordano said. The French government wanted the training program to show that it was possible to transfer technology from the industrial north to the developing countries of the south. "Paris hopes that our cooperation in this area will be exemplary," d'Ordano told *Le Monde.*

The full text of the Franco-Iraqi Nuclear Cooperation Treaty was not made public until eight months later, and then in the most discreet manner possible: an unannounced publication in the French public register, *Le Journal Officiel,* dated June 18, 1976. In one clause, the Iraqis insisted that "all persons of the Jewish race or the Mosaic religion" be excluded from participating in the program, either in Iraq or in France.[6]

The treaty committed the French to training six hundred Iraqi nuclear technicians, more than enough for a bomb program. "Some of them attended French universities," a high-level CEA official said. Others were slated to receive training at CEA research facilities, where they would inevitably glean nuclear weapons secrets from their French colleagues. "We also trained Iraqi chemists," the official said. This laconic admission is of capital importance, because extracting military plutonium from spent reactor fuel required complex chemical processes.

One final irony involved the large quantities of highly enriched uranium Saddam was seeking. For years the French had imported from the U.S. Department of Energy the 93 percent enriched uranium they used to power their Osiris reactor, since every gram of highly enriched uranium made in France was earmarked for military programs. The last thing they wanted was for the U.S. government to start poking its nose into their nuclear exports. So a secret deal was struck between the CEA's export agency, Techniatome, and their military branch at Vaujours, east of Paris. By special order, the Tammuz reactor fuel was manufactured at a French bomb plant.

Chirac found it easier to negotiate the nuclear deal than to complete details of the first Mirage sale to Iraq. One reason was that France had never signed the Nuclear Non-Proliferation Treaty, which went into effect in March 1970, and did not feel bound by all of its restrictions. Nuclear technology was a question of "national sovereignty," Chirac and his advisors argued. Harking back to 1966, when de Gaulle pulled France out of NATO's integrated military command structure because he refused to put French nuclear weapons under NATO's control, Chirac argued that Iraq had the right to similar independence. National sovereignty was sacred.

In fact, however, the French never really believed the Iraqis would succeed in building a nuclear weapon. But Chirac wanted to convince the Arab world that his conservative Gaullist party was on their side. It was the French Socialists, after all, who had built the Dimona nuclear research reactor in Israel in the 1950s, knowing full well that Israel hoped to develop a nuclear deterrent. If the Socialists could do that for Israel, Chirac and the Right could do it for Iraq. The payoff would be enormous, he reasoned, and the fallout slight. Besides, the world's nuclear trade was too heavily dominated by the United States. France had a right to export also.

It was an attitude that won Chirac many supporters in the French business community. He became known as "Mr. Iraq."

Back in Baghdad, Saddam called the Strategic Planning Committee into session. So far, their design to transform Iraq into a significant military power had met with great success. Major arms deals were in the pipeline with France and the USSR, and both trading partners had agreed to supply nuclear technology as well. The French Institut Merieux was already building Iraq's first bacteriological laboratory, in accordance with the protocol signed the year before. It was time to launch the next phase of Saddam's scheme: the acquisition of poison gas.

Chemical weapons could be a "force multiplier," Adnan Khairallah argued. Unlike the sophisticated electronics systems then being developed by the superpowers, the technology was well within the grasp of a developing nation like Iraq. The committee decided to make an all-out effort to acquire an extensive manufacturing capability for various types of poison gas, including suffocating agents, like mustard gas, and nerve agents, like the more sophisticated Tabun and Sarin.

An immediate practical decision was made at the end of 1975 to put these schemes into effect. Adnan Hamdani was shifted to the powerful Planning Ministry, where he could oversee Iraq's entire industrial development strategy. Hamdani's job was to slip strategic weapons projects into large contracts ostensibly aimed at developing Iraq's civilian manufacturing or agricultural potential. For this task, he was aided by two additional members of the Revolutionary Command Council, Izzat al-Douri, the new minister of the interior, who was also in charge of agricultural development; and Taha al-Jazrowi, who became minister of industry and minerals.

Hamdani buried the strategic weapons projects in Iraq's Second Five-Year Plan, scheduled to take the nation from 1976 through 1980. Under the heading "agricultural development," for instance, he inscribed a little-noticed entry that called for "the creation of six laboratories for chemical, physiological, and biological analysis." To operate the laboratories, the plan called for the training of 5,000 technicians by foreign companies. It was not a modest effort.

Under the heading "Chemical Industries," the plan called for the construction of a pesticides plant at Samarra capable of manufacturing 1,000 tons a year of organic phosphorus compounds. Most Western nations had stopped using these highly lethal compounds for pest control years before because of their high toxicity. Organic phosphorus chemicals form the basis of nerve gas compounds such as Sarin and Tabun.

Another project called for expanding the Basra oil refinery to manufacture 180,000 tons a year of benzene and toluene. Toluene is a petroleum derivative used in manufacturing dyes. But when nitrogen is added to it under specific conditions, it becomes trinitrotoluene, also known as trotyl, tolite, or TNT.

Yet another project called for establishing a huge production line at the Basra Petrochemicals-1 (PC1) complex, to manufacture 110,000 tons of ethylene per year. Without ethylene, there can be no petrochemicals industry. It is the most basic byproduct that results from petroleum refining and is obtained by "cracking" petroleum vapors. It is used to make polyethylene plastics and dozens of other household and industrial products. However, when mixed with air it forms an explosive mixture. Besides its use in liquid rocket fuel, ethylene is one of the chief ingredients of mustard gas when transformed into ethylene glycol.

Iraq's need for these base chemicals was so great that the 1976–1980 plan called for more production lines at another petrochemicals complex to be built at Basra. The plan called for producing an additional 400,000 tons per year of ethylene "for export purposes." Saddam was not content to become a manufacturer of death; he wanted to become an exporter as well.

Behind all this industrial wizardry was a German-trained chemist who took over the State Organization for Technical Industries (SOTI) in 1975. According to a French government brief prepared for businessmen interested in tapping the Iraqi market, SOTI had previously been known as the State Organization for War Industries. The change of names was a significant harbinger of things to come. Located at Midan Square, just off Rashid Street in downtown Baghdad, it was run by a general, Dr. Amer Hamoudi al-Saadi, who had never spent a day in uniform. His rank was honorary, a way of showing the military that the Baath party was the sole dispenser of military merit.

In late 1975 Adnan Hamdani asked Izzat al-Douri to purchase plans for a poison gas plant from the United States. Iraq had no diplomatic relations with the United States, so al-Douri had to go through France, where all the doors were wide open to the "personal friend" of Prime Minister Chirac. He lined up a French engineering company that had a subsidiary in the U.S. called NACE Corporation and had it scout an appropriate supplier.

NACE turned to Pfaudler Company of Rochester, New York. Pfaudler was one of the leading manufacturers of corrosion-resistant, glass-lined vats and other highly specialized equipment needed for mixing toxic chemicals. Pfaudler agreed to dispatch two chemical engineers to Baghdad to discuss the Samarra pesticides project with the Ministry of Agriculture.

That is how two Pfaudler employees, Joseph M. Culotta and Morris Gruver, became involved in what could have been the scandal of their lives. When they arrived in Baghdad in late 1975, they were greeted by an amiable official from the Ministry of Agriculture. Iraq was a developing country, with a great heritage, he told them. Did they know that Iraq was the site of the biblical Garden of Eden? The grandeur of old Mesopotamia was well known. But modern Iraq was still a backward country in many ways. Despite its great heritage, it could not feed its people because Iraqi farmers were unable to protect their crops from the ravages of desert locusts and other pests. "A modern pesticide plant could change that," the official said. Pfaudler could provide the solution to Iraq's problem.

As Gruver told the *Washington Post,* he had been doing volunteer work for his church on the problems of world hunger, so the Iraqi's argument about the need for pesticides "made a lot of sense." When the two engineers returned to Rochester, they set to work preparing the blueprints and equipment specifications for Iraq's first pesticides plant.

Culotta and Gruver had been in the chemicals business for years. One of the biggest problems in manufacturing pesticides, especially in inexperienced areas of the Third World, was safety. The chemicals were dangerous; some of them were toxic; a single accident could cause widespread deaths. To avoid mishap, they believed it was necessary to first build a pilot plant to train the local work force and identify potential problem areas. Only then could real pesticides production begin.

Pfaudler presented a proposal for a pilot plant on January 24, 1976. The detailed design specifications explained not only how to build the plant but what type of special equipment was necessary for blending toxic chemicals. "This looked to be a big dollar project for us," Culotta said. "It was kind of an attractive job."

But the Iraqis were in a hurry. They wanted to waste no time building a pilot plant, but to go into full-scale production right away. This haste disturbed the two chemists, as did the Iraqis' desire to manufacture four highly toxic organic compounds: Amiton, Demeton, Paraoxon, and Parathion. They wanted Pfaudler to build production lines big enough to turn out 1,200 tons of these chemicals per year. All four were chemical first cousins to nerve gas and could be readily transformed into deadly weapons.

The deal fell apart during a stormy meeting in mid-1976 in New York's Waldorf-Astoria Hotel when the Iraqi delegation, headed by a burly, gruff man named Hussein who represented the Ministry of Industry, said they wanted to launch a full-scale production plant immediately. "We want a commitment to proceed now," Gruver recalls "Hussein" insisting. The Iraqis felt that the Americans were too concerned about plant safety, so they broke off negotiations, perhaps anxious not to arouse suspicions as to their real intentions. Undeterred by the American rebuff, Saddam would have to look elsewhere in his quest for poison gas.[7]

THREE

Bonanza on the Gulf

Chirac returned to Baghdad for a three-day "private" visit on January 27, 1976, on his way home from an official trip to Delhi. He just wanted to pay his respects to his friend Saddam, Chirac told the press as he left India.

The Iraqi leader swept aside the pretense. He treated the French premier to a full state reception and sat him down to hear a detailed account of Iraq's weapons needs. Chirac had brought along his foreign trade minister, Raymond Barre, just in case the need arose. Barre, who would play an instrumental role in developing the Franco-Iraqi marriage of reason, took over as prime minister when Chirac was forced to resign later that year.

The French daily *Le Monde* dispatched a correspondent to cover the "private" event, who couldn't help but pick up on Chirac and Barre's enthusiasm. Billions of dollars worth of new industrial contracts were on the table, he wrote. They included a new airport for Baghdad, a subway system, more nuclear plants, a radio and television broadcasting system, a nationwide telecommunications grid, railroad lines, naval yards, and more. But even better, the French "horse," Saddam, had become "the sole man in charge of defense" in Iraq, *Le Monde* wrote. And he was seeking "to diversify his weapons supplies." That carefully chosen phrase, using Saddam's own words, was ripe with promise for French defense contractors.

The death lobby was about to be born.

Back in Paris, the French air force viewed the arduous Mirage negotiations with consternation. They had yet to receive their first F1s, and here the Iraqis were demanding the same advanced electronics that they had ordered themselves. The generals argued that France could not afford to export electronic countermeasures systems, which were costly to develop and easy to foil. Nor should it divulge the secrets of the latest Thomson-CSF combat radar. Top on the worry list of the French intelligence agency, SDECE, was the presence of numerous Soviet technicians on Iraqi air bases. Surely, SDECE chief Alexandre de Marenches argued, if a NATO member delivered state-of-the-art electronics gear to Iraq, the KGB would be climbing all over the planes within hours to glean their secrets.

In March the air force chief of staff, General Claude Grigaut, was dispatched to Baghdad to make a counterproposal. He pointed out to his Iraqi counterpart, General Hamid Shaaban, that the Iraqi air force was already equipped with an advanced Soviet interceptor, the MiG-25. What it really lacked was an advanced ground attack capability. Thomson-CSF was just then developing a new multirole radar for the Mirage that could handle air-to-air *and* ground attack requirements, Grigaut said, and that could provide the ideal solution for Iraq. It was like having two planes in one.

Although Shaaban was receptive to these arguments, the Iraqi leader turned a deaf ear. Saddam Hussein suspected that Grigaut was trying to sell him some downgraded "export" version of the French air force planes. He wanted the same planes the French were buying for themselves.

The slow pace of the Mirage negotiations frustrated the French aerospace industry. Without an aircraft to hang their equipment on, the major French manufacturers of missiles, radar, avionics, bombs, rockets, and flares were shut out of the Iraqi market. If they wanted to sell anything, they first needed to "convince" Saddam to buy the Mirage. To the French way of thinking, that meant distributing the spoils. And to do that, they needed help.

The French were not newcomers to the international arms bazaar. Dassault had barely averted a damaging kickbacks scandal during the NATO "contract of the century" negotiations. As the French arms trade analyst, Jean-François Dubos put it, competition was so fierce on the international marketplace that "intermediaries, official or not, are not overlooked, nor is the method of baksheesh." The arms salesmen decided to short-circuit the French government by influencing the decision makers close to Saddam.

One of the best-known experts on Iraqi affairs was an international trade consultant named Ramzi Daloul, a Palestinian exile who traveled on a Lebanese passport. Like many influential inter-mediaries plying their wares in the Gulf, Daloul worked out of London. His clients were among the biggest arms manufacturers in France, including Thomson-CSF, Sofma, Alcatel, and Matra. Early in the game Daloul had identified the weak link in Saddam's chain. It was Adnan Hamdani.

Daloul knew that Iraq was not like other Gulf states, where kings and princes had to be paid off. Saddam Hussein had some-thing of a Calvinist attitude toward money. Although members of his own family were on the take, and his father-in-law, Khairallah al-Tulfah, was raking in fabulous profits from a series of trading companies he had set up, Saddam insisted that government officials and members of the Baath party devote all their energies to the state. He expected total dedication. And to enforce it he crafted a special decree, known as Law Number 8, of January 15, 1976, which prohibited foreign companies from using unregistered inter-mediaries or agents for commercial negotiations with Iraq. The new law punished by "death or life imprisonment any person in the public sector who knowingly serves as an agent" for foreign com-panies. As Daloul and Hamdani would discover, it was not a joke. In Saddam's Iraq, being a middleman meant walking on eggs. Either you went direct, or you didn't go at all.

Saddam's contempt for the corruption of the Gulf oil monarchies extended to the West and to his arms suppliers. The ease with which he had been able to purchase the Osirak bomb plant from France was a case in point. With enough money, he saw, he could purchase allegiance. Everybody had his price, from heads of state on down. The trick was finding out how much they cost.

By January 1976 Saddam Hussein was in sole charge of Iraq's defense procurement. Under his guidance, Iraqi arms purchasing teams scoured the world in search of the best weapons technology Western arsenals had to offer. It was an era of monumental arms-for-oil swaps; and not only the French were involved. Saddam soon learned that everybody wanted a piece of the cake. Iraq had be-come one of the top five arms-importing nations in the world, and arms salesmen literally tripped over each other's feet in the lobbies of Baghdad's shabby hotels. With a little patience, and some luck, he found he could pit competing suppliers against each other. The Europeans were especially keen to answer Saddam's call because they had been virtually excluded from the world's biggest arms market, Iran, which had become a de facto U.S. monopoly.

Saddam also discovered that many Third World nations, such as Yugoslavia, Brazil, and Egypt, were capable of providing advanced technology nearly on a par with that available in the USSR or the West, at substantially lower prices. And as in France, these sales had no political strings attached. Money made the deals go through. Sometimes just credit was enough. Arms sales to Baghdad were a matter of pork-barrel politics. They were all about jobs. And in most cases, oil.

Little has been written about the Iraqi-Brazilian arms relationship, but interviews with Brazilian arms salesmen and U.S. intelligence sources show that Brazil played a key role in arming Iraq and in providing technologies for the Iraqi bomb. In return, Iraqi oil dollars were crucial to the Brazilian arms industry. Companies like Embraer, which made combat trainers and jet fighters, and Avibras, which made rocket launchers and missiles, were able to launch vast industrial expansion programs thanks to Iraqi development money. New factories were built, thousands of new workers trained, and nearly all of it to meet the demands of the Iraqi market.

One of those who knew best how to marry arms sales with national interest was Carlos Sant'Anna, the international sales director of Brazil's largest conglomerate, Petrobras. From his glass-walled quarters in the heart of Rio di Janeiro, Sant'Anna commanded an industrial empire. His salesmen stalked the world to find new markets for Brazilian manufactured goods in exchange for the oil the country desperately needed to fuel its growing economy. He brought in business for dozens of Brazil's export-oriented enterprises, and in the late 1970s one of his best markets was Iraq.

In July 1976 a team of Petrobras oil experts made a remarkable discovery that marked the beginning of the Iraqi-Brazilian honeymoon. Just below the marshlands close to the Iranian border, they stumbled on a new oil field of staggering proportions. The initial geological soundings made Carlos Sant'Anna drool. The Majnoon field was one of the largest in the Middle East, containing a minimum of 7 billion barrels of oil, or one-fifth of Iraq's proven oil reserves at the time. Petrobras hastened to conclude an exclusive exploitation agreement with the Iraq National Oil Company, which would eventually lead to production of 700,000 barrels of crude oil per day. The find was indeed "crazy," as the Arabic word *majnoon* signified, and Brazil had sewn it up.[1]

But to prevent a huge trade deficit with Iraq, Petrobras had to offset its oil purchases with sales of Brazilian manufactured goods and services. That was where Carlos Sant'Anna entered the picture. He made sure that Brazilian industry was well placed in Iraq's development plans, securing large infrastructure contracts for Brazilian construction companies and engineering firms. The first to profit from the oil bonanza was José Luiz Whitaker Ribeiro, who headed Brazil's bustling heavy manufacturing consortium, Engesa.

When Engesa was launched in 1967, it employed fewer than twenty people and was devoted to manufacturing oil field equipment. By the time the Majnoon deal was sealed, Engesa had grown dramatically and had branched out into the lucrative arms business. Engesa and, indeed, the entire Brazilian arms industry that grew up in the 1970s, plotted its development by targeting highly specialized niches in the international arms market. Whitaker was a marketing genius. He understood that Third World nations like Brazil and Iraq wanted to build large fleets of tanks and armored vehicles but could not afford to pay the hefty prices that the major suppliers were charging. His first brainchild was a wheeled armored car called the Cascavel. Whitaker's engineers took bits and pieces of existing technology and blended them together into a Brazilian soufflé. The Cascavel's 90-mm gun turret was purchased in France; the armor came from Britain; the drive chain and hydraulics came from Germany; and the whole was assembled in Brazil to sell for less than $200,000 a copy.

Saddam agreed to a trial purchase of some 150 Engesa-9 Cascavels in 1976, as part of a $836 million deal with Petrobras. Also included were 150 Urutu scout cars and 2,000 military trucks. Deliveries began at the rate of ten vehicles per month. It was the start of a long and mutually beneficial relationship that would have a dramatic impact on world peace.

*   *   *

Aleksey Kosygin was watching events in Iraq with a mixture of surprise and concern. He had been taken aback by Saddam Hussein's quick maneuvering to end the Kurdish revolt and alarmed by his peace agreement with the Shah of Iran. When Chirac visited Baghdad in January, Kosygin's advisors warned him that the USSR could ill afford to lose Iraq as a client for Soviet weapons and oil technology. So on May 29, 1976, Kosygin made the pilgrimage to Baghdad to bury the hatchet with Saddam Hussein. But Kosygin may have arrived too late; Raymond Barre had made it in to see Saddam the day before. The pot-bellied, jovial Barre played tag with Kosygin for the next three days, much to the dour Russian's displeasure.

Saddam told Kosygin he was willing to overlook the Soviet defection during the Kurdish war, but now insisted that their relations be placed on a purely commercial basis. Iraq would not support Soviet foreign policy goals in the region, but it would be happy to continue purchasing Soviet weapons. To Barre, Saddam reiterated his demand for state-of-the-art electronics on the Mirage, but softened his tone. If the technical review then under way reached a favorable conclusion about the French proposal, he said, they could do business, and fast.

On July 30, Saddam sent a trusted confidant, Information Minister Tarek Aziz, to Moscow to finalize the biggest package deal Iraq had ever concluded with the USSR. (Aziz was a Christian from the north, whose real first name was Johana.) According to the CIA, the sale was worth at least a billion dollars and included delivery to Iraq of the latest Soviet fighter, the MiG-23, as well as advanced air combat missiles, artillery pieces, tanks, and an accelerated training program for Iraqi air force officers and mechanics. The Soviets tried to get Aziz to expand Soviet visiting rights at the Oum Qasr naval base, but the Iraqi's answer was evasive. Saddam Hussein had no intention of returning to the old pattern of dependence on the USSR.[2]

On September 12 he sent Adnan Hamdani to Paris, to conclude the final details on the Mirage deal. Hamdani met with Barre, who had succeeded Chirac as prime minister in August.

Over the coming months the French managed to keep time with the fast-paced diplomatic and commercial ballet, thanks to their Palestinian advisor, Ramzi Daloul. Official delegations traveled between Paris and Baghdad, hammering out the technical details. Daloul's impressions were worth gold to his French business clients, as were his contacts, especially with Hamdani. What the Iraqis wanted most, Daloul said, was a show of political support (as opposed to political constraint). If France made it appear that they were seeking a strategic alliance with Iraq, then the arms deals would come by themselves.

Raymond Barre clinched the Mirage deal on June 26, 1977, during a working visit to Baghdad. With Daloul's help, the French had convinced Saddam to take the multirole version of the Mirage F1. Although the planes were essentially fighters, they could also carry out some ground attack functions. Saddam agreed to the sale on condition that more sophisticated versions of the plane would be sent later.

As it was announced in the French press a few weeks later, the most important elements in the $1.8 billion deal were the thirty-two jet fighters and the four twin-seater trainers. Dassault called the Iraqi jets the "EQ" planes, in keeping with the code-letter system his company used to designate export aircraft by country of purchase. Successive versions were numbered EQ2, EQ4, EQ5, and EQ6, to distinguish their avionics fit.

But the package included much more. The Iraqi army ordered 110 AMX-10P light amphibious tanks and a large consignment of Milan and HOT antitank launchers. Naval aviation put in for 14 Super Frelon helicopters, capable of launching the Exocet antiship missile from their bases near the Gulf. The air force placed its first orders for the expensive ordnance that hung beneath the wings of the Mirage fighters, including Matra's Magic I dogfight missile. The package deal included something for each of the three major branches of the Iraqi Armed Forces, with a little added perk — three Puma VIP helicopters, painted white, just like those used by the French president — thrown in for Saddam.

It was agreed that French defense contractors and government agencies would train Iraqi pilots and maintenance crews, and that certain ground installations (hangars, jigs for aircraft and engine repair, and communications) in Iraq would be modified to accommodate the first non-Soviet planes Iraq had purchased for more than a decade. For the French, it was much more than a foot in the air force door. For the Soviets, it was a dangerous precedent.

One clause of the new contract especially infuriated Kosygin. Iraq's deputy defense minister, Adnan Khairallah (whose antipathy for the Soviets was nearly as great as Saddam's) awarded the French a maintenance contract for "certain Soviet equipment already in service." French companies had performed a similar service for the Egyptian armed services after the Soviet pullout in 1973. The message to Moscow was clear: Soviet technicians were no longer indispensable in Iraq.

Kosygin tried to block the Mirage sale by offering Baghdad more MiG-23s at concessionary prices. When that didn't work, he threatened to call in Iraq's debts. As his frustration mounted, he even threatened to cut off further arms supplies if the Iraqis bought too heavily from the French. Saddam returned the compliment by stepping up criticism of Soviet foreign policy.

For Kosygin and his Middle East experts, it was a war of words. But for Saddam Hussein, it was a war of independence. He was determined to steer Iraq away from Soviet political domination, and in the French defense industry he had found a perfect partner. They saw a huge potential market for their goods in Iraq and lobbied the French government hard to agree to the sales. With a little luck and support, they argued, Iraq could become the Eldorado for French defense companies that Iran had become for their American counterparts. Arms sales to Iraq would create jobs, improve the balance of payments, and could even reduce development costs on new weapons programs.

Principal among the defense industry lobbyists was aviation wizard Marcel Dassault, a French Jew who fought the Nazis during the occupation, converted to Christianity, and built an industrial empire out of the ruins of Europe. He had supplied the French air force with every jet fighter they had ever owned, including a few the generals claimed they never wanted.

Dassault was a French institution. Besides heading the most prestigious industrial empire in postwar France, he sat in the French National Assembly. Although he rarely attended parliamentary debates, his presence among the elected made a powerful statement about the marriage between the military-industrial lobby and the French government. No one complained about a conflict of interest; not even Dassault's political enemies called on him to resign as head of his industrial empire if he wanted to remain in

Parliament. Industry and government were virtually one, a fact of the French political system that would have a major impact on arms sales policy over the next fifteen years.

Dassault, a tiny man with often cranky ideas, reigned like an icon over the French national conscience, perhaps because he had succeeded in the nearly impossible task of bridging the social and political chasm that divided the French Left from the Right. His political philosophy placed him on the Right, from whose ranks he was elected to Parliament, while the labor policies he pioneered at his aircraft and electronics factories had earned him the fidelity of the powerful Communist party trade union, the Confédération Général du Travail (CGT). When the government tried to reduce air force orders, Dassault's Communist workers would lead the protest to prevent defense cuts. When he proposed selling fighter-bombers to Israel, the CGT cheered. When he turned around and sold the same planes to South Africa, Libya, or Chile, the CGT cheered again. Dassault's foreign sales were in the national interest: they meant jobs.

After Dassault, the defense industry's most outspoken advocate was the president of Aérospatiale, General Jacques Mitterrand. The older brother of opposition leader François Mitterrand, the general served as a discreet bridge between the moderate conservatives and his brother's leftist coalition. He argued successfully for the commercial alliance with Saddam's Iraq. In the early days of the arms bonanza in the Gulf, Aérospatiale cashed in by selling Iraq thousands of antitank missiles and dozens of combat helicopters (see the Appendix). Now that the Mirage deal had gone through, the company was offering Saddam its most advanced weapon system: the sea-skimming Exocet missile, which soon proved its worth as an effective ship killer.

Dassault and Mitterrand received help in pushing through these sales from several key officials within the French government, including SDECE chief Alexandre de Marenches, who believed that France had a strategic interest in weaning Iraq from its Soviet masters, and André Giraud, who headed the vast nuclear lobby. But more important, they had the support of the two top men at the Defense Ministry's all-powerful Armaments Directorate (DGA), which was responsible for weapons programs, procurement, and foreign sales. The best ally of the French defense industry was none other than the head of the DGA, Engineer General Henri Martre. Martre believed that a marriage of reason with Iraq could help solve some of his ministry's cash-flow problems. Nuclear weapons research was expensive, and because France was determined to maintain an independent deterrent, the largest chunk of its research and development funds went toward perfecting a nuclear arsenal, while conventional weapons programs went begging for funds. Sales to Iraq offered a neat solution to this problem.

While Martre argued for the sales to Iraq from a strategic point of view, his director for international affairs, Hugues de l'Estoile, handled the details. The elegant, bespectacled de l'Estoile traveled again and again to Baghdad to help the Mirage negotiations along. His talents as a salesman were so appreciated that when he left government a few years later, he was snatched up by Marcel Dassault, for whom he became vice president in charge of international sales. De l'Estoile's activities hardly changed; he had just changed hats.

With the first Mirage sale, Iraq had become a multibillion-dollar portfolio. If you were French and your business was defense, Iraq soon became the only game in town. Nearly a thousand French defense contractors cashed in on the Iraqi bonanza, from the giants — Dassault, Aérospatiale, Thomson-CSF, Matra, and GIAT (Groupement des Industries d'Armement Terrestre) — down to manufacturers of microcircuits and camouflage nets. The real question was not who belonged to the pro-Iraq lobby, but who would dare to oppose it.

Saddam Hussein continued to believe that chemical weapons, because of their inherent simplicity, would help Iraq achieve final independence from its weapons suppliers. They were relatively easy to manufacture, and the raw materials could be purchased from a wide variety of sources on the world market. After Amer al-Saadi's purchasing team was rebuffed in New York by the two chemists from Pfaudler, they continued searching. In late 1976 they approached two British companies, Imperial Chemical Industries (ICI), and Babcock & Wilcox. Once again the Iraqis said they wanted to build a modern pesticides plant capable of producing Amiton, Demeton, Paraoxon, and parathion. An ICI spokesman, quoted by the *Washington Post,* said the company declined the offer "because of the sensitive nature of the materials and the potential for misuse."

But ICI did more than just decline the deal. According to intelligence sources in Washington, it also informed the British government of the unusual Iraqi request. ICI had no doubt that the type of pesticides plant Iraq was seeking could be easily converted to production of nerve gas. The specifications the Iraqis showed them (taken from the drawings supplied by Pfaudler the year before), called for the same type of corrosion-resistant reactor vessels, pipes, and pumps as were needed for nerve gas production. "It's clear that both the British and the U.S. intelligence communities were aware of the Iraqi procurement effort by late 1976, early 1977," the sources said. "But the information just got put in a drawer someplace."

On Capitol Hill, the hearings led by Senator Church into CIA dirty tricks were in full swing; it was not a time for the CIA to engage in more international skullduggery. The congressional investigation into CIA misdeeds, along with the extensive personnel cuts ordered by President Carter's intelligence chief, Stansfield Turner, had clipped the agency's wings. As for the British, it was not their habit to intervene in commercial contracts. But British intelligence discreetly made known its interest in Iraqi weapons plans, and this appears to have prompted the Iraqis to exercise greater caution in their procurement schemes.

After ICI in Britain turned them down, the Iraqis tried two companies in Italy. The giant chemical firm Montedison and the turnkey engineering concern Technipetrole, now known as TPL, both deny they had a hand in building a pesticides cum nerve gas plant in Iraq. Yet both have been named in various press accounts, and their names appear on the U.S. Senate Foreign Relations Committee roster of Iraq's chemical weapons suppliers.[3]

In the end, however, al-Saadi decided to go back to the land he knew best: Germany. According to Karl Heinz Lohs, the director of the Leipzig Institute for Poisonous Chemicals in East Germany and a frequent lecturer in Iraq, al-Saadi knew what he wanted from the very start. "You Germans have great expertise in the killing of Jews with gas," al-Saadi told him once. "This interests us in the same way. . . . How [can] this knowledge . . . be used to destroy Israel?"[4]

Lohs was horrified at the suggestion, and in his lectures he emphasized the terrible effects of chemical weapons use. It was only later, he told a West German reporter, that he realized his presence in Iraq had been a foil. Lohs now believes that the numerous East German chemical weapons experts who accompanied him on these trips used him to disguise the deepening cooperation between the East German government and Baghdad on chemical weapons production.

Germany is the world's specialist in poison gas. German generals were the first to introduce chlorine and mustard gas in combat during World War I, and German scientists continued to pioneer poison gas technologies afterward, despite the 1925 Geneva protocol prohibiting the use of chemical weapons in war. In 1937, the I. G. Farben Company of Germany discovered that certain organic phosphorus compounds, which were easy to obtain, could be transformed into a deadly gas that attacked the central nervous system. Hitler's Third Reich began manufacturing large quantities of the new nerve agent. But the führer never used it in combat. The chemistry involved in making the nerve gas compounds was so simple, he was told, that the Western powers must have already mastered it, which was true. Nevertheless, I. G. Farben patented the deadly mixture right after World War II. It was called Tabun.

Tabun and its first cousin, Sarin, were almost identical in composition to the organic phosphate compound parathion, a well-known but dangerous insecticide. Tabun and Sarin were so deadly that a single drop was enough to kill a man. Unlike mustard gas, chlorine, and phosgene — which had limited effect during World War I — nerve gas was odorless and colorless. It was easy to make and easy to spread. It made killing quick and efficient.

"People have made Sarin," says Julian Perry-Robinson, a chemical weapons expert at the University of Sussex in Great Britain. "One person has made Sarin in his mother's kitchen. It's in principle not all that difficult. That person, mind you, was trained in the skills of organic synthesis, and they are skills, but lots of people have them. Students of chemistry would have no particular problem, I don't think, university students, in producing Sarin quite easily."[5] Sarin and Tabun were obtained from organic phosphate compounds, which in turn derived from different types of phosphate minerals. Iraq had large phosphate deposits in its western desert, close to the Syrian border. By early 1977, al-Saadi had decided to divert them to nerve gas production. The story of this exploit shows how successful he became at disguising Saddam Hussein's murderous intentions behind ostensibly civilian projects.

The Belgian engineering firm Sybetra had already contracted to build a huge phosphates mine near the village of Shab al-Hiri. This plant, which now attracted al-Saadi's interest, came to be known as Akashat. It took its name from Wadi Akash, a dry riverbed where nuggets of raw phosphate mineral had glistened for centuries in the desert sun. Travelers who picked them up sold them at caravan towns, where they were known as "desert roses."

Phosphates mining was a perfectly acceptable enterprise for a developing country such as Iraq. There were plenty of examples around, including Morocco, which had become a major exporter of urea and fertilizer, manufactured from the phosphates deposits in the Sahara. Al-Saadi proposed creating the same sort of operation. Once work on the mine began in late 1976, he signed a second contract with Sybetra to build a giant fertilizer complex along the Euphrates at Al Qaim. The fact that the fertilizer plant was 150 kilometers from the phosphates mine aroused no suspicion. "We'll build a railroad," al-Saadi said when the Belgians asked how he would get the raw phosphates from the mine to Al Qaim. Iraq was a land of opportunity where it paid to think big.

Sybetra stood to make big profits from the Akashat / Al Qaim project, which it slated as a billion-dollar enterprise. As part of the Générale de Belgique group, the Brussels-based Sybetra had been set up to provide an export outlet for Belgian equipment manufacturers. Sybetra engineers turned the Akashat project over to the Union Minière of Belgium, which had run the mining industry in Zaire when that country was still a Belgian colony. The Al Qaim "fertilizer" plant was given to the Belgian chemicals company Mechime. Major construction work, buildings, internal rail lines, and roads were jobbed out to Six Construct International, another Brussels-based conglomerate, known as Sixco. Nobody batted an eye at the curious specifications, which called for reinforced concrete fortifications around certain buildings. Nor did they realize that al-Saadi and Saddam Hussein were acting on design when they decided to build the two plants so far from one another despite the extraordinary additional expense of constructing a dedicated rail link (built by Mendes Junior Constructora, of Brazil) to move the phosphate ore. But Saddam Hussein was following one of the basic principles of the ancient art of war: disperse your resources to make it more difficult and more costly for the enemy to take them out. By separating these critical facilities by 150 kilometers of desert, Saddam was hedging his bets. He was hoping to decrease the likelihood that enemy saboteurs could take them both out at once.

Little is known about the Akashat operation, although it has been publicly identified by U.S. officials as Iraq's first nerve gas plant. Former engineers from Sybetra said that Akashat was primarily a mining operation for the extraction, milling, and storage of phosphates. However, some accounts suggest that a separate $40 million plant for nerve gas production was built there.[6] The big chemical plant, however, was at Al Qaim.

Sybetra turned to fifty major subcontractors to build Al Qaim. Belgium's Mechime supplied plans and engineering for transforming raw phosphate ore into phosphoric acid, one of the basic components of fertilizer — and nerve gas. This production line was called Unit 100. For special equipment, Mechime turned to Copée Rust, part of France's Groupe Lafarge. Mechime built another large production line for sulfuric acid, used to transform phosphorous fluoride into hydrogen fluoride, a substance so corrosive it must be contained in special stainless steel or glass-lined reactor vessels. Hydrogen fluoride is one of the basic ingredients of Sarin.

From Davie Power Gas (DPG) in Great Britain, Sybetra ordered ammonium and potassium processing equipment, which was set up at Al Qaim's Unit 400. An American firm supplied a unit for producing another ammonium compound, believed to be ammonium perchlorate, or rocket fuel, while major Austrian, German, Swiss, Danish, and Swedish companies all contributed specialized equipment. As a former Sybetra project engineer noted, "It would indeed be easy to turn this type of equipment to another use besides fertilizer production." But nobody saw it at the time. It was the perfect example of dual-use technology. Al Qaim and Akashat had a perfectly legitimate purpose — to develop Iraq's enormous phosphates deposits into an industry — but they also fit a secret plan: to ensure supplies of basic chemicals for Saddam Hussein's poison gas machine.

As time went on, the Belgian engineer recalled, responsibility for Al Qaim was shifted from Iraq's State Organization for Minerals to a newly created outfit called SEPP. He knew it as the State Establishment for Phosphates Production. Others knew it by a different name.

Saddam Hussein's power was growing daily. President al-Bakr had trouble with his heart, and increasingly took a back seat to his younger protégé. By 1978 Saddam had managed to consolidate one crucial pocket of power. With scarcely a murmur from al-Bakr or the Baath party hierarchy, he succeeded in naming his brother-in-law and cousin, Adnan Khairallah, to replace al-Bakr as minister of defense.

Saddam knew that Soviet Premier Kosygin looked askance at his growing ties to the West. With almost magisterial control, Saddam alternated the signals he sent to Moscow. On the one hand, he stepped up persecution of the Iraqi Communist party by executing, in May 1978, twenty-one Communist military officers who had been languishing in jail since 1975. No political activity was allowed within the military, Saddam said, except that of the Arab Baath Socialist party. On June 7 the fate of the officers was announced by Naim Haddad, a member of the ruling RCC. In July the government turned the persecution into law, by retroactively extending the death penalty to all military personnel, other than Baathists, who had engaged in political activity since the 1968 putsch, "even if they had retired since that year." It was the last and final phase of Saddam's witch hunt against the Communists.[7]

On the other hand, Saddam increased arms purchases from the USSR. In 1978, according to the Stockholm International Peace Research Institute (SIPRI), Iraq ordered $3 billion worth of military equipment from the USSR, the biggest arms package Iraq had ever bought. It included 138 MiG-23/27 fighter-bombers (intended to rival the Mirage F1), a half-dozen SCUD-B missile launchers, up to 16 of the Soviet airlift command's largest troop and equipment transport, the Ilyushin-76 Candid, and large quantities of Mi8 troop transport helicopters. Another large order the next year included SA-6 antiaircraft missile batteries, MiG-25 reconnaissance planes, and a wide variety of ordnance for the MiG-23.

Saddam played it hot and cold with Kosygin and Brezhnev to keep the aging Soviet leaders on edge. In early 1978 he demanded that the Soviets move their embassy, which was located next door to the presidential palace. Saddam suspected the KGB of monitoring his conversations inside the palace and at the adjoining Baath party headquarters, and he wanted the embassy moved to make eavesdropping more difficult. When the Soviets refused, in April, the Iraqi authorities cut off water and electricity to their embassy compound. Within days the Soviets announced they would move.

When Saddam ventured to Moscow that December, he drove the message home. He would not tolerate Soviet "meddling" in domestic Iraqi politics through the ICP or the Kurds. Nor would he align his foreign policy to that of the USSR. Iraq had no intention of making "a larger contribution to the cause of national liberation," as Kosygin had requested. Iraq would steer its foreign policy and choose its investment partners as it saw fit. And, increasingly, it would turn to the West.[8]

Because Saddam was careful to make known his opposition to Soviet foreign policy goals, his extensive purchases of arms and technology from the USSR were viewed with only mild concern by Washington. Saddam's Iraq resembled no other Soviet client state and was increasingly seen as an anomaly. But then it was not a sure friend to the West, either. This became clear when the Camp David peace agreement between Israel and Egypt was announced in September 1978. Only two months later Saddam Hussein hosted radical Arab and Palestinian leaders at a Baghdad conference to form a "Front of Rejection." They pledged to punish Egypt's President Sadat for making peace with Israel and to punish the West for siding so openly with Israel. Palestinian terrorist groups were encouraged to strike Western targets. With the formation of the Baghdad front, Saddam Hussein realized one of his most cherished goals: to propel himself to the forefront of Arab politics.

Iraq's new radical role in Arab-Israeli politics would have attracted far greater attention and aroused concern in the West if it hadn't been for events taking place just across the border in Iran. As it was, the revolution that was brewing over there would change the face of Middle East politics for years to come.

FOUR

Saddam Takes the Helm

The Shah of Iran, with whom Saddam Hussein had negotiated a last-minute peace treaty in March 1975, fled Tehran in January 1979. A few days later, Ayatollah Ruhollah Khomeini made his triumphant return from exile to the Iranian capital. Revolutionaries faithful to the Ayatollah seized power in a bloody coup during the night of February 11–12, 1979, and the Islamic Republic of Iran was born. So was a major American foreign policy headache.

Washington was so preoccupied with the Iranian crisis that it had little time to worry about Saddam Hussein. The "Front of Rejection" launched during the Baghdad conference was a disappointment for President Carter, but not a major worry. American concern in the region focused on Syria and Jordan, which were urged to join the Camp David peace process and refused, and increasingly, on Iran.

The growing radicalism of the Iranian revolution and the expulsion of Egypt from the Arab League provided dramatic opportunities for Saddam Hussein, who was increasingly attracted by the idea of establishing a large defense manufacturing industry in Iraq. His only potential competitor in the Arab world for arms making was Egypt. But the Camp David peace agreements had seriously damaged Egypt's pan-Arab credentials. By launching the "Front of Rejection," Saddam hoped to reinforce Egypt's ostracism from the Arab fold and to take Egypt's place as the political and industrial center of the Arab world.

In 1975, three Arab oil states — Saudi Arabia, Qatar, and the United Arab Emirates — had pledged $335 million each to set up a new arms manufacturing group in Egypt, called the Arab Organization for Industrialization, or AOI. The idea, according to the AOI charter, was "to establish an industrial base within the Arab nation, to fulfill its needs in the field of advanced industries."

Egypt's arms industry, begun by Britain during the colonial era, was the oldest in the Middle East. Egyptian gunpowder plants had been operating for more than half a century. The country's first aircraft works was built in 1950. Although Egypt had the skilled labor force necessary to make large quantities of modern weapons, it lacked the money to invest in new equipment and industrial licenses. This is what the AOI had been designed to provide. With start-up capital of slightly more than $1 billion (Egypt's share of the joint venture consisted of existing industrial facilities), the AOI began a massive procurement effort, primarily in Europe. From France it bought licenses and knockdown kits for Gazelle antitank helicopters, Alphajet trainers, and a wide range of military engines; from the British it bought Swingfire antitank missiles, Jeeps, Land Rovers, and much more.

Saddam Hussein had objected to the AOI from the start, arguing somewhat feebly that Iraq was a better investment choice for the Arab Gulf states than Egypt. With Sadat's Egypt now banned from Arab politics as a result of the 1978 Camp David accords, Saddam urged the AOI partners to take their money out of Egypt and place it in Iraq. At the same time he launched negotiations with British Aerospace and Dassault to purchase an aircraft factory. The project would cost upward of $3 billion. Saddam figured he could launch negotiations first and pay later. It was a tactic he perfected as the years went on.

Building combat jets would confer on Saddam Hussein a prestige unheard of in the Arab world. His advisors told him that the best way to build a modern aeronautics industry was through licensed production of an advanced jet trainer. Even though the Iraqi air force had no pressing need for such a plane (they had just purchased L-39 jet trainers from Czechoslovakia), the manufacturing skills were similar to those required for more sophisticated fighters, which Saddam hoped to be able to build later on. It was an extremely ambitious program, and yet it raised no eyebrows in the West.

Asking the French to submit a bid for their Alphajet trainer, developed jointly with Dornier of West Germany, was a natural outgrowth of the extensive arms cooperation that already existed between the two countries. Asking British Aerospace to bid with their Hawk was more unusual, given Saddam's underlying hostility toward Great Britain.

As the colonial power that had carved out the modern state of Iraq from the ashes of the Ottoman Empire in 1916, Britain bore a large responsibility in Saddam's eyes for Iraq's most chronic problem: its limited access to the Gulf. Saddam felt that Britain had deprived Iraq of territory that was historically its own (that is, Kuwait). He had never forgiven the British government for thwarting an Iraqi attempt to seize Kuwait by force in 1963, and he accused the British of intervening to check his ambitions again in 1973, when Iraqi troops briefly crossed the border into the emirate a second time.

But there was another side of the coin. Without British insistence in 1916 in postcolonial negotiations with France, the Ottoman provinces of Basra, Baghdad, and Mosul would have been split into separate zones of influence, and modern Iraq would never have come into existence. The northern province of Mosul would have gone to France as the spoils of war, joining the French mandate of Syria-Lebanon, while Baghdad and Basra would have gone to Britain as part of its Middle East empire. It was "Churchill's folly," the saying went, to unite in one country two oil fields (Basra and Mosul) and three tribes (the Sunnis, Shiites, and Kurds) that had been separated by history, economic realities, and ethnology. Iraq was artificially large because of British stewardship. It was a secret debt, and Saddam hated it.

From 1916 until the revolution of 1958, Britain continued to dominate Iraqi affairs and Iraqi oil. That meant Britain was Iraq's principal arms supplier as well. But the first revolutionary regime in Baghdad had made a great show of casting out British military advisors and switching to Soviet weaponry. By 1960 most Middle East specialists considered it a foregone conclusion that Britain had been irremediably supplanted by the Soviets in Iraq. They concluded that Iraq had become a Soviet client. And they were wrong.

As one Soviet diplomat long acquainted with the region later admitted, "We never succeeded in penetrating the Iraqi high command, or the centers of decision-making within the Baath party. It is incorrect to speak of Soviet military personnel in Iraq as 'advisors' as you normally understand the term. They were more like contract employees working for an authoritarian employer who cared little about their welfare, subjected them to adverse conditions, and paid them a pittance for their labor."

If the Soviets failed in their attempts to penetrate the Iraqi Armed Forces, the British had succeeded beyond their wildest dreams. More than twenty years after they had been kicked out of Iraq, the Iraqi Staff College outside Baghdad was still using manuals on strategy and on battlefield tactics that had been prepared by the British War College. British army doctrine suffused Iraq's professional military structure. Many of Iraq's best officers had been educated at Sandhurst, the most prestigious military academy in the Commonwealth. Saddam Hussein was fascinated by the British, attracted by their characteristic efficiency and discretion, even though he loathed what he termed Britain's "hegemonistic intentions" toward Iraq.[1]

Saddam had another reason for inviting Britain to bid on the aircraft project. He suspected that his personal secretary, Adnan Hamdani, was on the take. According to information he had received from his intelligence chief, Barzan Ibrahim al-Tikriti (the oldest of his three half-brothers), Hamdani was taking kickbacks from the French.

At Thuwaitha, in the desert just fifteen miles south of Baghdad, work on Iraq's nuclear research center was progressing rapidly. So were the protests, which came ringing in through diplomatic channels from Israel, Great Britain, Saudi Arabia, Syria, and elsewhere. All expressed concern to the French that the Osirak reactor was really intended to make nuclear weapons.

To head off the protests, President Valéry Giscard d'Estaing ordered the French Atomic Energy Commission, the CEA, to develop a "clean" fuel for the Osirak reactor, so France could honor its lucrative nuclear contract without adding to fears of proliferation. The CEA began to experiment with a new fuel pack they called "Caramel," made of uranium enriched to a mere 7 percent. It was sufficient to power up the Osirak reactor, but totally useless for weapons production. The French urged Saddam to accept the new fuel to put his government "beyond all suspicion" of developing nuclear weapons. Saddam coldly refused. While he lavished public praise on his French "partners," privately he threatened to cancel juicy commercial contracts if the French didn't deliver his bomb-grade uranium. The only concession he finally accepted was to take delivery in smaller consignments.[2]

While the French were completing work on his reactors, Saddam concluded a ten-year nuclear cooperation agreement with Brazil. The 1979 agreement was so secret that future Brazilian governments claimed they were unaware of its contents. One clause, which Saddam may have required as a condition for signing large-scale arms contracts, committed Brazil to supplying Iraq with large quantities of natural and low-enriched uranium, reactor technologies, equipment, and training. Brazilian and Iraqi nuclear physicists were to "exchange visits to research and development facilities."[3]

The Brazilian agreement would be crucial for events to come. Brazil, too, had a secret nuclear weapons program, run by the navy. Since the early 1950s, Brazilian scientists had been working on ultracentrifuge technology to make bomb-grade fuel from the large supplies of natural uranium extracted from Brazilian mines. The Brazilian program had been started with the help of a former Third Reich scientist, Wilhelm Groth. In 1975 Brazil had signed the biggest nuclear deal in history with a consortium of West German firms, to build nuclear power reactors, research centers, reprocessing laboratories, and a centrifuge plant to enrich natural uranium. Iraq hoped to acquire West German nuclear technology through Brazil in a triangular relationship, benefitting from Third World solidarity.

Iraq signed other nuclear agreements with India and China, U.S. government sources say, although the details have never been revealed. Like Brazil and France, India and China were not signatories to the Nuclear Non-Proliferation Treaty. By April 1979 the only "missing link" in Iraq's plutonium-driven nuclear weapons program was a reprocessing laboratory to extract plutonium from spent reactor fuel or from irradiated "targets" placed around the reactor core. That link was supplied by the Italian nuclear clearinghouse, Snia Techint. According to documents provided by a former company manager, this subsidiary of the Fiat group agreed to sell four nuclear laboratories and three "hot cells" to the Iraqi Atomic Energy Commission. Hot cells are sophisticated concrete cubicles in which highly irradiated nuclear material can be manipulated by mechanical arms behind a thick glass window, after it has been removed from the reactor core.

Between 1978 and 1980, the United States tried to block this sale, but the Italian government argued that the nuclear transfers provided crucial leverage for Italy in the intense competition then underway on a $2.6 billion naval deal, to supply Iraq with what amounted to a turnkey modern navy. By providing the hot cells, Italy could demonstrate to Saddam that it was worthy of his trust.

Like the French, the Italians claimed that their technology would not help Iraq make the bomb. But according to Richard Wilson, director of the Department of Physics at Harvard University, who visited the Thuwaitha project not long after the hot cells were installed, the "Italian Project" was nothing less than a fuel fabrication plant and included sophisticated equipment for shaping highly enriched uranium, a key requirement for making a bomb. The Italian Project could provide Iraq with as much as 8 kilograms of plutonium per year, he believed, easily enough for one bomb. And it would all be operating within two years.[4]

When the twin Osirak reactor cores had been completed, the CEA made arrangements to have them hauled to the Mediterranean port of La Seyne-sur-Mer, near Toulon, to await the arrival of an Iraqi container ship. The CEA had done everything to avoid publicity, and security procedures were elaborate. The precious cargo arrived in the dead of night in a convoy of armored cars at the blue, orange, and white warehouse of the Compagnie des Constructions navales et industrielles de la Méditerranée (CNIM), a building designed to resist earthquakes. The plan was to load the reactor cores onto the Iraqi ship before dawn on the morning of April 9, 1979, before the day shift arrived.

At the Thuwaitha site in Iraq, everything was ready to receive the reactor cores. The huge reinforced concrete reactor pool, dug deep into the rocky earth, had been completed on time by the French contractors. The crane that was to hoist the reactors into place and manipulate spent fuel rods had been tested and greased to perfection. Test equipment was coming in from all over the world. A germanium detector had been purchased from ORTEC, a company in Oak Ridge, Tennessee, home of America's first bomb plant. Computers from Hewlett-Packard had been installed. The head of the Thuwaitha project, Dr. Ja'afar Dhia Ja'afar, told friends from the European Center for Nuclear Research (CERN) that a great day was about to dawn. But he spoke too soon.

On April 4, three young men stepped off the commuter flight from Paris at the tiny Toulon-Hyères airport. Without a word to each other, they hailed separate cabs and headed off to different hotels. All three carried European passports. On April 6, four other "tourists" arrived in Toulon. Without arousing suspicion, the seven young men met that evening near the CNIM warehouse and observed the habits of the night watchman guarding the building where the reactor cores were stored. Once they were sure the watchman had gone on his break, they climbed over the security fence and headed silently for the warehouse, which they opened with a replica of the key the watchman had used only a few hours earlier to close it down for the night.

Inside the hangar, they went straight to eight large crates. These contained the honeycomb structure of the reactor cores, where Dr. Ja'afar and his colleagues intended to place the zirconium-clad fuel rods a few months later, when they were scheduled to start up the Osirak bomb plant for the first time. Working quickly but carefully, the intruders packed specially designed high-explosive charges around the reactor cores. The explosives were powerful enough to penetrate armor plate.

At approximately 3:15 in the morning of April 7, an enormous blast rocked the CNIM warehouse, totally destroying the reactor cores but causing little other damage. No one was hurt. To this day the French police have found no trace of the bombers, and these details would never have come to light if it hadn't been for the "confession" in the German press by one member of the seven-man Israeli commando group a year later. Mossad had struck. The attack at La Seyne was code-named Operation Big Lift.

When Saddam learned of the bombing at La Seyne-sur-mer, he was furious. The French would of course have to replace the reactors, since they were responsible for them while they were on French soil. But the French would have to do more. Three weeks after the explosion, Saddam dispatched his cousin, Defense Minister Adnan Khairallah, to Paris to demand the replacement of the destroyed reactor cores and to deliver Iraq's final refusal to accept anything but bomb-grade fuel.

When Khairallah met with his French counterpart, Defense Minister Yvon Bourges, on May 4, the first item on the agenda was a detailed briefing on Dassault's latest plane, the Mirage 2000, then at an advanced stage of development. To soften Iraq's hard line on nuclear fuel, Khairallah told Bourges that Iraq was prepared to leap from the Mirage F1, which it had not yet received, to the Mirage 2000. But there was a hitch: Saddam wanted Dassault to build an assembly line in Iraq and train thousands of Iraqi workers.

To Bourges and his top arms salesman, Hugues de l'Estoile, the assembly line idea was out. They feared Iraq would dump its planes on Third World markets at a later date, undercutting by a wide margin the exorbitant prices Dassault demanded. What they told Khairallah, however, was different. The Mirage 2000 was several years from deployment, and Iraq needed a front-line fighter-bomber now. Instead of waiting for the new plane, Iraq would do better to buy more F1s, especially since Thomson-CSF was just then putting the finishing touches on a new radar, the Cyrano IV, that would enable the Iraqi planes to fly hundreds of miles at sand-dune level without being detected by enemy air defenses.

The new radar and low-level navigation package would give the Iraqi air force the ability to strike Israel. The deal sounded like music to Saddam's ears. He summoned the French premier to Baghdad on July 7 to accept the French proposal. Negotiations were over, Saddam told an enthralled Raymond Barre. The time of the payoff had come.

"We will never forget your positive attitude and your comprehension at the most difficult moments of our history," Saddam offered generously. "You were the only Western power to recognize the legitimacy of our decision, a few years back, when we nationalized the oil companies. You were the only ones not to provide support to the Kurdish rebellion, not to intrigue against the central government in Baghdad." Iraq and France had become strategic partners, Saddam said. And to prove it, he pledged to increase oil deliveries to France by half.

Barre received Saddam's offer graciously, for France had suffered more than most countries from the break in Iranian oil deliveries caused by the Ayatollah's revolution. Iraq now supplied France with roughly 25 percent of its oil. And France had become Iraq's third largest trading partner, after West Germany and Japan.

The rewards for so much French "comprehension" were on their way. By the end of Barre's trip, *Le Monde* announced that French suppliers were being considered for naval purchases worth between $1.4 and $2.3 billion. By October 1979, French nonmilitary exports to Iraq were up 53 percent from the previous year. In December the contract for twenty-four additional Mirage fighter-bombers was signed. It was billed by *Le Monde* as a way of "better preparing the purchase of the Mirage 2000 when the new combat aircraft from Dassault-Bréguet becomes operational."

No sooner had Raymond Barre left Baghdad than one of the most bizarre episodes in modern Iraqi history occurred.

In early July, only days before Iraq and Syria were scheduled to enter a treaty of union, Saddam claimed to have discovered a conspiracy to overthrow his ruling Baath party. In fact the plotters, who included seven of Saddam's closest colleagues on the ruling Revolutionary Command Council (RCC), had a far more limited aim. They had learned that Saddam Hussein was planning to take over the presidency from Ahmed Hassan al-Bakr before the treaty was signed with Syria. Already, as vice president, Saddam had sown death and destruction throughout Iraqi Kurdistan. His purges of Communists within the army had left widespread resentment among the professional officer corps. If unchecked, Saddam and his cronies from Tikrit would bring ruin upon the whole country, if not outright civil war, they feared. So Saddam's rivals, led by a secretary general of the RCC, Muhy Hussein al-Mashhadi, launched a "stop Saddam" campaign.

Saddam got wind of the plot as it was developing but waited patiently for the conspirators to play their hand. On July 12 Saddam convened a Baath party congress in Baghdad to consecrate his rise to power and al-Bakr's retirement.

The conspirators' plan was to get rid of Saddam through a bureaucratic trick. All they had to do, they believed, was to maintain al-Bakr in the presidency until the union with Syria was consummated. Then Saddam would be forced to take a back seat, not only to al-Bakr, who would become vice president of the union but, more important, to the iron-willed Syrian leader, Hafiz al-Assad, who would become its president. Under Assad's boot, they figured, Saddam was doomed.

As the voting on al-Bakr's retirement was about to begin, al-Mashhadi took the floor and demanded that the vote be unanimous, as called for in party regulations, rather than by simple majority. Al-Bakr, shocked, growled in protest. "What are you really after here?"

"You can't leave," al-Mashhadi rejoined. "If you are sick, why you don't you take a vacation instead?" In the brief, embarrassed silence that swept across the huge meeting hall, Saddam could read the depth of his victory. Al-Mashhadi had played his hand and lost. His co-conspirators said nothing.[5]

Saddam's promotion was confirmed later at the same meeting. His first act as president was to strip al-Mashhadi of all his party posts. Then he ordered his thugs to haul the offender away from the meeting hall. To make sure he had flushed out the conspiracy, he asked Barzan Ibrahim al-Tikriti, who had replaced Sadoun Shaker as head of Iraqi intelligence, to launch an "investigation." It was a license to arrest, interrogate, and torture at will, skills at which Barzan excelled. Within days he delivered a list of sixty-eight names to Saddam, including those of some very prominent Iraqis. All were involved in some way or other with the "plot."

Saddam Hussein owes his remarkable tenure to his ruthless extermination of opponents. In the early days the Communists were his favorite target, "a rotten, atheistic, yellow storm which has plagued Iraq."[6] After tricking them into joining his government, he paved the streets of Baghdad with their blood. To reduce the risks of succumbing to the ax of an unknown rival, he surrounded himself with sycophants and the family clan. *I and my brother against our cousin.* . . . When his own relatives turned against him, he never hesitated to snuff them out with his own hand.

Saddam inaugurated his presidency ten days later with an extraordinary psychodrama reminiscent of the most lavish festivals of Nazi hysteria. In front of a stunned audience of Baath party officials on July 22, Muhy al-Mashhadi was forced to read through a public "confession" of his crimes against the party and the state, while Saddam looked on from the speaker's podium, chewing his cigar. Then Saddam took the floor and told some home truths about party loyalty. "Treason is unjustifiable," he thundered into the microphone. "That's why there can be no degrees of betrayal."

No matter how slight the offense, crimes against the party or against his person (which by now had become one and the same) merited death.

He picked up the list Barzan had prepared and began to read out the names, one by one, with agonizing slowness. As each of the accused stood up, terrified, Saddam waved his hand derisively and shouted at him to get out. He repeated this procedure until the tension in the meeting hall verged on frenzy. Finally, one of Saddam's cousins, Ali Hassan al-Majid, stood up and shouted, "Everything that you did in the past was good and everything that will do in the future is good." In the official videotape Saddam had made of the party proceedings, pandemonium breaks out. Saddam himself begins to sob as loyal Baathists call on him to cleanse the party of the unfaithful.[7] On August 8, 1979, twenty-one of those on Barzan's list were executed by a firing squad.

Because the victims included fully one-third of the ruling Revolutionary Command Council, the risk of rebellion within party ranks was high. So Saddam called on every party congress throughout the country to send a delegate to man the firing squad. It was a stroke of political genius. Not only had Saddam smashed today's rivals, he had implicated future rivals by turning them into executioners. He led the firing squad personally, side by side with the remaining members of the RCC. It was a tactic he would use again and again, until there was not a single prominent politician in Iraq who did not have the blood of fellow Iraqis on his hands. Whether through family or through political violence, the bonds of Saddam's regime were made of blood.[8]

By the time Saddam took over as president of Iraq in 1979, he had concentrated power in his own hands. Key positions in the military, the security apparatus, and the party were filled from a pool of some five hundred candidates, all members of his family or his clan. It was a repeat of the tribal system of government that had ruled the Arab world for generations; and it was one of the dark secrets of his regime that Saddam tried to hide beneath a blanket of rhetoric about socialism and revolution.

Saddam believed he needed absolute power over his countrymen in order to fulfill his monumental ambition. "Your revolution," he told party militants shortly after assuming the presidency, "is more than ever the target of Zionism and of its international manifestations. It is also the target of the great powers, because it resolutely adheres to its independent nationalist line, opposed to all forms of foreign interference."[9] Enemies were everywhere, within Iraq and without, and all were out to get Saddam Hussein, he believed.

Saddam liked to say he was willing to pay 10 percent more for French weapons than for similar Soviet equipment because he knew he was "buying the best." It was a statement made in all innocence. When Saddam learned in the spring of 1979 that Adnan Hamdani, his bagman for purchases of high-tech equipment and arms, was skimming of the top, his fury knew no bounds. But as was his habit, he kept his suspicions to himself and close family until he had gathered enough evidence to strike.

What he discovered, sources familiar with the case say, was that Hamdani and the Palestinian middleman, Ramzi Daloul, were taking 10 percent off the top of every arms deal Iraq signed with France. Half went to Daloul and his partner, a Lebanese trader named Sarkis Soghenalian to cover expenses; half went to Hamdani. The 10 percent "surcharge" was passed on to the Iraqi government.

What incensed Saddam about the Hamdani case — besides the fact that he and his family were not getting a cut — was that a foreign government might have gained access to Iraqi state secrets. Hamdani knew as much as anyone about Saddam's strategic plans. He had personally negotiated many of the arms deals, and he knew in detail about Saddam's attempts to purchase chemical weapons and nuclear technologies from the West, China, and Brazil. After forcing Hamdani to make a complete confession, a furious Saddam summoned Daloul to Baghdad and demanded his money back. The terrified Palestinian is said to have forked up $8 million in cash and may have made other "contributions" to a secret Baath party fund held in a Swiss bank. He owed his life to the timely intervention of his political sponsor, PLO chairman Yasser Arafat. Besides making contributions to Arafat's Fatah Movement, Daloul sought additional protection by making substantial payments to one of Arafat's rivals, the radical Palestinian leader George Habash.

French defense contractors working in Iraq at the time heard rumors that Hamdani was to be executed and went out of their way to avoid him. "By the time you heard that this or that official was on the take," one arms salesman recalled, "it was already too late. Within weeks — months at the most — he disappeared."

Saddam angrily informed the French that he refused to pay Daloul's commission and that he was chopping 10 percent off the top of every outstanding payment. The French swallowed hard and agreed to charge no more commissions. Instead they made a secret arrangement with Daloul for future services, which some sources believe he continues to receive today.

When Saddam assumed the presidency in July 1979, the modernization of the Iraqi army after the debacle in Kurdistan was nearly complete. The Baathists were committing upward of 35 percent of the state budget to the purchase of arms from the Soviet Union, France, Italy, Yugoslavia, and Brazil. Many of the larger deals involved arms for oil swaps. But some were paid in cash, especially with the Soviet Union, with whom Saddam's relations had cooled to a chill, following the brief but humiliating Soviet arms embargo.

The list of Iraqi arms purchases from 1976 to 1980 would make any dictator drool. A two-bit force when General Qassem took power in 1958, the Iraqi army by 1980 had some 2,000 tanks, 130 self-propelled howitzers, 800 artillery pieces, and 1,200 anti-aircraft guns. The navy, hitherto nonexistent, had five Osa-class Russian missile boats, equipped with the Styx antiship missile, and 26 rapid patrol boats. Three submarines were on order from the Soviet Union, and plans had been drawn up to purchase four frigates and six corvettes from the West.

The air force undoubtedly had made the most impressive progress. A powerful strike force had been put together, composed of 12 supersonic Tupolev Tu-22 bombers and 80 MiG-23/27s organized in four ground attack squadrons. Added to this were five squadrons of Sukhoi-7B and Su-20 fighter-bombers, another 57 older MiG-19 and MiG-17s, nearly as many HS Hunter F.59s and T.69s from Great Britain, and 60 Mirage F1s on order from France. Air defense was handled by five squadrons of MiG-21s (more than 90 aircraft), which could double in a crunch as ground-attack aircraft, as they had during the Kurdish wars. Saddam had also begun to build a sizable helicopter fleet, which included some 80 Soviet transport and attack helicopters and a number of French and German helicopters equipped for antitank warfare.

It was a period of lavish spending, lavish growth, and extravagant ambition. As arms salesmen from East and West plied their wares in Baghdad, few realized — and fewer cared — that Saddam was purchasing all that equipment with a precise design.

FIVE

The Tilt Begins

Under Iraq's nuclear cooperation agreement with France, 600 Iraqi technicians and physicists were to be trained at various French institutions, including its experimental nuclear research center at Saclay. But by mid-1980 Iraq had sent only one-tenth that number. Despite Iraq's attempts to favor technical studies, as Hassib Sabbagh's APD had suggested, it still lacked nuclear physicists. Not to be deterred, Dr. Ja'afar and his colleagues turned to researchers from other Arab nations, "repatriating" them to Iraq. After all, Iraq's bomb was intended to be an Arab bomb, to reclaim the lost dignity of the whole Arab world. Naim Haddad, one of Saddam's closest associates, put it bluntly. "The Arabs must get an atom bomb."[1]

Foremost among those recruited were Egyptian nuclear physicists. That Saddam should turn to the Egyptians despite his outward rejection of Egypt's separate peace accord with Israel was a sign of his strong pragmatism. Saddam Hussein would deal with the devil in person if he thought it would further his own aims. Saddam ordered Ja'afar to hire one of Egypt's best-known nuclear physicists, Dr. Yahia al-Meshed, and enroll him at Saclay as part of the Iraqi program. Al-Meshed's specialty was the chemical reprocessing technique of obtaining bomb-grade plutonium from spent reactor fuel.

Al-Meshed returned to his room at the Hotel Meridien in Paris on Friday evening, June 13, 1980, after a full week of "research" at Saclay. Intending to get a good night's sleep so he could go out on the town the next day, he hung the "Do Not Disturb" sign on his door, kicked off his shoes, and went to bed. He never suspected it would be for the last time. The next day the chambermaid found al-Meshed's badly battered body at the foot of his bed. He had been beaten to death, a particularly brutal form of assassination. That evening Israel radio announced his death, commenting that "Iraqi projects to acquire an atomic bomb have been set back by two years."

Two transactions that spring heightened fears that Iraq intended to use the Osirak reactor to produce bomb-grade plutonium. An Italian company, in a semiclandestine deal, sold Iraq six tons of depleted uranium purchased from the West German nuclear consortium NUKEM. Fearing that NUKEM might not deliver the uranium if they knew it was intended for Iraq, the Italians claimed it was for domestic use in Italy. But they needn't have worried about NUKEM's scruples. The consortium was a wholly owned subsidiary of the German chemicals giant Degussa, which had invented and manufactured Zyklon B, the powerful cyanide gas that streamed out of the showerheads in Hitler's death camps, killing millions of European Jews. Degussa had also played a key role in the Nazi effort to build an atom bomb, stopped only when its Oranienburg works near Berlin were flattened by U.S. bombers in 1945. That same year, as the Third Reich was going up in flames, Degussa's chairman, Hermann Schlosser, donated 45,000 reichs-marks to Hitler's SS. Thirty-five years later Schlosser was still on the Degussa board, and in 1987 he was awarded the German Federal Merit Cross for his services to industry.[2]

One of Schlosser's services was shipping nuclear equipment and materials to almost every developing nation that was known to have a clandestine bomb program. Another was opening the vast Iraqi market to German firms. His readiness to supply nuclear materials to both India and Pakistan had impressed on Saddam Hussein that this was a man he could do business with.

Only months after the triangular deal with Italy, NUKEM offered to sell the Iraqis even more uranium. Why go through an expensive intermediary when you could buy direct? NUKEM was ready to sell Iraq 11,364 kilograms of depleted uranium fuel pins, the equivalent of 158 *years* of nuclear fuel for the Osirak reactors. To fill such a large order, NUKEM turned to a Montreal trading company called Eldorado, and to RMI Company of Ashtabula, Ohio, which specialized in nuclear waste. The Iraqis claimed the old fuel pins were to be used in a training reactor that was not yet built. According to Leonard S. Spector, an American expert on nuclear proliferation, "A more likely reason . . . was that the pins were intended to be inserted into Osirak." Spector pointed out that depleted uranium is worthless as a nuclear fuel "and could not have powered any Iraqi reactor, current or future. But depleted uranium, like natural uranium, can be irradiated to produce plutonium." In other words, it was just what the Iraqis needed to make a bomb.[3]

The deal would have gone through if it hadn't been for alert regulatory officials in the United States and Canada, who suspected NUKEM of hiding the real identity of its client. When they learned that the fuel pins were destined for Iraq, they blocked the sale. As one of the officials who worked on the case was quick to point out, "This came from the same people who brought us Zyklon B."

Like most European nations, West Germany was dependent on Gulf oil and had bartered technology for oil with the Arab world and Iran. Thirty-five years after the Holocaust, the West Germans were willing to sell technology that would allow Iraq to manufacture poison gas, ballistic missiles, even nuclear weapons. But West German law prohibited the export of arms.

The very existence of a weapons industry in West Germany was a closely guarded secret all through the 1950s and 1960s. As the years went by, most of the same technology concerns that had helped build Hitler's Third Reich were born again from the ashes of World War II. One of the largest firms was the aircraft maker Messerschmitt-Bölkow-Blohm, or MBB. By the late 1970s MBB had become a premier manufacturer of combat helicopters and tactical missiles.

MBB, observing the enormous amounts of money Iraq was spending on weapons, wondered why the French and Soviets should reap all the rewards, just because of the scruples of the West German parliament, which forbid foreign arms sales. One way MBB got around the export ban was by joining international marketing groups. It teamed with Aérospatiale in France to form the Euromissile consortium, which sold tens of thousands of antitank and anti-aircraft missiles worldwide — a high percentage to Iraq — all without disturbing the acute sensibilities of history-conscious Germans. As long as Germans weren't doing the actual selling, everything was fine. "We must respect our teaming agreements," was how MBB spokesmen liked to explain it. "We have no control over where our French or British or Italian partners decide to sell our systems."

The text of the Euromissile agreement, signed in 1972 by then Defense Minister Helmut Schmidt, was explicit. Once either partner signed a sales contract, "neither of the two governments will prevent the other from exporting or having exported war weapons or other armament materiel, which is the result of joint development or production."[4]

MBB had no such teaming arrangement for its helicopter division, so when Iraqi agents approached the company in 1980 to purchase attack helicopters, they had to scramble to find a partner on the international arms market. While the paperwork was being sorted out, work on the Iraqi choppers began — at MBB's main helicopter works just outside Munich.

MBB disguised a succession of helicopter deals with Iraq in a variety of ways. The first twenty Iraqi BO-105s were listed in the international arms registers compiled by the Stockholm International Peace Research Institute in 1981 as a production license granted to the Nurtania Aircraft Company in Indonesia, but this arrangement aroused suspicion among West German parliamentarians and pacifist groups, since Nurtania had not built its helicopter plant yet. For years MBB insisted it had never built and never delivered these aircraft to Iraq. Today, however, MBB officials acknowledge that they were shipped to Baghdad directly from Munich, but insist that they were unarmed "executive transport" helicopters (the West German army used them as antitank machines).

The Iraqi helicopters appear to have left the Munich factory in 1982 and 1983. But they didn't go directly to Iraq. First they made a stopover in Switzerland, where a retrofit firm called Transair Swiss mounted Swiss-built rapid-fire guns and other weaponry. Then the helicopters hopped over the border to Austria, so that the Denzel Company could add communications, navigation, and fire-control systems necessary for military operations. A pacifist group spotted the last of these helicopters in 1984 on the airstrip of Pichling, Austria, in full camouflage dress, as an Iraqi military cargo plan came to load them for the final journey to Baghdad. Although the revelation that MBB was selling combat helicopters to Iraq set off a scandal in West Germany, Messerschmitt managed to deliver dozens more to Iraq, using increasingly clandestine means.[5]

MBB ceded a license in 1981 to Spain's state-owned aircraft maker, CASA, officials at both companies concede, to handle military exports to the Middle East for the BO-105. The Iraqis signed an agreement the next year to purchase twenty-four helicopters armed with rapid-fire Oerlikon 20-mm cannons, with deliveries at almost the same time as those from Germany and Austria. Later MBB sales to Iraq included twelve BK-117 light transport helicopters, a model that had been developed jointly with Kawasaki in Japan. "These helicopters were sold to Iraq via our American subsidiary," said Christina Gotzheim, a spokesman for MBB's helicopter division. "They were fitted out with search and rescue winches in the United States, then shipped to Iraq via the United Kingdom in February 1990." Like the other MBB sales, this was a purely civilian deal. "The only armed MBB helicopters that went to Iraq came from Spain," Gotzheim advised.

The United States was mildly concerned about the Iraqi arms buildup but did nothing to temper Saddam's appetite. At the rare White House briefings that touched on Gulf affairs, the State Department arms control experts and Arab analysts argued that throughout the 1970s the U.S. arms exports to Iran had far outpaced European and Soviet arms sales to Iraq. Rather than worry about the arming of Saddam, which the United States was powerless to prevent, the government should keep tabs on the level and sophistication of Iraqi weaponry and make sure that the Shah of Iran bought better equipment from U.S. defense contractors. Given that Iran was three times the size of Iraq, and many times wealthier, the Shah could simply outspend Saddam Hussein. Besides, no one believed the Iraqis would ever master the sophisticated technology they were purchasing. The French technicians who were training Iraqi pilots and missile operators disdainfully described their students as "incompetents." In this the French wrongly assimilated Iraq with other Arab Gulf states, which were buying anything and

everything from European arms merchants and treating sophisticated weaponry like so many fancy toys.

The Islamic revolution in Iran upset the entire strategic equation
in the region. America's principal ally in the Gulf, the Shah, was
swept aside overnight, and no one else on the horizon could replace
him as the guarantor of U.S. interests in the region. The Carter
administration had tried to convince religious leaders in the early
days of the revolution to maintain security cooperation with the
United States, but any illusions of "working with" the revolutionaries in Iran were brutally dispelled on the morning of November 4, 1979, when 3,000 Iranian "students" stormed over the walls
of the United States Embassy compound in Tehran, occupying it in
the name of the struggle against imperialism. Revolutionary Iran
became America's enemy. Worse, Iran began to threaten the conservative oil monarchies just across the Gulf, creating real fears of an
"Islamic sweep" westward that would threaten regional stability
and Western oil supplies.[6]

These events cast Iraq in a new light. State Department analysts
pointed out that Saddam Hussein was a virulent anti-Communist.
When the Soviet Union invaded Afghanistan on Christmas Day of
1979, Saddam joined the chorus of conservative Arab leaders who
vigorously condemned the aggression. Better yet, the Iraqi was
strengthening his ties to Saudi Arabia, America's only remaining
ally in the Gulf. On March 25, 1980, Saddam signed what
amounted to an anti-Soviet pact with Saudi Arabia to prop up
neighboring North Yemen, which was struggling to repel a Soviet-
backed attack from Communist rebels in South Yemen. Saddam
pledged Iraqi military help "to liberate South Yemen from communist agents and their masters." His pact with the Saudis was the
only good news from the region for the State Department and the
Carter White House during that troubled season.

The greatest fear shared by President Carter and his national
security advisor, Zbigniew Brzezinski, was a Soviet takeover of
Iran. By April 1980 there was clear evidence that the embassy siege
had been engineered by Soviet intelligence agents, with the goal of
bringing down the moderate government of Mehdi Bazargan,
which had ruled Iran in the months following the forced departure
of the Shah. Evidence now available shows that the Soviets were
hoping to push the regime over the radical brink so that the

pro-Soviet mullahs could "block the normalization of relations with the United States."[7] Because of this situation, along with the Soviet invasion of Afghanistan and the Soviet-backed attack on North Yemen, the Carter administration feared that it was facing a concerted Soviet attempt to reverse the balance of power in the region. Brzezinski believed that the Soviets were trying to achieve their historic goal of reaching the warm waters of the Gulf through Iran, Afghanistan, and the Baluchistan region along the Pakistan-Iran border. For Carter's hard-line advisor, it was a strategic nightmare.

Although the United States still had no diplomatic relations with Baghdad (Iraq had broken ties after the Arab-Israeli Six-Day War in 1967), by mid-1980 Brzezinski began to look more favorably toward Saddam Hussein as a potential counterweight to the Ayatollah Khomeini and as a force to contain Soviet expansionism in the region. The American tilt toward Iraq began here, just as the Cold War was getting off to a new start.

The hint of a change in the U.S. attitude toward Iraq was warmly welcomed in Baghdad, although not for the reasons that Carter administration officials thought. Saddam Hussein believed that recognition by the United States of Iraq's role as a counter to radical, fundamentalist Iran would boost his ambition of becoming the acknowledged head of the Arab world. With Egypt banned from the Arab League and Syria embroiled in Lebanon, Iraq was the only contender for the Arab throne. To attain that goal, which would put Iraq on the front line with Israel, Saddam was willing to bend his tactics to meet what he perceived as U.S. requirements, especially if those requirements related to Iran.

Saddam had an old score to settle with the Iranians over his southern border. He had never liked the agreement signed with the Shah in 1975. He felt confident he could regain the lost territory and probably topple the anti-American regime in Tehran by taking swift military action. He had no illusions that the United States would openly support the war he proposed to start. But getting rid of the Ayatollah Khomeini was clearly in the American interest, and in many other ways the United States and Iraq could benefit each other, Saddam believed. It was time to renew diplomatic relations with Washington and to move on quickly to more elaborate forms of strategic cooperation.

Senator Stephen Solarz was the first person outside the Carter administration to get an inkling of just how close the government had come to forging a strategic alliance with Iraq. When Solarz visited Baghdad in 1982, Saddam Hussein explained why Iraq had been seeking stronger ties to Washington. In the months before he declared war on Iran in September 1980, Saddam said, he had been reviewing the entire question of Iraqi-American relations with other members of the Revolutionary Command Council. "I thought it was not right that Iraq's relations, as a nonaligned and independent country, should remain severed with one of the two superpowers in the world," he told Solarz. "Then the war broke out and the idea of discussing the issue in the leadership was put aside." Saddam hated to have it appear that he was seeking American help in time of need.[8]

With Baghdad leaning toward the United States and Washington tilting toward Iraq, the stage was set for a high-level meeting between the two administrations. It would be the first time that a Baath party representative had ever met with a U.S. government official. The top-secret negotiating session was Brzezinski's idea. According to the *New York Times* and to accounts of Iranian exiles, Brzezinski flew to Amman, Jordan, during the first week of July 1980 to meet with the Iraqi leader. The aim, the *Times* wrote, was to discuss ways the United States and Iraq could coordinate their activities "to oppose Iran's reckless policies." If that was the purpose of the meeting, it was tantamount to a council of war.

Brzezinski and former aides deny he ever met fact to face with Saddam, and surely the Iraqi leader would have milked such a clear recognition of his importance for all it was worth. But Brzezinski did pay a call on Jordan's King Hussein, and he may have met with a high-level Iraqi emissary as well, to discuss the likelihood of war between Iran and Iraq and American response to it. In Baghdad, the meeting was taken as heady encouragement to Saddam's war plans. As a former aide to Brzezinski, Gary Sick, said in an interview, "There was no doubt where Brzezinski's heart lay" when it came to Iran. The Islamic revolution was a threat to U.S. interests in the region, and a strong Iraq would check Khomeini's expansionist desires. "Brzezinski was letting Saddam assume there was a U.S. green light for his invasion of Iran, because there was no explicit red light. But to say the U.S. planned and plotted it all out

in advance is simply not true. Saddam had his own reasons for invading Iran, and they were sufficient."

Brzezinski's discussion with King Hussein provided the first hint that the United States was looking for new partners in the region that were able to police the Gulf. Despite American concern over Iraq's nuclear program and Saddam's rapidly growing military arsenal, Baghdad was clearly the best choice. For a hard-nosed strategist like Brzezinski, it was a high-stakes risk worth taking. Especially with U.S. hostages in Tehran and presidential elections coming up in November.

Saddam Hussein saw the United States as "a huge candy store full of high-tech goodies," as one American diplomat in Baghdad put it. His goal in improving relations with Washington was to gain access to the advanced technology that had guaranteed Israel's superiority over the Arabs in every war they had ever fought. The best way to determine whether the Americans were as serious about closer ties as Brzezinski had suggested was to request arms. Saddam decided to test the waters by slipping American components into a European arms contract. The first Iraqi attempt to "buy American" occurred just as tensions were rising with Iran.

Iraq was negotiating to buy a turnkey navy from the Italian government for $2.6 billion: it included four 2,500-ton Lupo-class frigates, six 650-ton Assad-class corvettes, an 8,700-ton supply ship, and a 6,000-ton floating dock. The eleven vessels were to be accompanied by complete port facilities, missiles, state-of-the-art electronics, radar, and all the necessary training and maintenance. Some 1,200 Iraqi naval officers would go to Italy for training. The Genoa-based Fincantieri Navali Riunti had undercut its French competitors by at least $200 million. The Soviets were left out in the cold.

Saddam's reasons for buying the ships from Italy instead of France or the USSR were strategic rather than technical. He wanted to broaden his supply base and expand his club of international supporters. With so much business tied to the Iraqi market, Saddam figured, the Italian government and business community would join the pro-Iraq lobby. If he couldn't create loyalty through ideology (Saddam's only ideological supporters were neo-Fascists and anti-American factions in France and Germany), then he would buy it.

To the Italians' dismay, the Iraqi Ministry of Defense insisted that the frigates be powered by General Electric gas turbine engines purchased in the United States. The eight engines, which Fincantieri agreed to buy for $11.2 million, were cleared for export by the U.S. Commerce Department in January 1980. A month later, however, members of the U.S. Senate blocked the sale because Iraq was on the State Department's list of countries supporting international terrorism. In the months that followed, the State Department and the White House worked behind the scenes to grease the skids. In July, Carter came out in favor of selling Iraq five Boeing airliners for its national airline, the first such sale since the Baathists had seized power. In August the State Department managed to overturn the Senate ruling on the GE engines, and in early September, only days before Saddam attacked Iran, Iraq announced that it had chosen Italy as its principal partner for the outfitting and training of an entire modern navy.

The U.S. "tilt" toward Iraq had borne its first fruits.

Meanwhile, in Tehran, Iranian President Abolhassan Bani Sadr was facing attacks from radical clergymen on the left and potential mutinies from American-trained military officers on the right. To "safeguard the Revolution," some 12,000 U.S.-trained officers were purged from the armed forces, with a heavy emphasis on majors and colonels. Of an estimated two hundred generals, "26 were executed and the rest forcibly retired."[9] The hostage crisis in Tehran caused Bani Sadr to fear that America would intervene, either directly (as they did in the failed attempt at Desert One in April 1980), or with the help of Iraq. To this day, Bani Sadr is convinced that the United States did try to overthrow his regime. Now in exile in Paris, he tells the story of an aborted coup, which he believes was part of a joint U.S.-Iraqi operation.

The plotters were led by the former head of the shah's army, General Gholam Ali Oveissi, who had moved to Baghdad along with the last of the shah's prime ministers, Shahpur Bakhtiar. They set up a military training camp near the Iraqi city of Sulaimaniya.[10] According to Bani Sadr, their sympathizers inside Iran established their headquarters at Nogeh air base, just outside the city of Hamadan, midway between Tehran and the border with Iraq. "We unveiled eight major cells" of the underground organization, the

former president recalls. "The largest of the cells was in the air force. But there were others at army bases in Kermanshah, Khuzistan, Azerbaijan, and Kurdistan, all along the Iraqi border. Their mission was to paralyze the army and the air force once Iraq launched its invasion. It was not a coup d'état but an organized Iraqi attack."

The first clue to the conspiracy came from an intercepted letter. By comparing the handwriting to samples in army files, Iranian intelligence officers were able to identify its author, whom they traced to a helicopter commando unit. "The problem was, we didn't know when the Iraqis intended to act. But we did know that they were planning to stage a coup to restore the shah, which would provide cover for the invasion."

Armed with intelligence provided by a Soviet diplomat, Bani Sadr struck quietly in July 1980, only days after Brzezinski's trip to Amman. In total secrecy he rounded up 600 pro-Bakhtiar officers who were attending a planning meeting at Nogeh air base. Among them were 25 air force pilots and 270 officers from the only regular army division then stationed in the southern border province of Khuzistan. The army officers had been ordered to dismantle Iranian defenses along the border with Iraq; Saddam Hussein was planning to march on Tehran, overthrow Khomeini, and win eternal gratitude from Washington.

One of the most haunting ironies of the Nogeh coup attempt did not emerge for a number of years. Bakhtiar's liaison agent with the conspirators in Hamadan was an Iranian businessman who had agreed to commit his fortune and organizational talents to the plan. He delivered messages back and forth across the Iran–Iraq border and distributed money to the various cells inside Iran. Later, under very different circumstances, he entered the international spotlight during the Iran-contra scandal, as one of the principal intermediaries between the United States, Israel, and Iran. The agent's name was Manucher Ghorbanifar.

Until August 1980, Iraq had chosen the obvious route for its dual-track industrialization program. Development plans focused on building a large chemical industry, based on Iraq's extensive deposits of oil and phosphates. "We built our industries big from the start," explained Amer al-Saadi, the chemical wizard behind

Iraq's poison gas effort. Al-Saadi was joined at SOTI by a promising young electronics engineer, Amer Rashid al-Ubeidi, who was given the rank of lieutenant general as a reward for his extraordinary expertise. He believed that Iraq should expand into defense electronics, since this was the key to modern weaponry. After a long negotiation, which pitted the French firm Thomson-CSF against Plessey of Great Britain, Iraq announced in August 1980 that it was awarding Thomson a major contract for "the creation of an Iraqi electronics industry." The project was given the code name Saad 13.

This $1 billion contract was barely mentioned in the French press and was treated as a virtual state secret in the years to come. At one point Thomson even tried to deny it had ever signed such a deal, although thousands of Thomson engineers were involved at different times, training Iraqi technicians in France and supervising production in Iraq.

The Saad 13 electronics plant was built some 140 kilometers north of Baghdad in the village of ad-Dawr, not far from Tikrit. The idea, said René Anastaze, the Thomson-CSF vice president in charge of the project, was to "give the Iraqis a tool for the future." Thomson engineers who worked at the site said it incorporated the most advanced production technology available in the West. "Saad 13 is one of the largest and most modern electronics assembly facilities anywhere in the world," they confided during walks through the streets of Baghdad and in conversations held on hotel balconies to escape the Mukhabarat eavesdroppers. It was certainly the most ambitious project of its kind undertaken in a Third World country. And its entire production was devoted to the needs of the Iraqi armed forces.

Amer Rashid al-Ubeidi, who was put in charge of industrial projects at SOTI, was feared and respected by the French engineers. "General Amer was so good," one engineer said, "he could take a blueprint of an electronic circuit and, after examining it for a few seconds, point out where you had made a mistake in the design."

The French counseled him to start production modestly at Saad 13. An all-Iraqi work force of around 1,500 employees began by assembling Thomson-CSF man-pack radios by early 1984, under the expert eyes of 100 Thomson engineers. As time went on, and the Iraqis gained experience, they built combat radios and other equipment from scratch. Separate production units were devoted to cutting military-grade quartz crystals and manufacturing hybrid integrated circuits. The Iraqis went on to strategic tasks such as the assembly of battlefield radar systems, electronic countermeasures, and avionics. Later a computer chip plant was scheduled to be added, including a high-tech silicon foundry.

Part of the contract involved training Iraqi technicians in France. During interviews in Baghdad, Iraqi military sources said that some 3,000 to 4,000 Iraqis had been sent to France for special training as part of the Saad 13 program. The training effort was so extensive and so lucrative that Thomson-CSF built an "educational center" in the Paris suburb of Jouy-en-Josas, near Versailles, exclusively to handle its Iraqi clients. The Iraqis took basic courses in electronics, then specialized in a particular branch of production technology. The more gifted students were sent to other Thomson training centers across France to learn the secrets of the latest combat radar then being supplied to Iraq for its Mirage fighter-bombers or to master the art of fooling the state-of-the-art electronic counter-measures, designed to protect NATO aircraft from attack by enemy missiles and planes.

Amer Rashid's plan was to build up a corps of electronics en-gineers who had mastered all the skills necessary for manufacturing combat electronics gear. As with Iraq's other military-industrial plans, the strategy was aimed at protecting Iraq from any embargo by suppliers later on. With factories like Saad 13 to serve Saddam's ambition, and helpers like Thomson-CSF, embargoes would be meaningless.

Tension between Iran and Iraq had been mounting for months by the time war broke out in September 1980. In April an Iranian-backed Shiite group in Iraq planted a bomb at Baghdad University that narrowly missed killing a key member of the Revolutionary Command Council, Tarek Aziz. In response to the bomb attack, Saddam ordered his half-brother, Barzan Ibrahim al-Tikriti, to unleash his Mukhabarat thugs on Iraq's Shiite clergy. Numerous arrests were made, and many clergymen assassinated, including the leader of Iraq's Shiite community, Ayatollah Mohammed Bakr al-Sadr. The repression of the Shiites created widespread resent-ment inside Iraq and hardened Iran's attitude toward the Baathist regime. Iran began calling for the overthrow of Saddam Hussein in daily Arabic-language broadcasts beamed into Iraq. Iraq returned the favor in Persian-language broadcasts to Iran.

Meanwhile Saddam Hussein's armies prepared for war. Troops were deployed all along the 1,200-kilometer border with Iran and were instructed to seize key pockets of disputed territory once hostilities were declared. Starting on September 4, Iranian and Iraqi troops traded artillery fire, while commando units from both sides launched cross-border raids. On September 17, Saddam made a historic speech before Iraq's rubber-stamp National Assembly. With great theatrical display, he held out the 1975 peace agreement he had personally negotiated with the shah and tore it up in front of the cameras. Iran had violated that agreement on numerous occasions already, Saddam explained. Iraq refused to award Iran the fruits of the 1975 accord (total sovereignty over the Shatt-al-Arab waterway) as long as Iran continued to occupy a series of border hamlets and villages.

It was a slim pretext for war, but it was enough for Saddam Hussein. Five days later he ordered his armies to cross the border into Iran. The troops were instructed to concentrate on the southern province of Khuzistan, where much of Iran's oil was located. (The Iraqis called the province Arabistan because it was largely populated by Iranians of Arabic, not Persian, descent. Saddam expected Iran's Arab population to rise up against Tehran. He was wrong.)

Saddam was still counting on the Iranian fifth column that his intelligence chief, Barzan, had established with the help of Shahpur Bakhtiar. Saddam fully expected the Iranians to lay down their arms in the early hours of combat. His Iranian allies had failed to inform him that the Nogeh coup attempt had been unmasked in July. He continued to believe the war would end in a matter of days with a crushing Iraqi victory and perhaps even the demise of the Islamic regime in Tehran. But instead of toppling that regime, the Iraqi invasion propped it up. Even pro-monarchists in the Iranian air force closed ranks in defense of their homeland.

Count Alexandre de Marenches, who headed French intelligence at the time, is a fine connoisseur of the Middle East. Portly and seeming world-weary, he likes to sit back and survey events from afar like an Olympian god. Born of a French aristocrat father and

an American mother, Marenches was General de Gaulle's inter-
preter during World War II. Along with General Vernon Walters in
the United States, he is the last surviving "prince" of the grand
intelligence game who personally knew the Big Four (Roosevelt,
Churchill, Stalin, and de Gaulle). Today, from a comfortable retirement on the French Riviera, he counsels world leaders and businessmen. When the Iran-Iraq war broke out, one of his "clients"
was Saddam Hussein. Marenches was so close to the Iraqis when
he headed the SDECE that they bought his million-dollar villa near
Grasse as the summer residence of Iraq's ambassador to France.[11]

"The war with Iran was born of a terrible misunderstanding,"
Marenches believes. Like many dictators, the Iraqi president had
created a vacuum of fear around himself, so even his closest advisors hesitated to tell him the truth. Saddam blundered into Iran,
Marenches argues, because of faulty intelligence. "This is the tragedy of authoritarian regimes. If the big leader is mistaken, the
consequences are incalculable." Saddam Hussein was led to believe
that "there would be a popular uprising to applaud the first Iraqi
soldier who came over the horizon." Marenches places the blame
for the error on Saddam's intelligence chief. Barzan flattered his
boss, Marenches laments, "whereas the principal quality of a director of intelligence is to tell the truth."[12]

Saddam did foresee one immediate consequence of his invasion
of Iran: the suspension of arms supplies from the USSR. When he
launched his attack, the Soviets were busy playing games in Iran.
They were not amused that the Iraqis upset their plans. For generations the KGB had been working to penetrate Iran's Shiite clergy. In
February 1979, when Ayatollah Khomeini took power and threw
the Americans out of Iran, the Soviets stood to gain more than they
had ever believed possible. One KGB agent, Mohammad Doai,
worked as secretary of Khomeini's cabinet. Others were spread
through the clergy, the armed forces, the press, and the government
bureaucracy. Still others controlled the intelligence services freshly
purged of suspected monarchist sympathizers. The pro-Soviet
Communist party (Tudeh), which had been working underground
since its inception in 1920, was now invited to join the Tehran
government. KGB boss Yuri Andropov and his top Iranian affairs
officer, Geidar Ali-Reza Aliev, were furious with Saddam for
threatening to shatter all those years of hard work.[13] Andropov,

who was a full member of the ruling Politburo in Moscow, had little difficulty in convincing Brezhnev and Kosygin to agree to an embargo on arms to Iraq in the days following Saddam's invasion of Iran. Besides cutting the Iraqi leader down to size, he argued, it would show the Iranians that the USSR was on their side.

But this second Soviet embargo had little effect. Over the previous five years Saddam Hussein had diversified his supplies of arms to an extent matched nowhere in the world. Furthermore, by paying cash for his weapons, he had avoided the political compromises that hampered other Third World leaders, who were beholden to their arms suppliers not only for the weapons but for the cash and subsidized loans to pay for them. Softening the blow of a Soviet arms embargo had been one of Saddam's major strategic goals; he succeeded so well that the Iraqi armed forces merely blinked when the Soviets cut them off, and continued their invasion of Iran. Saddam's buyers even managed to obtain tanks and other weapons from Soviet-bloc countries such as Poland and East Germany at the height of the embargo. As Saddam told a group of French journalists in July 1980, on the twelfth anniversary of the Baathist revolution, "Now when the Soviets refuse us a certain type of weapon we no longer make a fuss, we simply go elsewhere, especially to France."[14]

Between 1977 and 1980, when the country was at peace, Iraq had ordered $4 billion worth of French arms. Now in late September 1980, with Iraq at war, Saddam needed to know whether the French would deliver.

Saddam dispatched Tarek Aziz to Paris to find out. Aziz, who was then serving as vice president of Iraq had distinguished himself on difficult foreign missions in the past. The cigar-smoking Iraqi emissary's air of joviality and bonhomie fooled no one. Aziz was a tough negotiator, who could switch from trading banalities to trading threats in an instant. He was gifted with a sharp wit and a penchant for blunt language. The French both respected and feared him. They knew he could just as easily shovel abuse on the French government as lavish praise. More than anything, they feared that Aziz would threaten to reveal the amount of cash Iraq had pumped back into France in the form of campaign contributions for some very well-known politicians. Or that he would mention that the wife of a senior government official was receiving "gifts" from the

Iraqi ambassador to Paris, purchased from an exclusive jeweler at the Place Vendôme, just across from the Ritz Hotel.

When Aziz met with President Giscard d'Estaing and Prime Minister Raymond Barre on September 24, he politely reminded them that France was currently getting nearly 25 percent of its oil from Iraq. What a pity, he sighed, if Iraq had to revise that policy. President Saddam expected France to deliver the first Mirage fighter-bombers in the coming months, as planned.

Giscard complained that the Mirage contracts had been signed before Iraq was at war and that France sold weapons for defensive purposes only. But the Iraqi vice president was waiting for him. "You didn't hesitate one instant to break your own rules," he retorted, "when you decided to ship arms to Biafran separatists in 1968." The French had sent mercenaries, paid by the French treasury, to help overthrow the government of Nigeria, which was a sovereign state and a member of the United Nations, Aziz said. "We are not asking you to violate international law. We are just asking you to uphold your commitments." French understanding during Iraq's time of need would not go unrewarded. Aziz hinted that Iraq would be willing to award the $3 billion jet trainer contract to the French instead of the British, and he made sure that this part of the story hit the French press.

But Giscard was worried that Iran would consider arms deliveries to Iraq now as a sign of hostility. Worse, he was afraid that the Iraqi was trying to suck him into a strategic partnership. France would do better to remain neutral in the conflict than be seen as taking sides. Besides, Iran was sure to attack Iraq's oil terminals on the Gulf, Giscard argued, and France would have to look for other sources of oil anyway.

Aziz could have told the French president about the Soviet arms embargo, but he was under strict instructions to keep that secret for the time being. When Aziz left Paris, the question of whether or not the French would make good on the Mirage delivery was left in suspense.

Though the export of conventional arms was a politically sensitive issue in France for a variety of reasons, nuclear cooperation with the Third World did not rub the same political sensitivities. Giscard promised Aziz that France would uphold its commitment to complete the installation of the Osirak reactor complex, and the day after the Iraqi left Paris, Giscard ordered the delivery to Baghdad of the first 12.5 kilograms of highly enriched uranium fuel.[15] The Iraqi reactor was scheduled to go critical by mid-1981 and to begin producing plutonium for the Iraqi bomb immediately.

The Iranians and the Israelis were both worried about Iraq's nuclear weapons program. Some sources suggest the Israelis may have passed information about the program to Tehran, through Iranian agents they had cultivated during the time of the shah. On September 28, 1980, the head of Israeli military intelligence, General Yehoshua Saguy, told Israeli journalists that he was surprised the Iranians hadn't destroyed the Osirak reactor during the first week of the war, given the clear advantage they had demonstrated in the air. Two days later a pair of Iranian F-4 Phantom jets attacked the Osirak site, but their bombs fell harmlessly beyond the reactor perimeter. The raid was little more than a warning shot.

The French were not the only ones who benefited from the second Soviet arms embargo. One of the happiest men in the Middle East in the fall of 1980 was Egypt's president, Anwar Sadat. Egypt had purchased great quantities of Soviet weaponry throughout the 1960s and 1970s, and it still had large stockpiles of Soviet ammunition, spare parts, rocket launchers, and aircraft. Only days after the Soviet Union imposed the embargo in late September 1980, Sadat conferred with the Carter administration, then announced that Egypt would sell Iraq $1 billion worth of Soviet arms.

The sale was all the more extraordinary given the crucial role Saddam had played only the year before in having Sadat kicked out of the Arab League in retaliation for signing the Camp David peace agreement with Israel. But Saddam Hussein would show again and again that ideology counted little compared to issues of power. Egypt had something Saddam needed urgently, and Saddam was willing to eat a little crow to get it. The Egyptian weapons helped keep the Iraqi army going for eighteen months.

The Chinese also weighed in behind Saddam. During the early days of the war China shipped hundreds — later, thousands — of 1950s-generation main battle tanks, artillery pieces, and armored personnel carriers to Baghdad. Iraqi generals used tanks in two ways: as stationary artillery, buried in the desert with only the turret sticking out, and as a kind of top-heavy Range Rover, to ferry troops to the battlefield when the going got tough. Iraq bought at least 1,300 tanks from the Chinese and simply abandoned them on the battlefield when they broke down. In most cases it was cheaper to replace than to repair them.

The Chinese purchases were about more than just weapons. By turning to China with a lot of money (the first tank sale in the fall of 1980 was part of a $1 billion package) Iraq was telling the Soviets that their monopoly had run out. If they wanted to continue to have a share of the action in Iraq, they would have to end their arms embargo.

When the Soviets pulled their advisors out of Iraq following the September 1980 arms embargo, they lost more than just a client. They lost access to Iraq's port on the Gulf as well.

The Soviets had long coveted Oum Qasr. The first Soviet warship had visited it in 1968, and such visits to the isolated naval base at the northern end of the Gulf became more frequent after the 1972 Friendship and Cooperation Treaty. By the mid-1970s, Oum Qasr was considered by Pentagon strategists as a Soviet "facility" — not a base, properly speaking, but a friendly port where the Soviet blue-water navy could seek fuel, provisions, and repairs. And, most important, show the flag in a region of American predominance.

Saddam Hussein had never liked having Soviet officers on his military bases. He considered them, perhaps rightly, as at least part-time intelligence officers, whose tasks including subverting Baathist support in the armed forces in favor of the Iraqi Communists. With the embargo, he was rid of them. Iraq would wage war on its own, with a little help from its friends.

Tarek Aziz made at least two trips to Paris before Christmas to convince the French to deliver the Mirage fighters to Iraq. Just as the French had feared, the Iranian air force launched major attacks against Iraqi oil platforms in the Gulf, bringing Iraq's oil exports to a virtual standstill. Oil experts in France began to sound the alarm about finding other sources. André Giraud, who was serving as Giscard's "oil minister," evaluated the loss to France at 480,000 barrels per day, but scoffed at those who believed that France would run out of oil. Giraud was a technocrat who had graduated to a ministerial post from his position as the head of the French Atomic Energy Commission. He believed that as a technocrat who possessed the keys to highly specialized knowledge, he had only to tell the public not to worry, and their worries would disappear.

Saddam was getting desperate for his Mirages and his French-trained pilots. The Iraqi air force had performed miserably in the early battles of the war. Many squadrons had refused to fight, taking refuge in neighboring Jordan to avoid losses. Maintenance problems grounded other Iraqi aircraft, because the Soviets had taken the maintenance manuals of the MiG-23 when they were thrown out of Iraq. Despite the revolutionary purges of the Iranian air force, Iran's U.S.-trained pilots had far outclassed their adversaries.

In the end, the argument that convinced the French to deliver the planes was provided by Saudi Arabia's King Khaled and his cousin, the emir of Kuwait. When Tarek Aziz visited Prime Minister Barre a few days before Christmas, he came bearing gifts. His Arab brothers had agreed to make good most of Iraq's oil commitments. France would continue to get its oil at prewar prices — *if* Iraq got its Mirages. After a brief consultation with his "oil minister," who strongly urged him to take the Saudi and Kuwaiti crude, Giscard agreed.

Tarek Aziz was a born manipulator, and he loved to use the press to drive home his points. In a press conference in Paris on December 23, 1980, the Iraqi sent a message to the Soviets as well as to the French. The failure of the Soviet Union to make good on its commitments to Iraq "would have no impact . . . because Iraq had learned how to diversify its sources of military equipment and to create its own military industry." In response to the question whether Iraq expected to receive its Mirage fighter-bombers soon, Aziz noted with a smile that French arms deliveries "were continuing normally."[16]

But no one picked up on the most significant revelation contained in his statement, about creating Iraq's military industry. That effort, the deadliest of all, was progressing by leaps and bounds.

SIX

The Road to Osirak

Word that the American hostages in Tehran were about to be released came on January 21, 1981, just as Ronald Reagan was raising his right hand to take the oath of office. Twenty-five minutes later, the hostages boarded two airplanes at Tehran's Mehrabad Airport. After 444 days of captivity, they were heading home.

Reagan had won the 1980 election in part because of the humiliation the hostage crisis had caused Jimmy Carter.[1] Now that he had made it to the White House, he was not about to risk his presidency on the shoals of Middle Eastern politics. Iran and Iraq did not appear on the Reagan administration's agenda as top foreign policy priorities. Instead of activism, American involvement in the Middle East now focused on three containments: containing the Iran–Iraq war, curbing Israeli action in Lebanon, and keeping Iran's messianic version of Islam from contaminating America's moderate Arab allies: Saudi Arabia, Kuwait, Jordan, and Egypt.

The United States had no desire to promote an Iraqi victory in the war with Iran, fearing that too much success would go to Saddam's head. But neither did the Reagan administration want to see Ayatollah Khomeini establish a fundamentalist regime in Baghdad, because this would lead to regional upheaval. "Neither victor nor vanquished" became the U.S. credo toward the Iran–Iraq war. In practice, since the United States had no diplomatic presence in Baghdad or Tehran and could exert little influence on either regime, it meant winking at arms sales to both sides by its friends and allies, inadvertently fanning the flames of war. When Iran appeared to be headed for defeat on the battlefield, Washington approved Israel's covert arms sales to Tehran to bolster the regime. When the Iraqis' resolve weakened under the Iranian assault, Washington encouraged Paris to step up arms deliveries to Iraq. It was a weird brew of conflicting interests that barely merited the name "policy." In fact, after the hostage crisis in Tehran, the Gulf was an issue Washington preferred to avoid.

Interviews with officials and arms dealers suggest that the French waited until the American hostages in Tehran were released to deliver the first Mirage fighter-bombers to Iraq. A scant ten days after the release, the first four planes were ferried by French air force pilots to Larnaca, Cyprus, where Iraqi crews proudly took over and flew them for the last leg of the journey. When word that the planes had reached Baghdad leaked out, Iran protested loudly. The Islamic Republic of Iran Air Force, whose nearly five hundred modern jets were falling into disrepair because of the U.S. embargo on spare parts and maintenance, now faced almost three hundred thirty combat-worthy aircraft. The Mirages were arriving in Iraq at the rate of two per month, or twenty-four planes a year. With sixty planes on order, Iraq would continue to receive fresh aircraft through June 1983, giving them plenty of spares to compensate for combat losses. In the meantime, hundreds of Iraqi pilots and mechanics were being trained on the Mirages at centers in Brittany and Bordeaux. Those who passed the course returned to Iraq, where former French air force pilots perfected their tactical training.

"When the war with Iran started," one Dassault specialist recalled, "we did everything we could to get their pilots up to speed. We sat behind them on training missions. We helped them plan tactics. We taught them how to use new missiles. Sometimes we even leaned on the stick to help them maneuver into a better position. We did everything except pull the trigger." Indeed, it was as close to a strategic alliance as you could get, short of the actual deployment of French combat troops in Iraq.

As the Iraqi air force grew in size and quality, the French government slapped an embargo on three Combattante II missile boats scheduled for delivery to Iran, the last of a twelve-boat order placed by the shah. To all appearances, the French were taking sides in the war, and they were choosing Iraq.

The decision to support Iraq reaped substantial payoffs. Within weeks of the first Mirage delivery, the Franco-German Euromissile consortium announced that Iraq had agreed to purchase the Roland II low-level air defense missile, in a $2.9 billion deal that would make the Russians jealous. Besides the rush order of 113 Roland launchers (100 on MAN trucks made in West Germany, the other 13 on French-built AMX-30 tanks), the March 1981 package included a wide range of missiles for the Mirage fighters, Panhard armored cars equipped with HOT antitank missiles, and much more.

The Rolands were deployed around Baghdad on artificial mounds built to give the fire units a better view of the Mesopotamian plane. Before the Rolands arrived, Iranian aircraft had been able to attack Baghdad and other strategic sites virtually at will. The Iraqis hoped that the state-of-the-art French systems would make the Iranians think twice before they attacked again. Fixed launch sites were set up for Rolands at other strategic locations throughout Iraq, while thirteen mobile units were deployed on the front lines with Iraqi mechanized divisions.

Instead of the "lightning" victory Saddam had expected with his high-tech weapons, Iraqi troops were faring poorly on the battlefield. They were bogged down at the border town of Susangerd, southeast of Baghdad, and at Khorramshahr and Abadan farther to the south. The Iranians were putting up a much fiercer resistance than anyone had expected. The Iraqi invasion had stirred nationalistic feelings that cut across political lines. Iranian air force pilots who had been jailed as a result of the failed Nogeh coup in July 1980 were released on orders of President Bani Sadr. Despite the months in jail and threats of execution, they acquitted themselves well in combat.

Helping the Iranians were more than four hundred M-109 self-propelled howitzers the Shah had purchased from the United States. These sophisticated guns, which could "shoot and scoot," outdistanced and outshot everything in the Iraqi inventory, and the Iraqis felt the disadvantage keenly. Early in 1981 the Iraqi Ministry of Defense alerted all military attachés abroad to step up the search for new heavy artillery systems capable of beating the M-109s. One of the first places they looked was France. The French army was just then completing trials on a new long-range field howitzer it had mounted on its AMX-30 tank, called the 155 GCT (*grande cadence de tir*). They had already begun to advertise it on the arms market as the "fastest and most accurate gun in the world." Development work was partially funded by Saudi Arabia, since France was spending most of its R&D money on nuclear weapons, not conventional armor. The gun was being built by the French state arsenal, GIAT.

Always eager to expand foreign sales, which lowered the price of the weapon to the French army, GIAT turned to its state-controlled marketing outlets, Sofma and Sofresa, which enjoyed virtual monopoly status, splitting the world into regions controlled by one or the other. Sofresa had made the initial export sale of the 155-mm gun to Saudi Arabia in 1980; now it was Sofma's turn to contribute.

Sofma's first plan was to sell the gun to Argentina, an increasingly good customer for French weaponry. To make the sale, they tracked down a Lebanese middleman, Nicola Saker, who was known to have good contacts with the Argentine military. When Saker's deal fell through, Sofma turned to another Lebanese agent, Sarkis Soghenalian, who had been introduced by the man who had sewn up Iraq for the French, Ramzi Daloul. This was just the weapon the Iraqis were seeking, Sarkis said. All he had to do was work out a split with Shaker, who still had a letter of commission from Sofma guaranteeing him a 6 percent cut on any export sale, and he would be about $40 million richer. Sarkis decided to bring in his younger brother Zaven, who had good contacts with Iraqi army procurement officers.

In March 1981, Sarkis Soghenalian flew a group of Sofma officials to Baghdad on his private jet, the "Spirit of Free Enterprise," to present the new GIAT gun to Iraqi procurement officers. He was so familiar to the Iraqis that they allowed him to land at Baghdad's al-Muthena air base instead of using the international airport, so that he and the Frenchmen could avoid unwanted publicity and customs formalities. Among the French officials were General Daniel Huet, president of Sofma; Michel Beillan, the managing director; Colonel Jacques Masson-Regnault, a former artillery officer who was in charge of the "Vulcan Project," as the 155 sale came to be known, and his assistant, Michel Obilinski.

General Huet had to borrow a battery of six guns for the firing demonstration from his competitors at Sofresa, which had just filled an order for the Saudi army. The huge armored vehicles were loaded onto tank transporters and hauled across the Saudi desert to Basra in southern Iraq. Meanwhile a French army reserve artillery crew arrived in Baghdad by a commercial flight. They all flew down to Basra on Iraqi army helicopters for firing and mobility trials out in the desert.

The Iraqis loved the new gun. Mounted on an AMX-30 tank, it could fire a rapid barrage, duck for cover before enemy artillery spotters could locate it, then fire again from a new location in just a matter of minutes. The Iraqis set up target areas that resembled convoys of Iranian tanks and let the French reservists go to work. The Iraqis and the salesmen from Sofma watched the show from a bunker dug into the sand. The guns were so far away that no one really heard the firing begin, but all of a sudden a circle of explosions erupted in the target area, filling the desert with a deafening roar. The guns, firing at their maximum range of 24 kilometers, scored hit after hit on the Iranian "tanks," thanks to a sophisticated electronic fire control computer. When it was all over, the Iraqis applauded. It was the most impressive display of precision firepower they had seen.

"The Iraqis never bought anything off the shelf," one of the French arms salesmen recalled. "They always asked for modifications before they would agree to a sale." For all their enthusiasm, the Iraqis were critical of the AMX-30 chassis, which had problems operating in the heat and sand of the Iraqi desert. They wanted it fixed. And there was a problem with the barrel: after a few hundred rounds, it started to melt.

"If we didn't make the modifications," the salesman recalls, "we were afraid they would go to Oto Melara in Italy, since they had a competing project." So the French agreed to make the changes.

Sofma engaged in some sleight of hand to take care of the competition. Knowing that the Oto Melara gun was running several months behind schedule, they paid Zaven and Sarkis Soghenalian to take an Iraqi army delegation to Italy to see the competition for themselves — in an unfavorable light, of course. As they had expected, the Oto Melara gun was no match for the 155 GCT — at least, not at that time. To their relief, the Iraqis agreed.

Sarkis took the Sofma people back to Baghdad in June 1981, a few weeks after the election, on May 10, of Socialist President

François Mitterrand and only days before the Osirak bombing. No one on the airplane can forget the timing. "All French customs wanted to know as we were leaving Le Bourget was whether we were taking cash out of France," one of the Frenchmen said. The new Socialist government had imposed strict foreign exchange controls to prevent the flight of capital, since many French people believed that the left-wing coalition intended to plunder their fortunes.

Once again, after touching down in the "Spirit of Free Enterprise," Sarkis and the Frenchmen were put up in a government guest house at al-Muthena to avoid publicity. They were whisked from meeting to meeting with Iraqi officials in charge of various aspects of the project, such as training, maintenance, and integration. Then the real negotiations began, led by the Iraqi chief of staff, General Neguib Jenaab Thanoon. The French referred to him as "Charlie Chaplin" because of his short stature and brush mustache.

"General Jenaab was getting nowhere," one participant recalls, "so he called in Lieutenant General Amer Rashid." Rashid, who came to be known as the father of Iraq's French air force, was a technician at heart and enjoyed sweeping responsibilities; but when it came to negotiations, he was a cowboy.

"I know you French," he started in. "You are always trying to get us to pay for a Cadillac while you give us a Chevy." Rashid demanded a 40 percent discount on the $1.6 billion contract.

"That was for openers," the Frenchman recalls. "So I reminded him that I was in Baghdad as the representative of the French state arsenal and that our prices were fixed by the French government, controlled by the Finance Ministry, the Defense Ministry, and the comptroller's office. 'It's not going to be 40 percent, ' I said, 'or 10 percent, or 4 percent or even one-quarter of 1 percent. These are our prices, and they are firm. This said, if you can convince my government to make you a gift of half of the equipment, it's no skin off my back.'"

Amer Rashid was furious. He took the Frenchman's attitude as a humiliation. "You can take your bloody contract and fly with it back to Paris," he shouted.

The story quickly made the rounds, and when the head of the Sofma team met the French military attaché in Baghdad the next day, he received a frosty reception. "I hear you are a burnt-out case," the attaché said.

But Amer Rashid's fury dissipated almost as quickly as it had erupted. And when Sarkis Soghenalian and the men from Sofma returned to Baghdad a few weeks later, they were welcomed with open arms. Not only was everything forgotten, but the $1.6 billion Vulcan contract was signed, one of the best deals the French had ever negotiated in Iraq. "Normally, the Iraqis paid a 20 percent deposit, and another 20 percent in six months, leaving the rest until later," said a source familiar with the contract terms. "This time they paid us $800 million in cash. So you can see why we were so happy."

The eighty-three guns covered by the Vulcan deal meant business for a wide spectrum of French defense companies who supplied Sofma with the goods. Munitions makers had to double their production. GIAT had to build a new factory to meet the Iraqi rush order. (They later tried to convince Iraq to purchase the towed version of the same howitzer, but to no avail. At more than $2.5 million per copy, more than double the price of similar guns on the market, the Iraqis found it too pricey for their tastes.)

What the Iraqis liked best about their new French gun was the proximity fuze, a small throwaway electronic device screwed into the nose of the artillery shell that determines when it will explode. The Iraqis acquired, from the French firm TRT, extremely sophisticated fuzes that could detonate the shell just before it reached the ground. Although the fuze cost one-third of the price of each round of ammunition, the Iraqis felt it was worth it. "With a single GCT round, they could wipe out every Iranian within a kilometer," said one former French army artilleryman, who helped train Iraqi gunners in the desert near Basra. "This is how they stopped the human waves. They were firing like at Verdun. It was a real massacre."

Only months after Sofma showed them the new French gun, the Iraqis started looking for a cheaper towed howitzer to round out their arsenal. They wanted more firepower and longer ranges than even the French could provide so that they could fire on the Iranians without being fired on in return. An Austrian diplomat in Geneva came to their aid. Voest-Alpine, the artillery division of the Austrian state arsenal, Noricum, was putting the finishing touches on the gun they needed, he said. The Iraqis should come and have a look.

The Voest-Alpine gun, the GH N-45, was an artillery gunner's dream. Its extremely long barrel and specially designed munitions gave it the longest range of any artillery piece in the world — far longer than the 24 kilometers of the French guns. "We never heard the end of that one," one Sofma official said later. "Forty-two kilometers — we were nowhere near." The Iraqis signed up to buy two hundred of the guns on the spot, but because Austria's laws forbade arms sales to countries at war, Voest-Alpine registered the deal as a sale to Jordan. The flimsy ruse was good enough for the Austrian government, which did nothing to block it.

Halfway through the deliveries, however, the Iraqis became disenchanted with the Austrian guns. The Iraqi army complained that the gun barrels couldn't stand up to intensive combat use, especially when they used the specially designed munitions to reach maximum range. A technical evaluation showed that the barrels started to melt after 638 rounds on average; the Iraqi requirement called for a barrel life of 1,500 rounds. When Iraq refused to take delivery of the remaining 100 guns, Voest Alpine resold them to Iran.

In the meantime the Iraqis had traced the "secret" of the Austrian gun back to the Canadian-American artillery genius who had designed it. Gerald Bull was something of a black sheep in the international arms marketplace. After working in the 1960s for the Pentagon on a "ballistic cannon" project, which Bull claimed could launch satellites into earth orbit from a huge artillery tube, Bull went into private business in northern Vermont. He patented a revolutionary "base-bleed" artillery munition, which could boost the range of most artillery pieces by as much as 50 percent. To market his invention, he set up a company called Space Research Corporation, or SRC, in the late 1960s.

One of the first countries Bull turned to was South Africa. Throughout the 1970s South Africa was one of the Western world's best arms customers. It purchased Mirage fighters and helicopters from France, main battle tanks from Britain, and artillery pieces from the United States. The West saw in South Africa a bulwark against Communist expansion from Angola and Mozambique. Western governments were particularly anxious to maintain control of the strategic mineral reserves that constituted South Africa's wealth.

But in 1977 the United Nations imposed a worldwide arms embargo on South Africa, turning it overnight into a pariah state. The CIA, however, contacted Bull and asked him to sell advanced weaponry to South Africa in order to preserve Western strategic interests. Bull entered into a development contract with the South African Armaments Corporation, or Armscor, and sold them a 20 percent stake of SRC. As the CIA came under greater Congressional scrutiny in the late 1970s, however, it appears that they abandoned Bull. He was arrested for breaking the UN arms embargo on South Africa and sentenced to six months in jail.

When Gerald Bull left the minimum security prison in Allenwood, Pennsylvania, in early 1980, he was a bitter man. SRC was bankrupt. The Americans had led him into the South African business, then abandoned him; obviously they could no longer be trusted. So he moved his business operation to Europe, setting up shop in Uccle, a posh suburb of the Belgian capital, Brussels.

Meanwhile, artillery manufacturers around the world were applying for licenses to make base-bleed munitions and a revolutionary new long-range gun-howitzer, also patented by Bull. Millions of dollars in licensing fees began flooding into SRC coffers once again. Among those who purchased licenses were Voest-Alpine in Austria, GIAT in France, PRB in Belgium, Royal Ordnance in Britain, and the South African Armaments Corporation, Armscor.

Sarkis Soghenalian introduced the Iraqis to Gerald Bull in his Brussels office not long after they purchased the Voest-Alpine gun. They described the problem they were having with the Austrian howitzers, and the Canadian inventor explained that the Austrians had purchased only parts of his patented system and had gone into production before they had ironed out the problem of barrel wear. Bull informed them that Armscor had solved the problem.

The Belgian consortium Sybetra had worked hard at the Akashat and Al Qaim sites, building one of the largest phosphates production and processing plants in the world. By mid-1981 the project was ready for government acceptance, or commissioning, which in Iraq was a long process that involved intricate financial negotiations. The prime contractor had put up a 10 percent performance bond on the $1 billion project and was anxious to have the money released. But the Iraqis, always eager to delay payment as long as possible, did their best to stall. "At the last minute, they always managed to find something wrong, something not made according to specifications," a former project engineer explained. "More often than not, the Iraqis had simply changed the project specifications during construction, so it was impossible to tell what should have been completed at what time." If the government refused the project, the Iraqis kept the deposit. If the project was completed late, they charged substantial late penalties. Either way, Sybetra stood to lose.

Around this time, Belgian engineers at work on the site detected a curious tightening of Iraqi security. Barbed wire fences were erected, antiaircraft guns installed, and Iraqi security police were all over the site. One French engineer working for Sybetra remembers trying to return home for Christmas in 1980. The Iraqis refused to grant him an exit visa until he had finished installing his part of the project, a giant centrifuge, ostensibly for separating phosphates. He was forced to remain in Iraq for three years straight. "We used to go out for drives in the desert," the engineer recalled. "There were wolves and coyotes roaming wild. The emptiness of the place was astonishing. But all of a sudden, we were confined to Al Qaim. The Iraqis told us it was because of the war."

But the Belgian and French engineers at Al Qaim began hearing other rumors. The Iraqis had hired a Swiss firm, Alesa Alusuisse Engineering Ltd., that had begun work on a "uranium" project. The phosphates mined at Akashat were known to be rich in uranium ore, and the engineers suspected that the operation involved separating uranium from phosphates for further processing. The Swiss workers did not mix with the others, and their project was shrouded in secrecy.

Later it became known that Alesa had built a special production unit at Al Qaim to extract fluoride salts, including uranium fluoride, from liquid phosphoric acid. Al Qaim was going to play a key role in Iraq's nuclear weapons schemes, in addition to manufacturing large quantities of precursor chemicals for use in deadly nerve gas. It was just a matter of time.

The Osirak nuclear reactor was set to go critical on July 1, 1981. The fuel had been installed, and the cooling channel was ready to be filled with water. The nuclear physicists, such as Dr. Ja'afar Dhia Ja'afar, had made sure everything needed for plutonium production was available on site once the reactor started up. Iraqi agents were negotiating to purchase depleted uranium fuel pins from NUKEM in West Germany, and the Italian firm Snia TechInt was busy installing the last of the reprocessing and fuel manufacturing laboratories. Iraq was also purchasing, from Niger, Brazil, and Portugal, hundreds of metric tons of natural uranium, or yellowcake, which could be irradiated in the Osirak bomb plant to produce plutonium. If those sources dried up, uranium could be produced at Al Qaim, which could also transform the uranium ore into uranium hexafluoride, ready for enrichment.

Sources at the French Atomic Energy Commission working in Iraq at this time said they were surprised to find Brazilian nuclear physicists working at the Osirak site in the spring of 1981 in areas sealed off to the French. They didn't know what the Brazilians were doing there, for the nuclear pact Brazil and Iraq had signed two years earlier had been kept quiet. Brazil was hard at work on a top-secret project to enrich ordinary uranium to bomb-grade fuel by spinning uranium hexafluoride gas in specially designed ultra-centrifuges. The technology was being provided by a consortium of West German firms, according to the terms of a nuclear cooperation agreement that Brazil had signed with West Germany in the mid-1970s.

In the spring of 1981 the International Atomic Energy Agency completed its regular six-month inspection of Iraq's nuclear research center at Thuwaitha. According to the published version, all was well. Safeguards required by the Nuclear Non-Proliferation Treaty, which Iraq had signed, were enforced properly. Iraq posed no threat at this time as a potential proliferator, the agency concluded.

Privately, however, some IAEA officials were worried. One of the inspectors, Robert Richter, who had visited Iraq, broke ranks and went public with his fears. In statements leaked to the press and to Senator Alan Cranston of California, Richter accused Iraq of circumventing the Non-Proliferation Treaty and of maintaining secret facilities at Thuwaitha that were off limits to the IAEA inspectors. Worse, he said, the IAEA itself was at fault, because it had repeatedly failed to challenge the Iraqis about the hidden laboratories, which were believed to include additional hot cells for plutonium manufacturing. Given the sizable purchases of uranium yellowcake that Iraq had declared, and the Italian hot cells, Richter and others at the IAEA calculated that the Iraqis could manufacture a bomb by 1983. (In fact, Iraq was purchasing more than double the amount of yellowcake it had declared to the IAEA, through agents on the black market.) By 1985 Iraq could be making five bombs per year. Richter, an American citizen, was promptly fired from the IAEA after making these allegations, for failing to keep quiet about what he had seen in Iraq. As for the IAEA, it dismissed Richter's charges as groundless.[2] The Vienna-based agency has a vested interest in making the world believe that the Non-Proliferation Treaty is a success. Otherwise, thousands of international bureaucrats would be out of a job.

Richter was not alone in calling attention to the dangers of Iraq's nuclear program. In France, three physicists who had worked on developing the Osirak reactor submitted to President Mitterrand a report showing that the Iraqi "research" reactor was intended to make the bomb.[3]

Israeli Prime Minister Menachem Begin was also worried about the Osirak reactor. In April 1981, Begin concluded that Israel would have to destroy the Iraqi nuclear plant if it wanted to avoid a catastrophe later on. In concert with his hawkish chief of staff, General Rafael Eitan, Begin began planning Operation Babylon.

A Polish Jew who had survived the Holocaust, Begin was haunted by fears of extermination and was determined to thwart the Iraqi bomb. Overriding the objections of members of his intelligence community, which downplayed the threat, he had Eitan build a full-scale model of the Iraqi nuclear plant so air force pilots could practice bombing it. The pilots remarked how closely Osirak resembled Israel's own bomb plant at Dimona, which had been supplied by the French.[4]

The daring raid that crippled Tammuz I was executed by Israeli F-16s on June 7, 1981. On the 500-mile flight to their target, the Israeli pilots were never out of enemy territory for more than three minutes. The pilots had been chosen for their linguistic as well as their combat skills. When they were crossing Jordanian airspace, they conversed with each other in Saudi-accented Arabic and told Jordanian air controllers they were a Saudi patrol that had gone astray. When they entered Saudi Arabian airspace, they switched accents and pretended they were Jordanians.

When Iraq had purchased the Roland II air defense missiles from France earlier that year, one of the strategic sites they had wanted to protect was the reactor site at Thuwaitha. However, the missile batteries arrived too late, and the Israelis encountered no resistance when they approached their target. Eyewitnesses later reported that a first wave of Israeli F-16s punched a hold through the very center of the reactor dome of Tammuz I with precision-guided missiles. Through that hole a second wave of fighters dropped 2,000-pound "dumb" bombs with such accuracy that they destroyed the reactor core, its containing walls, and the gantry crane.[5] The damage was so great that Osirak was declared dead. Rather than repair it, with all the risks of radiation leaks, a team of French experts told the Iraqis they would do better to raze it and start over again.

The Israeli attack was almost universally denounced. One of the first to protest was the new French president, François Mitterrand, whose election had been greeted with jubilation in Israel. The first Socialist to win the French presidency since World War II, Mitterrand was known to be a strong supporter of Israel who had no soft spot for the Arab world. As interior minister in the 1950s, he had played an important role in the French attempt to crush the Algerian rebellion. Mitterrand's election worried Saddam Hussein, who had long been suspicious of the French Socialists' pro-Israeli sentiments. After all, it was a Socialist government that had engineered the secret sale of the Dimona reactor to Israel in the 1950s.

Begin had delayed Operation Babylon until Mitterrand was firmly in command and had informed the French president ahead of time, intelligence sources say. Hundreds of French workers were still present at the Tammuz plant at the time of the Israeli raid, but that Sunday morning they had decided — unusually — to hold Mass at a building far from the reactor dome. (Sunday was an ordinary working day in Iraq.) Only one Frenchman was killed during the raid. According to a former French intelligence official, he may have been an agent of SDECE, planting a homing beacon on the reactor core so the Israelis would know precisely where to strike.[6]

Mitterrand's protest, as expected, was limited. He called for no sanctions against Israel and made only the vaguest of promises to

Iraq to rebuild the Osirak reactor, although St. Gobain Nucléaire, a semi-private agency for French nuclear exports, tried to convince him otherwise.

Another event, only one week after the Osirak raid, gave the Iraqi leader further reason to fear that the new French government was about to change its policy toward Iraq. It was customary for the French president, accompanied by his defense minister and the head of the French Aerospace Association (GIFAS), to tour the Paris Air Show on the morning of opening day. As luck would have it, the acting president of GIFAS in June 1981 was General Jacques Mitterrand, the new president's older brother, who had recently retired as head of Aérospatiale. A fraternal relationship with the head of state should have been a glorious connection for French arms exporters: it was not.

The incoming president, wanting to make a political statement about his administration's intentions concerning arms exports, ordered his brother to have every weapon removed from the premises before the presidential tour began. All night long the arms exporters toiled, removing bombs, missiles, and rockets from the hundreds of aircraft on display on the tarmac of le Bourget airport. (Some were still at work when the Mitterrand brothers arrived. The presidential cortege neatly avoided the offenders.) The new Socialist government would no longer export weapons blindly to dictators all over the globe, Mitterrand said. Moral considerations would now dictate France's exports.

It didn't take long for the death lobby to go to work. General Mitterrand explained quietly to his brother that illustrious foreign guests, including the Iraqi chief of staff, General Abdul Neguib Jenaab Thanoon, had traveled to France just to see the latest in French weaponry. General Jenaab and the others would not understand the president's gesture. After all, they had standing orders with French exporters and had made substantial down payments for military equipment that even then was leaving French factories. Did the president want to make these clients believe that France would go back on its word?

The general won. As soon as the presidential cortege left the air show, he ordered the bombs and missiles and rockets returned to the display. For the arms business, it was going to be business as usual. And that meant major sales to Iraq.

SEVEN

Secrets of Samarra

The bombing of the Osirak reactor did not come as a surprise to Saddam Hussein — or at least he so pretended. "We have said for some time that 'Israel' would try to attack vital installations in Iraq," he explained to his Council of Ministers on June 23, 1981, "with the goal of paralyzing development and scientific and economic progress, which is a determining factor in Iraq's strength. This is why we contacted friendly countries to request they supply us with arms whose very possession was intended to deter 'Israel' from launching an attack of this kind. We were always clear about this."[1]

Saddam was convinced that Israeli aggression would not stop at the Osirak attack. Israel was "even trying to interfere in the internal affairs of Arab countries," he said. "The Zionists would have the Arabs do away with high school and university education in such subjects as chemistry, physics, mathematics, and astronomy, because these branches of science could be used for military ends against its security. The interference of 'Israel' goes so far as to demand the destitution of princes, leaders, kings and ministers, to replace them with others.... 'Israel' would even require that Arabs rewrite their history by a new light, including the story of the Prophet Mohammad and his struggle against the Jews of Medina, Banou Khouneika and Banou al-Nazir."

The Israeli attack on Thuwaitha proved once again that "the Zionist entity is thus the sworn enemy of the Arab Nation and of Iraq." Faced with Israeli aggression, "every nation that is truly seeking peace and security and that honestly respects freedom and the independence of peoples should help the Arabs in one way or another to acquire the atomic bomb, so that they can confront the real atomic bombs the Zionist entity possesses."

Later that day Saddam carried his message to an American television audience in an interview with Barbara Walters of ABC News. Israel wanted "to maintain the Arabs in a state of underdevelopment," he said, "to be able to dominate them and persecute them." In the wake of the Israeli attack, which was carried out "with the help of sophisticated American weapons," the American people "should ask themselves whether it is possible to maintain good relations between the USA and the Arabs, especially when the American administration is openly allying itself with 'Israel' by giving political, military, economic, scientific, and financial support."

When Saddam Hussein talked about Iraq's scientific and technical progress, what he meant had little to do with what most Westerners imagine. He was not referring to any great achievements by Iraqi researchers, nor even to his regime's laudable efforts to bring education to the masses. What he meant was the great strides Iraq had made toward the atomic bomb. Scientific progress for the Arabs meant developing this weapon, which was intended to put them on an equal footing with Israel. To Saddam's mind, that was the only scientific progress worthy of the name.

Until the Israeli destruction of Osirak, Iraq had pursued the plutonium route to the bomb, which required at least one large, highly visible resource, a reactor for irradiating uranium. Now Saddam wondered if Iraq should change its approach, to depend less on large strategic facilities that could be destroyed in the future. As he told Walters, the Israeli attack had taught "not only the Iraqis, but all Arabs, that they must shelter their vital projects from all attack, so that even an atomic bomb will not be able to knock them out." It was an important lesson, and Iraq would spend billions of dollars putting it into practice.

Saddam had been counting on obtaining the bomb within a matter of months, if not years. With that hope shattered, he had to turn elsewhere for strategic "reach." He wanted weapons capable of inflicting great damage on Israel. And what could be worse to Holocaust-conscious Jews such as Menachem Begin, he reasoned, than poison gas? In the drastic overhaul of Iraqi strategic weapons projects following the destruction of the Osirak reactor, he gave Dr.

Amer al-Saadi additional resources and told him to accelerate the poison gas programs. He was also told to take extraordinary precautions to protect existing facilities, burying them wherever possible, and to disperse new ones across Iraq. The more targets there were, Saddam now understood, the less damage a single strike could do.

After the earlier rebuffs from the United States and Britain, al-Saadi knew exactly where to turn to find willing partners for Iraq's most momentous enterprise: West Germany. Thirty-five years after the Holocaust, many West Germans were still ready and willing to help Iraq learn "how this knowledge . . . [can] be used to destroy Israel." One of them was a German trader named Anton Eyerle, who headed the Rhein-Bavaria Vehicle Construction Company. For Eyerle, who was fifty-seven when he started working for Iraq, Saddam Hussein was "a strong man for whom it is worth fighting." The Iraqis were "people who still have character." In his office in Kaufbeuren, Bavaria, Eyerle still kept a "people's receiver," a radio console popular during the Third Reich. He had fixed it so that he could play Hitler's booming speeches as if they were just being broadcast, as he had heard them thirty-five years earlier. Eyerle had served in Hermann Göring's Luftwaffe, and in an interview with the West German newsweekly *Der Spiegel* he explained his enthusiasm for Iraq and the Iraqi dictator. "This is as it was in my youth," he said.[2]

Saddam's men would find other partners in West Germany's chemicals, electronics, and military establishments. Over the next ten years, Germans worked shoulder to shoulder with Iraqi chemists, ballistics engineers, and nuclear scientists to develop one of the most diversified arsenals of unconventional weapons found anywhere in the world. Senator Jesse Helms, whose staff assistants spent months tracking them down, called these companies and their cohorts "Saddam's Foreign Legion."

In the mid-1970s, the Strategic Planning Committee had tucked several innocuous-sounding projects into a Five Year Plan. One of them was yet another pesticides plant to be constructed near the town of Suwaira, some 30 kilometers south of Baghdad, near the ancient site of Ctesiphon. This plant was initially supposed to make

3,500 tons a year of deadly organic phosphorus compounds. It was not a large facility as pesticides plants went, but it was huge when its real purpose was understood: the manufacture of poison gas.

Until the Israeli bombing of the Osirak reactor, however, the Suwaira project had been on the back burner. Negotiations had dragged on, and no contracts had been signed. Now the project was dusted off and assigned top priority. Al-Saadi turned to a respected West German company Thyssen Rheinstahl Technology, which signed a contract for 21.4 million deutschemarks in 1981, ostensibly for a "university" project. Contract documents showed that the "Diyala Chemical Laboratory" that Thyssen built in Salman Pak, a popular suburb of Suwaira, was fitted out with specialized manufacturing equipment capable of handling the most toxic substances. One of the chemicals manufactured at the laboratory was phosphorus pentachloride. According to Michael Braungart, a West German chemical engineer who was shown the project documents by the newsweekly *Stern,* the production line was unusual because phosphorus pentachloride "is a starting chemical for organic phosphorus chemical agents. There is no reason for such a special layout in normal laboratories," he concluded.[3] From the start, Salman Pak was designed as a nerve gas plant.

Did the Germans know what they were building? Thyssen claims that "no statements can be made" about the purpose of the laboratory. The company "had no information at any time" that might have suggested the laboratory was a poison gas plant. The project leader, civil engineer Peter Heinrich, told *Stern* that "it never occurred to me at that time that something terrible was installed there. Upon inquiry, we were told that the facility had to be resistant to sulfuric acid. . . . To me, it was a job like any other. I thought the whole thing was clean."[4]

From the day ground was broken at the plant in late 1981, the site was heavily guarded by Iraqi soldiers, and Soviet-built SA-2 missile batteries were installed to protect against air attack. To make sure there were no spies in their midst, the Iraqis kept a close watch on the German workers, accompanying them even when they went to the lavatory. Thyssen employees and their subcontractors had to sign a two-page letter guaranteeing that their companies had "no relations with Israel . . . no assembly workshop in Israel . . . no representative in Israel . . . no partnership in Israeli factories or enterprises [and] provide no advice nor . . .

supply anything to Israeli companies." The letter, which went far beyond the type of "Israel clause" imposed by many Arab contractors, highlighted Iraq's fear of espionage and the highly strategic nature of the Salman Pak project.

A further warning signal should have gone off when the Thyssen employees contemplated a project specification that called for an expensive air cleaning plant for the laboratories, to be built by one of the eight German subcontractors, Noske-Kaeser. The Iraqis were not known for caring about environmental protection. The only reason for such an elaborate air cleaning system was to prevent the highly volatile chemicals from poisoning workers and the local population.

If that was still not enough to arouse suspicion among the Germans working at the site, then the "animal house," where beagles and other test animals were kept, should have been. Once production began at Salman Pak, the beagles were used to test the lethality of the nerve gas agents. Their cadavers were thrown out on a garbage dump in plain view.

Not long after returning to Germany from the Diyala laboratory, a young German welder named Klaus contracted a mysterious blood disease and died. It was a deadly business. And it was only the beginning.

Two months after the Paris Air Show, Saddam sent Tarek Aziz, who had become one of the key players in his strategic designs, back to France. When difficult contracts were up for negotiation, Saddam always dispatched Aziz to make the deal. He had recently been promoted to foreign minister, and his talents as a negotiator were second to none. Aziz met with his new counterpart, Claude Cheysson, on August 19. Cheysson was an outspoken advocate of forging strong relations with the Third World, and he greeted Aziz warmly. Unlike Britain, a former colonial power, and the United States, whose policy Cheysson dismissed as "lopsided" in favor of Israel, France could play a positive role in the region, Cheysson believed. Being impartial, with neither colonial nor imperial ambitions, France was the perfect partner for a nation such as Iraq, which was just seeking Western assistance for its development needs.

Tarek Aziz was quick to understand that Iraq had found a new friend. Whereas Mitterrand showed reserve, Cheysson bubbled over with enthusiasm for the "Iraqi experiment." When Aziz asked him whether France would rebuild the Osirak reactor, Cheysson gave him an unqualified yes, without once referring back to his boss at the Élysée Palace. Iraq's nuclear reactor, Cheysson said, was a monument to peace. The Israelis had to learn that they could not treat the Arabs this way.

Mitterrand surrounded himself with other pro-Arab ministers as well. His minister of cooperation, Jean-Pierre Cot, elevated Cheysson's anti-imperialistic cant to the realm of doctrine. Jean-Pierre Chevènement, who was married to an Egyptian woman, was an unabashed admirer of Saddam Hussein. Although Chevènement served as minister of education in Mitterrand's first cabinet, he exerted a powerful influence on the ruling Socialist party because he controlled one of its largest factions.

Another pro-Arabist was Mitterrand's cranky minister of foreign trade, Michel Jobert, a political renegade who belonged to neither the left nor the right. He had served in the cabinet under Giscard d'Estaing and stayed on to work with Mitterrand. A small, bitter man who resented the United States' dominant position in post–World War II Europe, Jobert was a fierce opponent of Israel. Like Cheysson, he believed the Osirak reactor was a monument to peace. When he made his first official trip to Baghdad as foreign trade minister on October 1, 1981, he had on his agenda a wide range of arms deals and industrial projects intended to shore up Saddam Hussein's regime and to firmly place France ahead of its European competitors as Iraq's principal trading partner (West Germany and Japan led the pack in sales of industrial goods and heavy machinery to Iraq, areas where the French were traditionally weak). Jobert reinforced the message delivered in August by Cheysson: not only did the new Socialist government have no intention of going back on previous commitments to Iraq, but the Iraqi government had only to make its wishes known and France was ready to help and willing to sell.

President Mitterrand soon cast his principles aside, and within months of taking office approved the largest arms package the French had ever concocted for Iraq. The $2.6 billion deal was announced on February 21, 1982, during a widely publicized visit to Baghdad by Foreign Minister Cheysson and included the 83 heavy artillery pieces and sophisticated ammunition of the Vulcan

Project, in addition to hundreds of Exocet missiles, Panhard armored cars, and more.[5] France intended to make a public show of support for Iraq. The French noted with some alarm that most of Iraq's new industrial projects were going primarily to the West Germans, so they decided to sell what they knew how to make best: weapons.

Saddam Hussein's uncle and father-in-law, Khairallah al-Tulfah, had made the grade. From his humble origins in the village of Al-Auja, he had become one of the wealthiest businessmen in Iraq and, more recently, Baghdad's lord mayor. The father of Iraq's defense minister and of Saddam's wife controlled seventeen companies worth more than $500 million.

But money was not enough for the aging patriarch. In 1981 he decided it was time to make his contribution to eternal Baath party doctrine as well. He penned a scurrilous pamphlet that was widely distributed by local party cells. Its title was long but explicit: *Three God Should Not Have Made: Persians, Jews, and Flies.* Persians, al-Tulfah wrote, were "animals God created in the shape of humans." Jews were a "mixture of the dirt and leftovers of diverse peoples." As for flies, they were a trifling creation "whom we do not understand God's purpose in creating."[6]

For all three, the Baath party had a solution, which it broadcast throughout the Arab world, thanks to the powerful French transmitters of Baghdad's Voice of the Masses. "There is a certain insecticide for every type of insect," Baghdad Radio proclaimed. It was an Iraqi attempt at humor. Like most Baath party jokes, its punch line was death.

The German community in Baghdad was thriving, and West German trade with Iraq was up. More than a hundred German companies were doing business with Baghdad; dozens maintained full-time offices in the Iraqi capital. One such was Karl Kolb GmbH, a medium-sized chemicals concern from Dreieich, a trading estate close to the Frankfurt airport. Its Baghdad representative was a fifty-five-year-old German named Klaus Franzl.

Franzl was more than just a sales representative. Court documents show he was a major shareholder in the Karl Kolb company, having provided DM 540,000 in start-up capital. Franzl had been working in Baghdad for years and knew Amer al-Saadi and the Baathists well. One of his favorite hangouts was a belly-dancing joint called the Al Wia Club, where patrons could drink French champagne and eat *masgouf* while rubbing shoulders with some of the regime's most senior officials. This may be where he first heard of the Samarra project, one of the two pesticides plants that Amer al-Saadi planned to build. In the months following the Israeli raid on Osirak, Franzl succeeded in having his company appointed as the main contractor for that plant.

While the Samarra deal was certainly worth millions to Franzl and his colleagues, it may have appealed to him for other reasons as well. Customs investigators who searched Franzl's home in Dreieich years after Samarra had become a synonym for death found a large oil painting that showed Franzl wearing a Wehrmacht order from the Third Reich on his chest. Like Anton Eyerle's, his sympathy for Saddam Hussein's regime appears to have gone far beyond his taste for the excellent wages the Iraqis paid.[7]

Franzl's partners in Germany were all younger men. The most important was Helmut Maier, managing director of Karl Kolb. Born on December 28, 1932, Maier was too young to have fought in the Wehrmacht, but he was old enough to remember Germany's Nazi past.

Maier and Franzl contracted with a recently created Iraqi entity, the State Establishment for Pesticides Production (SEPP), to build an entire chemical weapons complex at Samarra. Of course the planned use of the Kolb facilities was never mentioned in the contract. For the two Germans, and for the host of subcontractors who helped build Samarra, this was merely a plant for making insecticides. They knew about flies, but they pleaded ignorance about Saddam's feelings toward Persians and Jews.

To help him in his day-to-day relations with the Iraqis, Franzl called on a German-educated Iraqi, Nazar al-Khadhi, who was soon appointed as his de facto deputy. Al-Khadhi's official title was head of the Baghdad office for Preussag AG and Water Engineering Trading, subcontractors for Kolb. W.E.T., as it was known, was run by an enterprising forty-two-year-old German named Peter Leifer, who traveled to Baghdad many times to supervise the fitting out of the Samarra plant.

Al-Khadi organized several trips to Germany for SEPP officials.

In September 1981, for instance, an Iraqi team led by the director of SEPP, Dr. Abdallah al-Ani, and a SEPP chemist, Dr. al-Nayeemi, visited UHDE, a subsidiary of the chemicals firm Hoescht. The company's Baghdad representative later telexed the head office in Frankfurt with information on the Samarra "pesticides" project and advised the company not to get involved. On May 4, 1982, German Customs documents show, the traveling Iraqis visited Preussag's Hannover office, claiming they represented the Baghdad Water Supply Administration. On another trip, SEPP's general manager, Mr. al-Attar, claimed he was from the State Establishment for Oil Refining and Gas Industry (SEORGI). Extensive documentary evidence shows that SEORGI was negotiating industrial contracts with some of the world's largest petrochemicals companies, including Technipetrole (TPL) in Italy. How many of these apparently innocent deals were linked to Iraq's poison gas program had yet to be determined by government investigators.

Helmut Maier understood that he had to proceed with caution, for poison gas was a subject of sensitivity to many Germans. To cover his tracks in the unlikely event that the German authorities decided to investigate Kolb's relationship with Iraq, Maier set up a front company called Pilot Plant, also located in Dreieich, to execute the Samarra contracts. Documents seized at Kolb headquarters in November 1987 by German Customs show that Maier was managing director of both companies.

Maier provided many services for the Iraqis, besides the equipment to manufacture chemical weapons. He advised them on the most efficient method of setting up their "pesticides" plant, designing it, and finding the right suppliers. And he served as a middleman for German firms hoping to get a piece of the cake. Heberger Bau GmbH, of Schifferstadt, was one such company introduced to SEPP through Maier's good offices. In return, Heberger paid Karl Kolb and Pilot Plant a 3 percent commission on its contracts with SEPP. The first of these, signed on February 2, 1982, was for construction of above-ground bunkers at the Samarra complex. Bertold and Egon Heberger were convinced that it was well worth paying a DM 120,000 commission to get a foothold in the Iraqi market, which could be worth millions to their company.

The sprawling Samarra complex that the Hebergers helped build was heavily guarded, in accordance with Saddam Hussein's new orders to protect Iraqi factories from attack. A single access road led into the complex through a double perimeter fence. Several fixed SA-2 missile batteries guarded the site from air attack. Spread across a 160-square-kilometer military "exclusion zone," the chemical weapons manufacturing and storage facilities themselves could have fit in an area one-sixth that size, but had been dispersed to make targeting more difficult. To the west of the central processing zone, German companies built fifteen underground silos of reinforced-concrete thick enough to withstand a direct air attack. A separate compound, built by Heberger Bau, contained a dozen strangely shaped storage bunkers. According to BBC television, which commissioned a commercial SPOT satellite photograph of the Samarra complex for an October 1986 "Panorama" program, these bunkers were up to a hundred yards long. Some were carefully crafted fakes, intended to mislead enemy bombers.[8]

Karl Kolb eventually built six separate chemical weapons manufacturing lines at Samarra, called Ahmed, Ani, Mohamed, Iesa, Meda, and Ghasi. The first was completed in 1983; the last, sometime in 1986. These plants made everything from mustard gas and prussic acid to the nerve gas compounds Sarin and Tabun. The plant was designed so that the poisons were funneled from the production "reactors" to an underground packing plant, where they were put into artillery shells, rockets, and other munitions. By the time the BBC commissioned its satellite photograph, the Samarra complex was without a doubt one of the largest chemical weapons manufacturing plants in the world.

The only real secret of Samarra was why the West German government did nothing to stop it.

Iraq's fortunes in the war with Iran took a dramatic turn for the worse on March 17, 1982, when Iran finally succeeded in rallying its forces, throwing the Iraqis into a rout. Victorious Iranian Revolutionary Guards soundly defeated the Iraqi Third Army at Khorramshahr, taking tens of thousands of prisoners. Then they wheeled around and chased the tattered Iraqi Fourth Army back across the border.

Fueled by his battlefield success, Ayatollah Khomeini called for the resignation of Saddam Hussein, whom he considered personally responsible for the war. Khomeini's call appears to have won some favor in Iraq. During a cabinet meeting in late March 1982, Saddam Hussein is said to have brought up the subject himself. "Khomeini seems to think peace will be possible if I resign. Maybe he is right," diplomatic cables reported Saddam as suggesting.

As he had done many times in the past, Saddam was trying to sound out potential opposition to his rule. Taken in by the ruse, his minister of health, Riyadh Ibrahim, responded enthusiastically. "Perhaps if your excellency stood aside for a few months, we could put the word of the Iranians to the test," he suggested. Saddam replied that this was a good idea, which he thought worthy of a more detailed discussion. Inviting the minister into his private office, he excused himself from the cabinet meeting. A few minutes later the other cabinet members heard a shot; then Saddam re-emerged and ordered his guards to take Ibrahim's body away. The minister's execution was announced a few days later, prompting speculation among foreign diplomats in Baghdad. He had imported "bad medicine" from abroad, the official statement read, which had "contaminated" brave Iraqi soldiers, causing their death.

The U.S. State Department viewed the dramatic events on the battlefield with alarm. "We were afraid of a spillover of radical Shiism," says Richard Murphy, then ambassador to Saudi Arabia, one of the architects of U.S. policy in the Middle East. "We knew the other states in the Gulf, with their large Shiite populations, could not stand much provocation. So our policy started to focus on putting an end to the war. That became our top priority."

The first step along that road was taken in March 1982, when the State Department took Iraq off its list of countries suspected of supporting international terrorism. Countries on that list are subject to "foreign policy controls" that make even the most innocuous commercial exchanges difficult and cannot receive any form of American foreign aid or assistance. If the United States wanted to funnel aid to Baghdad, it had to start by lifting the stigma of terrorism. To those who argued on Iraq's behalf, including the assistant secretary of state in charge of Middle East policy, Nicholas Veliotes, and, later, Undersecretary of State Michael Armacost, it may have appeared a purely administrative gesture; but by removing Iraq from the terrorism list, the State Department opened up a Pandora's box.

By May 1982, the situation on the battlefield had gotten even worse for Iraq. Iranian troops had crossed the border and began to put pressure on Basra, Iraq's second largest city and its only gateway to the Gulf. In desperation, Saddam sued Ayatollah Khomeini for peace. He announced the unilateral withdrawal of all Iraqi forces from Iran (a scarcely veiled retreat) and declared Iraq's acceptance of the international border with Iran. When Khomeini didn't accept, he lit another fire in the region, hoping to divert Iranian attention to a common enemy: Israel. On June 3 a Palestinian gunman mortally wounded Israel's ambassador to Great Britain, Shlomo Argov, on the steps of London's Dorchester Hotel. The assassination, seemingly the handiwork of Yasser Arafat's PLO, was all the Begin government needed to launch its long-planned military incursion into Lebanon to destroy the PLO infrastructure.

Within hours of the Israeli invasion on June 5, Saddam appealed publicly to Ayatollah Khomeini. Iran and Iraq should stop fighting each other, he argued, and join forces against Israel in a Holy War. The Iranian leader declined. It turned out later that the assassination of Argov was the handiwork of Saddam himself. The police investigation in London concluded that the gunman's weapon had been supplied by a military intelligence officer at the Iraqi Embassy in London. Iraqi agents had planned and financed the operation, which was carried out by a hired assassin from the Abu Nidal Organization, then based in Baghdad. Saddam's attempt to create a diversion from his losing war with Iran resulted in the deaths of thousands in Lebanon.

When the State Department decided to give Iraq a clean bill of health on the terrorism, it knew full well about Baghdad's support of Abu Nidal. Iraq's involvement in the Argov shooting was soon brought to the attention of the U.S. government by the British authorities, but as Richard Murphy confided, "There was never any discussion at State to put Iraq back on the terrorism list. The subject simply never came up."[9]

Saddam Hussein was a man with a mission. He believed that through fear, hardship, and war, the Baath party would redeem the Arab world from the humiliation it had suffered at the hands of the colonialists, the Zionists, and the imperialists. As the Iraqi leader told pamphleteer Charles St. Prot, whose glowing portrait of Saddam was distributed free by the Iraqi Embassy in Paris, the "new Arab man . . . must have a new mentality, a new set of values, a more responsible way of being. He must act as citizen, patriot, and builder."[10] He had to take part in the monumental enterprise Saddam had launched: building the greatest military power the Arab world had ever seen. As one Soviet diplomat would put it later, "Saddam Hussein is convinced he is a great world leader of the type that is born once in a generation."[11] If it was his mischance to be born in tiny Iraq, then he would transform that country into a mighty nation worthy of his ambitions.

Saddam was intent on becoming the new Saladin, the Muslim warrior who drove the Christian Crusaders out of the Holy Land in the twelfth century. As he liked to point out to Arab visitors, it was no coincidence that Saddam Hussein, like Saladin, was born near Tikrit. The destiny of the two Muslim leaders was intertwined in more ways than one. Through years of patient work in the shadow of his cousin, President al-Bakr, Saddam Hussein had built himself up into a larger-than-life figure, whose portrait dominated every public square, every street corner, every living room in Iraq. There was Saddam Hussein the devout Muslim, kneeling to pray at the mosque; he was the Arab warrior, making his triumphal entry into Jerusalem astride his white horse, as Nebuchadnezzar had done before him; he was the leader of the historic Qaddisiyah battle to drive out the Persian infidel, looming large over yet another battlefield. The Iraqi leader was everywhere, in every guise. He explained the cult of personality to a group of Kuwaiti newspaper editors in 1982:

> You might think that [Iraqi] journalists speak of Saddam Hussein because they are government employees. But have you ever seen a little girl singing a patriotic song where the name of Saddam Hussein doesn't appear? Is this because she is a government employee, too? Have you ever heard a poet recite a poem where the name of Saddam Hussein doesn't appear many times? Have you ever seen a peasant or a simple worker or a woman who has lost her husband or her son in battle speak of the Revolution without mentioning the name of Saddam Hussein? . . . Speak to our women, to the widows of these martyrs. They won't tell you that their husbands died for the Fatherland. The first thing they'll say is that they died for

Saddam Hussein. . . . Saddam Hussein should be a symbol for all Iraqis, because Iraqis have a greater need for such a symbol than the average Muscovite.[12]

The regime was Saddam and he was it. All of Iraq's vast resources, its oil, its skilled labor force, its plentiful water, were under his control. All had been put at the service of his driving ambition to become the dominant military power in the Middle East, the new policeman of the Gulf.

In June 1982, Saddam launched a costly program to build a network of underground bunkers to shelter the country's strategic resources from future air attacks. In part this was one of the lessons learned from the Osirak attack. But the Israeli raid did not explain everything. Every new government building in Baghdad was to be equipped with an underground bunker, according to British engineers who built many of them. According to Colin Croft, chairman of Britain's Federation of Nuclear Shelter Consultants and Contractors, British companies submitted designs for enough underground bunkers to hide 48,000 soldiers. Each bunker consisted of ten steel tubes and would be capable of holding up to 1,200 people. "The designs included command posts, sick bays, decontamination rooms, armouries, kitchens and stores for dried food and water: everything necessary for a long stay."[13]

One of Saddam's personal bunkers was built beneath a cinema in the basement of the Al Sijood administrative complex, right next to the presidential palace. Small by Saddam's standards (30 feet by 15 feet), it nevertheless contained enough electronic equipment, computers, teleprinters, and fiber optic communications links for Saddam to maintain contact with his troops in every corner of Iraq.

Saddam had a German company, Boswau and Knauer, from Augsburg, construct a far more sumptuous hideaway beneath the new presidential palace he had begun to build.[14] This complex was buried sixteen floors — more than 300 feet — beneath the Tigris River. According to a German engineer who worked for Saddam as a security advisor at the time, "Saddam would feel only a jolt" if a Hiroshima-sized bomb were detonated just a quarter of a mile away from the bunker, which was modeled on the American NORAD command and control headquarters, deep inside Cheyenne Mountain at Colorado Springs. Huge springs, two feet in diameter, on a cushion of hard molded rubber, supported the foundations of Saddam's underground cube. For further protection, a gap between the bunker and the surrounding riverbed allowed for movement of the earth. The outside walls were made of six to eight feet of reinforced concrete.

Two escape routes from the palace led down into the German bunker: an earthquake-proof elevator, built into the wall of Saddam's ground-floor office, and a staircase that could be reached only from the palace basement; it was guarded at every turn by automatically controlled machine-gun posts.

Once below ground, the Iraqi president still needed to remember a complex series of codes for the cipher locks that opened the six-foot-thick vault doors. They led into an airlock fitted out with showers and a decontamination room in the event of nuclear or chemical attack, and then to a guard post. Just in case an intruder managed to penetrate the area, every corner was under surveillance by video cameras and could be sprayed with bullets from machine guns built into the walls.

The first level of the underground shelter contained the guard headquarters, with dormitories, a canteen, and more decontamination showers. On the floor below were located the president's own living quarters. Besides a luxurious private apartment, complete with imported marble, there was a command and control headquarters that had been fitted out to rival the best that NATO command posts could offer. The third level down contained food stores, generators, and fuel and water reserves. Japanese engineers installing security cameras said they came upon a paved tunnel in one of these bunkers, giving rise to speculation that the various underground shelters in the Baghdad area were linked to one another like a gigantic ant farm.

Remembering that conspirators had tried to ambush President al-Bakr at the airport upon his return from a trip to Bulgaria ten years earlier, Saddam ordered the French construction companies Fougerolle and Spie Batignolles to redesign the VIP lounge at Saddam International Airport, then under construction, to include an underground escape route and a completely separate access road. Company engineers still recall the unusual specifications of the airport facilities. "If the airport came under attack, Saddam could escape through a 15-kilometer-long tunnel beneath the VIP lounge that led to a secret helicopter landing pad out in the desert," one said. Huge reinforced concrete bunkers were built underneath the three passenger terminals, while the 60-meter-wide runway — probably the widest of any civilian airport in the world — was designed to accommodate two bombers taking off side by side, using reinforced concrete one meter thick.

Saddam's "bunker mentality" went further than his personal protection. In June 1982 he signed a $380 million contract with the same Belgian construction firm that had built most of the Al Qaim chemicals complex. The aim of this extravagant program, code-named Project 505, was to bury Iraq's advanced warplanes in a series of eight hardened antinuclear bases 50 meters below ground. Six Construct International (Sixco), began work on Project 505 in October 1982 along with a French construction company called Nord France. The Belgian company benefited from a government export credit guarantee, issued by the Office du Ducroire. By the time it was completed, sometime in 1986 or 1987, Iraq had spent more than $2.5 billion on its strategic shelter program, despite the lack of any clear threat from the Iranian air force.

Sixco ran the project out of an office on Haifa Street in downtown Baghdad, and over the next four years built a total of seventeen air bases and headquarters for several armored divisions. The first Sixco bases were Tel Affar (in Mosul), Ad Hain (Samarra), Al Hai (southwest of Baghdad), KM 160 (located at milepost 160 along the Baghdad-Ar Rutbah-Amman highway), Tuz (Kirkuk), As Salman (near the Saudi border), Al Yussuf (north of Basra), and Qalat Saleh, along the border with Iran. French engineers who worked on the site said the underground portion of the Qalat Saleh base was large enough to house two dozen aircraft, as well as missile stores, fuel, and all necessary maintenance equipment; it was designed to be totally self-sufficient under nuclear-biological-chemical (NBC) attack. The only facilities above ground were the entry ramp (secured by a concrete door 1.5 meters thick), and low-lying crew quarters linked to the shelter by tunnels. The Iraqi Mirages housed at this base during the war with Iran took off from an underground ramp, with their brakes on and afterburners lit. A blast wall protected the shelters from the heat of takeoff. Eyewitnesses say the planes seemed to be airborne by the time they emerged from the ramp; the 3000-meter-long runways were built behind mounds of desert clay, making them virtually invisible to observers more than a few dozen meters away.[15]

Contract drawings later published in the Belgian press show that all eight Sixco bases were of similar construction. Each was a square whose sides were five to six kilometers long and surrounded by barbed wire, with a single, heavily guarded watchtower over the central entrance. Narrow asphalt roads inside the base connected the underground personnel bunkers, ammunition bunkers, fuel tanks, and twin power stations that sustained all base activities. Twelve reinforced concrete aircraft hangars, built in groups of three, stood at each end of the twin crisscrossing runways. The hangars, made of reinforced concrete more than half a meter thick, were covered with a thick layer of desert clay and lime, making them virtually indistinguishable when viewed from the air.

The separation of vital facilities made the bases less vulnerable to air attack, and one eyewitness who visited the Qalat Saleh base in 1985 said that an Iranian missile had landed "within meters" of the blast door of an aircraft hangar without doing any noticeable damage. Each base was capable of sustaining a 300-man combat team of pilots, mechanics, and support personnel. During the war with Iran, Iraqi pilots were able to take off from these bases with a maximum munitions load, using special boosters to provide additional thrust. The boosters consisted of compressed-air "rockets," which were refilled from specially designed trucks provided by former Luftwaffe pilot Anton Eyerle of the Rhein-Bayern Vehicle Construction Company.

Sixco was not the only firm building hardened air bases. Others were being constructed by Yugoslav and British companies (Projects 404 and 303). Swiss companies provided airlocks to protect against chemical and nuclear attack; Italian companies built the blast doors; French companies provided a special honeycomb structure for the aircraft hangars; and German and British companies supplied power generators and communications gear. Everybody had a piece of the pie.

One of the more remarkable aspects of the Sixco deal involved government-sponsored visits by Iraqi military officials to NATO air bases in Belgium and West Germany to see firsthand how NATO provided NBC protection for its air forces. Iraq built a total of 300 hardened aircraft shelters in addition to another 300 light-weight "Potemkin" shelters intended to fool attacking aircraft. The whole project, including the use of dummies, was based on NATO doctrine and built by NATO suppliers.

Military sources in Baghdad said that these bases, as well as vital industrial plants, were also protected against electromagnetic pulse, or EMP. A nuclear explosion sets off an electromagnetic shock wave that melts silicon chips and renders most conventional military electronics and communications systems totally useless. Nothing short of a nuclear explosion can create EMP.

For many years after news first trickled out about Iraq's shelter program in 1985, nuclear proliferation experts would be gnawed with doubt. The idea that Saddam Hussein was spending billions on hardening his defenses because he feared an Israeli attack on vital military installations was almost plausible. If, however, Iraq was continuing its nuclear weapons program in secret, all the building and hardening added up to one thing: a strategy to wage nuclear war and win.

For eighteen months, the fortunes of war slowly turned against Iraq, as the Soviet Union continued its arms embargo. The USSR also slashed imports from Iraq (mostly oil) from 247 million rubles in 1980 to zero by January 1981. The Soviets claimed they were responding to American pleas for "strict neutrality" toward the Gulf war, to keep the conflict from spreading to neighboring countries. But this public policy was a convenience for both superpowers; each was working furiously behind the scenes to further its own interests. The Soviets were by far the more successful. They were making overtures to the mullahs in Iran in an effort to fill the vacuum left by the departure of the United States. Because it borders Afghanistan, which the Soviets had invaded in December 1979, and has 1,200 miles of common frontier with the Soviet Union, Iran was tempting prey.

At the same time, the Kremlin leaders knew that Iraq could not hold out forever without heavy equipment, spare parts, and munitions. Saddam could turn to the French; he could even solicit the United States; but he could not change the fact that 95 percent of the equipment his ground forces were using was Soviet-made. Even the vast stores of Soviet weapons purchased from Egypt in the early days of the war could not fulfill Saddam's need. The Soviets were waiting for the results of their "Iranian gambit" to become clear and were expecting Saddam's generals to waste huge quantities of arms and munitions on the battlefield, drawing down Iraqi stockpiles just as they had during the 1974–75 Kurdish war. They were waiting for the fortunes of war to turn against Saddam, putting him (they hoped) in a position of need.

In June 1982 the Soviets opened the arms tap once again, from necessity as much as choice. By this time the Iranians had seized the initiative on the ground, Israel had invaded Lebanon and defeated the Syrian air force without a warning from Moscow, and some Iranians were publicly calling for support of the Afghan rebels in their fight against the Soviet invader. The Soviets could afford to teach Saddam Hussein a lesson, but they could not afford to lose yet another war. If the Iraqi armed forces did not get immediate and significant resupply, they faced defeat at the hands of Iran. Failure to honor a long-standing commitment would have inalterably damaged Soviet credibility in the Third World. "Not supplying arms to a signatory of a Treaty of Friendship was one thing, but permitting that signatory to be invaded and toppled would be quite another," Iranian analyst Shahram Chubin wrote.[16] Brezhnev would leave power with the taint of a Jimmy Carter if he failed to go to Baghdad's aid.

The Soviet decision to resume supplying arms to Iraq came too late from a political point of view. Baghdad was not going to accept Soviet control of its armed forces any longer. From now on, any Soviet equipment would have to reach Iraq without any strings attached, for Saddam could now turn to any number of other suppliers who were more than happy to fulfill his needs. In the struggle for power and influence between Baghdad and Moscow, Saddam Hussein appears to have won. Although his new arms suppliers could not replace Iraq's enormous arsenal of Soviet-built equipment overnight, they had helped him break the bonds of dependence.

By November 1982, 1,000 to 1,200 Soviet advisors had returned to Iraq, discreetly tucked away on military bases, air fields, and at division headquarters. Some 400 T-55 and 250 T-72 tanks had arrived, while an impressive array of Grad, Frog 7, SAM 9, and SCUD B missiles were on their way, along with MiG-25 reconnaissance fighters and Mi-24 helicopter gunships. The Kremlin's Arabists argued that Iraq's "withdrawal" (retreat) to the international border on June 29 provided the perfect occasion for a policy reassessment. The Soviets felt that they had reached a dead end in their attempts to penetrate Iran, and they worried that Iraq was preparing to turn to the United States for aid.[17] That last fear was more than justified, as future events would show.

Sarkis Soghenalian was a big man with a booming voice. When he made friends, it was for life. After leaving Beirut to make his fortune in America because of the Lebanese civil war, which began in April 1975, Sarkis had settled on Miami as his true home. He dressed like an American, he spoke and joked like an American. But deep down he remained Lebanese. And like a good Lebanese patriarch, he had a family business. *I and my brother against our cousin, with our cousin against the world . . .*

Sarkis and his younger brother, Zaven, were fixtures at the Hughes Aircraft corporate chalet just off the tarmac at Farnborough military airport outside London. Farnborough alternated with Paris as the host for the world's biggest air show.

It was September 1982, and business had never been better for Sarkis. He and Zaven had just concluded negotiations with Sofma to sell Iraq the most accurate (and most expensive) gun in the world. That deal was going to net them more than $60 million in commissions. Sarkis didn't really need to make another sale, but selling was in his blood. As he chatted with an Iraqi procurements officer in the Hughes chalet, the idea suddenly came to him that Iraq should consider buying some American helicopters. Hughes had a great little model, the 500 MD Defender, which was perfect for battlefield observation. If the Iraqis wanted, Sarkis explained, he could arrange to fit it out with the latest model TOW antitank missile.

The Iraqi general, Hamed Abdullah Mohammed, thought it was a great idea. But he had to check with Baghdad to see if it was all right to purchase weapons from the United States, with whom Iraq still did not have diplomatic relations. Meanwhile, Sarkis sounded out friends in Langley, Virginia, home of the CIA, to see whether the sale would win U.S. government approval.

The answer was not long in coming from both quarters: go ahead. So over the next few months Sarkis and General Mohammed put together a deal for sixty Hughes helicopters. Iraq asked to pay in oil. As long as payment went through an American oil company (Chevron), Hughes had no objection.

The Reagan administration notified Congress of the potential sale in December 1982. Four Republican senators opposed selling weapons to Iraq because it was "not in the best interests of the United States." But the aerospace lobby went to work, and within weeks the deal received official blessings from the Commerce Department and the State Department. Commerce soon informed the senators that their objections were irrelevant, since the sale of aircraft weighing less than 10,000 pounds did not require an export license to countries not subject to foreign policy restrictions (which had been lifted when Iraq was taken off the terrorism list in March). All sixty helicopters were delivered by the end of 1983.

The Hughes helicopter deal was more than just an arms sale. It involved spare parts, training, and support equipment and gave the Iraqis a first taste of the type of high-technology support the Shah of Iran had received from the United States during the five years preceding his fall. Although Hughes did not deliver the helicopters equipped with TOW missiles, which would have been illegal, Iraqi agents purchased the missiles on the international black market; Sarkis was later charged in a Florida court with having helped the Iraqis purchase and install TOW missile launchers. A separate indictment accused him of conspiring to arrange the sale of an additional 103 armed helicopters to Iraq through Kuwait.[18] According to French arms salesmen who negotiated directly with Sarkis on other contracts, the helicopter deals also involved an intelligence tradeoff. On one trip to Iraq on the "Spirit of Free Enterprise," Sarkis picked up an advanced Soviet artillery weapon and flew it back to France, where it was turned over to the CIA at the French military airport in Bourges.

American diplomats in Baghdad at the time readily admitted that the helicopter sale "was not gratuitous." The Iraqis had repeatedly told American diplomats in private that they would like to procure sophisticated U.S. weapons, including advanced fighter aircraft, but they realized that a large weapons package would meet with stiff resistance in Congress. "The Iraqis certainly want to get their hands on the cookie jar," one diplomat said, "but they aren't willing to get burnt by reaching for it."

Instead they took a more gradual route, building up support in the aerospace lobby, the midwestern farm belt, and key manufacturing associations in the United States. In short, they set about creating a pro-Iraq lobby within the U.S. business community. Anyone watching the Iraqis at work in late 1982 or early 1983 would have called it an arduous task. But it worked better than even the Iraqis could have hoped.

EIGHT

Countering the Ayatollah

That first helicopter sale by Hughes to Iraq was followed by many more such deals. In a very real way, it opened a door that had been shut since 1967 between the United States and Iraq. It was as if the two governments — Saddam Hussein in Baghdad and the Reagan administration in Washington — were engaged in a slow dance around a dimly lit hall, gradually pressing closer, whispering in each other's ear and ignoring the other dancers, until they swooned in each other's embrace. From hostility to indifference, then mild interest, Washington now eagerly pursued relations with Baghdad.

The Reagan administration first considered following up on Brzezinski's Iraq gambit in 1982. The State Department's chief Arabist, Nicholas Veliotes, warned Secretary of State George Shultz about the Iranian advances on the battlefield, arguing that the United States should quietly support Saddam Hussein. Iraq's retreat from Iranian territory that spring raised fears for the first time that Iraq could actually lose the war; and the last thing Washington wanted to see was a victorious Iran spreading its fundamentalist revolution westward into the Arab heartland. Saddam Hussein's call for a negotiated settlement to the war and his retreat of that year lifted one major obstacle to better relations between the United States and Iraq, since in theory Iraq was no longer the aggressor in the war. In July Iranian troops pushed over the border into Iraq for the first time. These events, reviewed in a staff report by the Senate Foreign Relations Committee, explained the policy tilt toward Iraq that intensified in 1982. "The United States has undertaken a number of steps to shore up Iraq and to forestall an Iranian victory," the report said.[1]

The helicopter sale was one step. Another, far less bruited measure of U.S. support for Iraq was conducted in the arcana of the foreign policy establishment. It involved billions of dollars in credits, guarantees, and loans. To help Iraq weather the Iranian storm, the State Department policy planning staff turned to the Department of Agriculture, which had a little-known program for helping U.S. grain exporters find new markets in the Third World. It was a remarkable sleight of hand, which not only enlisted the help of the government bureaucracy in implementing the administration's foreign policy goals, but helped to broaden support for Iraq by signing up one of the most powerful lobbying groups in American politics: midwestern farmers. It couldn't have come at a better time, since Iraq was on the verge of bankruptcy.

In December 1982 the Commodity Credit Corporation (CCC), a branch of the Department of Agriculture, quietly authorized a $300 million line of credit for Iraqi purchases of American wheat and rice. It was not the type of announcement that made headlines, but word soon got out to the grain exporters. Agribusiness is one of America's strongest commercial suits. The embargo on grain sales to the USSR imposed in December 1979 by the Carter administration to punish the Soviets for their invasion of Afghanistan had left the industry swimming in surplus wheat, soybeans, and rice. America's grain belt was eager to boost exports to the Middle East to make up for the lost sales. But because of the region's political instability, the exports needed U.S. government backing. This is what the CCC program, known as GSM-102, provided.

The CCC guarantee was not a loan, but it gave Iraq "most favored nation" status as far as the grain exporters were concerned. Before the announcement, Iraq had been considered a high-risk country that most U.S. banks preferred to avoid. Almost overnight, Iraq won favor on the financial marketplace. If Baghdad failed to pay for the grain within three years, the U.S. government would foot the bill.

Richard Murphy would throw his weight behind the food credit program as an elegant way of helping Baghdad without dipping into the State Department's foreign aid budget. The effect was to turn the day-to-day management of U.S. policy toward Iraq over to the huge agro-industrial conglomerates such as Cargill, Arabfina, and Dreyfus.

This and other disguised aid programs to Iraq were possible only because Iraq had been taken off the terrorism list in March. In testimony to Congress, the CCC general sales manager, F. Paul Dickerson, emphasized the political nature of the GSM-102 and GSM-103 programs, explaining that the loan guarantees began at a time "when the United States and Iraq were working to re-establish diplomatic relations." In mid-1983 the Department of Agriculture increased Iraq's credit line by 20 percent. They doubled that amount at the end of the year, bringing the total food credits to more than $1 billion. Meanwhile, the State Department Arabists were lobbying hard to rehabilitate the "terrorist" Saddam Hussein.

On March 21, 1983, a Soviet-built Mi-8 Hip military helicopter crashed in Italy's Dolomite Mountains, killing the pilot and the seven other people on board. It had not been shot down for intruding into NATO airspace; the eight men were all Iraqis, and their helicopter belonged to the Iraqi air force. Their ill-fated flight from Venice to Milan was part of a top-secret training mission organized by the Italian government. The crash tore the lid off a "black" program few had suspected.

From *New York Times* reports on the following days, it became apparent that the Mi-8 was one of several being fitted out in Italy with some of NATO's most advanced electronic warfare equipment. Iraq wanted to give its Soviet choppers a night-flying capability to rival that of NATO's most sophisticated attack helicopter, the AH-64 Apache. The Iraqi pilots were being trained to perform low-altitude "nap-of-the-earth" flights to avoid detection by enemy radar. Such flights rely on an extremely accurate Doppler-augmented inertial navigation system and an automatic pilot to keep the machines from crashing as they zoom along at top speed just above treetop (or sand dune) level. Learning to master the techniques sometimes proved fatal even for the most experienced pilots. Before turning to Italy, Iraq had lacked this equipment and the expertise to use it.

The retrofit market is one of the most lucrative sideshows of the world arms bazaar, as well as one of the most shadowy. New companies spring up overnight, offering tantalizing solutions to countries, such as Iraq, that are eager to modernize their older weapons. The retrofit specialists seldom appear in the reference works published each year cataloguing the world's largest defense contractors. They rarely advertise and do most of their business by word of mouth. Often they work on the fringes of the law. The Rome-based company Caproni Vizzola l'Eletronica was small, discreet, and willing to act in total silence — for a fee. But Caproni was only a front. Most of the night-vision and navigation equipment it installed on the Iraqi helicopters was provided by Agusta Bell, the Italian subsidiary of the American helicopter manufacturer Bell Textron. It gave the Iraqis a taste for more of the best, made in the USA.

In Beirut the broad windows and large balconies of the American Embassy gave onto the jewellike Mediterranean. The palm-lined avenue along the sea, which Beirutis called the Corniche, was packed with strollers. Pushcart vendors sold bananas and oranges and pirated cassettes. A sense of security hovered over the Lebanese capital, which by the spring of 1983 had finally begun to pull itself together after eight years of civil war. The United States and its European allies — Great Britain, France, and Italy — had helped "pacify" the city and the immediate surroundings following the Israeli withdrawal in the fall. Marines jogged proudly along the beach at dawn, trading jokes with neighborhood kids who tried to keep up. Italian medics had set up shop in the poor southern suburbs of the city, where their services were much sought after by the predominantly Shiite population, many of whom had never seen a real doctor in years. French bomb experts were cheered as they dug up ancient booby traps and dismantled the minefields cutting the city in half. For the first time in eight years ordinary Beirutis could travel without fear from one side of the city to the other. Brand-new public buses began shuttling between the Moslem and Christian sectors of the city. The future looked bright.

That brief idyll — it lasted barely six months — was smashed in a few seconds' time when a truck laden with explosives broke through the front gate of the U.S. Embassy and rammed into the cafeteria, ripping a seven-story hole in the face of the building.

It was noontime on Monday, April 18, 1983. Three kilometers away, in his sheltered apartment on the edge of Ashrafiyeh, former Lebanese president Camille Chamoun cocked an ear when the bomb went off. Chamoun had heard bombs before, but this one was extremely powerful. After a moment, the former president smiled as if to reassure himself. "It's the French. They've found another Israeli bomb and have defused it."[2]

Within minutes, however, the telephone rang, and Chamoun's face fell. Outside sirens were screaming, and ambulances had begun to race toward the embassy from different parts of the city. Ten minutes later the dust had not yet settled from the blast. The front end of the building had collapsed in on itself, and huge slabs of concrete dangled in midair, suspended by their twisted reinforcement cables. It would take rescue workers several days to pull the dead from the wreckage; some of the body bags contained little more than severed limbs. The Reverend Ed Leis, a navy commander who stayed up all night performing last rites, was a witness to the grisly scene. "We make the sign of the cross on the forehead, and if there's no forehead, then on the next best place."

At first it was unclear who had launched the bomb. Back in Washington, the CIA went to work. Communications intercepts from all over the Middle East were scrutinized by experts at the National Security Agency. The bombing occurred just as the director of the CIA's Near East and South Asia analysis bureau, Robert Clayton Ames, had been chairing a meeting in the soundproof "bubble" on the seventh floor of the Beirut embassy building with agency station chiefs who had arrived that morning from all over the Middle East. In one blow, the unknown bombers managed to wipe out most of the CIA's best Middle East experts. It was a disaster for U.S. intelligence. The CIA was determined to find out who was to blame.

Within weeks, thanks to satellite intercepts of telephone conversations, the answer came in: the terrorists had been guided by Iran, which had gone on a rampage against the West. Halting the spread of the Iranian revolution, especially its use of terror, was no longer an abstract concern for the United States: it had become a top priority.[3] Added to this was the alarming series of Iranian successes against Iraq. Taken together, these events dramatically altered America's perception of the Middle East. They would seal the as-yet-unspoken pact between Washington and Baghdad, providing the final incentive for the tilt toward Iraq.

Secretary of State George Shultz met secretly with Iraqi Foreign Minister Tarek Aziz on May 10, 1983, during a trip to Paris, where he had gone to discuss the Iranian threat with America's European allies at the Organization for Economic Cooperation and Development (OECD). The Iraqi was sympathetic to Shultz's concerns and offered to provide information on Iranian-backed terrorist groups. Before the meeting broke up, Shultz asked about Abu Nidal. The United States was well aware of Iraq's support for the radical Palestinian terrorist group, Shultz reminded the Iraqi. Baghdad had given the order to Abu Nidal operatives a year earlier to assassinate Shlomo Argov. Only two months later Iraq had ordered Abu Nidal to launch a machine-gun and grenade attack on Joe Goldenberg's, a restaurant in Paris, which took the lives of six innocent victims and wounded twenty-two others. If Baghdad wanted to improve relations with the United States, Shultz said, it could start by expelling Abu Nidal. Before the year was out, Baghdad complied.

In September, Richard Murphy was called back to Washington from Saudi Arabia, where he had been serving as ambassador since 1981. He knew many Arab leaders and their families personally. Shultz put him in charge of forging a new U.S. policy toward the Gulf. Replacing Veliotes as assistant secretary of state for Near Eastern and South Asian affairs, Murphy would be the State Department's top gun in the area. After two years in Saudi Arabia, he was sympathetic to the Saudis' fear of aggression from neighboring Iran. He was less sympathetic to the regime in Baghdad, which the Saudis were shoring up with billions of dollars in protection money (the Saudis and the Kuwaitis were delivering their own oil to Iraqi customers free of charge, allowing Baghdad to maintain oil revenues while it rebuilt its oil export network). But he believed, as did the Saudis, that without the Iraqi rampart to hold the Iranians back, the delicate balance of the Middle East would be shattered.

Murphy helped devise a multitrack policy aimed at weakening Iran and shoring up Iraq, which was greatly in need of Western credit and Western arms. "Our primary goal was to end the war because it was generating instability. No matter what anybody says now, with perfect hindsight, this is what it was all about. We wanted to see an end to this unpredictable war, before it got out of hand. We wanted to contain Iran."[4]

Accordingly, Murphy says, the Reagan administration launched "an interagency effort, with the participation of Defense, CIA, and State," to help Iraq. One key element was a far-ranging intelligence-sharing agreement worked out by CIA Director William Casey, which included supplying the Iraqis with sensitive intelligence data on the activity of the Iranian air force gathered by U.S. AWACS planes based in Saudi Arabia.[5] Other aspects of the effort were more public, such as backing Iraqi appeals at the United Nations to arrange a cease-fire in the war with Iran. The United States also encouraged Iraq's principal Western arms supplier, France, to extend new loans to Baghdad. It gave the green light to Egypt to continue its massive arms shipments to Iraq. But by far the most important part of the plan, as far as Iraq-U.S. relations were concerned, was the CCC credits. Having depleted its $35 billion reserve of foreign currency by mid-1983 and exhausted the patience of Saudi and Kuwaiti lenders, Iraq was desperately in need of cash. And the United States soon became one of its best sources of funds.

As is so often the case, a subtle nod from official Washington was all the professional lobbyists needed to get into the game. The U.S. tilt toward Iraq soon became a race to see who could sell the most and the fastest to America's newest client. Well-paid Washington lawyers and influence peddlers championed causes ranging from farm exports to high technology trade. All kinds of deals were possible now that Iraq was off the terrorism list and national security export controls no longer applied.

Along with Richard Murphy and the State Department Arabists, the Pentagon's Richard Armitage joined those within the Reagan administration who argued convincingly for closer ties with Iraq. The United States should take the initiative in renewing diplomatic relations with Baghdad, they believed, while gradually opening the tap to greater sales of U.S. technology to Saddam Hussein. "Our aim was to improve relations with Iraq," Murphy recalls, "so the old Iraq of the 1970s didn't re-emerge after the war. Beyond that, of course, Iraq was an interesting market for U.S. exporters."

No one understood that by extending credit to Saddam the Reagan administration had legitimized the Baghdad regime and was helping to bankroll Saddam Hussein's death machine. No one saw it coming.

Just as the CCC credits were getting under way in mid-1983, work on the "pesticides" plants at Samarra and Salman Pak was nearing completion, with the help of dozens of German chemicals companies. As the newsweekly *Stern* put it, "If they had special wishes, the Iraqis preferred businessmen who had already been doing business with Iraq for some time, who maintained offices in Iraq, who had good relations with the Iraqi authorities, who had Iraqi partners in their companies, or who were married to Iraqi women. The Iraqi connection comprised three to four dozen companies." None of them once asked their Iraqi partners to explain the real nature of the projects they were helping to build. They just did not want to know.[6]

The equipment going to Samarra and Salman Pak was so specialized and so unusual that the shipments should have sounded alarm bells all through the German government. Indeed, the Federal Economics Agency had a special licensing bureau at Eschborn that was responsible for spotting illicit exports from West Germany, whether they were headed for the Soviet bloc or for Iraq. But the Eschborn inspectors were asleep at the helm. "We have more than one million export movements every month at German ports, airports, and on the ground," complained Hans Schumaker, a spokesman for the German Foreign Ministry. "You can't expect us to open every container leaving the port of Hamburg. Of course some things are going to get through, but our export control laws are just about the toughest in the world."

That was not the experience of Dr. al-Ani or of his colleagues at SEPP, Dr. Ali Nouri and the managing director, Dr. al-Attar. They understood German export controls perfectly. And they understood that German export controls were perfectly meaningless. To receive shipments of sensitive equipment from West Germany, all they had to do was pay off an inspector at Eschborn or falsify documents, since nobody checked what was actually being shipped. In all the years that Karl Kolb and Preussag and Pilot Plant and dozens of other West German companies were shipping containers of death to Iraq, not once did Eschborn send an inspector to their headquarters in Germany or to their manufacturing plants or to their freight forwarders.[7]

By mid-1983, Saddam Hussein was prodding his chemical genies to get to work. He wanted to gas the hordes of Iranian troops massing along Iraq's southern border. He was worried — rightfully, as it turned out — that Iran's new tactic of launching human

wave attacks against Iraqi troops in their foxholes would eventually overwhelm the defenders. He was afraid the Iraqi lines would
break around Basra and in the desert near Al Amarah. If Iranian
troops managed to breach the Shatt-al-Arab waterway or the Tigris, which flowed into it at Al Qurna, just north of Basra, they
could slip a noose around Iraq's second largest city. With Basra cut
off from Baghdad, the country would be split in two. This was
Saddam's nightmare.

Murphy and his assistant, James Placke, were also preoccupied
with this possibility, which may have contributed to a certain
laissez-faire attitude toward Iraqi purchases of poison gas materials
from West Germany, which they learned about from diplomatic
cables and the CIA. Their belief was that as long as Iraq was using
chemical weapons to defend its own territory and on a limited
basis, its actions were "understandable." After all, they argued,
what would the United States do if it was faced with a "human
wave" invasion from Mexico? And this was the Middle East.

In late 1983 Dr. al-Ani turned to an Iraqi-born commodities
broker in Nashville, Tennessee. Saheeb Al Haddad was a pillar of
the local business community. A naturalized American, he was as
patriotic toward his new homeland as any citizen. His Al Haddad
Brothers Trading Company was doing a booming business with
Iraq, primarily supplying grain through the CCC program. Al
Haddad was particularly proud of the motto he had devised for his
company: "Linking the special needs of the East to the awesome
talents of the West."

It is not known whether the Iraqis exerted any particular pressure on Al Haddad through family members still living in Iraq to
meet their "special needs." However, when Dr. al-Ani sent Al
Haddad a telex requesting that he procure certain chemicals, the
Nashville trader processed the deal as he had hundreds of Iraqi
requests for agricultural products. One shipment Haddad arranged
in mid-1983 contained dimethyl methylphosphonate, one of many
chemicals that in combination could be used to manufacture Sarin.
In the United States, its export was subject to certain controls. A
follow-on shipment contained 6.5 tons of potassium fluoride,
another Sarin precursor. That shipment was discovered and blocked by Customs inspectors at New York's Kennedy Airport during a
routine check inside the cargo warehouse of the Dutch airlines

KLM. The seventy-four drums of deadly chemicals were addressed to the State Establishment for Pesticides Production, Baghdad, Iraq.[8]

Dr. al-Ani was hard at work lining up other companies willing to supply the chemical grist for Iraq's poison gas mills. In early 1983, he and a team from SEPP traveled to the seaside industrial town of Terneuzen in the Netherlands, home of a Dutch trading company well known in Iraq, KBS. Al-Ani asked the KBS export manager, M. L. Sakhel, to buy 500 tons of thiodiglycol on behalf of Iraq. Mustard gas is made from thiodiglycol by mixing it with hydrochloric acid. In small quantities, thiodiglycol is also used to make ink for ball point pens. KBS agreed and purchased the chemical from the Belgian subsidiary of Phillips Petroleum for slightly more than $1 million. The first truck left Belgium for Baghdad in July 1983 without a hitch.

In August, Heberger Bau, which owed its good fortune in Iraq to Helmut Maier of Karl Kolb, received a new contract to build a "scrubbing" unit at the Samarra poison gas works. This purification plant eventually included four production buildings, a staff housing complex, streets, and other infrastructure work. Documents submitted to a German court by a chemical weapons specialist show that the plant was an integral part of the Tabun production lines. Heberger Bau jobbed out much of the construction work to Ludwig Hammer GmbH, of Kleinostheim, while Heberger supplied equipment worth DM 2.7 million. According to the 1987 German Customs report, the sales of an air filtration system and four poison gas scrubbers to Iraq were forbidden by export control laws governing highly toxic equipment and materials. But Heberger Bau exported them with no inquiry.

In September 1983 the Samarra poison gas factory went into production, with engineers from Karl Kolb, Preussag, and other German companies on hand to supervise the start-up. Other specialists may have been there as well. Documents obtained in Germany showed that a "French" and a "Soviet" production line were operating at the Samarra gas works. Kurdish opposition sources say that twenty-two Soviet engineers worked at Samarra and may have provided the secrets of Soviet chemical warfare mixes. Several reports suggest that East German chemical warfare specialists built an earlier chemical plant at Samarra and trained Iraqi officers in the battlefield applications of nerve and mustard gases, including methods of dispersing poison gas in public areas such as airports or subway systems as a means of creating widespread panic during terrorist attacks.

The first product off the line was an experimental batch of deadly yperite, or mustard gas, which Iraqi troops began lobbing onto the Iranian human waves in December 1983. "Mustard gas attacks the skin and creates great blisters, or, if you breathe it in, it attacks the respiratory system and then goes on to attack bone marrow," says Dr. Graham Pearson, director of Britain's Chemical Defence Establishment at Porton Down. Once it attacks the bone marrow, mustard gas goes on "to produce anemia and so on to death."[9]

Iraq's poison gas program had not gone entirely unnoticed. In September 1983, according to the BBC, the Reagan administration ordered a multi-agency National Intelligence Estimate on the spread of chemical weapons in the Third World. When it came to Iraq, the report noted with alarm the steady "process of direct purchases of chemical agent precursors, munitions for filling and production facilities from Western Europe and Egypt." The report was particularly critical of the Bonn government, which had failed to restrain the activities of West German companies in Iraq. Some of the details were macabre. "West Germans have provided technical assistance in field trials of nerve agent" — a scarcely veiled euphemism for mass murder.

While one side of the Reagan administration was working to strengthen relations with Iraq, another was discovering with horror the extent of Iraq's chemical weapons program and the aid that West German companies had provided. This side of the administration delivered a series of diplomatic notes to the German Foreign Ministry via the U.S. Embassy in Bonn. The Germans laughingly called the notes "non-papers." When the demarches eventually reached the German export licensing office in Eschborn, they lost even that minimal status. As one licensing officer wrote jokingly in a memo to his bosses back in Bonn, "These anonymous papers have the art of winding up in the wastebasket."[10]

In October 1983, Tarek Aziz went to New York to meet again with George Shultz, this time at the United Nations. Iraq was seeking approval of Security Council Resolution 540, condemning Iran for continuing the war. Shultz, pleased by Iraq's recent expulsion of Abu Nidal, offered U.S. support. Aziz suggested that the secretary of state go to Baghdad for talks with Saddam. There were many issues that the Iraqi president would like to discuss with him, especially the covert aid Iraq believed Washington was offering Iran through Israel. Aziz presented a long list of alleged Israeli arms deliveries to Iran. We cannot believe you do not know what the Israelis are doing, Aziz said sharply, when Shultz pretended ignorance. The Iraqis were convinced that Israel would not lift a finger without asking permission from Washington. And Israel was not the only U.S. ally helping Iran with modern weapons and spare parts, Aziz added. The Western press was full of accounts of arms deliveries to Iran from Italy, Great Britain, and elsewhere. By helping Iran, the West was courting disaster. Did the United States want to see a Khomeini-style regime in Baghdad? Nonplussed, Shultz promised he would look into the matter.

The hard-nosed Iraqi diplomat brought up another issue at this meeting. News had leaked out in the preceding weeks that Iraq was seeking the loan of five Super-Étendard fighter-bombers from France. As the delivery date approached, tensions were mounting around the world because Iran was threatening to blockade the Strait of Hormuz, the chokepoint through which more than half the world's oil flowed. Fearing that the blockade would create a worldwide oil shortage, the British Foreign office put pressure on the French not to deliver the planes, while the United States, in a gesture intended to reassure the world oil markets, made its own contribution to raising the temperature by dispatching the aircraft carrier *Ranger* and an entire battle group from Central America to the Indian Ocean.

Aziz asked why the delivery of five combat aircraft, of a type no longer produced, was so important in a war in which human losses could be counted in the hundreds of thousands. He was convinced that the enemies of Iraq, principal among them Israel, were behind all the fuss; Aziz feared that the French would back off from delivering the aircraft if they felt the United States was truly opposed to the deal. Aziz told Shultz that if he wanted to make a gesture of good faith toward Iraq, he could tell the French that the United States had no objection to the loan.

For the Iraqis, the Super-Étendards would be the first aircraft in their inventory capable of delivering the powerful Exocet antiship missiles, which had proved so deadly during the June 1982 Falkland Islands war. Armed with the Exocet, the Iraqis would be able to strike devastating blows against Iran's economy, since all of Iran's oil was hauled to foreign markets by ship. Instead of extending the war, Aziz argued with Shultz, Iraqi attacks on Iranian shipping could shorten it. Without the money to purchase arms on the black market, Iran would soon be forced to drop out of the fighting. Shultz agreed to make a pitch to the French.

Back in Paris, others were applying pressure on the French government to deliver the promised planes to Iraq. Hugues de l'Estoile, who had left the Defense Ministry to become Dassault's principal arms salesman, had already done a lot of arm twisting to convince the French navy to do without the five planes for a few years. Only eighty-nine Super-Étendards had ever been produced, and all of them belonged to the navy. De l'Estoile had negotiated earlier that year to sell Iraq twenty-nine more Mirage F1 fighter-bombers, a deal worth nearly $2 billion. But the new Mirages, redesigned to carry the Exocet, would not be ready until late 1984. Until then, de l'Estoile argued, Iraq needed the Super-Étendard to keep Iran from winning the war; in fact, their delivery had been a condition of the Mirage sale.

De l'Estoile had even managed to enlist the help of President Mitterrand in agreeing to the loan. After meeting with the new Egyptian president, Hosni Mubarak, in Cairo in November 1982, Mitterrand had made his clearest commitment ever to the Iraqi cause. "We do not want Iraq to lose the war," he declared. "The age-old balance between the Arab and the Persian worlds must absolutely be maintained." The Iraq lobbyists would repeat the Mitterrand statement like a litany for years to come. Iraq had become a national French cause.

On October 13, 1983, Saddam Hussein summoned thirty-two French journalists to Baghdad to hear a remarkable performance. Although the journalists didn't know it, and Saddam certainly didn't let on, the French government had already decided to deliver the Super-Étendards. In fact, subsequent accounts suggest the planes were actually on their way by that time, but Saddam's complaint was planned to suggest just the opposite.

"These are our weapons, and we have paid for them," he told the journalists angrily, chewing on his cigar. If the Super-Étendards did not arrive immediately, Iraq would be forced to take drastic measures to punish the French. "What is this country that doesn't keep its promises? France must not bow to pressure. It's a question of national independence. Otherwise, its friends will be tempted to go elsewhere, such as the United States or the USSR." Besides, Saddam said, he failed to understand all the fuss made over planes "which can't even carry a nuclear weapon." France had better deliver them by the end of the month, or else.[11]

Saddam's strategy succeeded. Iran, thinking that the French were wavering in their support of Iraq, backed off from the threat to block the Strait of Hormuz. And France quietly delivered the planes when no one was looking. For months, French newspapers reported sightings of the planes, one time in Brittany, another time in Bordeaux, when in fact they were flying under Iraqi colors in the Persian Gulf. By the end of 1983, Iraqi pilots had begun picking off tankers at Iran's only oil terminal, at Kharg Island, using Exocet missiles. It was the start of the "tanker war," aimed at crippling Iran's oil exports and boosting Iraqi morale.

The U.S. government export credit guarantees for grain had a major impact on Iraqi morale at a time when food shortages had become a sore point with ordinary Iraqis. One week there would be no butter on the shelves, and the next week, no meat. Items such as cooking oil or even eggs were often hard to find. To meet the escalating costs of the war and to free up dwindling hard currency earnings to purchase arms and weapons-manufacturing technology, Saddam had ordered a drastic cutback in imports of consumer products in late 1982. But the Iraqi leader knew the limits of his own people. His goal throughout the war, as one U.S. diplomat in Baghdad put it, was to provide "guns *and* butter." And the only way he could do that was to buy the butter on credit. This is how the U.S. government came to Saddam's rescue. U.S. food credits and government-backed loans allowed Saddam to devote his remaining cash resources to the war against Iran, and to his long-term strategic goal of becoming the major military power of the Middle East.

As U.S. diplomats stationed in Baghdad explained in interviews at the time: "The Iraqis like us for several reasons: (1) they've had bad harvests for several years because of the war, and need to import ever-increasing amounts of food, (2) we extend credit, which encourages other 'friends' to do the same, (3) having staples available on the home front keeps up morale with the troops on the battlefield, [and] (4) the U.S. has made an effort to discourage its friends from selling weapons or dual use items to Iran."

The Iraqis liked America for another reason as well. The United States was beginning to make discreet overtures about providing the Baathist regime with American weapons. In October 1983 William Eagleton, then the top U.S. diplomat in Baghdad, recommended that the government help Iraq acquire the same kind of U.S. spare parts and equipment it was denying Iran. Eagleton reportedly sent a classified cable to Washington: "We can selectively lift restrictions on third party transfers of U.S. licensed military equipment to Iraq." He suggested that "we go ahead and we do it through Egypt."

The Iraqis also wanted spare parts and ammunition for the U.S.-built tanks, field guns, self-propelled howitzers and TOW missile launchers they had captured from Iran on the battlefield. Similar parts were being shipped to Egypt regularly as part of the $2 billion-a-year Camp David peace package. In return for the proposed arms deliveries, the United States wanted front-line Soviet weaponry from Iraq's arsenal, especially the latest-model T-72 tank (sometimes referred to as the T-72B46 or T-80). "Getting our hands on the latest T-72, with its improved fire control system and layer-on reactive armor, was definitely a top priority," former Pentagon officials said. The CIA, the Defense Intelligence Agency, and other, more covert U.S. operators were attempting to swap American weapons for state-of-the-art Soviet systems with Iran and Syria as well. In one proposed swap, the United States offered the Iraqi defense minister, Adnan Khairallah, thirty American-made 175 mm howitzers for $46 million. The deal apparently fell through when an enterprising Pentagon officer, General Richard Stilwell, started examining the books and realized that the United States was undercharging Iraq by about $8 million. When Stilwell upped the price to $54 million, the Iraqis backed out, insulted by what they considered an unjustified surcharge. In fact, the $8 million difference covered the price of four T-72 tanks. But Stilwell seems to have been unaware that the trade was to be included in the price.[12]

When Donald Rumsfeld, President Reagan's special envoy to the Middle East, arrived in Baghdad in December 1983, he was carrying a hand-written letter for President Saddam Hussein, proposing that the United States and Iraq renew diplomatic relations. Reagan wanted to expand military, technical, and commercial ties between the two countries, and Saddam was receptive to the idea. After three years of war with Iran he had shown that Iraq could weather a Soviet arms embargo and Iranian human wave attacks, without collapsing or calling for help. Iraq could renew relations "from a position of equality" with the United States, with no loss of face; Saddam hated appearing like a beggar. He still remembered his peasant upbringing, his lack of education. Over the years he had refined his childhood resentments into a full-blown inferiority complex, which translated into bluster and pride.

State Department officials who accompanied Rumsfeld to Baghdad said Saddam insisted that the United States make a show of good faith before he would agree to renew diplomatic ties. Almost word for word, he repeated the arguments Tarek Aziz had used with George Shultz in New York two months earlier. It is in the United States' power to cut off arms supplies to Tehran, Saddam said. If the United States really wants to show its "neutrality" in the war and its good will toward Iraq, it should stop supplying weapons to Iran; then everything becomes possible between the two great nations.

It made little difference that the weapons were reaching Iran from Italy, Israel, or Great Britain. In Saddam's mind, they originated in Washington. The American president was so powerful that if he truly wanted the war to end, it *would* end immediately, he told Rumsfeld. Conversely, Saddam reasoned, if the war was still going on, it was because the U.S. wanted it to continue.

Rumsfeld's visit with Saddam Hussein and Tarek Aziz convinced U.S. policy planners that it was necessary to launch a major effort to block arms supplies from reaching Iran. "The idea had been germinating for some time," recalled Tom Miller, a diplomat who accompanied Rumsfeld to Baghdad. "But this is where the idea jelled. It was our attempt to prove to the Iraqis that we were really serious about ending the war."

The arms interdiction effort, known as Operation Staunch, was handed over to one of the State Department's top Arabists, Ambassador Richard Fairbanks. Assisting him were Charles Patriza, a State Department lawyer, and James Placke, the deputy assistant secretary of state for northern Gulf affairs, who had served in Saudi Arabia, Kuwait, and Iraq. It was the final piece of the tilt to Iraq that so impressed the Senate Foreign Relations Committee in their 1984 report on U.S. policy toward the Iran–Iraq war.

The idea was to weaken the Ayatollah by cutting off his weapons supplies. Armed mainly by the United States during the 1960s and 1970s, Iran needed American spare parts and weapons to continue fighting. After the Tehran hostage crisis, Iran had turned to the black market, where U.S. weapons and spares were available illegally from foreign defense contractors making them under license. The Iranians also turned to Israel, Turkey, and NATO countries to purchase "surplus" U.S. weaponry from national stockpiles through various intermediaries. Saddam and his advisors assumed that the United States was secretly encouraging its allies to sell weapons and spares to Iran. Operation Staunch set out to convince those allies (or, if necessary, to pressure them) to stop the sales. The plan was a double victory for the Arabists, for it meant that the United States was effectively siding with Iraq, all the while putting pressure on Israel as well. For Israel had been doing a booming business selling arms to Iran. In 1980, the sales had received tacit approval from Washington anxious to keep some channel of communication open to Tehran. Now the Israeli sales were stigmatized as "counterproductive."

In separate interviews, Fairbanks, Placke, and Patriza agreed that they "leaned pretty heavily on Israel. . . . We told them they just didn't want to be selling arms to Iran." As Fairbanks put it, "We shared with them our geopolitical stand, that it makes sense to us to get this war ended, because it's a dangerous one to continue. . . . The only winner possible at this stage is Iran."[13]

For Saddam, the news of Operation Staunch was too good to be true, so good that at first he didn't believe it.

NINE

The Condor Takes Off

To tighten the economic noose around Khomeini's neck, in January 1984 the Reagan administration added Iran to the list of countries that "provide support for acts of international terrorism," an action that had far-reaching consequences for U.S. trade with that country. A wide range of products and spare parts that had been available to Iran despite the 1979–81 hostage crisis was now forbidden. Iran could no longer turn to U.S. manufacturers for communications equipment, inflatable boats, off-road vehicles, diesel engines, electric generators, and other "dual-use" equipment.

The ban, which dramatically reinforced the arms embargo in force since 1980, was meant to show Iraq that the United States would carry out its pledge to bring the Ayatollah to his knees. Iran now had to turn to black marketeers even to keep its civilian airplanes functioning. Not only did these dubious traders charge exorbitant prices, but they were frequently caught in sting operations mounted by the U.S. Customs Service. Following the trade ban, "the Iranians sent out all their smurfs" in search of American technology, said the head of Customs' Strategic Investigation Bureau, Jack Kelly. More often than not, they got caught.

The trade ban provided one more clue to the diplomatic enigma that became a virtual American alliance with Saddam Hussein. The United States, counting on Saddam Hussein to get rid of Ayatollah Khomeini in Iran, was willing to help his cause in a variety of discreet ways.

* * *

Richard Murphy made his first official trip to Baghdad as assistant secretary of state in February 1984, just as Iran was launching a surprise attack against the Majnoon Islands. These two thin strips of strategic territory, loaded with oil, commanded the northern approach to Basra.

The Iranians attacked at night. Commandos in small fiberglass boats slid silently through the Howeiza marshes, taking the few Iraqis guarding the levees by surprise. By dawn the Iranians were fully in control of both islands, the north and the south, and dug in. They erected a pontoon bridge to bring up supplies and fresh troops. Within days, they had increased the bridgehead to some 30,000 troops and had built a dirt causeway linking the Majnoon Islands to the mainland in Iran. The Iraqis counterattacked time after time, trying to drive the Iranians into the swamps and back over the border. But the reed-choked marshes got the better of them. The heavy undergrowth fouled the propellers of Iraq's amphibious tanks, making them easy targets for Iranian gunners. To the Iraq military planners only one solution remained: gas.

From Soviet, French, and German-built helicopters, Iraqi pilots dumped canisters of poison gas fresh off the production lines at Samarra and Salman Pak. A small electric pump inside the drums triggered on impact, dispersing the mixture into a deadly cloud. In other attacks, helicopters sprayed the Iranians with a greasy yellow liquid that filled the area with the odor of garlic. Later the Iraqis would drop crude chemical bombs from Sukhoi-7 and Sukhoi-20 attack aircraft. The Iranians, who wore no protective clothing, felt ill almost immediately. Within minutes they began vomiting a yellowish liquid, and their skin turned red. By the time medics reached the battlefield, some of the troops were already dead, their faces horribly blackened by the gas. Others had amber-colored blisters all over their bodies and were having trouble breathing.

It was the first time Iraq had used poison gas against Iranian troops on a large scale. And it was not limited to the Majnoon. In other parts of the front, where Iran was coordinating human wave attacks to close the noose on Basra, the Iraqis attempted to break the advance by using gas as well. Militarily, the results were not conclusive, and the Iranians held onto the Majnoon Islands. But according to foreign military attachés in Baghdad, the poison gas attacks were frequent, large-scale, and "flagrant."[1]

The timing could not have been worse for Murphy, who had gone to Baghdad to negotiate an official date for the renewal of diplomatic relations between Iraq and the United States. The poison gas was an embarrassment and put a temporary kink in the diplomatic schedule. It may also have been why Murphy was not taken to see Saddam Hussein. Instead he met with Tarek Aziz and the first deputy premier, Taha Yassin Ramadan.

"My personal reaction to the use of chemical weapons was one of horror," Murphy recalls. "This is something I am particularly sensitive to. I had a family member who was gassed during World War I." Murphy says that he never brought up the issue of chemical weapons in subsequent meetings with Saddam, but he did raise it with Aziz that February. "I told him that there are many ways to kill a man, but this is the one that is totally unacceptable to a Westerner. We've been accused of rolling over and ignoring Iraq's use of chemical weapons. This is simply not true."

American diplomats in Baghdad agreed with Murphy's recollection. "Iraq's use of CW is the one serious hitch in our relations," embassy staff members said in 1984. "The Iraqis feel we have gone too far out in front on this issue. They suspect we have some hidden agenda, some second thoughts about U.S.-Iraqi trade and cooperation. Because of our protests, the Iraqis stepped up their cooperation with the USSR, just as we were finally achieving really warm relations for the first time in seventeen years."

Despite the apparent firmness of the protests delivered by Rumsfeld and Murphy, the Iraqis continued to use chemical weapons on the battlefield. "We simply did not have the leverage to force them to do anything," a former diplomat complained, somewhat defensively. "The first item on our agenda had to be the restoration of diplomatic ties." The United States was so intent on reopening a full-fledged embassy in Baghdad, diplomats said, that it was willing to overlook Saddam Hussein's flagrant violation of international law, which the State Department called a "predictable sin."

Iran protested Iraq's use of chemical weapons to the United Nations, citing the 1925 Geneva Convention, which both Iran and Iraq had signed, forbidding the use of chemical and bacteriological agents on the battlefield. In early March the UN secretary general dispatched a team of four observers to the area. They examined surviving gas victims, collected soil samples, and ran tests on unexploded chemical bombs. In one famous wire-service photo published at the time, the UN team and Western journalists wearing gas masks snapped photographs of an unexploded Iraqi chemical bomb. If it hadn't been for a defective fuse, the bomb would have exploded like many others. The UN investigators discovered markings on the bomb casing showing that it had been made in Spain.

The bomb casings had been flown into Baghdad a few weeks earlier on an Iraqi Airways cargo jet. On January 21 the Iraqi plane had left the Torrejon base in Spain, home of the 401st Tactical Fighter Wing of the U.S. Air Force. The plane was so heavily loaded it needed the full length of the jetway to take off. On board were Spanish munitions ready to be filled with deadly chemical agents in Iraq. The shipment included several pallets of fuses — small electronic "triggers" to make the bombs explode — manufactured by the Spanish company Explosivos Alavesas, or EXPAL. It was a defective EXPAL fuse that led to the discovery of Spain's involvement in Iraq's chemical weapons program.[2]

For researcher Julian Perry-Robinson of the University of Sussex, chemical weapons such as those used by Iraq in early 1984 were "a morale weapon, not a firepower weapon. They serve a propaganda purpose more than a military one." The idea was to break Iranian morale through the sheer horror of a chemical attack. In the early stages of Iraq's use of gas, this did not work.

Professor Aubin Heyndrickx, of the Toxicology Laboratory of the State University of Gent, Belgium, was one of the specialists chosen by the UN secretary general to examine Iranian victims of poison gas attacks. He believes the proliferation of chemical weapons is a bigger problem than nuclear proliferation, "because chemical weapons are cheap, easy to obtain, and viciously effective. And they don't generate the same awesome fear that prohibits nuclear weapons use." Heyndrickx, who soon became an unwitting accountant of death, noted that these early Iraqi attacks with chemical weapons were only partially effective. "Fatalities barely reached 20 percent," he said. "The Iraqis were experimenting with various mixes of chemical agents to find the most lethal compound. During these first attacks they used a mix of yellow rain, yperite, and Tabun, which were packed separately into munitions and mixed by the force of the explosion. They found that by mixing different poisons during the same attack, it made treatment more difficult.

Later on, they found a more effective mixture. By 1985 they were using a mix of hydrogen cyanide, mustard gas, Sarin, and Tabun in their attacks. This brought fatalities up to the 60 percent level. Over the years, they bombarded some 2,000 villages in Iran with this deadly mixture."[3]

Heyndrickx pointed out that the hydrogen cyanide compound the Iraqis were using bore a close resemblance to Zyklon B, the dreaded compound used by the Nazis to exterminate millions of Jews in gas chambers. Then as now, Zyklon B was made by the German firm Degussa, which along with its nuclear subsidiary, NUKEM, was heavily involved in trade with Iraq.

Iran, hoping to capitalize in the court of world public opinion on the horror generated by Iraq's chemical attacks, began sending gas victims to hospitals in Paris, London, Lausanne, Vienna, Stockholm, and Tokyo in early March. They even sent one group of gassed soldiers to Germany, despite mounting evidence that German firms had helped Iraq build its poison gas works. Television showed victims with horrible blisters on their faces, arms, backs, and legs. Some had little left of their faces because of the gas attacks. It was a sobering spectacle, but it had little effect on public opinion. Perhaps because Europeans harbored few illusions about Iraq's respect for human rights, the gas attacks did not come as a shock. Like the State Department Arabists, they considered the Iraqis' behavior predictable. And there was little public sympathy for Iran, which was being linked almost daily to murderous terrorist attacks, hijackings, and car bombings in Lebanon and, increasingly, in Europe. Iran's decision to use terrorism to wrest diplomatic and financial concessions from the European nations may have cost it thousands of lives on the battlefield with Iraq.

Iraq even managed to put its own spin on the tales of poison gas. Certain newspapers close to the arms-exporting lobby said that the victims had not been gassed by Iraqi bombs; they were victims of an explosion in an Iranian chemical plant. It was all a publicity stunt by Iran to win public support for its war against Iraq, which was protecting the "Eastern flank of the Arab world" from an invasion by the Iranian terrorist horde.[4]

On March 30, 1984, the *New York Times* cited "U.S. intelligence sources" in a report alleging that a German company had built a chemical weapons plant in Iraq. The company, identified for the first time as Karl Kolb GmbH, was leading a consortium of German firms that had contracted with an Iraqi state entity to build a "pesticides" plant, the *Times* wrote. Intelligence sources said that the facility had been converted to production of poison gas and that Karl Kolb had been working in Iraq since 1977. Iraq was believed to have five poison gas plants operating or close to completion at that point.

In a blustering statement that barely concealed his anger, Chancellor Helmut Kohl of Germany promised to look into the matter. He was not angered by the activities of Karl Kolb — after all, the company had merely done what German businesses did best in cornering a lucrative export market. Kohl was furious with the effrontery of the *New York Times* and with the CIA for having leaked "sensitive intelligence information" — sensitive because it involved the double dealings of the West German state. In private, Kohl complained vigorously to U.S. officials. His economics minister, Martin Bangemann of the Free Democratic Party, was more outspoken. He declared it a clear case of "professional jealousy" on the part of the Americans, who would have preferred to get the Samarra contract themselves.[5] (Like the U.S. Department of Commerce, the German Economics Ministry performed the double function of promoting exports and controlling them.)

Meanwhile, Iraq, heartened by what it considered success on the battlefield with Iran and on the battlefield of world public opinion, began scouring the European market for precursor chemicals to make more poison gas.

In March, KBS of Holland received an order so big that the company's president, J. A. Bravenboer, a former army officer, went to the Foreign Ministry in the Hague to make sure it was all right to ship the chemicals to Iraq. Bravenboer showed the Iraqi shopping list to a friend in a laboratory in Delft, who told him there were enough raw materials in the order to spray every tree and shrub in the Middle East with pesticide for the next five years. The list included hundreds of tons of thiodiglycol to make mustard gas, 250 tons of phosphorus oxychloride ($POCL_3$), an important ingredient of Tabun, and large quantities of two Sarin precursors, trimethyl phosphite and potassium fluoride. Except for the $POCL_3$, export of these chemicals was legal in Europe at the time. Some were controlled in the United States (as the Iraqis found out when the shipment from Al Haddad Trading was blocked at Kennedy Airport in February 1984).

But fearing that the Iraqi shopping list was for poison gas, Bravenboer turned down the lucrative order. According to BBC researcher Herbert Krosney, the Iraqis tried in vain to convince Bravenboer that the chemicals were intended for civilian use. In one telex from SEPP to KBS dated March 20, 1984, Dr. al-Ani states that the chemicals were to be used for making "rubber, drugs, pesticides, fertilizers, paper, sugar, vegetable oil, batteries, dry cells and petrochemicals." To clarify the situation, KBS export manager M. L. Sakhel traveled to Iraq not long afterward and was apparently satisfied by what he saw. The company continued to ship to Iraq smaller quantities of chemicals that were not subject to government controls, including dimethylamine, a Tabun precursor, and isopropanol, which was needed for making Sarin.[6]

Sensing the reticence of KBS to fill large orders, al-Ani turned to another Dutch chemicals trader, Melchemie, which had been doing business with Iraq since 1969. Located in Arnhem, Melchemie had some 250 employees and a full-time branch office in Baghdad. Melchemie sold only civilian chemicals according to its director, I. O. Zandkamp, who openly acknowledged filling a $10 million Iraqi order in 1984.

Of the eight items on the list telexed to Melchemie's Arnhem office on March 9 from SEPP, six were probably intended for Iraq's poison gas plants, although the Iraqis were careful to give each a civilian designation. One precursor on the list was intended for "etching glass and petrochemicals," the Iraqis claimed. Company records show that the list included 1,000 tons of thionyl chloride, 20 tons of potassium hydrogen fluoride, 60 tons of phosphorus oxychloride, 5 tons of hydrogen fluoride, and 150 tons of isopropyl alcohol. German court records show that these chemicals were sent to Samarra, where in all likelihood they were used to manufacture poison gas.

On April 19, SEPP reconfirmed with Melchemie its order of phosphorus oxychloride, the only chemical on the list that the Dutch government banned from export because of its use in manufacturing Tabun. Melchemie contacted chemical supply houses all over Europe in search of the banned substance, unsuccessfully. On July 2 the Dutch trader telexed SEPP to apologize for the delay.

"You certainly know that the products in question are subject to obtain export licence from the government in the exporting country. This explains the unusual delay in answering to your enquiries and to request you to understand." The telex was signed by Mel-chemie export manager Bas Weijman.

The Iraqis were undeterred. If a source dried up, or a shipment was delayed, they knew where they could turn for deadly chemicals to exterminate "Persians, Jews, and Flies." The Karl Kolb company signed yet another sizable contract with SEPP on April 4, 1984, just as Chancellor Kohl was protesting that such a sale was impossible. (After all, he and other West German officials told American leaders in private, Germans have a sense of history.) Contract documents seized later by German Customs show that the new contract covered an expansion of the production lines at the Samarra poison gas works. The documents detail how Kolb, Preussag, and other companies continued to deliver manufacturing equipment to Samarra for several years, even though the Western German export control bureau rejected many license requests. During a court case against the company in 1990, a Swiss chemical engineer, Dr. Werner Richarz, hired by German Customs to analyze blueprints and other documents concerning the production plants at Samarra, concluded, "There was not a single plant set up in the entire Samarra complex that was designed for the production of modern pesticides." That was only a convenient fiction to disguise sophisticated facilities whose sole purpose was to manufacture mustard gas, Tabun, and prussic acid.

Chemical bombs were not the only weapons the Iraqis experimented with in 1984. The Iraqi High Command also began using its Soviet-supplied SCUD-B ballistic missiles to attack Iranian cities close to the border. But because Iran had almost completely evacuated these border cities, the missile attacks had little effect on Iranian morale. The Soviet SCUD-B could hit targets up to 180 miles away with its one-ton warhead, but Iran's largest cities, including Tehran, were out of range.

In 1983 Lieutenant General Amer Rashid al-Ubeidi had reopened discussions with British Aerospace and Dassault to build an aircraft factory in Iraq despite Iraq's precarious financial condition. "It was all a question of time," he said in retrospect, explaining the decision to devote scarce resources to the program. "The longer we waited to build our military factories, the more expense we incurred in buying weapons." In 1984 Amer Rashid was pushing hard for Iraq to develop its own ballistic missiles as well. As he explained in an interview a few years later: "The Persian people had been deluded by their leaders, who told them the war would never affect them. The blows we inflicted at the borders were absorbed and never reached the interior. We wanted to bring the war to the people in Persia, to make them realize the folly of their leaders. And only ballistic missiles offered us this opportunity."[7]

To build a missile with a long enough range to reach Tehran (360 miles beyond the border), Iraq needed outside help. Through German engineers working in Baghdad, the Iraqis learned of a project then under way in Argentina. In early 1984 they asked to join.

Not far from the city of Córdoba, in the Sierra Chica mountains, the Argentine air force had built a top-secret industrial site. From the valley, through which a flat road led to the village of Falda del Carmen, the area appeared ordinary enough except for a high wire fence that completely closed off the site. To gain access to the two-lane road leading up to the watchtower and the secret hillside fortress, cars had to pass through an air force checkpoint a few kilometers away. Even from the air, little more was visible than a few low-lying hangars built into the slope. But deep inside the mountain, protected by reinforced concrete doors, the air force had buried a complete plant for designing and manufacturing ballistic missiles.

In the early months of 1984, say Argentinean construction workers who helped build the plant, trucks loaded with sealed containers came frequently from the direction of the capital, Buenos Aires. Under cover of darkness, they unloaded their precious cargo of computers and test equipment according to an NBC News report. Inside the mountain, teams of engineers were hard at work designing a new ballistic missile. But the engineers were not Argentineans; they were German.[8]

The project requiring so much secrecy, and so much expense, was called Condor. And it was of vital importance to Iraq.

Argentina's military dictatorship launched the Condor program in the late 1970s at the same time it intensified research into nuclear weapons. The intent was to build a missile capable of carrying a nuclear warhead. In 1979 the air force signed a sweeping research and development agreement with a little-known engineering firm based in Zug, Switzerland, which soon became known as the Consen group, and work on the top-secret Falda del Carmen manufacturing plant began the next year. Consen had been launched by former employees of Bohlen Industrie — the heirs to Germany's arms-making Krupp family — and of the West German missile and weapons manufacturer MBB.

Consen was drawn into the missile program thanks to a handful of German engineers, former Nazis, who had taken refuge in Argentina years before. Some had gone to work for the Instituto de Investigaciónes Aeronáuticas y Espaciales (IIAE), the air force agency in charge of the ballistic missile project. These engineers understood the complex nature of manufacturing a ballistic missile very well, and they argued that the Argentineans would be deluding themselves to think they could go it alone. The best bet was to seek West German help, since pioneering German research during the Third Reich still formed the basis for every ballistic missile in the world.

Seeking that help openly, however, was out of the question. The West German government was not eager to stir up reminders of its Nazi heritage, which a cooperative program to build a ballistic missile in the Third World would have done. So Consen was set up as a front, to channel West German technology to the missile project. The company, which has shifted its base of operations on several occasions in an effort to escape scrutiny by journalists and law enforcement officials, filed for bankruptcy in Switzerland on June 30, 1989. The secret of who really owned and controlled Consen and its sixteen or more affiliates was so thick that even Dunn & Bradstreet investigators had an empty file on the group. The German daily *Die Welt* revealed in February 1991 that the public prosecutor in Munich was investigating PBG Project Betruungs GmbH–Bohlen Industrie GmbH of Essen for its ownership of the Consen group, but company officer Eckbert von Bohlen und Halbach denied the affiliation. "Consen was set up by a man named Reiser who worked for our companies some ten or twelve years ago," von Bohlen insisted in an interview. "That is the only connection Consen has ever had with us."

Consen design engineers, recruited from MBB and other top

German firms, moved to Córdoba in 1981, to begin work on the Condor program. The first missile they built, called Condor I, was modest by most standards. It could deliver a relatively small warhead (400 kilograms) to a distance of about 100 miles. But even so it required sophisticated technologies far beyond the reach of the fledgling Argentine defense industry. To get the missile into the air required solid-fuel propellants of the type found only in intercontinental ballistic missiles (ICBMs). To steer it accurately to its target, they needed inertial guidance equipment of military specifications, which the handful of manufacturers in the West were not allowed to export freely. They also needed precision vanes and nozzles to direct the rocket exhaust and carbon-carbon composite materials to coat the missile nose cone, to keep it from swaying off course as it reentered the earth's atmosphere.

By 1983 Consen had completed the design and ordered procurement officers in Switzerland and Germany to start lining up suppliers of the high-tech items needed to begin building the first missiles. Many European companies jumped at the chance to work on the Condor program, despite the 1982 war between Argentina and Britain over the Falkland Islands. MBB detailed the head of its armament programs, Karl-Adolf Hammer — a specialist in rocket design — to the Consen group. At the same time it was helping to piece together the first Third World missile capable of carrying a nuclear warhead, MBB was working for the Pentagon on highly classified military projects.

As time went on, Consen became little more than a stand-in for MBB, which was providing the bulk of the Condor technology. By channeling its sales and cooperation through Consen, MBB could claim ignorance of the real nature of the project, which it would later describe as a "meteorological rocket." It could also claim, as a review of MBB promotional literature shows, that its principal export markets were in the industrialized West (Consen companies were registered in Switzerland, Austria, and Monaco), when in fact MBB was fueling an indigenous Third World armament program.

This multibillion-dollar company, employing 37,000 highly skilled workers, was the German defense industry's most influential lobbyist in Bonn. It was also a prime cooperation partner for the Pentagon and other defense ministries around the world, and it knew how to lobby on Capitol Hill. When the going got tough,

MBB hired the former economics counselor at the U.S. Embassy in Bonn as its principal lobbyist in Washington. This former American diplomat, well versed in the export licensing business, made the rounds of congressional staffers, quietly pushing the cause of MBB and its parent company, Daimler-Benz.[9]

MBB was embarrassed when its deep involvement in the Condor program was exposed, starting in 1989, for the company had a significant share in some of the Pentagon's most advanced weapons projects and was loath to lose the good business. MBB's aircraft division, for instance, knew all the secrets of U.S. military jets flying in Germany. It had been selected in 1983 to upgrade the Phantom F-4F with the latest avionics and armaments, including sensitive electronic countermeasures. Other MBB divisions were working with Raytheon to build the Patriot and Hawk missiles, with Texas Instruments to build the HARM antiradiation missile (used to knock out enemy antiaircraft batteries before they could shoot at U.S. planes), and with General Dynamics to develop a combat reconnaissance drone called LOCUST. MBB was bidding to manufacture the Maverick antitank missile and the U.S. Army's new Multiple Rocket Launch System (MLRS), the most potent long-range artillery system in the world. It was also a major subcontractor for the U.S. Army's latest intermediate-range ballistic missile, the Pershing II.

While MBB was participating in these highly classified weapons projects, it was transferring advanced ballistic missile technology, design, manufacturing, and test equipment to Argentina, Egypt, and Iraq through Consen and the Condor project. The record now suggests that much of the expertise MBB gleaned from its Pentagon contracts ended up in the hands of Saddam Hussein. Design work for Condor was performed by MBB in a feasibility study signed with the Argentine air force.[10] MBB claims that when it found out that Condor II — the longer-range successor to Condor I — was intended to carry weapons of mass destruction, it turned down a subsequent contract to build the missile. But the company continued to sell sophisticated technology to the Condor team, including special computers needed to enhance the missile guidance systems.[11]

Italian companies also contributed to the Condor program, starting with Italy's largest defense contractor, Snia BpD, another large Pentagon supplier. Snia developed a special solid-fuel propellant for Condor I in a contract dated 1981. When queried about the sale, a Snia spokesman acknowledged the contribution to Condor. "But this was not our own rocket fuel. We bought this propellant from the Baker-Perkins Company in Saginaw, Michigan."[12]

The French defense electronics firm Sagem, already heavily involved in direct military sales to Iraq, supplied inertial guidance systems for the Condor. In West Germany, MAN and Wegmann sold tractor-erector vehicles for use as mobile launchers. In Sweden, the automotive and aerospace conglomerate Saab-Scania contributed the cabs.

By the time the Iraqis joined the program in 1984, the MBB design team, working through Consen and directly for the Argentine air force, was ironing out the final details on the one-stage solid-fuel missile, Condor I. Now they were getting ready to hit the export market.[13]

Amer al-Saadi and Amer Rashid maintained a close working relationship for nearly a decade. Although al-Saadi was in charge of the missile programs, his background as a chemist was of no use in ballistics, guidance, or systems engineering. This is where Amer Rashid made his contribution; he could take one glance at a gyroscope and figure out how to make it guide a ballistic missile. Together, the two Amers scrutinized the performance of the Argentine-German project.

Condor I was a good beginning, they told the Argentineans. But for Iraq to be interested, the missile would have to have a much longer range, say, five times the 150-kilometer reach of Condor I. Long enough to hit Tehran, Amer Rashid said pointedly. Or Tel Aviv, al-Saadi added.

That will take money, said Colonel Luis Guerrero, who had been head of the Condor project since the end of the Falklands war. After some quick calculations, he said Condor I could be transformed into the second stage of a larger rocket if they developed a first-stage booster to extend the range. They could probably use a liquid-fuel booster, something like the Soviet SCUD-B. But there was a problem, Guerrero added. Large purchases of missile technology by Argentina and Iraq would attract attention from the

United States and, especially, Great Britain, since the extended-range Condor would be capable of reaching the Falkland Islands.

Fine, the two Amers responded. Iraq would participate in the Condor project through an Egyptian friend, Field Marshal Abu Ghazaleh, who was then serving as Egypt's minister of defense. The new missile, Condor II, would be developed as a joint Argentine-Egyptian project. This would calm British fears, since the missile was designed for export only, and would reassure the Americans because the Egyptians were their ally. Iraq would stay on the sidelines and provide the necessary funds — and, Amer Rashid added to himself, siphon off every bit of technology it could. And so, on February 15, 1984, the Egyptian Ministry of Defense signed a contract with one of the Consen group companies, IFAT, company documents show, for a turnkey production plant to manufacture the rocket engines and for design and development of a 1,000-kilometer-range ballistic missile. Condor II was about to take off.

Kicking the Condor project into high gear required some creative management. The Consen group was reorganized, and a host of front companies in different countries set up to hide the trail of missile technologies headed for Egypt, and to disguise the Iraqi funding that was behind the project.

Documents prepared by the Consen group, explaining its "global reach" to potential clients, give an unusual insight into the shadowy world of the missile business. The lead company, Consen SA, received direct design and technical support from MBB. In addition, it had cooperation agreements with Wegmann and MAN in West Germany, Snia BpD in Italy, Bofors in Sweden, and Sagem in France, the documents show.[14] No fewer than ten wholly owned subsidiaries were listed as members of Consen's international purchasing network, whose principal goal was to funnel sophisticated missile technology to the Condor design and production teams now in Egypt and Iraq. In Monaco there was Consen S.A.M. and Consen Investment, which helped with the money flow. In Zug (home of many mailbox companies), Consen operated with three affiliates, Condor Projekt AG, IFAT Corporation (Institute for Advanced Technology), and Desintec AG. Desintec was put out of commission almost immediately, when it was caught trying to buy rocket nozzles for the Condor from a California company in 1984. IFAT, which provided the conduit to the Egyptian Ministry of

Defense, owned other companies and served as a procurement office in the United States.

In Salzburg, Austria, Consen owned Delta System and Delta Consult GmbH. Delta hired many of the engineers who would later travel to Iraq. (At one point, Delta Consult was reported to have 150 electronics and computer specialists in Iraq.) These engineers, former employees of MBB and other defense contractors in Germany, Austria, and Italy, were paid salaries of up to $19,000 per month, to work in Iraq on the missile projects.[15] In the Channel Island of Jersey, Consen owned Transtechno Ltd., which gave it an opening into Great Britain. In Munich it ran yet another procurement front called GPA. Finally, in Córdoba, Argentina, Consen had bought out an engineering firm called Intesa SA, which was restructured as a joint venture with IIAE, the technical agency of the Argentine air force. In Buenos Aires, Consen owned a second engineering firm called Consultech SA, run by an enterprising young engineer, Dario Humberto Oddera and a thirty-four-year-old businessman, Roberto Antonio Colla. Consultech helped to import high-tech from Europe by organizing the needed End-Use Certificates and other paperwork from the Argentine government. From there equipment could be reexported to Egypt or to Iraq without a care, where the missile assembly plants were to be built.

It was an extraordinary example of international cooperation. Its aim was to provide Iraq — the only participant determined enough to actually build the missile — with a weapon capable of wreaking mass destruction upon its neighbors, its enemies.

The Egyptians called their version of the project Badr 2000, suggesting that the new missile's range was 2,000 kilometers (in fact, Condor II is believed to have been designed to fly 1,000 kilometers, or around 600 miles). But the Iraqis were not content to let their Egyptian friends pursue such a strategic project alone; Amer Rashid had no intention of relying on promises, even contractual ones, that were outside his direct control. So at the same time he and Amer al-Saadi joined the Condor II project as silent partners providing development funds, they launched a far-ranging, international effort to bring the same technology home to Iraq. They called it Project 395. The plan was to lay the foundations for an entire ballistic missile manufacturing industry in Iraq. Long range was absolutely crucial. For the missiles to win Saddam's approval, they had to be capable of reaching Israel.

Saddam's doomsday project was complex and expensive. But with credit from the United States to put food on the table of ordinary Iraqis, Saddam felt confident that he could free up the necessary funds. Without that billion-dollar-per-year aid, the Iraqi leader would have been less likely to go ahead. For by 1984 he was spending some $14 billion on new weapons each year, fully one-half of his gross domestic product.[16]

The Saad General Establishment belonged to the State Organization for Technical Industries (SOTI), which supervised Iraq's growing defense industry.

At SOTI, Amer Rashid and Amer al-Saadi were assisted in the procurement of unconventional technologies by the foreign branches of the Iraqi secret service, the Mukhabarat, which until December 1983 was run with an iron fist by Barzan Ibrahim al-Tikriti. His successor, Dr. Fadil Barrak, was a professional intelligence officer "in the business of naming people and making lists."[17] He also knew a few things about corporate law and appears to have assisted the two Amers in their effort to purchase strategic companies in Europe to get access to restricted military technology and hardware.

In early 1984, the Saad General Establishment signed contract number 16/1/84 with Gildemeister Projecta of Bielefeld, West Germany, a wholly owned subsidiary of the German machine-tool manufacturer Gildemeister AG, or GIPRO. The contract called for the design, construction, and fitting out of an entire missile research, development, and testing center just outside the northern Iraqi city of Mosul. The project was called Saad 16. The Saad General Establishment was building other military factories, such as Saad 13, the French-built electronics plant. Each factory was given a number; the prefix "Saad" denoted a military facility. Saad 16 set the Iraqis back some $253 million, and some accounts allege that the total cost of the missile program reached $950 million.[18]

To disguise the military nature of the project, Gildemeister dressed it up as a "university research" complex. In documents submitted to export licensing authorities, Gildemeister insisted that Saad 16 comprised "laboratories and workshops comparable to facilities at universities, technical education establishments, and testing institutes — that is to say, facilities which are not specifically built for military purposes."[19] But had any official in the West German government wanted to know what it was all about, they had only to ask Gildemeister for a more complete identification of the Iraqi purchaser.

But of course, the West German government asked no questions. The deal was worth too much in hard currency to German manufacturers, who in 1984 sold some $860 million worth of German technology to Saddam Hussein. MBB, through its subsidiary MBB-Transtechnica, won one contract worth $48.7 million, to supply "laboratory equipment." And much more was to come. The German and Austrian press identified thirty-eight West Germany companies working on Saad 16, including many of West Germany's largest industrial concerns, such as MBB, Siemens, Thyssen, and Rheinmetall. These firms formed a powerful lobby in favor of industrial sales to the Baghdad regime. Back in Germany, they organized "a comprehensive training program for Iraqi experts" in some of the most advanced manufacturing plants in the West. Like France, Germany was embarking on a strategic alliance with Iraq, but unlike the French, the Germans were doing it all through the back door. One reason for the subterfuge was not to anger Iran, where German companies (often, the same ones who were selling to Iraq) were doing a booming business. Fueling military industrial projects on both sides of a war required a delicate diplomatic balancing act.[20]

Work on Saad 16 began before the ink was dry on the Gildemeister contract. An isolated site was found in a valley some 15 kilometers north of Mosul, in Iraqi Kurdistan, far from the border with Iran and out of reach, Baghdad hoped, of Israeli warplanes. A Vienna-based engineering group called Consultco, in which Iraq had recently bought a stake, was hired by GIPRO to provide the blueprints. Consultco's major shareholder was Austria's largest state-run bank, Girocentrale — another powerful lobbyist in Iraq's favor. With Girocentrale's help, most of the construction work for the complex, estimated at $144 million, was done by Austrian firms.

Construction workers and engineers who worked at the site say it was heavily guarded at all times. In addition to numerous antiaircraft batteries and troops posted in watchtowers, the Iraqis used video cameras and electronic sensors to detect intruders all along the 3.3-kilometer perimeter fence. The main entrance was equipped with quick-rising metal barriers, to prevent a suicide attack such as the one that destroyed the U.S. Embassy in Beirut. Inside the complex, Iraqi intelligence teams patrolled constantly in Mercedes Unimog armored cars equipped with ground-surveillance radar. A complete hospital unit and a fire brigade were set up on the site, so no outside help would have to be brought in during an emergency.

The centerpiece of the project was a 100-meter-long hall for the assembly of missile prototypes. To the north of that an even larger gallery, 120 meters long, tunneled directly into the mountainside. Its inside walls, protected by honeycomb soundproofing, looked as if they were papered with concrete egg cartons. This was the test-firing range for rocket motors. In an adjacent valley to the west of the main hall, twenty-eight buildings were constructed in huge pits, then covered over with cement and dirt to protect them from air attack. (In 1990 the German and Austrian press published photographs of these bunkers taken as they were being built, clearly showing how they were carved out of the ground.) These "university laboratories" were all designed with steeply sloping cement roofs to deflect a direct bomb attack, and thick concrete walls on three sides. The fourth wall, made of aluminum, was designed to "blow out" in the event of an explosion, venting the blast in a harmless direction. The blow-out walls were supplied by the Austrian firm Ilbau. The buried bunkers, linked by a network of underground tunnels, concealed a missile-fuel test plant.

Everywhere they went on the Saad 16 grounds, the German and Austrian engineers were followed by Iraqi security guards. More than once the foreigners had to look down the barrel of a gun just to get onto the construction site. One building close to the electronics labs housed a soundproof room supplied by West Germany's largest electronics firm, Siemens. "Only if one is inside this room," a project engineer said, "can one overlook that this is a military project."[21]

Siemens acknowledged that it supplied specially designed power switch gear to provide an independent energy source for a "large industrial facility." In fact, the "facility" was a fuel-mixing plant, where Iraqi and German scientists would later experiment with potent new blends of rocket fuel. "Siemens didn't know what was in that facility before all the articles in the press and publication of the German intelligence report," said an official spokesman, Enzio Kuehlmann-Stumm. Siemens engineers, among the first to serve at Saad 16, were apparently among the last to know what they were really doing.

MBB lobbied hard to get its fair share of the Saad 16 cake. Yet it later claimed that it was merely a "legitimate subcontractor" to Gildemeister. MBB officials said that "one shouldn't make links between the company and people who have worked in our company and are now delivering to Iraq. Those people are simply buying on the open market." A smart shopper could stock up on the latest in advanced weapons technology without raising an eyebrow in Bonn.

Incredibly, Gildemeister applied for, and received, a blanket permit to export whatever it desired to Saad 16, with no further licensing requirements. Building a ballistic missile design and testing center was ruled to be a legitimate business project for German companies, according to the Federal Economic Agency, which supplied permit number 48422 to Gildemeister. To prevent prying eyes in German Customs from taking a harder look at some of the high-tech jewels going to Saddam Hussein, the permit states that "according to current rules, machinery, electrical equipment, regulation, measuring, and testing instruments for a research, development, and training institute with eight main sections, name: Project Saad 16, do not need an export permission."[22] It was a license to build Saddam's death machine. Germany's powerful industrial lobby had won a major battle.

TEN

Corporate High Jinks

In March 1984, when Keith Smith dropped in on friends at the Honeywell office in Bracknell, outside of London, he proposed to do them a great favor. If they wanted to expand their brand-new British operation, he had just what they needed. Saudi Arabia was backing a ballistic missile program in Egypt and was in the process of depositing $1 billion in Swiss banks to cover the costs. Honeywell UK could get a piece of the action, Smith suggested. But to prove that they could contribute to the new missile, which the Egyptians wanted to build from off-the-shelf components to cut costs, Honeywell engineers would have to provide a technical study on various types of explosives for ballistic missiles. Of course, Smith added, Honeywell would be paid for the study.

Keith Smith, a systems engineer, had formerly worked for a British company called Hunting Engineering. Systems engineers must know a bit about many different technical fields, to understand how a complex weapons system fits together. Smith was versed in ballistics and in the technologies of guidance, propellants, and warheads; he could serve as a procurement agent for an entire missile project. His job was not to design the missile or its components; it was to track down the specialists who could.

While he was at Hunting, Smith became friendly with a colleague named Gareth Thornton, who eventually left the company and went to work for Honeywell. Thornton rose in the ranks to become the supervisor of Honeywell's Operations Analysis Group at Bracknell, which he helped establish in 1982. Meanwhile, Smith branched off into business by himself, and through Thornton got occasional consulting jobs with Honeywell UK.

But Smith's principal employer in March 1984 was the Swiss-based Institute For Advanced Technology (IFAT), which he described as part of the Bowas Group of West Germany, a manufacturer of military explosives and propellants. Most of his fellow employees at IFAT were "former members of MBB in Munich." IFAT had been set up to serve as a prime contractor for the Egyptian government, and Smith's job was to place development and procurement contracts with industry, he told Thornton. He just wanted "to help you and your group get going" by sending a little business their way. He failed to mention IFAT's connection to Consen or to the Condor missile projects.

Smith proposed that Honeywell complete two studies for IFAT. The first he described as a "parametric study of three months duration to review currently available payloads for a ballistic missile," according to internal Honeywell memos. The idea was to analyze which missile warheads gave the most bang for the buck when directed against high-value fixed targets such as cities, ports, oil refineries, and air bases. When Smith saw a shadow of alarm pass over Gareth Thornton's face, he assured him that the Egyptians would probably never fire the missile in anger. They just wanted it as a deterrent against aggression, much as the United States and the USSR kept nuclear weapons trained on each other to guarantee that they would never be used.

The second study was to be even more precise. Honeywell documents refer to it as a "pre-design study for FAE payload for ballistic missile." FAE is defense-contracting jargon for fuel-air explosive, an arcane type of weapon that Honeywell helped develop in the 1960s that was used on a limited basis in Southeast Asia. Vietnam veterans still refer to it as "foo gas." Small FAE bombs were used to clear helicopter landing sites out of the dense Indochina jungle. The blast melted everything (and everybody) within 100 meters of impact.

Fuel-air explosives use simple ingredients, like kerosene, gasoline, or ethylene oxide, but pack three to five times the punch of conventional explosives because of their peculiar chemistry. Ordinary explosives like TNT contain nearly 40 percent oxygen, incorporated into their molecular structure to make them ignite; fuel-air explosives obtain oxygen by sucking it out of the air. "So," the Honeywell study reads, "kilogram for kilogram, FAE releases many times more energy than conventional High Explosive."

An FAE bomb case is packed with a compressed liquid fuel mixture, which is ignited in midair by two pyrotechnic charges. The first disperses the fuel into the air to form a large aerosol cloud. A fraction of a second later, when the cloud reaches the right density, a second charge ignites it, setting off an enormous blast. Small amounts of fuel-air explosive packed onto a missile warhead could have devastating results, Pentagon experts say. If used against troops in the desert, for instance, FAE could have the effect "of a small nuke."

Few countries possessed FAE technology. The USSR was believed to have it, China and France were suspected of having it. On August 6, 1982, Israel dropped a fuel-air bomb against a PLO headquarters building in the Saniyeh district of Beirut, just missing an American correspondent who had been held hostage in the cellar only hours earlier. The six-story building was totally demolished, causing reporters to speak of a mysterious new weapon developed by the Israelis, which some called a "vacuum" bomb.[1]

All in all, it was a great weapon to use against "Persians, Jews, and flies." But igniting the fuel-air cloud required special technology, which only a few companies around the world possessed. Honeywell was one of them.

Keith Smith knew about Honeywell's expertise; he also understood the reservations Honeywell engineers might have about sharing classified data with a foreign entity. To overcome their reticence, he agreed that the proposed study should rely solely on unclassified research and should not include specific information on American FAE weapons past, present, or future.

On March 28 and 29, 1984, Smith and Thornton traveled to Minneapolis to discuss the IFAT project with Honeywell engineers and the corporate hierarchy. One of the engineers was Louis Lavoie, now retired, who lives in the Minneapolis area.

"He was a con artist," Lavoie told reporters, describing Keith Smith. He said that Smith's colleagues in Europe referred to him as "an international bounder or scoundrel." As for IFAT, Lavoie's impressions were no better. "IFAT people sounded like something out of a James Bond movie to me." In a memo he sent on to his division chief, John D. Beckmann, Lavoie panned the whole project, noting with disdain that Keith Smith was "fronting" for IFAT.

"In the proposal, IFAT is identified as the 'buyer' but the 'operational user' is not identified," Lavoie's memo reads. "Honeywell corporate fathers have imposed severe restrictions on working military programs with other nations. The State Department also imposes restrictions (Technical Assistance Agreements) even though the work may be 'unclassified.' . . . There is no benefit to DSD [Honeywell's Defense System Division] other than the money offered for the analysis ($100,000). Recommendation: This program appears to be some sort of shady deal. I recommend that we avoid it."[2]

Lavoie says he tried to locate IFAT via the Swiss embassy but was unsuccessful. Nor was he able to verify Smith's assurances that IFAT was solely representing the Egyptian government. And even if IFAT did represent Egypt, Lavoie was not sure that would square with Honeywell's policy of restricting sensitive defense technology to American users.

In a memo drafted on April 4, 1984, only days after Smith and Thornton's visit, John Beckmann noted that "the deal sounded shady and probably violated Honeywell principles regarding the international arms business." When he raised these objections with Smith, Beckmann says, the enterprising man from IFAT promised that "all Honeywell logos and corporate symbols would be removed" by the time the FAE study was passed on to the Egyptians. Far from reassuring Beckmann, Smith's promises turned him off. He concluded: "The IFAT proposition as presented by Keith Smith has a malodorous quality about it. Frankly, I think the proposition is immoral, violates Honeywell principles, and is not in the best interest of Honeywell."

Lavoie's appraisal *and* Beckmann's memo passed up the corporate ladder, with cover letters, addenda, memoranda, and glosses. Finally, according to reports in the *Minneapolis Star Tribune*, it reached the desk of Warde Wheaten, the now retired head of the company's Aerospace and Defense Group. He approved the project, and the study intended for Iraq's missile program went ahead. The contract was signed in August, and the final report delivered by the end of the year. Years later, when news of the IFAT deal broke, Honeywell's chairman, James Renier, tried to deny it, then just shook his head. "It was a mistake," he told reporter Tom Hamburger of the *Minneapolis Star Tribune*. "Clearly, some people assumed that since this report was not classified it was all right to go ahead." Renier should have been embarrassed about the FAE deal with IFAT. The man who co-authored the study, Lavoie, added, "I'm troubled that Saddam Hussein has this." So was the U.S military.

The 300-page Honeywell study was not a recipe for a fuel-air explosive, nor did it contain specific design features of the complex fuzing sequence, the fuel container construction, the burster charge design, or the cloud detonation mechanism design, as a damage assessment later commissioned by Honeywell pointed out. But it was clearly aimed at helping IFAT, and thus Iraq, to make the proper design choices for an FAE weapons system.

In the introduction to the study, the authors note that "work to-date does indicate that a FAE warhead is capable of offering a worthwhile payload for the Ballistic Missile." Later on they note that IFAT stipulated a maximum net warhead of 360 kilograms (the charge carried by the Condor I). With scientific diligence, they go on to explain the ways IFAT might get around that limit, packing more punch into a smaller bomb by "densifying" the fuel. Other sections describe in detail the blast effect of an FAE explosion, "target vulnerability," and damage assessment, while another describes "the methodology to be used for assessing the optimum design of FAE warhead and the most cost effective solution for the targets of interest."

Although the Honeywell study took IFAT only through the "pre-design" phase, it gave Iraqi engineers all they needed to know to resolve the remaining technical problems of developing an FAE weapon. In the section devoted to "detonation" (the most difficult part of developing an FAE weapon), the study notes that a 400-kilogram FAE warhead "would probably be detonated by 4 kilograms of TNT about 100 to 200 milliseconds after the fuel is dispersed by the burster charge." That information, of course, was not classified because it did not provide the exact detonation sequence down to the millisecond, as it would for a U.S. Army weapon.

Recommendations for further research and development were written into every "theoretical" chapter. Design assistance of this sort could help a country like Iraq shave years off the lengthy process of developing weapons. Indeed, one of IFAT's major contributions to the Iraqi weapons program was gathering all available design information in the West so Iraqi technicians and their German tutors could put it to practical use.

The Honeywell study may not have been a blueprint for an actual weapons system, but it made a remarkable contribution to Iraq's FAE program. Iraq was seeking a new weapon of mass destruction to complement its arsenal of poison gas, and Honeywell should have seen it from the start. But they never bothered to ask questions at the Pentagon or anywhere else.

Saddam Hussein's war against the ayatollahs set the stage for the greatest arms bazaar in the history of the world. Over the eight bloody years the conflict dragged on, some thirty-nine countries sold weapons to Iran or Iraq, most of them to both sides at once. By 1984, as Operation Staunch frightened many potential suppliers away from selling weapons and spare parts to Iran, Baghdad became the favorite watering hole for the world's arms salesmen. Throughout the Iran–Iraq war, Iraq was considered the perfectly licit arms purchaser, whereas Iran was the international pariah.

In addition to purchasing arms from France and the West, Iraq petrodollars helped establish armaments industries in developing countries, some of which could barely feed their own populations. For Brazil, Chile, China, South Africa, and Egypt, the Iraqi business was a windfall. Some, such as China, provided cheap guns and political support; others went much further in satisfying Saddam's appetites, providing sophisticated Western technology (usually American) not directly available to Iraq.

Carlos R. Cardoen, handsome and well traveled, was forty-two when he began his long love affair with Iraq. After earning an engineering degree in the United States, the Chilean entrepreneur entered the arms business in 1977 and was soon making a fortune on crumbs from the Iraqi pie. When a U.S. television interviewer charged him with making immense profits during the Iran–Iraq war, Cardoen dismissed it with a disdainful wave of his hand. "One hundred million? Are you joking? I made much more than that!"

Until Cardoen developed his Iraqi connection, Chile hardly merited consideration as an arms supplier. Its weapons industry had failed to take off, in part because of a UN arms embargo imposed in the early 1970s to protest the human rights violations of the Pinochet government. "Arms exports from Chile were until 1984 limited to small batches of ammunition and small arms," researchers Michael Brzoska and Thomas Ohlson of the Stockholm International Peace Research Institute wrote in their study, *Arms Production in the Third World*. Once Carlos Cardoen entered the scene, that would all change.

From the start, the enterprising Chilean knew how to meet critical Iraqi needs. When Saddam's army was faced with human wave attacks, it needed a weapon capable of killing large numbers of foot soldiers. The French company Matra had sold Saddam a cluster bomb called the Beluga, which spread lethal steel fragments over a wide area. But at $26,000 each (a conservative estimate — it was probably much more), the Iraqi air force hesitated to use them in any significant quantity.

Industrias Cardoen came to the rescue. In March 1984 Cardoen's crack Middle East salesman, a former cigarette vendor from Lebanon named Nasser Beydoun, offered to sell Saddam the Chilean version of the cluster bomb for about $7,100 apiece.[3] The Iraqis agreed on condition that deliveries start immediately. Within months, Iraqi Airways added a new international route: Baghdad to Santiago, Chile. Empty Boeing 747 cargo jets crossed the desert, the ocean, and the Andes to Santiago's international airport. Iraqi secret policemen and Chilean soldiers surrounded the planes as carefully screened workers loaded the military cargo under the gun. According to a *Time* magazine report, Cardoen made eighteen deliveries to Iraq during the summer of 1984.[4] Over the years, court records show that the cluster bomb sales earned Cardoen a total of $467 million. In gratitude for his services to the Iraqi nation, Saddam gave the Chilean an engraved plaque, which Cardoen proudly hung, along with an autographed photograph of Saddam, on the wall behind his desk.

A cluster bomb is little more than a fiberglass-reinforced metal container into which a large number of high-explosive "bomblets" can be packed. As the bomb falls to earth, the bomblets are released in spaced bursts, or "clusters." Instead of the single large blast made by a conventional bomb (which often misses its target), the clusters cause hundreds of smaller blasts over a wide area, each potentially lethal. The Cardoen CB-500 contained 240 bomblets, each weighing less than a pound and a half, but powerful enough to pierce armor plate. The key to their effectiveness was the digital electronic fuze that timed the release of each cluster of bomblets. In one variant, "sleeper" submunitions could be set to explode hours after the bomb hit, wreaking havoc among civilians and soldiers who thought they were safe.

Many companies trying to make cluster bombs stumbled when it came to acquiring the fuzes, but this wasn't a problem for Carlos Cardoen. Despite the UN arms embargo prohibiting sales to Chile, he purchased them from a Pentagon contractor in Lancaster, Pennsylvania, called International Signals Corporation. This secretive company, managed by James H. Guerin, had developed the fuze for the Rockeye cluster bomb on a second-source contract for the U.S. Navy. (The primary source of U.S. cluster bomb technology was Honeywell.) ISC also had a long history of involvement with the murky netherworld of semiofficial arms deals. Arms experts called it the gray market, because it involved deals that were not public, and not officially approved by governments, but having tacit or sometimes secret government backing. Guerin's biggest customers were Carlos Cardoen and the South African Armaments Corporation. Both Chile and South Africa were normally out of bounds to U.S. arms exporters, but James Guerin was a specialist in bending the rules. He knew how to ship American weaponry and technology anywhere in the world, claiming he had received quiet approval from the CIA.[5]

Established as a private venture by Guerin in 1971, ISC's official business — consumer electronics and educational aids — seemed innocuous enough, but opportunities on the world arms market soon turned the company into an $800-million-a-year enterprise. Much of it, according to federal investigators looking into Guerin's business deals, was either illegal or based on fraud. To pump up the book value of ISC for a projected merger with the British defense electronics firm, Ferranti, Guerin didn't hesitate to record hundreds of millions of dollars in nonexistent sales, to countries including the United Arab Emirates and Pakistan. Government investigators reporting to a federal grand jury called it "the biggest defense industry fraud in history." Meanwhile, Guerin's "real" business focused on blacklisted countries.

Guerin's South African connection went back to the mid-seventies, when his top associate, rocket expert Claude Ivy, moved to

Pretoria to set up a rocket industry for the state-owned Armaments Corporation, Armscor. The new South African company was incorporated on April 1, 1978, under the name Kentron. A separate guidance division, Eloptro, was pulled under its wing the following year. With Ivy's help, Kentron and Eloptro made everything from multiple-launch rocket systems (the Valkyrie), to an improved version of the Sidewinder air-to-air missile, the Kukri. ISC funneled technology to these and other South African weapons programs through a series of front companies in the United States and abroad. In interviews conducted at Kentron headquarters in late 1985, company executives acknowledged that they had been purchasing American technology despite the UN arms embargo. "But we do not buy production licenses. Since 1979, we have only bought one." ISC shipped much of the same embargoed technology to Carlos Cardoen, who in turn sent it on to Iraq.[6]

Sometimes the "gray" deals left traces. On August 2, 1983, for instance, Cardoen was nabbed by U.S. customs officers in Miami and indicted for attempting to smuggle night-vision goggles to Chile. He wriggled out of that in a plea bargain that cost his company $100,000 in fines. The charges were dropped, and he was allowed to continue his commercial activities unhindered by U.S. authorities.

By the time ISC fuzes for cluster bombs were being shipped to Iraq in 1984, James Guerin and Carlos Cardoen were old friends. According to Thomas L. Flannery, who has investigated Guerin for the Lancaster, Pennsylvania, *Intelligencer Journal,* the two arms contractors made a sweeping agreement "to split the world cluster bomb market in two." Cardoen would take Latin America and "special" countries like Iraq. Guerin would take the rest of the Gulf, Pakistan, and the Republic of South Africa.

Some of the Cardoen cluster bombs sold to Iraq may have been manufactured in the United States, Customs officers and other government investigators concluded after raiding the offices of Swissco Development, a Cardoen company in Miami Lakes, Florida. A lawyer for Swissco claimed that the company dealt only in real estate and had nothing to do with arms deals. But the search turned up a shipment of cluster-bomb impeller molds on their way back to Cardoen from Iraq, apparently because of a manufacturing defect.[7] (Impeller molds slow the bomb's descent, so the attacking aircraft can make lower passes without fear of blowback from the exploding bomblets.) Faced with charges on ABC's "Nightline" of having helped Cardoen ship U.S. weapons to Iraq, the CIA took the unusual step of issuing a blunt denial on July 16, 1991. "Allegations that the Central Intelligence Agency provided or facilitated the transfer of military equipment or technology to Iraq, with or without authorization, are totally false. . . . Moreover, the CIA has never had a relationship of any type with Carlos Cardoen."

Cardoen, Guerin, and their friends at the South African Armaments Corporation had something else in common besides intelligence connections and their interest in cluster bombs. All were in business with the renegade gun maker Gerald Bull.

"Iraq is a nation of artillery gunners," French arms salesmen liked to say. "They can shoot off more artillery rounds in a month than most NATO armies use in a year." Throughout the bonanza years of the Iran–Iraq war, Saddam's men bought thousands of artillery pieces around the world. They sent purchasing teams to the USSR, China, Yugoslavia and South Africa as well, despite the UN embargo slapped on trade with the apartheid state in 1977.

The Iraqis believed that artillery was the cheapest and most effective means of countering Iran's human wave attacks. They would pound and pound again the Iranian positions from miles away. It was cheaper to buy ammunition than to lose lives, especially when you were outnumbered three to one.

The Iraqis had first become interested in South African weapons in 1981. But Sarkis Soghenalian had steered them away, arguing that commercial relations with the apartheid state would damage Iraq's standing in the Third World. In fact, Sarkis was just trying to protect his commissions, which came primarily from France and the United States.

In early 1984 the Iraqi procurements chief, General Neguib Jenaab Thanoon, traveled in civilian clothes and a bush jacket to an isolated shooting range outside Johannesburg, to watch the fourth South African Infantry Training Brigade put Gerald Bull's 155 mm field howitzer through its paces. The South Africans called it the G-5, and they had launched full-scale production of the gun under license from SRC in 1981. By the time the Iraqis came around, Armscor had already made many improvements to the gun's design, including a hardened steel barrel.

Before the UN embargo, South Africa had manufactured modest amounts of ammunition and had helped to assemble some of its Mirage fighters in an experimental plant. But not until the UN cut them off from their traditional arms suppliers in 1977 did the South Africans launch a massive effort to expand their own weapons factories, buying sophisticated machine tools from the United States and Western Europe, since manufacturing equipment was not covered by the arms embargo. In many ways, Iraq took the South African example to heart.

One of Armscor's more remarkable achievements was the G-5 gun, which used Bull's base-bleed ammunition, giving it the longest known range of any artillery piece in the world. With its unusually long (45 caliber) barrel, the G-5 could hit targets 42 kilometers away, nearly 10 kilometers farther than any gun in U.S. inventory — or in Iran's. It meant that Iraqi gunners could lob shells at their enemies with little risk of getting hit in return.

General Jenaab watched attentively as the guns arrived in a cloud of dust at the South African test site, noting the time when the last German-built Unimog truck rocked to a halt beneath a scraggly tree and the gun crew leapt out of the cab. He ticked off the seconds it took the troopies to dig the stabilizing spades into the dry earth and lower the firing plate. He counted the minutes as they brought up the white bag propellant and placed the plastic-cased high-explosive round into the semiautomatic loader, which rammed it home. Mobility was the key to good gunnery, he knew. The gun crew had to be able to get in, fire their barrage, and get the hell out before the enemy located them and fired back.

Seven minutes after the last gun arrived, Major Jacob of the fourth Training Brigade came up to his guest. "Want to pull the cord, General?" he said. The Iraqi broke into a smile. At the signal, he yanked on the rope with both hands, and the mighty gun went off.

"That's the sound of freedom," Major Jacob beamed as the other guns responded. "That's what I always tell the locals, I do, no matter how they complain about it rattlin' their windows. As long as you hear that" — he pointed to the gun — "you don't have to worry."

The South African, of course, was thinking about the bush war his country had been fighting for nearly a decade with the South West Africa People's Organization, SWAPO. The Iraqi wanted to know how long the South Africans normally trained their crews.

"We field them after four weeks," Major Jacobs said. "In a pinch, they can get by in two. That's for your raw recruits. For a real gun crew," he snapped his fingers, "it's as simple as that."

It was the quick training that convinced the Iraqis to buy the gun, Jacobs said later. He and other South African officials who played instrumental roles in Armscor's biggest export sale would never forget how much of a hurry the Iraqis were in. "They kept on asking us when they could get the first guns," one salesman recalled. "We had to gear up a special production line just to meet the Iraqi order."

And it was well worth it, the chairman of Armscor, Commandant Piet Marais, acknowledged. The Iraqi deal brought in $520 million, most of which was paid in much-needed oil. And that was only for the initial shipment of one hundred guns, training, aiming computers, and an enormous load of ammunition. Follow-on contracts would continue for years.

Piet Marais liked to take the rare defense correspondents who visited Armscor on a tour of South Africa's newest and most prized addition, a totally automated munitions plant in Boskop, a suburb of the black township of Soweto. The entire plant, which used automated machine tools purchased from West Germany, was run by a crew of sixteen men, including the supervisor. Separate production units made different kinds of explosives. The newest unit was devoted to filling 155 mm artillery shells with a liquid mixture of TNT and RDX explosives. For the Iraqi order, it was churning out 500 shells per eight-hour shift.

"It's all for export," the plant manager said. "Our biggest success on the export market, ever." Outside, in the shipping area, he pointed vaguely toward hundreds of pallets of artillery shells waiting to be hauled off to port. Black stamped letters on the side of each wooden crate announced the destination for anyone to see: "Ministry of Defense, Baghdad, Iraq."[8]

The Iraqis were no angels, but the cynicism of European arms dealers made them sick. They watched some of their best suppliers turn around and sell the same weapons to Iran. When the Germans or the French or the Italians did this, the Iraqis could bring little leverage to bear, although they tried; the South Africans were a different story. They were fairly new to the arms export business, and since Iraq was prepared to buy every round of heavy artillery ammunition Armscor could make, it had clout. When he signed the contract, General Jenaab insisted that Armscor stop all sales to Iran. Marais agreed on the spot, and unlike other arms salesmen, he scrupulously kept his word.

A Swedish arms dealer, Karl-Erik Schmitz, discovered the South African pledge to his dismay in June 1984. As Iran's principal buyer of military explosives, Schmitz had signed contracts with Armscor for 3,700 tons of military gunpowder, part of a large shipment destined for Iranian munitions plants. But in June 1984, as a cargo vessel was heading for South Africa, Pretoria informed him the deal was off.

To make up for the shortfall, Schmitz appealed to a little-known cartel of European munitions producers that had grown out of a trade organization set up in Brussels in 1975. The European Association for the Study of Safety Problems in the Production of Propellant Powder (EASSP) was ostensibly a forum for sharing information on problems in explosives manufacturing and on international customs and transportation regulations. But when the Iran–Iraq war broke out, the association became a convenient cover for a cartel whose sole purpose was to keep both belligerents supplied with gunpowder and ammunition.

By 1981 only thirteen companies of the more than fifty original members remained. But they were Europe's largest producers of military gunpowder. Among the chosen were Nobel Chemie in Sweden, PRB in Belgium, SNPE in France, Nobel Explosives of Scotland, Muiden Chemie in Holland, Forcit and Kemira in Finland, Rio Tinto in Italy, Snia BpD in Italy, Vinnis in Switzerland, and Vass AG in West Germany.

"Cartel members in Sweden, France, Germany, Holland, and Belgium would meet regularly to eat and drink together and plan how they would keep Iran and Iraq supplied with munitions," said the Swedish Customs official who first cracked the case. "They knew that no single company could produce enough gunpowder to meet the enormous demand without raising production quotas and attracting attention. So they decided to spread the work around."

While the gunpowder manufacturers had to take extraordinary pains to hide their shipments to Iran, most sales to Iraq were conducted openly.

It was a death lobby of the crudest and most basic sort. These companies were not acting on government policy, or even on a secret tilt, to help one belligerent against the other. Their interest was to make sure that *both* countries were getting enough bullets, bombs, mines, and rockets to continue slogging it out on the battlefield, since war was the only thing keeping their factories open. In one particularly scandalous case, an Italian munitions maker, Valsella Meccanotecnica, packed cartel explosives into tens of thousands of underwater mines and shipped them to both Baghdad and Tehran.[9]

During their long business lunches, cartel members would portion out the monthly gunpowder needs of Iran and Iraq. Ten percent might go to a firm in Sweden, 20 percent to France, another 10 percent each to Holland, Finland, Germany, and Belgium. Western intelligence specialists estimate that during periods of intensive fighting, Iraq and Iran each consumed nearly half a million heavy artillery shells per month — as much as most major European armies used in a year for training exercises.

Former U.S. attorney general John Mitchell was a man of many resources. After leaving government in the dog days of the Watergate scandal, he set up a consulting company whose ambitions were broadcast in the name: Global Research International. His partner was Colonel Jack Brennan, an ex-Marine who had risen beyond the ranks to become a military aide to President Richard Nixon. He followed the former president into his internal exile, serving as his personal chief of staff at San Clemente.

In 1983 Brennan got to know Sarkis Soghenalian, who was looking for friends with powerful connections to help push his first helicopter deal with Iraq. Brennan and Mitchell lent Soghenalian a hand, expecting to get a fat commission for their services. Sarkis was slow to pay, saying that the Iraqis were putting him off. Meanwhile he took Brennan on numerous trips to Baghdad on the "Spirit of Free Enterprise" to meet Iraqi procurement officers, whetting his appetite for greater deals to come.

On their way to Baghdad in March 1983, Brennan says they

stopped off in Geneva, where Brennan received a call from former vice president Spiro Agnew. Like Mitchell, Agnew had gone into the consulting business, helping corporate clients by applying a little old-fashioned grease to the political skids. Agnew said he was representing a Tennessee company called Pan-East, which wanted to sell military uniforms to Iraq. He wondered if Brennan could help. They struck a deal, but eventually the Iraqis wanted so many uniforms that the Tennessee manufacturer had to turn elsewhere to keep them supplied. Pan-East sounded out companies in South Korea and Taiwan, but none could meet the $181 million Iraqi order in time. "When we exhausted our other options," Brennan said, "I thought, jeez, we should try the East Bloc. Labor prices there are virtually zero."[10]

That was how Richard Nixon got involved on the fringes of the military supply pipeline to Iraq. On May 3, 1984, he wrote a letter to Nicolae Ceausescu, whom he considered his personal friend, introducing Brennan and Mitchell to the Romanian leader. "I trust that this relationship which involves the production of military uniforms and accessories will be a very successful and long-standing one," he wrote. "I can assure you that Colonel Brennan and former Attorney General John Mitchell will be responsible and constructive in working on this project with your representatives." The Nixon letter helped; Ceausescu agreed to cooperate, adding Romania to the long list of Iraq's military suppliers.

Sarkis Soghenalian was so popular in Baghdad that Iraqi officers regularly feted him on his birthday at a nightclub rented for the occasion. At one of these parties, the Iraqis put apples on the heads of Filipino waitresses and started waving their revolvers, to see who could shoot the apples off. The Lebanese arms dealer has never related what happened next.

In February 1984, Agusta Bell, the Italian subsidiary of Bell Textron, made a $164 million sale to Iraq. This deal, which required U.S. government approval since it involved U.S.-licensed equipment, involved eight AB-212 military helicopters fitted out for antisubmarine warfare. They were intended to equip the Lupo-class frigates Iraq had purchased from Italy four years earlier, which were almost ready to head down the slip.

Sarkis does not appear to have represented Agusta Bell in Iraq, but he paid a great deal of attention to this sale. When it became clear that the U.S. government was prepared to issue an export license, Sarkis understood that he would have no problem shipping less offensive equipment. Through his contacts at Iraq's newly formed Army Aviation Directorate, Sarkis learned that the Iraqis were eager to close a deal on forty-eight Bell Textron 214-ST helicopters. A version of this helicopter, sold around the world as a military transport and commando support machine, had recently been reclassified as a civilian aircraft. Sarkis proposed selling the 214-STs to Iraq for "recreational" purposes and "VIP transport." This claim made hackles rise in some quarters of Congress. Representative Howard L. Berman of California wrote to Secretary of State George Shultz in November 1984 to express his incredulity at Iraq's claim that these helicopters were for civilian use. In a written reply to Berman, the State Department announced that "increased American penetration of the extremely competitive civilian aircraft market would serve the United States' interests by improving our balance of trade, and lessening unemployment in the aircraft industry."

U.S. diplomats also had second thoughts about the sale. In interviews in Baghdad at the time, they pointed out that the Iraqis "would love to get any American military equipment they could obtain. They have drawn a number of comparisons between the performance of Western and Soviet equipment, to the detriment of the Soviets." At worst the Bell 214 could be used for medical evacuation missions, the diplomats said. "It would be foolish of the Iraqis to use them in a fight. We are much more worried about the Hughes 500 MD 500 sold the year before. This is the same helicopter we were flying in Vietnam. Hughes advertises it as a dedicated tank killer, and flogs pictures of it with twin TOW launchers. As of mid-1984 the United States had no evidence that the Iraqis had converted these helicopters to military use, but U.S. officials were concerned that they would do so in the future.

A former Pentagon official says Secretary of Defense Caspar Weinberger "went ballistic when he heard about the helicopter sales," but never took action to block them. "He was ready to hang Richard Armitage by the toes for having signed off on this one," the official says. The Pentagon suspected the Iraqis wanted the Bell 214 because it was identical to the helicopters sold to Iran in the

1970s and so could be used by Iraqi special forces on covert operations inside Iran. Former officials blamed the U.S. aerospace lobby for having lobbied to decontrol sales of helicopters weighing less than 10,000 pounds. "They argued that U.S. manufacturers were suffering from unfair competition from the French. And in a way they were right. The French never hesitated to sell combat helicopters to Iraq, and French manufacturers had no parliamentary watchdogs to keep tabs on them."

Before George Shultz took over as secretary of state in 1982, he worked for one of the largest engineering and construction companies in the world, the California-based Bechtel group. Bechtel didn't build every oil pipeline and refinery in the Middle East, but it had made competitive bids on most of them, and company officials certainly believed that what was good for Bechtel was good for the United States.

Bechtel had won a $1 billion contract with Iraq to build an oil pipeline to the Jordanian port city of Aqaba. By mid-1984 the company was deep in negotiations with the governments of Iraq, Jordan, the United States, and Israel to "create the necessary conditions," as the diplomats liked to say, to ensure the success of the pipeline project. It was one of the most complicated deals in the complex history of Middle Eastern oil.

Iraq's goal was to remove as much of its oil as possible from the Persian Gulf, by piping it directly to ports on the Mediterranean or the Red Sea. This would eliminate the strategic importance of the Strait of Hormuz, which Iran periodically threatened to close to force Western nations dependent on Gulf oil to take a more positive attitude toward the Islamic revolution. To please Iran, the West would have had to scale back diplomatic support, arms sales, and trade with Iraq — moves that Iraq did its best to prevent.

The Aqaba pipeline project won almost universal favor. The Gulf states liked it because it meant Iraq would increase its oil revenues and would therefore stop begging for handouts. The Europeans liked it because it meant more stable oil prices. The Americans liked it because Bechtel would get the contract, which would give the United States a solid position on the potentially huge construction market in Iraq. Even the USSR liked it, diplomats and Iraqi officials in Baghdad said at the time, because Iraq would be able to pay back some of its estimated $9 billion military debt. King Hussein of Jordan liked it the most, because the pipeline was going to be built smack across his kingdom and would fill his depleted treasury with enormous royalty payments.

But for reasons that still remain unclear, Bechtel's plans called for the pipeline to run right along the border between Jordan and Israel to the Red Sea, which greatly complicated matters. As the Iraqis argued convincingly, the pipeline would pass so close to settlements up on the ridges of the West Bank that the Israelis could knock it out just by lobbing a few hand grenades.

In a speech in 1984 to mark the sixteenth anniversary of the July 17 Baathist revolution, Saddam Hussein said that Iraq was "considering practical guarantees" to protect the proposed pipeline from Israeli attack. In a scarcely veiled reference to the United States, he said the guarantees should involve "the interests of several effective international parties."

American diplomats in Baghdad provided their own spin on Saddam's comments. "The Iraqis are not asking the United States to intervene with Israel," they insisted. "Even if Israel came out and offered explicit guarantees the Iraqis would not accept them; they need to maintain their virginity in the eyes of their Arab allies. What they do want, however, is to intertwine private and public U.S. interests with their own, so that if the Israelis do anything to interfere with the project, those interests will suffer as much as Iraq's. This they feel is the best possible guarantee."[11]

The Reagan administration was anxious for the Aqaba pipeline deal to succeed, for they construed it as a test of Iraqi intentions. Putting such a strategic resource within shouting distance of the Israeli army "could signify a change in Iraqi policy," American diplomats in Baghdad liked to believe; it could mean the first real step toward Arab acceptance of the state of Israel. For that reason, the diplomats argued in cables to the Near East Affairs office in Washington, the United States should do everything in its power to encourage the Iraqis to go through with the deal. The pipeline was like a mortgage against future Iraqi behavior, they wrote. If the Iraqis defaulted on the unwritten contract with Israel, they risked losing their collateral.

ELEVEN

Captains of Industry

Brazil had been deeply in debt for so long that it had forgotten what it was like to be solvent. Each year brought billions more in overdue interest payments, and Western banks had become so wary of Brazilian "development" projects that new money was increasingly hard to find. The only bright spot on the horizon was Iraq, the privileged partner of Brazil's national oil company, Petrobras, and the best market for Brazilian arms.

By 1984 Petrobras was the largest single purchaser of Iraqi oil, even though the Iranians were occupying the Majnoon oil fields, which Brazil had contracted to develop and exploit. Brazil's daily purchases of Iraqi crude from the Iskenderun terminal in Turkey were about 160,000 barrels — nearly one-third of Brazil's oil imports — at a cost of almost $1.7 billion per year. Interbras, the trading wing of the Brazilian oil conglomerate, scoured the horizon for commercial deals to offset this huge debt to Iraq, stepping up its activities when the Petrobras concession at Majnoon expired.

Two of the largest barter agreements involved companies outside the Petrobras empire, Mendes Junior Constructora, and Volkswagen Brazil. The first won a $1.2 billion contract in 1981 to build a number of railway lines, including a top-secret cargo link between the uranium and phosphates mines at Akashat in Iraq's western desert and the processing plants at Al Qaim. Volkswagen Brazil sold the Iraqi government 150,000 Passat sedans, which were distributed as wartime perks to government officials and army officers. The Baathist regime had never entirely made its peace with the army, but it was hoping it could buy the silence of the professional officer corps. Along with the Passats, offered at one-third the normal price, the government proposed many other perks to the army men, including full credit for officers who wanted to purchase a house.

To pay for Brazil's oil purchases, Interbras supplied a diverse range of products to Iraq. Not all were for army consumption. In 1984, Interbras companies shipped to Iraq 216,000 tons of refined sugar, 30,000 tons of beef, 542,000 cases of corned beef, and 120,000 tons of frozen chicken. A subsidiary company delivered steel and steel products, such as reinforcing rods. Other subsidiaries sold refrigerators, household appliances, and electric batteries. Still others completed construction of the Baghdad and Basra "Novotel" hotels and were negotiating sales of electric and telephone cables, API tubes, and earth-moving equipment.

Sometimes the Brazilians had to employ all their ingenuity to ensure that their products arrived safely in what was, after all, a battle zone. In one "peak effort" described in the 1984 annual report, Interbras rushed a large order of meat from Brazil to Turkey by ship, hired a fleet of refrigerator trucks from local entrepreneurs, and then *drove* the 30,000 tons of frozen beef to military bases in Mosul, Baghdad, and even Basra, more than 1,000 miles away. Such sales, brokered in part by a well-known Lebanese businessman in Paris named Ahed Baroudi, were in addition to Brazil's arms dealings with Iraq, which by 1984, were larger than ever.

The Brazilian aerospace industry did not begin until 1969, but it has grown by leaps and bounds ever since. The industry was heavily subsidized by the state when it began, but key sectors were privatized almost immediately. By the end of the seventies, Brazil's largest aerospace companies — Embraer, Avibras, and Engesa — had become the cash cows of the export economy. Their largest markets were Libya and Iraq.

Despite privatization, the Brazilian armed forces maintained a heavy presence within the industry, which employed nearly 100,000 workers in 350 firms. The major contractors all set up shop in São José dos Campos, an industrial city some 90 kilometers northeast of São Paolo. They chose that city because a number of government-sponsored weapons laboratories were located nearby. The most important was a Brazilian air force outfit called CTA

(Centro Téchnico Aeronáutico). CTA developed many of the designs that were later marketed by "private" Brazilian companies as their own inventions.

When foreign dignitaries flew into the military air base at São José dos Campos, they were given special presentations of the latest in Brazilian weaponry. One frequent visitor was General Neguib Jenaab Thanoon and his political boss, Lieutenant General Abdel Jabbar Shenshall.

Shenshall, now the minister of state for military affairs in charge of arms procurement, was more remarkable for his incredible bulk than for his charm, influence, or military skills. (He was not a military man. Saddam had awarded him the rank years earlier — he was sixty-four by now — for his loyalty to the party.) French arms merchants who suffered through endless negotiation sessions with the gruff minister called him the "half-ton general" because he was always bursting out of his suits. In less charitable moments, they called him the "Kurdish hostage" of the Iraqi government. He spoke no French and little English. Former Baathists tell of one cabinet meeting in Baghdad at which Shenshall was called upon to explain the details of a weapons proposal. As he prepared to extract a pair of reading glasses from his pocket, Saddam commented in a theatrical whisper to those next to him: "I didn't know anyone here wore glasses." Shenshall's hand froze and hovered over his shirt pocket for the rest of the meeting. Like most of his fellow cabinet members, he was absolutely terrified of Saddam.

Despite his limited power, when Shenshall was dispatched on a buying mission by *his* boss, Defense Minister Adnan Khairallah, he was the man in charge. Shenshall traveled more than any Iraqi government official except Tarek Aziz, but he was on a short leash, and he knew it. His every move was followed by Saddam's intelligence agents, who would report any attempt he might make to strike up a friendship or take a bribe.

His relations with CTA went back several years. In 1981 Shenshall had shuffled into a tiny conference room in a wing of the old Finance Ministry in downtown Rio to hear an intriguing presentation by an air force brigadier from CTA named Hugo de Oliveira Piva. Brigadier Piva was a rocket man, and his agency was in charge of Brazil's ballistic missile research program. With him was a nuclear expert from the National Intelligence Service, Colonel Luis de Alencar Araripe, who explained in elliptical terms some of Brazil's most recent breakthroughs in developing a nuclear weapon. Brazil is a poor country, Piva told the Iraqis. But we are rich in brain power and ingenuity. With your oil money and our know-how, we could work wonders together.

He went on to explain an ostensibly civilian missile project called the Sonda-3, which CTA was then developing as a space probe, or "sounding" rocket. Much of the technology for the Sonda series had been provided by the German aerospace firm MBB, Piva said. Brazil was also receiving invaluable assistance from the West German Aeronautical Research and Testing Laboratory in the areas of composite materials, rocket steering mechanisms, ballistics, and inertial guidance.[1]

The Iraqis didn't bite on the rocket project this time. But they did begin sending their physicists to Brazil to study the gas centrifuge technique of uranium enrichment, which Brazil had purchased on the open market from West Germany. Centrifuge enrichment was a complex process that took many years to master. Shenshall said that the missile project was not suited to Iraq's needs. The military version of the Sonda-3, which Piva called the SS-60, could not travel as far as Iraq's Soviet-built Frog missiles and carried only a fraction of the payload. There was no need to spend all that money to help Brazil develop something Iraq already had.

By June 1984, however, the situation had changed. CTA had made dramatic advances in the rocket business by teaming up with the "private" companies Avibras and Embraer. Piva managed to convince engineer Ozilio Carlos da Silva, who headed Embraer's foreign trade division, to kick in fresh development money. Avibras did the same. As a result, Brazil now had a flurry of competing missile projects, based on technology initially developed by CTA, to propose to the Iraqis. And Iraq, the Brazilians knew, had a pressing need for new weapons that would take them out of range of Iranian artillery.

On the tarmac at São José dos Campos, Brigadier Piva was king. With Embraer, he told the Iraqis, CTA was getting ready to test-launch the next generation of the Sonda series (Sonda IV). Initially these rockets would be capable of delivering a 500-kilogram warhead 174 miles, and later, 625 miles. Piva was certainly aware of the missile work taking place in neighboring Argentina, and he may even have known of Iraq's participation in the Condor project. At any rate, the performance specifications he cited were almost identical to those of Condor II.

Also like the Condor II, the Sonda series was solid-fuel rockets. Solid propellants are tricky to mix, but once molded into boosters they are easier to store and manipulate than liquid rocket fuel. And they can be used for a variety of applications, including air-to-air missiles, antitank missiles, and virtually anything else that flies and packs a punch. Iraq was manufacturing modest quantities of single-base propellants for use in mortar bombs and small-caliber munitions, and Amer al-Saadi was planning to expand these plants. Getting propellant technology from Brazil would appeal to him, Shenshall knew; but he was a bit concerned that the Brazilian brigadier might be presenting just another paper project. Where was the new Sonda IV rocket? Shenshall wondered. Would Brazil be willing to transfer the technology for the propellant?

Instead of answering, Piva took his Iraqi visitors around to the other side of the apron to meet with engineers from Avibras. In their hangar, hidden beneath a giant drop cloth, was their latest creation. What Shenshall discovered when they unveiled it looked like a modern version of the old Soviet standard, the katyusha rocket launcher. The Avibras men called it the Astros II.

In fact, a 1987 report by the Congressional Research Service on ballistic missile proliferation shows that the Astros II was yet another military application of CTA's basic research into sounding rockets. Avibras stripped the sounding-rocket bodies of their expensive guidance systems and loaded them onto the back of a truck; then they added a ballistics computer and fold-down armor plates for the windshield to protect the driver during launch. Like the katyusha, the Astros II could ripple-fire its rockets against distant targets. But unlike the 40-kilometer-range katyusha, which both Iraq and Iran had purchased in large quantities, the Astros II could reach targets as far as 60 kilometers away. Improvements in ballistics design also meant that the Brazilian rocket launcher was far more accurate than the original Soviet weapon, which tended to stray far afield by the time it reached the target area. It was the perfect weapon for Iraq, Piva argued. With a modest cash advance, production could start the next day.

Shenshall agreed to a trial purchase of sixty rocket launchers at the modest price of $1 million each. But Brazilian engineers say that this was not just a run-of-the-mill arms sale. "The Iraqis became our partners in the final development phase of the Astros II," said one. "We supplied the system, but they sent over their own engineers to work out the final details and to make a few changes to meet their specific needs."

The plan was to eventually coproduce the rocket launcher in Iraq. And that was not all. Brigadier Piva opened the doors to CTA's Technical Training Center to Iraq as well. Starting in mid-1984, engineers from Amer Rashid's Scientific Development Committee began arriving for training at the Instituto Tecnologico de Aeronáutica (ITA). One hundred more Iraqis were sent to Avibras, where they stayed for periods of up to three years. Here, say Brazilian engineers who participated in the joint program, the Iraqis learned "everything about ballistics, weapons design, warhead technology, you name it. This was a south-south weapons development project." Both the Brazilians and the Iraqis were proud to be launching it on an equal footing.

Iraq's Missile Corps got its real start here, just off the tarmac at São José dos Campos. The Brazilians turned Iraq's Western-educated engineers into ballistics specialists.

The Soviet Union reopened the arms pipeline to Iraq in a big way in 1983, replacing every piece of ground equipment Iraq had lost during the first two years of the war with Iran. They shipped hundreds of T-55 and T-62 tanks, artillery pieces, and katyusha rocket launchers, which previously had been embargoed. In December the Soviets concluded their first large arms deal with Iraq since before the war, for several thousand tank transporters. Seldom mentioned in weapons inventories, these workhorses of the armored calvary give tank commanders the ability to move tanks along paved roads in the middle of the night from one end of the battlefront to the other without being seen. When used to their best advantage, as Iraq would show later during the war with Iran, they became a weapon of strategic significance.

In March 1984 the Soviets went further. Concerned that Iraq was leaning too heavily toward the United States, a top-level Soviet delegation led by the chairman of the State Committee for Foreign Economic Relations, Yacov Ryabov, traveled to Baghdad to offer

$4.5 billion worth of new weapons.[2] (Ryabov, a senior officer in the KGB, was named ambassador to France in June 1986.) It was the biggest arms package the Soviets had ever proposed. Better yet, given the nervousness in Baghdad over Iran's continued occupation of the Majnoon Islands and oil fields, Ryabov informed Saddam Hussein that the USSR was prepared to rush deliveries of additional MiG-21 and MiG-23 fighters, Mi-25 Hind helicopter gunships, and 350 SCUD-B missiles. Ryabov also proposed a program to upgrade Iraq's Soviet-built nuclear research reactor at Thuwaitha to five megawatts. These agreements, and a much needed $2 billion long-term loan, were signed by Saddam's top deputy, Taha Yassin Ramadan, during an April 27 trip to Moscow. The political payoff came quickly. In an interview with the *Washington Post* a few days later, Saddam Hussein blamed the United States for the continuation of the war and spoke warmly of his new, good relations with the USSR.[3]

So eager were the Soviets to lure Iraq back to the fold that they raced to deliver the new weapons, filling one rush order placed by Ramadan in scarcely four months. This was for 200 PT-76 light amphibious tanks Iraq needed to launch an assault on the flooded Majnoon Island oil fields. The tanks were delivered during August, foreign defense attachés in Baghdad said. By this time, Soviet military cargo bound for Iraq was said to account for 70 percent of the total traffic at the Jordanian port of Aqaba. Endless truck convoys traveled across the desert to Baghdad. The Soviets were making up for lost time.

The United States Embassy in Bonn was like a fortress sprawling along the banks of the Rhine. Built big to signify America's strong presence in postwar Germany, it was the center of wide-ranging intelligence activity, not all of which met with the approval of the center-right federal chancellor, Helmut Kohl.

American diplomats from the Bonn embassy knocked on Kohl's door almost every week to speak with his intelligence coordinator; others took the short drive over to the Foreign Office, where the veteran Hans-Dietrich Genscher continued to steer West German foreign policy. Genscher was a holdover from the Social Democratic government of Helmut Schmidt. When the political winds shifted to the right, Genscher changed partners and teamed up with

Helmut Kohl's Christian Democrats (his defection brought down the Schmidt government in October 1982). The visits by U.S. diplomats brought no pleasure to Chancellor Kohl: they came to deliver diplomatic notes about the involvement of West German companies in Iraqi poison gas plants.

The demarches began as requests for information about West German companies active in Iraq, but they became more specific as time went on. By August 1984, some of the notes complained that the West German authorities were not lifting a finger to stop the companies from their deadly trade, even though their names and the true nature of their activities in Iraq were now known. Indeed, some of the companies had been mentioned in the *New York Times*.

Chancellor Kohl gave orders to his deputy for security affairs, Waldma Schreckenberger, to take the American "nonpapers" and palm them off on another office. As a subsequent internal investigation conducted by the federal chancellor's office showed, Kohl understood very well what the "nonpapers" contained and knew that he did not want to be caught knowing it. It was much easier to protest his innocence that way; besides, the Federal Republic of Germany was an export economy, with literally millions of transactions every month, making it extremely difficult to track a few suspicious cases such as those that worried the Americans. Kohl was convinced there was no proof to establish that these companies were doing anything wrong.

Of course, there *was* proof, and some of it was contained in the demarches. American diplomats and other officials with access to the original documents said in interviews that the demarches provided detailed information on the German companies and their contracts in Iraq. In some cases copies of contract documents and bills of lading were appended to the diplomatic notes, but the West German authorities said that such evidence, showing that German companies were building chemical weapons plants in Iraq, was "not specific enough" to warrant further action. It was a refrain American officials heard repeatedly, in defiance of all common sense.

A few years later Richard Perle, then serving as assistant secretary of defense in charge of international policy, was asked during hearings before the Senate Committee on Government Affairs how often the United States had protested to the Germans: so often that he had lost count, he replied. And Iraq was not the only country that German business was supplying with strategic high-technology goods. There were exports of beryllium reflectors to India's nuclear weapons program, of tritium reprocessing equipment for Pakistan, of German-built machine tools to a MiG-29 plant in the USSR. German companies were supplying inflight refueling probes and training to the Libyan air force. Other companies had designed and equipped a poison gas plant for Colonel Qaddafi at Rabta. "We demarched them, we demarched them, we demarched them," Perle said with a sigh, "and then it all turned into marshmallows."

When U.S. diplomats presented specific evidence of the involvement of Dutch and Belgian firms in Iraq's chemical weapons programs, those governments responded by strengthening export controls on eight particularly noxious chemicals used to make poison gas. On August 6, 1984, West Germany was forced to follow suit. Chancellor Kohl announced the new export control laws with considerable brio. From now on, he said with the self-satisfaction that had become his trademark, no German company can stand accused of selling chemical weapons. The chancellor wanted to lay to rest these unfounded accusations. West Germany now had the toughest laws on its books of any nation in the world.

Laws are one thing, but enforcement requires the political will to take the heat that the companies and their powerful lobbyists are accustomed to applying. No sooner had Kohl announced the new laws (theoretically intended to catch companies like Karl Kolb), than his foreign minister welcomed Tarek Aziz to Bonn. Genscher reassured Aziz in September that business would continue as usual between West Germany and Iraq, despite all the fluff about chemical weapons deliveries. Even better: he hoped that the new laws would create a climate of greater mutual confidence so that West German companies could operate in Iraq without the terrible suspicion the Americans had created. Trade between Germany and Iraq should not only continue, it should expand. You must blame the Americans, not us, for all these misunderstandings.

That fall the German government launched an official investigation into the activities of the Karl Kolb group in Iraq. The initial report from the German Customs Institute, duly communicated to the U.S. Embassy in Bonn, stated that Karl Kolb, Pilot Plant, Preussag, and their suppliers had done nothing illegal. The plant and equipment shipped to Iraq, the report declared, had been designed for the manufacture of insecticide; not poison gas. According to the law then on the books, such exports were legal, unless the equipment was *specially designed* to manufacture chemical weapons. That was why the Kohl government had recently changed the law to ban exports that were *suitable* for the manufacture of chemical weapons.

The legal distinction appeared ludicrous to the first secretary at the U.S. Embassy, who knew that equipment was still being delivered to Iraq in spite of the change in the law. If the West German government wanted to prove its good faith, it could issue a temporary restraining order to block the exports while the legal question was sorted out. The Germans accepted that suggestion and retained all pending shipments from German companies to the Samarra poison gas works. Then, German export control officials say, "Something incredible happened."

Karl Kolb took the German government to court, challenging the export ban. The company alleged that the change in export control regulations had not been approved by the German parliament and that contracts then in effect were unfairly jeopardized by the ban. To support its case, Kolb organized a visit to Samarra by two German experts during the last week of October 1984. The Iraqis restricted their movements and refused to open some areas of the plant for inspection, on the pretext that they were still under construction. The "experts" concluded that what they had seen of the Samarra plant was consistent with normal pesticides production. Nothing had been "specially designed" for the manufacture of poison gas.

It was a good thing the two "experts" didn't get a very close look, because at the same time they were touring the Samarra plant, Karl Kolb had dispatched a management team to Baghdad to sign a contract to build two additional poison-gas-processing lines at Samarra, called Ahmed 1 and Ahmed 2. Each was designed to transform up to 4,000 liters of raw materials per month into toxic gas. The Kolb management obviously felt no compunction about this particular bit of trickery.

With the hired experts' help, in January 1985 Kolb won its

lawsuit against the West German government, opening the doors for virtually any enterprising German company that wished to help Saddam Hussein find more efficient ways of exterminating Persians, Jews, and flies. As Karl Kolb's company motto so eloquently put it, they were just "Serving Mankind by Serving Science."

The court victory cooled the efforts of already hesitant German officials examining the company's activities in Iraq. The "quirk" in West German law that prompted such caution was described by Richard Perle during the Senate committee hearings a few years later. To Senator John Glenn, the legal niceties of the German system verged on the incredible. In this exchange with Perle, he kept coming back to the legal barriers preventing a West German bureaucrat from chasing companies believed to be engaged in illegal export activity:

Senator Glenn: If that government official turns out to be wrong, he is liable for a personal damage suit?

Richard Perle: Even if he has acted in good faith.

Senator Glenn: Personally, even if he thought he was carrying out international agreements or whatever, this company could come back and sue him personally?

Mr. Perle: And the result is predictable: bureaucrats are cautious by nature, and they are certainly not going to stick their neck out if they can be held personally responsible. . . . If I could be so rude as to suggest, Senator Glenn, I do not think this is idiosyncratic or quirky. I think this is a deliberate German policy to erect barriers to export controls.[4]

The results *were* predictable. By 1985, 150 German companies had opened offices in Baghdad, and scores of them would later be cited for their involvement in building Iraq's growing arsenal of unconventional weapons. It was more death as usual along the Rhine.

By the end of 1984, the Samarra poison gas works was gearing up for full production. British and American intelligence sources estimated that about sixty tons of mustard gas were being produced per month; the production of Sarin and Tabun, which had just begun, was slated to reach eight tons per month within a year. To keep these death works supplied, Iraq needed increasing quantities of chemical precursors. For the time being, it continued to import them from Europe, despite new export controls enacted by Germany, Holland, Great Britain, and the European Community as a whole. Apologists for the industry, such as Martin Trowbridge of Britain's Chemical Industries Association, pointed to the enormous international trade in chemicals. With some 9,000 chemicals moving about the world, worth more than $150 billion every year, finding the chemical weapons precursor in a batch of legitimate products was like "looking for a needle in a huge pile of needles."[5]

The chemicals Iraq needed, however, were so special that even the most eager sellers, such as Melchemie of Holland, took extraordinary precautions to ensure that word did not leak out. After his initial efforts to obtain deadly phosphorus oxychloride for Iraq were frustrated by the new export controls, Bas Weijman, Melchemie's export manager, hopped on a plane to Milan on October 10, 1984, to meet with a representative from the Italian chemical conglomerate Montedison.

As a member of the European Community, Italy was legally bound to respect the new controls on eight chemicals notorious for their use in poison gas, including phosphorus oxychloride. But Enrique Gagliardi of the Montedison subsidiary Ausidet did not seem concerned. He told Weijman that Ausidet / Montedison would be happy to supply Melchemie with sixty tons of the forbidden substance, purchased from the partially state-owned French company Atochem. The details of these shipments of deadly chemicals were first revealed by the BBC "Panorama" team in 1986.

Six days after this critical meeting in Milan, Weijman was back in Holland, warning his Iraqi customer, the State Enterprise for Pesticides Production, to take special care not to broadcast the deal. "As we have no export permit from our government, we suggest that the financing for this product is done in the same way as we agreed for order of potassium hydrogen fluoride and potassium fluoride. This is the only way to ship $POCl_3$ without complications." This letter, quoted by "Panorama," was discovered by Dutch Customs on February 26, 1985, when they raided Melchemie offices in Armhem and the homes of three company officials.

Other documents seized by Dutch Customs show that the first part of the order, twenty tons of phosphorus oxychloride, were shipped from Venice to the port of Mersin, Turkey, in two trips by the SS *Aetos*. The two containers arrived in Baghdad by truck on January 5 and 7, 1985. Montedison later claimed that when they discovered the deadly chemicals were headed for a Middle Eastern country they canceled the order and convinced the Iraqis to send the chemicals back. One of these return shipments was seized as evidence by Italian Customs in Novara on November 4, 1985.

Angered by the Customs raid, the Iraqi Foreign Ministry delivered a stern warning to the Dutch Embassy in Baghdad. "In case your government not stopping actions against our country, blocking our economy and our good reputation, we foresee serious consequences for our bilateral relationship between our two countries."

Abdel Jabbar Shenshall was pleased to be back in Cairo, but he wasn't so sure he liked the role his government had asked him to play. As head of the Iraqi delegation to the First International Defense Equipment Exhibition in Cairo in November 1984, he was expected to beat the pavement and press the meat; and the Egyptians, with all their natural curiosity and basic enthusiasm, were all over the dour Kurd. They hung on him as if he were some kind of Christmas tree — which in a way he was. Nothing was too good for the Iraqi buyer as he waddled from stand to stand, surrounded by bodyguards. He was drowned in sweet tea and buried in rich pastries, dripping with honey and pistachios.

The defense show was the idea of Egypt's defense minister, Field Marshal Abdelhalim Abu Ghazaleh. Its purpose was twofold: to show off the accomplishments of Egypt's fledgling defense industry and to let Western suppliers know that from now on they would have to sell weapons manufacturing technology if they wanted to sell Egypt anything at all. Egypt had come of age.

Egyptian factories were now making a variety of weaponry, including katyusha rocket launchers and munitions, jeeps, antitank missiles, and Gazelle helicopters under license from France. A chemicals plant at Abu Zaabal, built by the Pacific Engineering Company of Nevada (PEPCON), was making ammonium perchlorate, a solid-fuel propellant for missiles and rockets. Other factories were churning out artillery ammunition, bullets, bombs, mortars, and rudimentary electronics. An aircraft factory was assembling Tucano trainers under license from Brazil. All of it was going to Iraq, and Shenshall was in Cairo to place new orders. The Iraqi business was worth nearly $600 million every year, Egyptian officials said.

Iraq had started purchasing arms from Egypt at the start of the Iran–Iraq war, but by 1984 there were political overtones. Egypt was still an outcast from the Arab League, and Iraq, like the other Arab states, had no diplomatic relations with Cairo. But it made no secret of refusing to enforce the Arab economic boycott of Egypt, and the influx of Iraqi money had financed a dramatic expansion of the Egyptian Military Production Authority, run by a modest, almost shy, engineer named Dr. Gamel el Sayed. Business was so good, el Sayed said in interviews, that new weapons projects were being born almost every day. What he didn't say quite so openly was that most of these projects were funded by Iraq.

Washington smiled on the Egyptian–Iraqi arms connection. State Department diplomats confided to reporters that they saw it as part of a new, moderate Arab alliance that would tie Iraq to American friends in Egypt, Jordan, and Saudi Arabia. American defense companies, such as BMY, which made the M109 self-propelled howitzer, were encouraged to compete on Egyptian weapons projects. General Dynamics was going to build a tank factory in Egypt, so that the Egyptians could assemble the U.S. Army's latest main battle tank, the M1A1, for export throughout the Arab world.

The only country less than happy about the bullish Egyptian arms market was France. Because France was not offering easy credit or foreign aid to Egypt, French defense contractors were virtually shut out of the market. They viewed the growth of the Egyptian arms manufacturing industry with alarm. Said one disgruntled arms salesman watching the show, "The Egyptians are no longer buying things, they are buying whole assembly lines. Their goal is to become the largest arms producer in the Middle East. We can only stand by and watch."

Shenshall's first stop at the show was the tiny Iraqi stand, sponsored by the SOTI, Iraq's fledgling military production authority. On display for the first time ever were Iraqi-built mortars, aerial bombs, and ammunition. Few took notice of the Iraqi presence in Cairo in November 1984. But as Shenshall surveyed what was little more than a coming-out party for the Egyptian defense industry, he concluded that Iraq could do just as well, if not better, on its own, and he said as much when interviewed at the show.

Shenshall's message was clear when he reported back to Khairallah. Instead of investing in Egypt's arms industry, Iraq could spend the same money expanding its own military production and use Egypt as a front for procuring advanced technologies from the West. Shenshall's report did not fall on deaf ears. Iraq's top two technicians, Amer Rashid and Amer al-Saadi, were happy to find a political sponsor for the idea they had been pushing all along.

Another coming-out party had been organized in Washington. This one was for Iraq; and it had all the trappings of a debutante ball. An Iraqi Airways jet flew into Dulles Airport on November 25, 1984, bearing Iraqi Foreign Minister Tarek Aziz and a host of aides, who had come to consecrate the renewal of diplomatic ties with the United States after a break of seventeen years.

When Aziz was ushered into the Oval Office the next day, he found Ronald Reagan exuberant from his recent electoral triumph. A fire was lit in the fireplace, and the president beamed at the stolid Iraqi as he ushered him toward the fireplace for the ritual photograph. Aziz looked more like a Corsican thug dressed up in a suit for some brother's marriage than a professional diplomat. The Iraqi could not relax as the White House press pool clicked and flashed, turning the meeting into history. Ever since the day in April 1980 when a booby-trapped cassette player carried by an Iranian reporter had blown up in his face at Baghdad University, Aziz had preferred to keep reporters at a safe distance.

Attending the ceremony on the American side were the two men who had worked the hardest to seal the new entente between Washington and Baghdad: Richard Murphy and Michael Armacost, who had taken over as undersecretary of state for political affairs in May. "We were convinced that Iraq was changing," Murphy says today. "Not all Iraqis were playing games on this."

Asked by reporters what he hoped would come of the new relationship between Washington and Baghdad, Aziz was deliberately low key. He said Iraq was "not expecting much" from the United States. "What interests us is that the U.S. does not support a continuation of the war." Iraq had waited this long so it could renew relations with Washington from a position of strength. President Saddam had not sent him to the White House hat in hand.

The Iraqi who probably did the most to convince Washington that the Baathist radicalism of the 1970s had been swept away was the forty-year-old Iraqi chargé d'affaires in Washington, Nizar Hamdoon. He was the one who had insisted on Aziz's meeting with Reagan, well aware that it would wrap American-Iraqi relations in a mantle of respectability. He watched the handshaking and photo session from the sidelines, basking in his success. Later he arranged for Aziz and the Foreign Ministry undersecretary, Ismat Katami, to meet with reporters at the National Press Club.

Hamdoon had been sent to Washington the year before to improve relations with the United States. Saddam's aim in sending Hamdoon, a member of his inner circle and a fellow Tikriti, was not just political, it was strategic. As an admiring *Washington Post* profile written not long afterward explained, Hamdoon's job "was to turn a foe into a customer for Iraq's vast supply of oil, to persuade Americans to sell agricultural and high-technology goods on long-term credit and to sway the country's highest leaders away from their strong support of Israel."[6]

But Hamdoon was not a diplomat by trade; Washington was his first posting abroad. The short, quick-witted Iraqi, the son of an army general from Tikrit, had joined Saddam Hussein's Jihaz Hanoon, the secret intelligence wing of the Baath party, while he was still a student in the mid-1960s. Before the Baathist putsch in 1968, he ran the Iraqi Federation of Students. From then on, Hamdoon rose in the party ranks, and in the mid-1970s he was put in charge of the party section handling Syrian affairs, at a time when Saddam feared a Syrian-backed plot to overthrow him. He undoubtedly played a key role in the 1979 party purge orchestrated by his fellow Tikritis, Sadoun Shaker and Barzan Ibrahim al-Tikriti. Some believe that Hamdoon served as an active intelligence agent throughout his term as chargé d'affaires and then ambassador to the United States. As Samir Vincent, an Iraqi-American businessman who was to play a major role in Iraqi weapons programs, said later, Hamdoon "comes from a position of authority. He's not just any ambassador."

If anyone had wanted to check on Hamdoon's claims of Iraqi moderation, all they had to do was look at a transcript of Saddam Hussein's speech, delivered only months earlier on the occasion of the sixteenth anniversary of the Baathist revolution.

The "historic experience" of the revolution, Saddam said,

> has been difficult and rough, because its enemies have tried from the
> very start to snuff it out. But they failed; their arrows were lost. They
> tried another tactic, by fomenting disorder, and they failed again. So
> then they tried to introduce poison and sickness to make us deviate
> from our course, just as they had deviated other [revolutionary]
> experiences in the past. Again they failed, because this historic
> experience had a solid base and pure blood. When they realized that
> [the Baathist Revolution] had survived all these difficulties and
> conspiracies, like a giant force, they fomented against it one of the
> most dangerous plots in modern times.

That plot, Saddam continued, was the Iranian revolution, and he
was laying the blame for it squarely on the United States which was
still bowing to the dictates of "world Zionism."

Saddam did not trust the United States, but he wanted American
technology to fuel his weapons programs and to expand his oil
industry. Laying the political foundation to do this and to secure
the needed funds was Nizar Hamdoon's job.

A few days after the diplomatic festivities in Washington, a pair of
bankers from Atlanta strode into the lobby of the Sheraton Hotel in
New York. The two men had come with high hopes of cashing in
on the Iraqi's buying spree. Christopher Drogoul, born in New
Jersey to a Franco-Lebanese father and a German mother, was
destined from an early age for the glittering world of international
business. After attending college in Montpellier, France, he returned to the States in the mid-1970s to begin his career in banking.
For many years he worked at the Atlanta branch of Barclay's Bank.
Then in 1981, he got his first break. Italy's largest state-owned
bank, Banca Nazionale del Lavoro, was seeking to expand its
operations in the United States and decided to open an office in
Atlanta. Drogoul joined BNL and helped set up the new branch,
which opened for business on May 20, 1982. Two years later, when
he was just thirty-four years old, he was appointed branch
manager.

With him that morning in the New York Sheraton was Paul Von
Wedel, a Brooklyn boy who had flown to the South many years

before. He had lost most of his hair but had retained his Brooklyn accent and his taste for a crude joke. Von Wedel was in charge of trade financing at BNL Atlanta. Although Drogoul was some ten years younger, he was Von Wedel's boss. Drogoul was not as smooth as he might have liked to appear, but he was enthusiastic and willing to work hard. Von Wedel was the cynic who had seen it all. Together they made a good pair.

Drogoul had arranged a meeting with two Iraqi bankers through a contact at Continental Grain, which was doing a hefty business with Baghdad at the time. He was looking for new clients to put the Atlanta branch on a more solid footing. Currency trading and bad short-term loans by his predecessor (an Italian) had plunged the bank into the red. Drogoul was determined to change that. As a former associate put it, Drogoul "was savvy and aggressive — a businessman more than a banker." Always one to take a risk, he had been entranced by the tales he had heard from friends at Continental of the grain trade with Iraq. With the renewal of relations between the two countries, he figured Iraq was a good bet, especially with the U.S. Department of Agriculture backing 98 percent of the loans.

Sadiq Taha and Jasim Khalaf had not come to New York just to meet the two Atlantans. They were deep in negotiations with their American sponsors at the Morgan Guaranty Trust, which had cleared more than $1 billion in agricultural credits to Iraq since the CCC program had begun in December 1982. Sadiq Taha represented Iraq's Central Bank, which had to guarantee the loans for Iraq's grain purchases, while Khalaf was from Rafidain Bank, Iraq's only commercial banking institution.

As Drogoul recalls it, at this fateful first meeting the Iraqis were "not especially eager" to do business with BNL Atlanta. Drogoul was prepared to offer a $100 million line of credit at a rock-bottom interest rate, but the Iraqis were more interested at first in talking about more general topics, to sound out the Atlantans. As the discussion wore on, Drogoul asked questions about the other banks helping to fund Iraq's CCC grain purchases in the United States, but received little more than a polite response. Then Von Wedel had the bright idea of asking Taha about the war.

The Iraqi warmed to the subject, and before long Taha was telling them how Iraqi troops had beaten back the Iranian offensives around Basra and the Shatt-al-Arab area, causing Iran such heavy losses in the marshlands from helicopter attacks that Iranian morale was broken. Taha was eager to impress the two bankers with Iraq's success on the battlefield. After all, if Iraq did not survive the war with Iran, it could never repay its debts.

After two hours, the bankers got down to business, and Drogoul made a snap decision to pare his interest rate to a bare one-sixteenth over the commercial lending rate — barely enough to scrape a meager profit, and only if Iraq made its payments on time. When the Iraqis agreed, Von Wedel rushed to Atlanta to draw up the agreements, which he finished at 4:30 the next morning. He had just enough time to drive to Atlanta's Hartland Airport and put the documents on the early-bird Delta Dash for New York at 6:10 A.M. Four hours later Drogoul called to tell him the contract had arrived and that he was taking it over to the Sheraton for the Iraqis to sign.

The $4 billion BNL blunder had begun.

TWELVE

The DoC Missile Caper

Dassault's chief salesman, Hugues de l'Estoile, was riding high by the time Christmas 1984 rolled around. He had just spent two weeks escorting Lieutenant General Amer Rashid al-Ubeidi around Paris to visit with defense contractors and government officials. As the head of the French Foreign Ministry's Research and Intelligence Bureau, Philippe Coste, would reveal a few years later, Amer Rashid was the "father of Iraq's first real military procurement plan, which introduced French weapons on a massive scale into Iraq's Soviet arsenal." The Iraqi general was just about the most important visitor Dassault, Matra, Aérospatiale, and the other French arms manufacturers could hope to welcome.

Short and slight of build, Amer Rashid always appeared dwarfed by the Western business suits he was obliged to wear during these arms-buying forays. But he had the eyes of a hawk and was quick to pierce through pretense and incompetence. When he was angry, his severe, steel-rimmed glasses flashed. "In truth," said a Frenchman who had extensive dealings with the Iraqi, "we were terrified of him."

Amer was accompanied by a team of air force technicians who had come to evaluate a French proposal to sell Iraq its latest combat jet, the long-awaited Mirage 2000, which had just gone into service in the French air force. The 2000 did not yet have a multimode radar, which the French hoped would turn it into a strong competitor of the F-16 and the Soviet MiG-29 on the international arms market.

General Amer was already sold on the package Dassault had put together. The Iraqi version of the Mirage 2000 would not be equipped as a multirole fighter, like the planes of the French air force, but as a low-level penetration bomber. Iraq was interested in sixty planes. When munitions, spares, and training were thrown in, the sale could be worth up to $6 billion, company officials said.

De l'Estoile took the Iraqi to visit his old boss, Henri Martre, now in charge of Aérospatiale, which was reaping exceptional profits from its business with Baghdad. Iraq was now buying three of every four Exocet missiles to come off the Aérospatiale assembly lines, and that order alone was grossing the company some $250 million every year. Added to that, Iraq was buying thousands of HOT and Milan antitank missiles, Roland II air defense systems, and Gazelle helicopters, making Iraq Aérospatiale's largest customer for defense products.

Amer Rashid explained that he was ready to kick in sizable funds to speed up development of Aérospatiale's nuclear-tipped air-launched cruise missile, which could be launched from the Mirage 2000. The mockup, called the ASMP (Air-Sol Moyen Portée), would be able to hit targets some 200 kilometers from where it was launched, skimming over treetops and sand dunes to escape detection. Amer, perceiving how uncomfortable Martre was with the Iraqi demand, reassured him that Iraq was not interested in the *nuclear* version. The new arms package, French arms sellers interviewed in Baghdad at the time readily admitted, was "a highly offensive shopping list. It has not been put together with Iran in mind, but to attack Israel."

But there was a hitch — several hitches, as it turned out. Amer Rashid had brought along a team from the Iraqi Finance Ministry to negotiate a new loan from the French government to cover the arms package. Iraq would be pumping most of the money back into the French economy, Amer pledged. Nonsense, replied the French finance minister, Pierre Bérégovoy. Using French government loans to purchase French-made planes for Iraq was just a way of robbing Peter to pay Paul, and Bérégovoy wanted none of it.

Bérégovoy and his accountants argued that Iraq should not rush into new financial commitments until it tied in to the Saudi Petroline later in 1985. The pipeline would boost Iraqi oil exports (and revenues) by 500,000 barrels per day. But France could consume only so much Iraqi oil. The last big Iraqi arms purchases the French Socialists had agreed to underwrite were still being paid for with

Iraqi oil.[1] Better to finish the business already in the works than to bite off more than the Iraqi economy could chew, the accountants said.

De l'Estoile and the defense lobby came charging back. They argued that without the new sale, France would lose the privileged position on the Iraqi market it had earned through years of patient work. The dispute over the new Iraqi planes went all the way to the Élysée Palace and was the subject of a December 1984 meeting of President Mitterrand's inner cabinet. Defense Minister Charles Hernu took up the cause of industry, crossing swords with the finance minister over the sale. Finally the prime minister, Laurent Fabius, suggested they compromise by cutting the Iraqi order by half. In three years' time, when the first planes were delivered, they could always reconsider the rest.

A French Defense Ministry mission to Baghdad was scheduled for early February 1985. The compromise solution was to be delivered personally by the head of the ministry's International Sales Directorate, General Pierre-René Audran. But Audran missed the plane.

The French had their own Iran-contra scandal, although it never made the headlines in quite the same way and certainly never packed the same political punch. At the same time French defense contractors were selling billions of dollars worth of advanced weaponry to Iraq, the government was trying to open a discreet channel to Tehran through private intermediaries and government officials. This back-door policy, which paralleled the beginnings of President Reagan's "Iran initiative," also included officially sanctioned gray-market arms sales to Iran, primarily through the French munitions manufacturer Luchaire.

It all began in June 1984 when Roland Dumas, a personal advisor to President Mitterrand, invited a secret emissary from the Iranian government for a discreet chat at the Élysée Palace. (The emissary, Sadegh Tabatabai, was a well-known arms dealer, who also happened to be a nephew of Ayatollah Khomeini.) A few months later Dumas, who had been promoted to foreign minister, made a "secret" stop in Tehran while on a state visit to Saudi Arabia. It wasn't long before the secret was out, and the pro-Iraq lobby jumped on it. Opposition leader Jacques Chirac wrote in a

November 1984 article that France should not fail in its "moral and material support of Iraq." He criticized those who were building bridges toward Iran. "Instead of dreaming about the post-Khomeini era," he wrote in *Politique Internationale,* they "would do better to worry first about Khomeini." Whether or not it was because the secret was out, the French "initiative" toward Iran soon turned to tragedy.

Pierre-René Audran had championed the Mirage 2000 sale to such an extent that he had earned the nickname "Mr. Iraq." But in the months before his scheduled trip to Baghdad in February 1985, he also made three secret trips to Tehran to discuss opening a discreet arms pipeline to Iran. In December 1984, however, the Socialist government decided to back away from the "initiative." When Audran's negotiating partner in Tehran, Mohsen Rafiq Doust, learned of this decision, he was furious. As head of Iran's Revolutionary Guards Corps, he commanded not only hundreds of thousands of soldiers on the battle front with Iraq, but also a phalanx of terrorists across the globe. Doust told the French emissary who delivered the bad news to Tehran that he held Audran personally responsible for the double-dealing of the French government and intended to "make him pay."[2] On January 28, only days before he was to leave for Baghdad, Audran was gunned down outside his home in a Paris suburb as he was leaving for work.

The assassination shook the French arms establishment to the core and prompted President Mitterrand to suspend negotiations with Iraq on the Mirage 2000. That message was carried to Baghdad on February 9, 1985, by Audran's temporary replacement at the International Sales Directorate, General Bernard Carlier, who spent three days hiding in Room 1010 of the Rashid Hotel. When his presence in Baghdad was discovered, he canceled invitations to the grand reception that had been planned in his honor at the French Embassy. He was terrified that the Iranians knew the reason for this top-secret mission and were following his every move.[3]

Baghdad wasted no time in putting its new relationship with Washington to the test. Even before he had raised the Iraqi flag at the embassy on Massachusetts Avenue, Nizar Hamdoon's operation shifted into high gear. The commercial section worked overtime to locate American companies willing to sell high-technology goods to Iraq. Dozens of Silicon Valley computer firms signed up for a computer trade fair in Baghdad in March 1985 to show off their wares. Hewlett-Packard soon opened a Baghdad office.

But Iraq's commercial interest in the United States had a sinister underside that should have been apparent from the start. After all, Iraq was a nation at war, and its leadership had never earned points for its trustworthiness or its support of democratic values. On the contrary, Iraq was known for making enormous arms purchases, for repeatedly using chemical weapons, and for having prompted an Israeli preemptive strike because of its nuclear weapons program.

Despite all these reasons for caution, in the early months of 1985 the Reagan administration opened the doors wide to Iraqi purchases of American high-technology goods, including equipment that could not be exported to the Soviet Union or the Eastern bloc. Droves of Iraqis came to buy — directly or through U.S. agents, the Germans, the Austrians, the French, and the U.S. Embassy in Baghdad — any and every way possible. They wanted the keys to the candy store, and they were willing to pay for them.

General Amer Rashid prepared the way. His Scientific Research Council, a new procurement agency carved out of his empire at SOTI, began applying to the U.S. Department of Commerce in August and September 1984 to buy modest quantities of computers, oscilloscopes, and electronic test equipment. These initial export licensing requests were greeted with heavy skepticism by the agencies that reviewed them for national security reasons or to ascertain whether the equipment could contribute to a nuclear weapons program. A 104-page listing of the Iraq licenses, released by the Commerce Department after months of tense negotiations, shows that the United States government was not approving high-tech sales to Iraq before March 1985; then the licenses started to go through as if someone had suddenly turned a switch. From its previous status as a country to watch, Iraq became a legitimate market for the sale of high-technology goods, despite the clear military applications of many of the products being sold. That was one of the immediate prizes the Iraqis collected by renewing diplomatic relations with the United States.

On September 20, 1984, General Amer's Scientific Research Council applied for a $5,000 oscilloscope; the application was approved on March 4, 1985. In another case an application for $21,000 worth of advanced computers, for use at the French-built Saad 13 electronics factory, was put in on July 13, 1984, and would have been rejected if it hadn't been for the policy switch (Commerce approved it the following May 7). Case after case shows the same pattern. The reviewing agencies were wary about high-tech sales to Iraq, delaying approval if not rejecting the applications outright — until the early months of 1985, when the Commerce Department succeeded in overruling them. From then on, Commerce simply stopped referring many critical Iraqi license requests to other agencies for review.[5] When it did refer a case, and another agency objected to it, Commerce either disregarded the objection or escalated the debate to a higher bureaucratic level. At that point the Reagan administration's ideological commitment to free trade and its political debts to American exporters outweighed isolated concerns about the Iraqi weapons programs. Amer Rashid's Scientific Research Council obtained twenty-one separate licenses for computer equipment during this period, and it was only one of many active procurement fronts. Some $94 million worth of sophisticated American computer hardware was sold directly to Iraqi weapons plants with Commerce Department approval. A report by a subcommittee of the House Committee on Government Operations now says that these computers helped Iraq develop long-range ballistic missiles and advance its nuclear weapon program.[4]

One of the staunchest advocates of the new "sell all" policy to Iraq in early 1985 was a California congressman, Ed Zschau. He lobbied hard to have the Defense Department barred from the export review process, according to former DoD officials and congressional sources, in order to open a new export market to his Silicon Valley constituency. His congressional assistant, James Lemunyon, went on to become deputy assistant secretary of commerce in the Bush administration, where he was put in charge of export licensing at the Bureau of Export Administration. (At least one license that was rejected by the Defense Department, DoC case number B119803, was approved four years later when Lemunyon took over this key position at the Commerce Department. Singled out by an interagency investigation, this case has apparently been erased from the DoC computer and cannot be found on any of the department's lists subpoenaed by Congress. It concerns a "computer designed for image enhancement," according to a confidential memo of August 9, 1988, submitted to the Government Accounting Office. The computer was made by the Silicon Valley firm International Imaging and was sent to Iraq's ballistic missile research center, Saad 16.)

Dr. Stephen Bryen was serving as deputy undersecretary of defense for trade security policy when the alarm bells first went off. In mid-1985 he heard that the Commerce Department had decided to license the sale to Iraq of a hybrid computer whose combined analog and digital functions would allow Iraqi engineers to plot ballistic missile trajectories without pinpoint accuracy. The computer, which was almost identical to one sold to the White Sands missile test range in Nevada, was made by Electronic Associates, Inc., of West Long Branch, New Jersey. According to the license application submitted on May 8, 1985, the official purchaser was the West German company Gildemeister Projecta, which was the prime contractor of Iraq's Saad 16 missile research and design center.

The EAI computer was only one of a long series of export license applications filed that spring for the Saad 16 complex. In a letter dated February 27, 1985, that was appended to the applications, the director general of the Saad General Establishment informed Gildemeister that the center was dedicated to "checking of basic materials such as ferrous, nonferrous metals, plastics, etc and scientific instruments and apparatuses, development and modernization of scientific instruments and apparatuses." The complex had been under construction since February 1985, he stated (actually, work had begun in late 1984), and would contain seventy-six laboratories and workshops. Gildemeister was to use his letter in applying for export licenses.

The EAI application, DoC case number A897642, was approved on August 26, at the peak of the summer holidays, despite a Defense Department recommendation two months earlier that it be refused because of the strategic implications.

Bryen and the Defense Technology Security Administration (DTSA), just across the Beltway from the Pentagon, began taking a closer look at the license applications that were routinely being approved for Iraq, and what he saw alarmed him. Strategic American technology was going directly to Iraq's Atomic Energy Agency, to the Iraqi air force, and to establishments and laboratories suspected of doing weapons research. DTSA recommended that dozens of applications be rejected outright and that others be returned without action. But the Pentagon was simply overruled. So on September 19, 1985, Bryen fired off a memo to his counterpart in charge of the Bureau of Export Administration, Undersecretary of Commerce Paul Freedenberg. "In light of U.S. policy toward Iran and Iraq regarding military end-use," Bryen wrote, "I am very concerned that Commerce has taken such a casual attitude toward providing such sophisticated equipment [to Iraq] for an end-use . . . with such military significance." More than thirty licenses for Saad 16 were approved for advanced computers, test instruments, microwave communications and manufacturing equipment, satellite mapping devices, image enhancement, a radio scaler, spectrum analyzers, and telemetry equipment.

Freedenberg just shrugged off the memo, and today admits that Iraq "just wasn't a big issue" during his tenure at the Commerce Department (he resigned to go into business as a private trade consultant on May 1, 1989). As for the millions of dollars' worth of computers and sophisticated test equipment going to Saad 16, Freedenberg lays the blame squarely on the intelligence community. "They raised no red flag on Saad 16. It was considered just one of many research centers." Freedenberg liked to remind his critics that the United States had a policy of forgoing many lucrative high-tech sales to the Soviet Union and Eastern Europe at the time, and its allies were snatching them up. In Iraq, American companies were competing against a multitude of potential suppliers. "So there was no reason to deny U.S. firms access to this new computer market," Freedenberg argues, by subjecting them to unreasonable licensing requirements.

But Saad 16 was no ordinary research center, and it took no particular technical expertise to understand that. In the seven-page description that Gildemeister sent to the Commerce Department when it started applying for export licenses, the project director of Saad 16, M. B. Namody, detailed the "academic" research laboratories he was seeking to equip with American high-tech instruments. They included the following:

LABORATORY	DESCRIPTION SUPPLIED BY IRAQ
0101	Mechanical workshop
0102	Heat treatment shop
0103	Surface treatment shop
0108	Chemical analysis
0111	Laboratory for the rapid determination of carbon and sulphur content in metals
0112	Laboratory for fissure detection in metals
0113	Laboratory for hardness testing of metals
0302	Laboratory for measuring the dependence of acceleration on drive
0303	Laboratory for testing movement sequences under atmospheric conditions
0502	Laboratory for calometric testing of fuels
0504	Laboratory for testing storage properties in raised temperatures
0505	Laboratory for testing the behavior of materials during transport (vibration and friction)
0506	Laboratory for determining the speed with which fire spreads
0507	Laboratory for testing the chemical stability of compounds and mechanical mixtures
0510	Equipment for laboratory production of homogeneous fuels and additives
0513–0516	Laboratory for calometric testing of starting material and fuel mixtures
0517	Laboratory for spectrographic testing of fuels
0602	Fluid mechanics laboratory for measuring aerodynamic quantities on models, e.g. lift correction value, resistance value, etc.
0603	Laboratory for measuring systems connected with the development and trials of vehicles, including data transmission, etc.
0608	Automatic control system simulation laboratory
0610–0612	Control system and navigation laboratory
0701–0711	Laboratory for examination of electro-optical aids, e.g., the production of lenses, optical filters, glass laboratory equipment
0712	Laboratory for microwave engineering
0713	Laboratory for low and high frequency engineering, e.g., in the radio and television frequency band
0714	Laboratory and workshop for electronic measuring instruments
0716–0717	Laboratory for antennae and antennae parts, and assembly and testing
0718	Test laboratory for printed circuit board engineering
0721	Calibration laboratory
0902	Laboratory for measuring the dependence of acceleration on drive

An analysis conducted by the Pentagon Office for Non-Proliferation Policy on August 9, 1988, concluded unequivocally that "almost all of the labs named deal with areas applicable to missile research and production, such as: fuel production, vibration and friction effects, the stability of mixtures, machine and vehicle construction, data transmission, automatic control, control and navigation, aerodynamic quantities, turbo machines, antennas, and microwaves. A lab for 'seismographic soil tests' is also listed, possibly indicating nuclear research."

The real purpose of the Saad 16 complex was clear. The Iraqis were into the missile game in a big way, and American companies were providing much of the technology they needed. The sales were perfectly legal, done with the knowledge and approval of the U.S. Department of Commerce. "When I look at the case list to Iraq," says congressional investigator Ted Jacobs, "I have to conclude that no one cared. The Iraqis didn't have to hide what they were doing, and still it got approved." For the Silicon Valley firms involved, it meant a few hundred million dollars' worth of computer sales. But for those on the receiving end of the Iraqi missiles they helped design, it was a matter of life or death.

The Commerce Department's attitude was inexplicable for another reason. Since 1982, in response to a National Security Decision Directive issued by President Reagan, the State Department had been negotiating international controls tailored to slow the proliferation of ballistic missiles in the Third World. By March 1985 all the details of the Missile Technology Control Regime (MTCR) had been hammered out by the United States and its G-7 allies: Canada, France, Great Britain, Italy, Japan, and West Germany. The export of complete missile systems as well as major components was banned, and a detailed watch list of missile technologies was compiled. The key figures for the MTCR were 500 kilograms and 300 kilometers: missiles with smaller warheads or with a shorter range fell outside the scope of the agreement.

Once the technology list was approved, President Reagan instructed U.S. government agencies to enforce the MTCR immediately, even before formal adoption of the control regime. The spread of ballistic missiles was of such urgent concern that waiting for adoption of MTCR by the allies would be folly. (He was right:

France and West Germany held up its adoption for another two years.) So as of March 1985, export license requests for countries such as Iraq were supposed to be scrutinized for potential missile applications. More often than not, however, the Commerce Department failed to pass license applications to the appropriate technical review agencies. Instead, Commerce Department officials say that they and their counterparts at State simply checked the items proposed for export against the MTCR list; unless they found a direct hit, they approved the license with the annotation: "Not restricted for MTCR, Chemical/Biological, or nuclear nonproliferation." The Iraqis loved it and kept coming back for more.

In addition to the high-tech purchases for their missile R&D center in Mosul, the Iraqis came to the United States in search of computer-assisted design equipment for a large weapons complex at Taji, an industrial suburb just north of Baghdad, on the road to Samarra. Work on the Taji complex had begun in 1981 with an $81 million steel foundry built by the West German conglomerate Thyssen Rheinstahl (the same company that was building a chemical laboratory at nearby Salman Pak). The Thyssen foundry was completed in 1984, and early the next year the site was turned over to the Nassr State Enterprise for Mechanical Engineering.

The head of Nassr was an enterprising Iraqi named Dr. Safa Haboby, who was to heavy engineering what Amer al-Saadi was to chemicals and Amer Rashid to defense electronics. Haboby understood the importance of machine tools, and the computers that controlled them, in making gun barrels, missile bodies, even ammunition. He set about acquiring sophisticated machine tools wherever he could, primarily in West Germany, Great Britain, and the United States.

The machine tools that the Nassr State Enterprise was seeking to purchase in the United States in early 1985 were normally restricted for export by the Coordinating Committee for Multilateral Export Controls (COCOM), an ad hoc body comprising delegates from the United States, its NATO allies, and Japan, since 1949. They could not be exported to the Soviet Union or to the Eastern bloc because of their obvious application to weapons manufacturing. But since they were not considered applicable to atomic weapons development and there was little risk of Iraq's diverting them to the USSR, the Commerce Department now says it had "no regulatory basis" on which to deny their export to Iraq.

But even this explanation falls short of the mark. In testimony before a subcommittee of the Joint Economic Committee on April 23, 1991, Professor Gary Milhollin, who heads the Wisconsin Project on Nuclear Arms Control and has been investigating Iraqi weapons development programs, presented evidence showing that Commerce simply lied about many of the licenses for Nassr and other Iraqi weapons plants. Milhollin presented a dozen cases in which Commerce approved licenses by declaring that the equipment was "not restricted" by the MTCR, when in fact the items did appear on the missile control list and should never have been exported to Iraq. "Commerce was simply not telling the truth," Milhollin concluded. To disguise its error, Commerce Department officials refused to share information on these cases with the Department of Defense and never passed them on for review.

Dr. Haboby had big hopes for the Taji complex. In early 1985 he signed a contract with a consortium of German companies led by Ferrostaal to build a second foundry and a die-forging plant. The initial 350,000-square-foot plant was to be more than doubled in size. Contributing to the project were Jürgen Hippenstiel-Imhausen, the German chemicals manufacturer whose company was then building Libya's poison gas plant at Rabta, and the cream of German heavy industry: the state-owned Salzgitter AG, MAN, Hochtief, Klöckner Industrie, Mannesmann, Buderus, SMS Hasenclever, and West Germany's premier manufacturer of gunpowder and munitions, Rheinmetall, of Düsseldorf.

Rheinmetall's participation should have tipped off the German authorities as to the true nature of the Taji plant, but it did not. The export control agency in Eschborn approved the deal without any questions. Official German government documents refer to the plant as a "universal smelting plant" (*Universalschmiede*), but Taji had been designed for the manufacture of artillery barrels, rocket casings, and other large military forgings and rolled steel products. The Germans and the Americans were so easygoing that the Iraqis dropped all pretense concerning this project, and in the license applications they declared that the computers, machine tools, and controllers were to be used "for general military applications such as jet engine repair, rocket cases, etc." The Commerce Department thought such projects were appropriate markets for American business. The U.S. relationship to Iraq was no longer a tilt but an alliance.

Francis Hurtut, first secretary at the French Embassy in Baghdad, was worried. "The Americans are coming," he whispered to reporters over drinks at the Meridien Hotel, just around the corner from the embassy. Short and trim, sporting a healthy tan, Hurtut often repaired to the Meridien pool deck on stifling summer afternoons, when the temperature often reached 110 degrees Fahrenheit. He liked to play a game with one female reporter from a Paris daily: spotting the American businessmen who were now flocking to Baghdad. "That one's from Bell Textron," he said, pointing to a leather-faced Texan wearing a loud shirt. "They just sold forty-eight combat helicopters to Iraq on the pretext they were for civilian transport. There's not a civilian helicopter in this country, and they know it."

Back in the French embassy around the corner, Hurtut liked to show reporters a press book he had been putting together. "Over the past six months, there have been two articles on French technology in the local Iraqi press, one on nuclear research, and the other on the Paris metro system. Over the same period, there have been forty-five articles on the United States and U.S. technology *every month*. When we hear Tarek Aziz saying that Iraq wants American technology, and for Iraqi students to attend American universities, we begin to wonder what crumbs from the table will be left for us. For a country such as France, which has done lots of favors for Iraq, we are certainly not getting any freebies," he concluded. "On the economic front, we are clearly competing with the U.S." And France was losing the competition.[6]

There was more than just Gallic chagrin to Hurtut's complaint, and French businessmen in Baghdad echoed his refrain. The Americans were coming, all right, and in force. Countries such as France, which were reluctant to offer unlimited new credits to Iraq, could only watch from the sidelines as the commercial cake was divvied up among the Americans, the Germans, and the Japanese.

David Newton was the U.S. chargé d'affaires in Baghdad who shepherded relations between the two countries into the greener pastures of mutual profit. In 1985 he was elevated to ambassador status. One of the rare speakers of Kurdish in the Foreign Service, Newton kept close tabs on internal repression, especially against the Kurds. Though he had no particular fondness for the Baathist regime, he believed that Saddam had undergone a change of heart, a message he conveyed in numerous cables to his boss at Foggy Bottom, Richard Murphy.

"Iraq is a country with good development prospects," he noted. Having tasted the fruits of cooperation with the United States, Saddam "would prefer to act as a member of the club," Newton believed. "Terrorism is a policy of weak nations that have little say within the system. Saddam would rather use the power of the state instead of acting as a subversive."[7]

Newton made no attempt to gloss over Saddam's ruthless gangland rule, but he felt that Iraq would "loosen up" after the war with Iran ended. Many foreign policy experts in the United States and elsewhere agreed. "This is a regime which does not need to terrorize people on a daily level to prove it is in charge," Newton said. "Everyone knows who is in charge."

Newton believed that expanded trade with the United States was the best way to nudge Saddam into more civilized behavior. "We are working hard on getting business for U.S. companies," he said. "We want to bring U.S. technology to Iraq for mutual benefit. But we have been hampered by the low level of credits from the Export-Import Bank," a U.S. government bank aimed at promoting trade with high-risk countries. "Any U.S. company wanting to do business here must be able to offer their own complete credit package, and for some of them it's a tall order." Newton recommended that American companies concentrate on high technology. "This is the only area where we can compete successfully," he said.

The Commerce Department seized on Newton's recommendation with a vengeance, sponsoring trade fairs, sending delegations of businessmen to Iraq, and relaxing the licensing requirements. In 1985 American companies even sold $700,000 worth of high-tech gear to Iraq's French-built defense electronics factory, Saad 13, including one $161,550 order for high-speed capacitors, similar to the krytron triggers used to detonate a nuclear explosion. Today, faced with their abysmal record on Iraq, Commerce Department officials hark back to Newton's advice. "Commerce doesn't initiate policy," they say, "it merely implements policy." If the United

States sold too much high tech to Iraq, they argued, it was the State Department's fault.

On August 15, 1985, the Iraqi air force launched its first successful attack against Iran's oil terminal at Kharg Island. It was a major accomplishment for the Iraqi flyers. Bomb damage assessment photographs made available at the time by Iraqi officials showed that the Mirage F1s had scored pinpoint hits against both the "T" and the "H" loading jetties on either side of the island, where supertankers had come to feed all through the war. Huge clouds of smoke were clearly visible, rising from the jetties after the attacks. After more than a year of threats and repeated warnings, the Iraqis had succeeded in piercing Iran's Hawk and Swiss-built Oerlikon air defense batteries. Iraqi pilots had not only honed their skills on the Super Etendards (which were returned to France in 1985); they had also begun to take risks that they wouldn't have taken two years earlier.

Such pinpoint accuracy could be achieved only with the most modern, laser-guided weapons. In fact, the Iraqis were the first to use these weapons — obtained from France — in real combat (well before American and British pilots turned them against Iraq with such striking effect). Aérospatiale's AS-30L missile was so advanced that the French air force was just receiving its first missiles by the time the Iraqis used them against Kharg Island. It soon became one of the most potent weapons in the Iraqi arsenal. The French missile rides to its target on a laser beam generated by a "laser designator" pod carried by the launch aircraft or by a separate plane. In either case, the laser beam locks onto its target regardless of how the aircraft moves, leaving the pilot free to break away and take evasive action once he has launched the missile. "The AS-30L is so precise," Aérospatiale executives liked to boast, "it can knock out a command and control bunker by flying in through the window and exploding inside. It can destroy a bridge by knocking out the pylons holding it up." The AS-30L could also hit targets such as an oil-loading jetty no more than a few meters wide.

But the AS-30L was not purely a French creation. The sophisticated laser technology that went into the ATLIS (Auto Tracking Laser Illumination System) pod was developed by Martin Marietta in America for Thomson-CSF in France, in a $37 million contract signed in 1975. By 1978 the first successful flight tests on the laser designator were performed, and in 1979 the ATLIS program was turned over to the French air force for final development. Thomson then turned around and resold the technology to Iraq. Today Martin Marietta insists it had "no knowledge" that Thomson was selling ATLIS to Iraq. Transfer of American laser technology to a third country was "restricted by the U.S. government," the company insists, because it mirrored the high-tech weapons then being developed for the U.S. Air Force.[8] In other words, the Thomson sales to Iraq were probably illegal. But Thomson-CSF was a major supplier of defense equipment to the Pentagon and may have been acting with tacit U.S. government approval; not one word of official or even officious protest was ever uttered. According to senior American diplomats then stationed in France, the United States was actively following the shipments of French arms to Iraq, seeing them as a means of preventing an Iraqi collapse. "The French deliveries helped Iraq remain strong enough to resist. So what did we do? We nodded to the French."

In later attacks on Kharg, the Iraqis used yet another sophisticated, long-range French missile, the Armat, which was designed to detect and home in on enemy radar emissions of the type used by Hawk or Patriot air defense missile batteries. The specifications for the missile are so highly classified that Matra has never released a photograph of it or given its true range (believed to be upwards of 100 miles). In a classified inventory of Iraqi weaponry prepared by French military intelligence in August 1990, the number of Armats delivered to Iraq was left blank. To further disguise the sale of this strategic missile to Iraq, French intelligence identified it in the inventory by the code name Bazar. It was a missile that gave attacking fighters the edge in combat, allowing them to knock out an enemy's air defenses before they could be used. Allied air forces used precisely this type of missile to disable Iraq's extensive network of air defense radars and missile batteries at the start of the air war in January 1991. In U.S. inventory it is called the HARM (High-Speed Anti-Radiation Missile) and is launched by F-4G Wild Weasel aircraft and the F-15E.

The Armat was not the only Iraqi air force system specifically tailored to counter American weaponry. In response to an Iraqi request, Thomson-CSF designed and built electronic countermeasures (ECM) pods for the Iraqi Mirages that were capable of jamming and deceiving NATO fighters. The Iraqis claimed they needed this equipment, which did not exist in France (since the French air force needed to jam Soviet planes, not American ones), to defend against future Israeli air attacks. "They could no longer pretend they needed protection against Iranian air strikes," defense industry sources said, "since the Iranian air force had been grounded since late 1983 for lack of spares." Thomson designed an extensive array of sophisticated ECM pods for Iraq, capable of deceiving front-line American fighters such as the F-15 and F-16, and even claimed they could be used to counter AWACS command and control planes. The only AWACS in the region were based in Saudi Arabia, where they were flown by the U.S. Air Force, and in Israel.

The continuing attacks on Kharg gave a much-needed boost to Iraqi morale. To reach Kharg safely, French technicians then in Iraq explained, the Iraqi planes took off from Mosul, in the north, then refueled and took on weapons at bases in the south. "From there, they launched attacks on the Gulf, against oil tankers and against Kharg."

Even if refueled and loaded at Iraq's southernmost Mirage base, Qalit Saleh, it was still a 750-kilometer round-trip flight to Kharg, stretching the limits of the Mirage. One mistake, one extra maneuver, and the Iraqi planes would drop into the sea for lack of gas. It is doubtful that Iraqi pilots were prepared for such a tense mission. Kuwaiti air force officers today admit that the Iraqis were using Kuwait's Ali al-Salem air force base virtually at will throughout the Iran–Iraq war. This was where Kuwait based its own Mirage F1 fleet, and its location at the head of the Gulf shortened the missions against Kharg by nearly 200 kilometers, a welcome boost for Iraqi fliers. Colonel Jack Brennan, John Mitchell's partner in certain Iraqi deals, recalls Iraqi officers boasting that they "owned the Kuwaiti air force" and had "an entire squadron in Kuwait" during the Iran–Iraq war. Suspicions that Kuwait was colluding with Iraq prompted Iran to threaten the emir with direct military intervention and, when that failed, to launch a spate of terrorist attacks on Kuwaiti soil. Iran considered Kuwait a co-belligerent with Iraq, because it had extended military and financial support to the Baathist regime.

On September 24, 1985, Marcel Dassault made his last appearance on the international stage. At a prescheduled press conference at Dassault corporate offices on the Champs-Élysées in Paris, the gnomelike patriarch announced in his whiny nasal voice the last good news his firm would hear for many years to come. Iraq had just agreed to purchase another twenty-four Mirage F1 fighter-bombers, in the latest EQ5 and EQ6 configuration.[9] The sale was worth roughly $1.5 billion. This was not the last Mirage sale to Iraq, but it was certainly the last one to be announced. Dassault, eighty-eight, was rich beyond imagination and could afford risk of a public announcement to bolster confidence in his company's performance on the increasingly difficult export market.

The fourth Mirage sale was as important for what it did not include as for what it did. It was not the Mirage 2000. At this point, as the war continued and oil prices dropped, the Mirage 2000 sale had been given the ax because it was far too expensive. The French government was not about to set up a $6 billion export credit facility for these planes, and Iraq could not come up with the financing itself. There was no discussion about the moral or political implications of selling a low-level penetration fighter to Iraq; for the French it was purely a matter of financial realism.

The major reason for the lack of discussion is that France's political structure does not allow it. The French parliament provides a forum for opponents of the government to express their dissatisfaction, but it is powerless to block the sale of sophisticated weaponry to dictators and repressive regimes across the globe. To this day, French deputies have no say about arms exports. They can hold no hearings and call no witnesses; they don't even have the right to get information. All arms sales are handled behind closed doors, in discreet discussions between the manufacturers and the government. The lack of public scrutiny certainly made it easier for Dassault to sell 133 Mirage fighters to Saddam Hussein, worth some $5.2 billion to his company alone, and billions more to the manufacturers of airborne missiles. (The last of the French planes was ferried to Baghdad in July 1990, only days before the invasion of Kuwait.)

From the first Mirage sale on, the French offered Iraq the "best and the brightest" of their defense industry, sending highly trained technicians to maintain Iraqi equipment, and dedicated instructors who used the most advanced simulators and air mission computers and spoke highly of their Iraqi pupils. The French commitment was sealed in blood in June 1985, when two French trainers demonstrating a 155 mm howitzer in southern Iraq lost their lives when a faulty breach gasket caused the gun to explode in their faces.

French companies were ready to take substantial commercial losses in order to please their Iraqi customers. In 1985, for instance, Thomson-CSF was approached on two separate occasions by Iranian buying teams, who came to the company's Paris headquarters to buy sophisticated frequency-hopping radios. "They claimed to be Iraqis," said one Thomson executive who met with the Iranians, "but their suitcases full of dollars made us suspicious." Finally, Thomson said they would check the request with the Iraqi military attaché in Paris. "We never heard from the phony buyers again."[10]

Hassib Sabbagh, the Palestinian entrepreneur who helped revamp Iraq's higher education system in the 1970s, continued to wheel and deal with Saddam in the 1980s. In 1984, his Athens-based Consolidated Contractors Company put together a bid with the German technology and construction firm Mannesmann to build the Iraqi segment of the trans-Saudi pipeline. This $508 million contract would have made Sabbagh's fortune all over again, but the Iraqis gave the deal to an Italian consortium led by SAIPEM. Although CCC and Mannesmann underbid the Italians, SAIPEM offered complete financing guaranteed by future Iraqi oil deliveries. Sabbagh believes there was a political angle as well. "The Iraqis were very angry with [West German foreign minister] Genscher for receiving the Iranian foreign minister in Bonn," he says.

In order to patch things up, sources say, Sabbagh arranged a secret meeting between Tarek Aziz, Genscher, and Mannesmann executives in Paris in 1985, in the sumptuous dining room of the Renaissance palace that housed the Iraqi ambassador to France, Mohammed al-Maschat. Genscher pleaded with Aziz to intercede with Saddam on behalf of the German firm, which was eager to win the pipeline contract. Surely, if Iraq wanted to maintain its high technological standards, he argued, it should expand its business with West German companies. German exports to Iraq had plunged from $1.5 billion in 1983 to scarcely $860 million in 1984. Aziz listened to Genscher coolly, sure he could capitalize on the German's eagerness to do business at any cost. "I'll see what I can do," Aziz said finally.

Mannesmann did not win that contract, but it was rewarded with many other contracts in later years. Beyond oil industry construction, which was their specialty, Mannesmann companies became major suppliers of the Taji military complex. The Iraqi ambassador's residence just off posh Ranelagh Gardens in Paris became a favorite tryst for the two foreign ministers. Genscher and Tarek Aziz met there again on July 29, 1987, to discuss further contracts. The two could meet more discreetly in Paris than in Bonn or Baghdad, especially when they had particularly delicate business to discuss. And the German–Iraqi connection would become increasingly delicate as time went on.

Not all West German officials scoffed at the mounting evidence of the country's involvement in Iraqi strategic weapons programs. In 1985 the West German chargé d'affaires in Baghdad, Dr. Arndt, became suspicious of the activities of some of his compatriots, who were boasting in hotel bars of their work at a secret industrial center outside Baghdad. One afternoon, diplomats in Baghdad say, Dr. Arndt took an unmarked embassy car and set out for Samarra, traveling on back roads. Did the German diplomat learn the secret of the poison gas works and report back to Bonn? Perhaps not. But he learned enough that when the Iraqi police caught up with him in the vicinity of the Samarra complex they arrested him on the spot. He was expelled from the country within days, a fact the German Foreign Ministry has tried to keep quiet until now. The official story on Arndt's expulsion was that he was caught in black-market currency trading.

By September 1985 the billion-dollar Aqaba pipeline project had run into political snags. At the suggestion of the Overseas Private Investment Corporation, a U.S. government agency that insures American companies working abroad against political risks, Bechtel, the prime contractor, was looking for ways to reassure Iraq that Israel would not interfere with the new pipeline nor threaten it once it was built.

Fearing an Arab boycott if it was found to be involved in a business relationship with Israel, Bechtel went to a Geneva-based businessman named Bruce Rappaport to secure the Israeli government's guarantees. Rappaport, whose Intermaritime Bank faced Geneva's Lac Leman, was a close friend of Israeli Prime Minister Shimon Peres. He got Peres to write a letter promising that Israel would leave the Iraqi pipeline alone. But the Iraqis wanted more than a promise; they wanted a financial guarantee to the tune of $400 million if the Israelis attacked, a commitment Israel was not prepared to make.

Bechtel then turned to a San Francisco lawyer named E. Robert Wallach, a close friend of Attorney General Edwin Meese, to get the U.S. government to back up the Israeli promise. On June 24, 1985, with a little help from Meese, Wallach and Rappaport were invited to the White House to meet with Robert McFarlane, President Reagan's national security advisor. McFarlane gave the pipeline project his wholehearted support, and three days later informed officials of the Overseas Private Investment Corporation that the project was a matter of national security. The pipeline case was then handed over to David Whigg, a former business associate of CIA Director William Casey. Whigg was detailed to the NSC to handle the delicate negotiations involving two countries that were technically at war (Iraq had never signed the armistice with Israel in 1948) and the United States, which was mediating between them. Casey had known Rappaport before coming to the CIA in 1981, and knew that he stood to gain from the deal by building a refinery in Aqaba to process Iraqi crude from the new pipeline.

On September 25, 1985, Wallach sent Meese a "For Your Eyes Only" memo, informing the attorney general of unusual developments on the Israeli side of the project. Ten days earlier the Reverend Benjamin Weir had been released by his terrorist captors in Lebanon, the first success scored by McFarlane and the NSC in their top-secret arms-for-hostage deal with Iran. Wallach wrote Meese that the Israelis insisted on taking credit. In a meeting with Rappaport, Peres "emphatically indicated that the release of Weir was a result of the efforts of the state of Israel and no one else." Wallach went on to suggest that Peres was hoping the United States would return the favor by convincing Iraq and Jordan to funnel a portion of the royalty payments from the pipeline into the coffers of Peres's Labor party. Total royalties could reach $650 million to $700 million over ten years, Wallach surmised. His memo to Meese was subsequently turned over to the special prosecutor in the Iran-contra investigation, Lawrence Walsh.[11]

That fall the Iraqis grew increasingly wary of Israeli intentions, and government officials told a visiting American trade delegation in Baghdad that they now had serious reservations about the deal. Tarek Aziz reiterated these misgivings to U.S. officials during a trip to Washington in early October.

When Hassib Sabbagh, the Palestinian entrepreneur, saw the pipeline deal going down the tubes, he says that his company "submitted a proposal to King Hussein that we own the pipeline, along with a group of Jordanian investors. We were ready to build it, and own it, and pay for it," Sabbagh says. Bechtel backed the idea, probably as a last resort, but the Iraqi government refused. By the end of the year, the deal was dead.

Marshall Wiley's career at the State Department peaked in 1979, when he was appointed U.S. ambassador to Oman. During his service there the United States negotiated military base agreements with the Omani government and kept track of the Iranian revolution from listening posts at the Strait of Hormuz. Wiley retired from the Foreign Service in 1981 and became a trade consultant with Sidley and Austin, one of Washington's largest lobbying law firms. His specialty was the Arab world, and he maintained good contacts with former colleagues in the Near East Affairs Bureau at State, who helped him keep abreast of business opportunities in the Gulf. Once the United States renewed diplomatic relations with Iraq in November 1984, he became an impassioned but eminently reasonable advocate of expanded trade.

Having served in Baghdad from 1975 to 1977, Wiley understood well the peculiar mentality of the Iraqi Baathists and was quick to seize a golden opportunity. "The Iraqis were not at ease working with the U.S. private sector," he said, "because their experience until then had been primarily with the central planning structures of Eastern Europe. So I thought we needed an organization to help to get to know each other better. That's how I got the idea for the Forum."

The Forum was the U.S.–Iraq Business Forum, which Wiley set up in May 1985. After finding two corporate sponsors — Westinghouse and Mobil Oil — he took the idea to Ambassador Nizar Hamdoon, who knew a good deal when he saw one. Wiley was basically offering to run a public relations campaign for Iraq free of charge. So even before the Forum officially opened its doors, Hamdoon gave Wiley a letter of endorsement written on embassy stationery. The letter advised "any United States company interested in doing business with Iraq" that it "would do well to join the Forum."

Wiley wasted no time in putting Hamdoon's letter to use. He began contacting Fortune 500 companies and proposing his services. Before the year was out, he had enough clients to warrant a meeting in Baghdad with one of the most powerful of Saddam's cronies, Deputy Premier Ramadan. "I told Ramadan we were not asking for money. But we needed his cooperation to sign up U.S. companies" for the Forum. By cooperation, Wiley meant access to Iraqi leaders and Iraqi markets. Ramadan agreed enthusiastically.

The access agreement worked both ways. "The Iraqis set up meetings for us when we brought trade missions to Baghdad," Wiley said. "In return, they would inform us ahead of time of their visits to Washington so we could set up meetings for them. All things being equal, the Iraqis preferred doing business with Forum members. They liked what we were doing." Iraqi officials made sure American companies got the message that if they didn't join the Forum, they might as well be in Siberia.

Wiley never registered as a lobbyist, although he probably did more than any single individual in the United States to promote U.S.–Iraqi trade. "We were never a lobbying group," Wiley insists today. "Sure we kept our members informed in a timely manner of legislation that was pending up on the Hill. But they did the lobbying, not us."

The U.S.–Iraq Business Forum attracted some of America's largest exporters as members. The oil industry was represented by Amoco, Exxon, Hunt Oil, Mobil, Occidental and Texaco. The Forum also signed up AT&T, Bechtel, Brown & Root, Caterpillar, Bankers Trust, General Motors, Comet Rice, and numerous defense contractors, such as BMY, Bell Textron, Lockheed, and United Technologies Corporation. A former chairman of the Senate

Foreign Relations Committee, Charles Percy, joined under the aegis of his consulting firm, Charles Percy & Associates. Percy now worked for American firms eager to get business in the Middle East. Many of the companies that received funding from the Atlanta branch of the Banca Nazionale del Lavoro also joined the Forum.

The Forum represented a powerful, well-organized, and effective pro-Iraq lobby, capable of twisting arms in high places when the need arose. And the members never hesitated to use their clout. One of the Forum's archenemies soon became Stephen Bryen's Defense Technology Security Administration, which was throwing cold water on many Iraqi requests for U.S. high-technology products. "People at the Department of Defense were trying to block everything to Iraq," Wiley recalls. "But unless you are not going to sell any capital goods at all, you can never tell what will end up in military factories." The only solution, Wiley argued, was to sell more. The sheer mass of U.S. equipment going to Iraq would dilute the relatively small amount that was fueling Saddam's military dreams. "The Middle East has lots of brutal people ruling countries," Wiley reasoned, "but that is not cause to stop all trade. If we limited our sales to countries that shared the same ideas of civil rights as we do, it would mean restricting our trade to North America, Europe, and a few other places."

The Commerce Department's record of export license applications shows that Wiley's friends and former colleagues at the State Department used their bureaucratic clout to push through high-tech sales to Iraq for Forum members. Among the licenses championed by the State Department's Near East Bureau were sales of Bell Textron 214-ST helicopters, General Motors military trucks, and the billion-dollar Aqaba oil pipeline to be built by Bechtel.

Wiley performed direct services for the Iraqis as well. When he wrote an opinion column in the *Washington Post* opposing sanctions against Iraq in 1989, he identified himself as a former ambassador to Oman but neglected to mention his present functions as president of the U.S.–Iraq Business Forum, an omission the *Post* should have spotted. He also introduced Ambassador Hamdoon to some of Washington's movers and shakers.

Hamdoon understood that the best way to ensure Iraqi access to the high technology it sought was to lull the American Jewish community into believing that Saddam Hussein was far less of a threat to Israel than Ayatollah Khomeini. So he quietly began to court American Jewish leaders and friends of Israel on Capitol Hill, inviting them to discreet dinners at his residence up on Embassy Row. When he had their attention, he would pull out a map he claimed had been taken from an Iranian soldier on the battlefield, showing the geography of Ayatollah Khomeini's frequent claim that the road to Jerusalem passed through Karbala, Iraq. Bold arrows on the map clearly indicated the westward sweep of the Islamic revolution, through Iraq, through Saudi Arabia and Jordan, until it reached its cherished goal, Jerusalem. We are all on the same side of this one, Hamdoon told his audience. Iraq is on the side of moderation. The *Washington Post* called him "the Artful Ambassador."

One unusual party, organized in November 1985 with Wiley's help, was thrown in honor of Representative Stephen Solarz. Wiley made sure there were high-level administration figures present. Seated on the blue-and-white imitation Louis XV chairs were Peter Rodman, head of policy planning at State, Howard Teicher, the top Middle East analyst at the NSC, and Robert Pelletreau, a deputy assistant secretary of state for Near East and South Asian affairs. To round out the party, there was Alfred H. Moses, a lawyer and former liaison to the Jewish community during the Carter administration; Judith Kipper, a Middle East specialist at the Brookings Institution; and three prominent journalists: Ken Wollack, co-editor of the *Middle East Policy Survey*, Don Oberdorfer of the *Washington Post,* and David Ignatius of the *Wall Street Journal.* "It was an amazing evening," said one guest. "Here's Steve Solarz, a Jewish congressman from New York, with pro-Israelis around him, talking with an Arab from Iraq." In Marshall Wiley, Baghdad had one of the most effective advocates it could have hoped to find.[12]

In September 1985, one of Wiley's former colleagues, Ambassador Richard Fairbanks, retired from the State Department to join the Washington and New York lobbying firm of Paul, Hastings, Janofsky & Walker. Like Wiley, he became a trade consultant. Like Wiley, his specialty was the Arab world. After two years of hard work on Operation Staunch, Fairbanks had succeeded in winning the confidence of the Iraqis and other friends of Iraq in the Middle

East: Saudi Arabia, Egypt, and Kuwait. The United States *was* trying to limit the sale of weapons systems to Iran, Fairbanks insisted, and he had been the organizer of that effort.

Fairbanks was quick to capitalize on his role within the Reagan administration and, like Wiley, he knew he could count on the Iraqi ambassador. "Hamdoon was impressive," Fairbanks recalls. "He was probably one of the most outstanding ambassadors from any Arab country we'd ever seen in this town. And his message was right to the point: Iraq wanted to expand trade with the West, and it wanted to start right here, with the U.S."

Unlike Wiley, Fairbanks went to work as a paid lobbyist for Nizar Hamdoon and registered as a foreign agent. "The Iraqi Embassy paid me the royal sum of $5,000 a month," Fairbanks says, "until I fired them as a client in February 1990." Fairbanks says his role was limited to providing court documents on the Iran-contra case and, later, counseling Iraq on the USS *Stark* incident and the BNL affair. He also served as an unpaid advisor to the board of the U.S.–Iraq Business Forum. "We were trying to wean Iraq back into the Middle East peace process, and I felt completely comfortable repping them," Fairbanks says now. "I am not ashamed of what I did. It is all on the public record. American policy was to try to draw Iraq back into reasonable concourse and the community of nations. I am convinced even now that it was better to try and to fail, than not to have tried at all."[13]

Fairbanks was soon joined at the law office by James A. Placke, who had served as deputy chief of mission in Riyadh under Richard Murphy and had risen to become deputy assistant secretary of state for South West Asia and northern Gulf affairs by the time he retired. Placke was articulate and energetic and had a keen business sense. He also knew how to maintain his contacts at the State Department and in the intelligence community. Besides his friendship with Murphy, Placke kept in touch almost daily with his successor in charge of northern Gulf affairs, Peter Burleigh.

If it hadn't been for the Reagan administration's "secret" initiative toward Iran, Iraq would have been the only game in town. Baghdad was receiving active support from the Department of Commerce, the Department of State, the White House, and the CIA — virtually everyone who counted in the halls of power, except for Secretary of Defense Caspar Weinberger, whose high-tech watchdogs were the only ones keeping tabs on the Iraqi account. Dennis Kloske, who took over as undersecretary of commerce in May 1989, had another phrase to describe the Pentagon boys; he called them "ankle-biters."

THIRTEEN

BNL Builds the War Machine

Saddam Hussein wasn't quite sure how he would pay for all his arms and technology, but when he looked at the huge sums in foreign aid the U.S. government regularly awarded Israel and Egypt, he probably figured that Uncle Sam's deep pockets would have something for him. After all, Iraq was acting in America's strategic interest by preventing an Iranian victory in the Iran–Iraq war, which would have jeopardized the stability of U.S. allies in the Gulf. If the U.S. government wouldn't openly sell offensive weapons to Iraq, as France and other Western powers were doing, the grain credits from the Department of Agriculture, which freed up other Iraqi assets for arms purchases, were the next best thing. By late 1985 Iraq was spending nearly 60 percent of its gross oil revenues to buy weapons and weapons-manufacturing technology and had little other source of income. The war with Iran and Saddam's war industry were immensely costly. But Saddam had good reason to believe that the U.S. government would help pay the bills. Until now, Washington had not turned down a single loan request.

Saddam Hussein was not the only one to benefit from the CCC farm credit program. Christopher Drogoul of BNL Atlanta was making a career of the Iraqi loans, and he was a happy man when he traveled to Washington in December 1985 with Paul Von Wedel. The Iraqi program was booming, and his bosses in Rome seemed pleased with the CCC business. When Drogoul had brought up the subject at the BNL annual North American managers' meeting in New York in the summer, the head of the International Department offered encouragement, given the success of Drogoul's first $100 million loan to Iraq. Von Wedel recalled in an unpublished memoir recounting the BNL affair that the amount would come to nearly $600 million, but BNL's exposure was limited to a mere $12 million since the CCC guaranteed 98 percent of the amount. The U.S. government guarantees made it easier to forget that Iraq was sitting atop a mountain of debt.

Drogoul and Von Wedel had gone to Washington to expand their network of business contacts. Their host was the U.S. Wheat Board, which was throwing a reception for a team of Iraqi buyers led by Ghanin Aziz of the Agriculture Ministry. It was the first of many Washington bashes hosted in the Iraqis' honor over the next four years by American grain exporters, for whom Iraq was a new and good market. The two bankers from Atlanta seized the occasion to get out the word that BNL was now the privileged bank for the Iraqi loans.

On December 12 they got together with Central Bank officials Sadiq Taha and Abdul Munim Rasheed. Taha wanted the BNL to take the unusual step of committing in writing to future loans it had not examined yet, and Drogoul was quick to accept. Before the day was out, he had signed a pledge that obligated BNL Atlanta to fund $556 million of Iraqi government purchases of American goods, which were to be guaranteed by the USDA's commodity credit program. That was ten million shopping carts full of food.

After the signing, Drogoul took the shuttle to New York to discuss the good news with one of his best clients, Yavuz Tezeller, who ran the American office of Entrade. This Turkish food emporium was a major supplier of U.S. grain products to Iraq, and he may have helped funnel precious high-tech goods to Iraqi weapons plants as well. At this and subsequent meetings, Drogoul and Tezeller allegedly discussed how to divert more than $1 million in CCC credits to their personal use by double-charging Drogoul's business and travel expenses. For the complicated series of credits and debits, Drogoul set up a special "transformation account" at BNL Atlanta. What it transformed was the bank's money, turning it into private money with a touch of the magician's wand.[1]

By early 1986, BNL Atlanta was funding exports worth hundreds of millions of dollars to Iraq, primarily from U.S. grain exporters. Although Drogoul had discussed the booming business with his superiors in New York and Rome, he had not yet secured their written approval to go beyond the $100 million ceiling BNL had placed on CCC-guaranteed loans to Iraq. In March Drogoul asked his credit manager, Raffaello Galiano, to telex Rome to seek formal approval to exceed the ceiling. The answer soon came in; it was no.

BNL's refusal was directly linked to a deepening dispute between the Italian and Iraqi governments over the $2.65 billion naval contract signed in 1981. By 1986 the four Lupo frigates and six corvettes had gone down the slip at the Genoa shipyard, and the Italian government was seeking ways to deliver them to Iraq. Some of them made steam for Alexandria, Egypt, with Italian crews, while others headed for Tunis. But the Iraqis knew they would have to fight their way through the Iranian-controlled Strait of Hormuz to get the warships home, and they didn't want to put their new high-tech navy at risk. So they stalled for time by insisting that the Italians adhere to the initial terms of the contract, which called for delivery at Oum Qasr, Iraq's only port on the Gulf. Until the ships reached Oum Qasr, the Iraqis argued, they could not commission them, and until they were commissioned, the Iraqis refused to pay. In the meantime, the Italian government was forced to pick up the tab.[2]

"The controversy over the Lupo contract had the effect of shrinking Italian credits for Iraq," explained the editor of *Southern Banker,* Kenneth Cline. To intensify pressure on the Iraqis, in 1986 the Italian government slapped a double embargo on Iraq: no new loans and no ships until the Lupo contract was paid up.

The Italian embargo left Drogoul out on a limb. He had loaned hundreds of millions of BNL money to Iraq, thinking he had Rome's approval, and now the Italian government had decided to change course in an effort to pressure Baghdad into paying its debts. BNL lawyers don't dispute these facts. "By this point," says Walter Driver, of the Atlanta law firm King & Spalding, "Iraq was considered a bad risk. Commercial banks were quoting 15 to 25 percent interest rates for loans to Iraq, so the only place Iraq could borrow money was through government-sponsored loans" such as those provided by BNL. His opinion of Iraq's credit worthiness was confirmed in numerous interviews with international bankers and commodity traders in Paris, London, New York, and Geneva.

A few weeks after the Italian embargo was slapped on, the BNL

Atlanta office received official notice from Rome that its loans to Iraq exceeded approvals by about $500 million. The Atlanta bankers tried to sell off their Iraqi portfolio and apparently succeeded in getting the Central Bank of Cooperatives in Denver to finance some of the grain deals. But this arrangement fell far short of the $500 million excess. The indictment against Drogoul and other bank officers alleges that it was at this time that they began to set up a parallel accounting system for the Iraqi loans, putting them beyond the scrutiny of the BNL head office in Rome, its regional office in New York, and the Federal Reserve Bank.

With the flick of an eraser and the push of a few computer keys, the Iraqi loans were simply taken off the books. To keep track of them, Drogoul and other BNL Atlanta employees kept a secret record they called the "gray books." This consisted of a few file boxes and computer floppy disks, which they removed from the office when the auditors came, transporting them in the trunks of cars and sometimes keeping them in their garages. Whenever money was paid to one of Iraq's supplier, a chit went into the box. Whenever the Iraqis repaid part of the loans, another chit was made out. Drogoul and his colleagues referred to the off-book loans as "Perugina," the name of a popular brand of Italian candy. Normal loans were called "non-Perugina."[3] The system worked so well that it really was a bit like taking candy from a baby.

Italy was not alone in reviewing its loan policy toward Iraq, and the credit crunch hit hard in the early months of 1986, as debts contracted earlier in the war with Iran came due. France, Britain, and West Germany followed suit, and Iraq fell far behind in its debt payments. Few banks other than BNL Atlanta were willing to confirm letters of credit issued by the Central Bank of Iraq. The Iraqi government had already slashed civilian development projects by 30 percent in 1984 and had dramatically reduced imports of food and consumer goods. All of the state's resources were now going to what Saddam needed most: arms and arms-manufacturing technology.

Iraq's precarious financial situation was made worse by a disastrous turn of events on the battlefield. On the night of February 8–9, Iranian troops did what all military observers until then had hoped was impossible: they swept across the southern border with Iraq and occupied the industrial town of Fao, within gunshot range of Kuwait. The nocturnal assault — dramatic, swift, and effective — was led by combat divers, who were followed across the Shatt-al Arab waterway by thousands of well-trained Revolutionary Guardsmen in small fiberglass boats. Overpowering the handful of Iraqi defenders in the palm groves surrounding the deserted town of Fao, the Iranians erected a pontoon bridge back to the Iranian mainland and dug in.

The Iraqis immediately declared a national state of emergency. Defense Minister Khairallah rushed down to Basra to marshal the troops, along with a top Baathist general, Saadi Tuma al-Jaboori. But several days of bad weather complicated the counterattack. Although the Iraqi air force flew a record 725 combat sorties in a single day, it repeatedly failed to knock out the improvised pontoon bridges. Within a week the Iranians had managed to move four divisions — upwards of 30,000 men — into the Fao peninsula across those bridges, which were little more than blocks of Styrofoam roped together and covered with roofing tin. Still, the pontoons were sturdy enough to support trucks and small artillery pieces, with which the Iranians began to shell Basra as well as neighboring Kuwait, as punishment for its brazen support of Iraq.

On February 11, Iranian President Ali Khamene'i sent a personal envoy to warn the Kuwaiti emir that "Kuwait will bear the consequences" of any aid to Iraq. He pointed out that the advance of Iranian troops to the Khawr Abdallah Channel, across from Kuwait's Bubiyan Island, now made Iran and Kuwait neighboring countries, and he warned against letting Iraq use Bubiyan as a safe haven for its navy. In response to these direct threats, the Kuwaitis kept quiet, shivering in their palaces as the guns boomed and hoping the Iranians would go away. The emir knew he could not throw the Iraqis out of Bubiyan or prohibit Iraqi planes from using Kuwaiti air bases as staging areas for attacks on Iranian oil installations without greatly angering Saddam.

As the weeks went by and the Iranians shored up their bridgehead on the Fao peninsula, there was real concern in Kuwait and the West that Iran might be winning the war. The prospects of an Iranian victory — however unrealistic they may have been — drove fear into the hearts of Iraq's creditors, who anxiously began calculating what an Iraqi default would mean to their balance sheets.

*   *   *

In March, Iraq received its first piece of good news in months. The French Socialists lost the parliamentary elections, and Saddam's "personal friend" Jacques Chirac returned to power. Chirac's first act as prime minister was to approve a major arms sale package for Iraq, despite the lack of realistic financing. Iraq was a "friend and ally," Chirac said, with whom relations went much deeper than the pocketbook. With the Iranians camped out on the Fao peninsula (and with Iraq already some $5 billion in debt to France), Chirac argued that it was no time to abandon Saddam Hussein.

The new deals were relatively modest compared to what the French arms industry had become accustomed to, totaling a mere $430 million. They included a half dozen Aérospatiale Dauphin helicopters equipped with a new generation of antiship missile (the AS-15TT), and high-precision 120 mm mortars made by Thomson-Brandt. The contracts were given colorful code names: Jacinthe and Tulip for the helicopters, and Jupiter for the mortars. Chirac also promised that France would keep open its production line for the Mirage F1, even though Dassault had no more orders on its books. Iraq needed the planes to replace its war losses.

Tarek Aziz could hardly restrain his enthusiasm at finding Chirac back at the Matignon palace. When he came to Paris soon afterward to sign the Jupiter contract, he bubbled with praise. "There are no clouds on the horizon of Franco-Iraqi relations," he told a press conference on June 10. "My visit has been crowned with success. My objectives have all been attained." In case the message was not clear enough, he added: "You could call that concrete results. . . . Arms orders are following their normal course. All the financial problems have been resolved."

The threat of Iranian terrorism prompted Chirac to greater discretion. Once the news of the Jupiter and Jacinthe deals was out, he gave strict orders to keep future contracts under wraps. Except for Aziz's periodic pilgrimages to Paris, the entire subject of French relations with Iraq became one of the most closely held secrets of Chirac's second premiership. Companies like Dassault, which sorely needed to announce a new export sale to restore investor's confidence, were ordered to keep silent as they continued to supply weapons to Iraq.

Those supplies did continue, and on a daily basis. A former NATO airfield, built by the U.S. Army Corps of Engineers at

Châteauroux in central France, was the primary loading point for French-built missiles, cluster bombs, fuzes, radar equipment, and avionics, which traveled on Iraqi air force Antonovs that flew to France just to load arms. The deliveries became so intensive by mid-1986 that commercial Paris–Baghdad flights were also used to haul arms. Although virtually empty of passengers, the Iraqi Airlines jets were so heavily laden they barely made it off the runway at Orly and had to refuel in Athens or Istanbul for what was normally a nonstop flight. French intelligence sources estimated in mid-1986 that "if France cut off the arms pipeline to Iraq for a mere three weeks, Baghdad would collapse."

Unable to expel the Iranians from Fao, Iraq struck back hard against Iranian oil tankers and export terminals in the Gulf, using its French-built warplanes and Exocet missiles. The French delivered nearly 270 Exocets to Iraq in 1986, 75 percent of Aérospatiale's total production. Within the confines of the defense community it became common knowledge that Iraq was now the biggest customer for the accurate but expensive Thomson-Brandt mortars. Many companies hoping to pick up the crumbs, showed Iraqi delegations all manner of special devices: dune buggies to pull the mortars across the desert, harnesses and special parachutes to drop them from helicopters, even reinforced Zodiacs so the Iraqis could use the mortars in the Howeiza marshes.

But the Iraqis were becoming less happy about buying arms. Even though Saddam had successfully diversified his supplies of weapons, he resented even the limited political influence a supplier could wield. Worse, news of weapons deals tended to leak, and large, highly visible transfers of equipment and money could allow Saddam's enemies (the world was full of them) to discover his true intentions. The tightening of international financial markets reinforced his determination to build an indigenous armaments industry.

By early 1986, it appeared that Saddam was getting closer to this goal. Western diplomats in Baghdad reported to their governments that Iraq was now using locally manufactured ammunition and bombs in the war. The reports were sketchy, but they confirmed what many arms salesmen had known for years: Iraq was buying fewer weapons, but more technology to make the weapons themselves. One embassy reported that Iraq had set up a special plant to reequip its Soviet-made T-55 tanks with a more powerful 105 mm main gun. With the new guns, believed to have been supplied by Rheinmetall, Iraq's Soviet tanks could fire armor-piercing rounds bought in the West, turning the tanks into effective tank-killers.

In addition to the Taji complex to the north of Baghdad, a number of other weapons plants had gone into limited production. Some 25 kilometers south of Baghdad at al-Yusufiah was the Badr factory, which made "dumb" bombs and was gearing up to make artillery pieces. A bit farther south, near the industrial town of al-Hillah, was Iraq's principal munitions works, the al-Qaqaa State Establishment, where Iraqi technicians were fitting out assembly lines to manufacture solid rocket fuel and a wide variety of explosives. At nearby Iskandariyah, the Huteen State Establishment was tooling up to make the Cardoen cluster bombs under license. At Saad 16, near Mosul, work on missile projects was advancing at a rapid pace, while at Saad 13, French-trained electronics technicians were assembling battlefield radios and radar gear.

Perhaps the most ambitious of all was the brand-new chemicals complex at al-Fallujah, 60 kilometers west of Baghdad on the road to Ramadi, near the Habbaniya air base. A consortium of West German companies led by WTB (Walter-Thosti-Boswau) and a consulting outfit called Infraplan were building a gigantic complex that went by the code name Project 9230. In contract documents, it was also called Project 33/85. (Iraq used the number system and multiple names to deceive potential investigators.) As time went on, other weapons-manufacturing lines would be added to the al-Fallujah complex, which was managed by the al-Muthena State Establishment.

The core plant had been designed by an old hand from the Samarra gas works, Water Engineering Trading (W.E.T.) of Hamburg, to manufacture the type of nerve gas precursors whose export was now controlled throughout most of the European community. W.E.T. was actually little more than a shell company, to cover private deals made with Iraq by two employees of the West German chemical producer Preussag AG. W.E.T. had few employees of its own so it had to purchase its expertise elsewhere. From the French chemicals manufacturer Atochem (a wholly owned subsidiary of the French national oil company Elf-Aquitaine), W.E.T. learned how to handle the extremely dangerous substances it would be working on in Iraq. When completed, the al-Fallujah plant was capable of churning out 17.6 tons of nerve gas precursor chemicals each day.[4]

The plan was crucial to Iraq's independence from any international embargo. By making Sarin and Tabun precursors themselves, the Iraqis no longer had to rely on suppliers in Europe or the United States. Among the chemicals manufactured there were phosphorus trichloride and phosphorus oxychloride, substances so toxic and of such little use except for nerve gas production that even the Soviet Union controlled their export. One hundred West German technicians and workers were sent to Iraq to supervise construction and installation of the production lines.

Other chemical weapons agents were being manufactured in significant quantities in a top-secret plant near the Akashat / al-Qaim phosphate works. According to U.S. intelligence sources, this plant was built in the early 1980s by Klöckner Industrie, a petro-chemicals firms based in Duisburg, West Germany. "This is a duplicate facility, a clear carbon copy of al Qaim," the sources said. "We know that chemical weapons are being manufactured at both the al Qaim and the Akashat plants."[5] A report prepared by the House Republican Research Committee entitled "Iraq's Expanding Chemical Weapons Arsenal" called the Akashat plant "the most autonomous production unit currently operational in Iraq."[6] This report situated it to the south of Akashat, near the Ar Rutbah air force base, which is close to the Jordanian border.

In an interview in Baghdad in February 1986, the head of the Scientific Research Council, General Amer Rashid, gave a rare glimpse of this flurry of activity. Iraq was already fitting French missiles onto Soviet aircraft and vice versa. It was upgrading Soviet tanks at repair depots built and equipped by West European companies and was developing its own electronics industry. Not a single piece of equipment purchased abroad fully met Iraqi expectations or requirements. "We systematically modify everything we buy. Everything," General Amer said. "We do this operationally, by using it in a different way, or technically, by actually modifying certain features. In nearly six years of war, we have yet to find any equipment that exceeded our expectations."

It was unusual for such a powerful but shadowy figure as Amer Rashid to speak on the record to a Western journalist but, even more surprisingly, he referred specifically to the Saad 13 factory set up by Thomson-CSF. "We are certainly trying to develop our own electronics industry, not to become self-sufficient, but to produce those parts or assemblies that will best contribute to our independence and free action now and in the future. Technology has become a very important weapon for us in and of itself, and military technology has become one of our government's top priorities. So we will try to master whatever technology that can contribute to the development of our industry."

For the most part, such claims were considered empty boasts. The conventional wisdom among Iraq's arms suppliers was that the Iraqis were scarcely capable of correctly using the sophisticated weaponry they had purchased in the West, let alone designing and building their own. Even foreign engineers were not certain about the real status of Iraqi weapons programs, because of tight government security and compartmentalization. "They call us in when they have a problem," one French engineer said, "they refuse to tell us what went wrong. 'Security, security,' they shout. Well, because of all that security the infrared seekers of our missiles are collecting dust, because they are storing them in secret warehouses out in the open desert they won't let us visit."

Much of the weapons-manufacturing technology was purchased on the open market and billed as "development" projects. It was a tried and true tactic that had served the Iraqis by making them eligible for government-sponsored export credits from West Germany, the United Kingdom, and the United States. But to obtain particularly sensitive technology, they had to use more clandestine methods, especially when the aim was to build a nuclear weapon and a missile powerful enough to be used against Tehran, Ankara, Riyadh, or Tel Aviv.

Only months after Keith Smith went to Honeywell to acquire the plans for a fuel-air explosive warhead for the Condor II ballistic missile, which was still under development in Argentina and Egypt, the Iraqis and their Egyptian partners decided to make a play to acquire FAE bombs directly from the Pentagon.

The Egyptians learned that some 9,000 CBU-72/B FAE bombs were being stored at the Hawthorne military depot in Nevada. Designed by Honeywell for the U.S. Air Force during the Vietnam

War, these bombs had been assembled by a Philadelphia munitions company, Day & Zimmerman. The Egyptian Ministry of Defense told the Pentagon that they urgently needed the FAE bombs for clearing mines in the Egyptian desert.

They were so confident of obtaining U.S. approval of the sale that they provided maps showing the areas they wanted to de-mine. But even though the United States had no current use for the FAE bombs, on August 12, 1985, the State Department's Office of Munitions Control issued a "negative advisory opinion" to the Philadelphia exporter. This was not a binding, final rejection, but it clearly showed the Egyptians and their American suppliers that the proposed $14 million deal involved the national security of the United States.

Egypt's share of the Condor II project focused on the procurement of sensitive technologies; it was being run by the minister of defense, Field Marshal Abdelhalim Abu Ghazaleh. He appointed Colonel Ahmed Hussam Khairat as his personal liaison officer with the clandestine network through which Egypt and Iraq were purchasing strategic, and often embargoed, goods in Europe. Colonel Khairat rented an office in Salzburg, Austria, to cover his operations. He shared the office with IFAT and Consen, the Condor II missile procurement front companies based in Zug, Switzerland. Khairat worked with IFAT's Keith Smith on a daily basis. But since Smith was already working on Honeywell to get the plans to manufacture FAE explosives, Khairat decided to go outside the Condor network to purchase the bombs. He called on an old friend, Dr. Abdelkader Helmy, who worked as a scientist with the Teledyne Corporation of Hollister, California. Helmy, an American citizen of Egyptian origin, spoke fluent Arabic. He also had a U.S. government top-secret security clearance because of his work at the Jet Propulsion Laboratory.

Helmy agreed to help Egypt obtain copies of the American patents for the FAE bomb and to investigate whether Egypt could manufacture its own. Soon, however, he realized that the Egyptians needed a different sort of help. He introduced Khairat to another former Teledyne employee who had launched his own consulting firm, Madison Technical Services, Inc. Sam Hazelrig knew how the Munitions Control Office worked, and he drew up a plan for the Egyptians on how best to approach the FAE deal. Court records show that Hazelrig submitted his strategy report to the Egyptians on March 7, 1986. Hazelrig was nothing if not thorough. He provided a detailed chronology of Egypt's year-long effort to obtain the FAE bombs and presented a detailed interpretation of the State Department's Munitions Control List. But he argued his conclusions in an extraordinary manner.

"The CBU-72/B FAE bomb is on the Munitions Control List inasmuch as it is classified a bomb. . . . It is easy to relate the FAE 'ball of fire image' to the release of nuclear energy; therefore, most personnel with little practical experience with FAE would have negative connotations on the subject. It is obvious," he concluded, without transition or further development "that the sale of FAE bombs to Egypt would not compromise national security."

His second point was argued just as dubiously. "The President of the United States through his representative, the Secretary of State, makes U.S. foreign policy. Munitions that could obviously upset the balance of power in the world, such as nuclear weapons, are made a matter of foreign policy. Therefore, the CBU-72/B FAE bomb is not thought to be a consideration of foreign policy." Hazelrig suggested that the Egyptian government renew its demand but on a more official basis, instead of going through the exporter. "The initiation of this procurement action should be taken by the Egyptian Ambassador to the United States through existing channels of communication adhering to established protocol . . . that would allow the U.S. Department of State to evaluate the military-politico requirements, including the end-use and user."[7]

Hazelrig delivered his report personally to Khairat at the IFAT offices in Monaco, the record shows, then traveled to Cairo to meet with other officers working on the Condor II project, including General Abdel El Ghohari, Egypt's project coordinator. From these discussions, Hazelrig told U.S. government investigators, he understood that the FAEs were really intended for a ballistic missile project and not for mine clearing.[8] What he apparently failed to realize was that both the FAE and the missile project were really intended for Iraq.

IFAT was having trouble procuring other technologies that were critical to the development of Condor II. In particular, they needed specialized software, available only in the United States, to help in the development of the missile. Again Colonel Khairat called Abdelkader Helmy, and again he managed to arrange an introduction. Through another former Teledyne colleague named Jim Huffman who had the right contacts, Helmy arranged for Khairat to explain his needs to a small software house located in Huntsville, Alabama, the home of the U.S. Army's Strategic Defense Command, then engaged in transforming the Patriot missile into a ballistic missile killer.

In April 1986, Khairat traveled to Hunstville with Keith Smith to meet T. J. Coleman, who ran an outfit called Coleman Research Corporation. To keep things clean, Smith decided not to use his IFAT calling cards and instead presented himself as a representative to Transtechno U.K., of Milton Keynes, near London. Transtechno was just another Consen front.

Smith and Khairat asked Coleman to provide them with software tailored for ballistic missile design and for analysis and control of flight trajectories. They also asked Coleman to quote a price for building an entire manufacturing facility for strap-down inertial guidance systems to be used on the missile and to design a program for optimizing warhead trajectories. It was a heady shopping list.

But Coleman wrote back almost immediately. The whole package, minus the inertial guidance manufacturing plant, came to $6.5 million, he replied on May 22. The most expensive portion by far was the "thrust termination" software, which included $1.5 million for wind-tunnel tests of a missile mockup. But there was a hitch. The Condor II shopping list required four export licenses. "Four separate Letters of Intent are suggested," Coleman wrote, if they wanted to facilitate the licensing procedure. Khairat and Smith let the matter drop. They had already revealed too much of their true plan. Instead, they took the Coleman proposal, just as they had the Honeywell FAE study, and used it as a procurement guide. This was a common Iraqi practice: buy the blueprints from one source and the equipment from several others. That way there were fewer leaks, since no one understood the big picture.

Since taking over the presidency in 1979, Saddam had been skimming 5 percent off the top of Iraq's $15 billion yearly oil revenues, according to a former planning minister, Jawad Hashim, and placing the money in special Swiss accounts. He had also been taking a 2.5 percent kickback on contracts with Japanese companies and had worked out a scam on the foreign letters of credit used to finance Iraqi development schemes.

Hashim said the billions constituted a special Baath party tax intended "to give the regime enough funds that if they are ousted from power then they could use [them] to make their comeback." Over fifteen years, according to Hashim's calculations, the war chest amounted to $31 *billion*. As much as "four billion in various currencies, but mainly foreign currencies" was in cash, much of it kept in Saddam's palace in Baghdad. "I have seen briefcases with foreign currency cash exceeding a million dollars," Hashim said. Saddam was especially likely to bribe African leaders, such as former Chadian President Kolingba. Hashim never revealed what Saddam got for his money.[9]

In a CBS "60 Minutes" interview, Wall Street financial investigator Jules Kroll revealed that the multibillion-dollar slush fund was controlled by Saddam's half-brother Barzan. Some of the money was invested in legitimate business concerns through front companies operating out of Switzerland. An estimated $1 billion went into bank accounts controlled by Saddam himself, for his personal and family use.[10]

Two Iraqi fronts, Midco Financial and Montana Management, Inc., organized the stock purchases. Montana had been set up as a mailbox company in Panama shortly after Saddam took over as president; Barzan created Midco in Switzerland in 1982. The Geneva commercial registry shows that the Midco seed money — 2.1 million Swiss francs — was paid in cash into a numbered Swiss account by an Iraqi named Aladine Hussein Alwan, whose name also appears on the Panamanian commercial registry as the secretary general of Montana Management. Alwan, whose real name was Aladine Hussein Ali Maki Khamas, was in fact a retired major general in the Iraqi army and had gone to work as Barzan's bagman. (He briefly entered the international spotlight in August 1990, when Saddam appointed him interim ruler of Kuwait.) The two front companies were controlled from Baghdad by Khalaf al-Doulimi and Mohammed Turki Habib, Barzan's aides.

Over the years, these Iraqi investment companies acquired substantial industrial shareholdings in many different countries. Jules Kroll believes they salted away as much as $10 billion disguised as legitimate business investments — 5 percent of the $200 billion Iraq earned during the 1980s. His investigators managed to locate

$2.4 billion in Iraqi-controlled deposits stashed in fifty banks around the world. One of the companies that attracted Saddam's private investment purse was Daimler-Benz, which owned missile and helicopter manufacturer MBB. Another was the French publishing conglomerate Hachette, which controlled several publishing houses and had stakes in newspapers, radio stations, and television networks. Hachette's owner and chief executive officer, Jean-Luc Lagadère, also controlled one of the top French defense companies, Matra. By buying into Hachette, the Iraqis couldn't guarantee access to the latest Matra missiles, but their 8.4 percent stake, worth around $67 million, was large enough to wield as a weapon of financial terror. If the Iraqis sold short, Hachette stock would tumble. Lagadère and his board say the Iraqis never wielded this weapon. But throughout the 1980s, Matra never refused an Iraqi order, no matter how sophisticated the equipment.[11]

As undersecretary of state for security assistance, science and technology, William Schneider was the department's point man when it came to foreign military sales. If Egypt wanted a new squadron of F-16s or if Israel wanted more helicopters, they had to go through Schneider's shop on the ground floor of the State Department.

Schneider had also taken over Operation Staunch, the effort to block military supplies from reaching Iran, when Richard Fairbanks retired to private law practice and lobbying. American diplomats in Baghdad said this is what brought Schneider to the Iraqi capitol during the first week of February 1986, only days before the Iranian attack on Fao. "He came to discuss expanding U.S. trade with Iraq, and to remind the Iraqis that we are still pursuing Operation Staunch." The diplomats also suggested with a few winks and nods that Schneider might have entertained Iraqi requests to acquire American weapons at some later date. "Don't forget that Bell Helicopter now has a full-time rep right here in Baghdad," one pointed out. "This is giving the Iraqis a taste of what U.S. technology is all about."

Schneider met with Tarek Aziz, who seemed to have a finger in every Iraqi arms purchase, and with the trade minister, Hassan Ali. The timing of Schneider's trip was deliberate, U.S. diplomats said. "Saddam had just returned from an official visit to Moscow in January — one of the rare trips abroad he has taken since the beginning of the war. We wanted to make sure we were present in a very visible way when he returned. Just to remind him that there is an alternative to the USSR."

Schneider's visit was significant for another reason as well. He was not an Arabist, nor was he a diplomat in the ordinary sense. His business was technology, which was what the Iraqis wanted most from the United States. In an interview shortly before his trip to Baghdad, Schneider was clearly uncomfortable with the sale of American-built helicopters to Iraq. "The Hughes 500 sneaked in under our noses because helicopters weighing less than 10,000 lbs don't technically need our approval. They can be shipped with an ordinary Commerce Department license." Schneider went on to explain that he had received unequivocal information that these small battlefield-observation helicopters had "definitely been diverted to military purposes," although he wouldn't say whether or not the Iraqis had managed to equip them with TOW antitank missiles, as the manufacturer's literature suggests. As for the Bell 214, Schneider said the State Department had cleared this sale only "with substantial Iraqi promises that they would not be used for military ends. So far, this seems to be respected."

But American high-tech goods were another matter entirely. Despite the favorable treatment they were receiving from the Commerce Department, the Iraqis complained to Schneider that they were not getting all the equipment they sought from the United States because of bureaucratic red tape. Purchases of computers for their oil industry and machine tools for their steel factories were being blocked (thanks to Steve Bryen and Richard Perle at the Pentagon), and the Iraqis wanted to know why. The United States claimed it was not supporting Iran, yet American weapons were still getting through to the ayatollahs. How could Iraq believe that the United States was supporting Baghdad, Tarek Aziz wanted to know, when purely civilian sales of American computers to Iraq could not get approval? Aziz never missed an opportunity to hammer his message home. He had made the same point in almost identical words only a few months earlier to Richard Murphy, during an unpublicized visit to Washington in October 1985.

When he returned to Washington, Schneider threw his considerable weight behind a "trade-off" with Iraq: the United States would ship the Iraqis no weapons, but it would allow extensive technology sales. Richard Murphy and the Near Eastern Affairs experts on the fifth floor of the State Department were overjoyed. Schneider stood a bureaucratic head higher than the Pentagon's Steve Bryen, whom they saw as their archenemy. In the fall of 1985, in a long interview devoted to developments inside Iran, one of Murphy's principal deputies found time to single out Bryen and Richard Perle for their obstructive behavior. "They are not interested in the Gulf," this Arabist lamented, "except when it comes to technology transfer. They are dead set against the sale of perfectly ordinary computers to Iraq."

The "perfectly ordinary computers" were in fact headed for the Saad 16 missile complex, Commerce Department documents subpoenaed by Congress now show. "Murphy fought dogs and cats to get these computers and imaging systems approved," Bryen asserts. "The State Department knew from explicit DoD warnings where that equipment was going, and it certainly wasn't intended for university research." Bryen has since tried to get the warnings he sent over to Commerce and the State Department released through the Freedom of Information Act, but to no avail. "My own letters are now classified as state secrets," he commented wryly.

In July 1986 the Pentagon lost the turf battle on Iraq. Like many Washington battles, the fight was joined in the corridors and lost at the conference table — in this case, at a meeting of the National Security Council, in which the Pentagon received a severe dressing-down for its "obstruction" of Iraqi high-tech license applications. At the request of the State Department, which backed the Commerce Department to the hilt, Admiral Poindexter issued a National Security Decision Directive enjoining all government agencies "to be more forthcoming" on Iraqi license requests. The Pentagon, and Bryen's DTSA, were not mentioned by name. But a number of Saad 16 licenses they had rejected were listed as examples of the type of high tech that ought to be allowed to reach Iraq.

The message was clear: it was okay for U.S. companies to help Iraq design and build a ballistic missile despite the administration's stated position on the MTCR. After all, it might teach the Iranians a lesson.

At the Iraqis' request, the U.S. exchanged defense attachés soon after the renewal of diplomatic ties. Colonel Mark Pough, the first

U.S. military attaché in Baghdad in nearly twenty years, took to his new job with a passion. He had gone on a crash course in Arabic before arriving in Baghdad and was scouring the local papers for hints of what was going on at the front during the attack on Fao. The Iraqis happily introduced Pough and other U.S. officers to mid-level commanders and some senior staff officers at staff headquarters in Baghdad.

Some of the Iraqis, such as Major General Aladine Maki Khamas, had been educated in the West. General Ala, as his subordinates called him, had gone to Sandhurst in Britain, and later attended a six-month armor training course at Fort Knox. An older-generation officer ostensibly in charge of the army's Historical Directorate, General Ala was a tank driver who had commanded the only Iraqi armored division that reached Damascus before a UN ceasefire ended the 1973 Arab–Israeli war. Colonel Pough had no way of knowing that General Ala was also one of the principal operators of Saddam's clandestine financial network in Europe.

But the U.S. military men in Baghdad were not the ones running the show. The real masters of the U.S.–Iraqi alliance were the CIA. Bob Woodward of the *Washington Post* reported in August 1986 that the United States had established a secret intelligence link with Baghdad and was giving the Iraqis intelligence on Iranian troop formations and economic targets derived from U.S. satellite photographs. CIA Director William Casey negotiated the intelligence-sharing deal personally with Barzan during a trip to Amman, Jordan, in 1982, French intelligence officials say. (On the way to meet Barzan, Casey stopped off in Paris to confer with the former head of French intelligence, Alexandre de Marenches.) Casey made subsequent trips to Baghdad to see how the intelligence link was operating. "Before the U.S. had a full-time ambassador in Baghdad," a source who knew about the arrangement said, "it had a full-time chief of the station" (as the top CIA officer in U.S. embassies is known). The COS enjoyed a privileged status among Saddam's cronies and was generally consulted before Iraq launched a major offensive on the battlefield or on the diplomatic front. "The United States did in Baghdad what it did in other Arab capitals over the past three decades: it made the CIA station chief more important in local eyes than the U.S. ambassador."[12]

The satellite link came on top of a long-standing agreement to provide the Iraqis with information on Iranian air force movements gathered by U.S.-manned AWACS planes flying out of Riyadh, Saudi Arabia, and patrolling the Gulf. U.S. tactical intelligence of this sort allowed Iraq to counter potentially devastating Iranian human wave attacks in 1983 and 1984; it was so sensitive that "King Hussein of Jordan personally oversaw the transfer to Baghdad" of U.S. intelligence data. In August 1986, information from U.S. satellite photographs probably helped the Iraqis plan their first air strike against Sirri Island at the head of the Gulf, where Iran had shifted the bulk of its oil-loading operations in an effort to get them off Kharg Island and beyond the range of the Iraqi air force. To make the extra distance, half the Iraqi Mirage fighter-bombers served as fuel tanks for the planes launching the attack, using a special "buddy-buddy" refueling kit supplied by Dassault.

Alan Clark headed Britain's Department of Trade and Industry (DTI), which paralleled the U.S. Commerce Department in many ways. Like Commerce, it was responsible for promoting trade; and like Commerce, it was the lead agency in licensing the export of sensitive technology. Promoting trade and controlling trade created just as many conflicts of interest in Britain as they did in the United States. The two jobs were frankly contradictory.

Alan Clark was no "wet," as his prime minister, Margaret Thatcher, called cabinet ministers she suspected of latent liberalism. Indeed, he was an outspoken advocate of free trade, a philosophy prominently on display in the conservative pantheon. But trade promotion often conflicted with national security, as Clark would discover the hard way.

The lurid lights and blaring headlines of a major scandal were the last thing from Clark's mind as he strode down the red carpet at Saddam International Airport in November 1986. He had come to Baghdad with a mission. He wanted to convince the Iraqis to support the British machine-tool industry, instead of buying just from the Germans and the Swiss as was their habit. Clark succeeded beyond his most imprudent dreams. The Iraqis bit, and they bit hard.

Clark was greeted by his Iraqi counterpart, Trade Minister Hassan Ali, and ushered into the VIP lounge for a brief champagne reception. In Clark's briefcase was a substantial "gift" for Saddam Hussein: a new credit guarantee to finance British exports to Iraq, offered by the DTI's Export Credit Guarantee Department (ECGD). If Iraq accepted the terms, it would bring British credits to Iraq since 1983 to more than $1.2 billion (£750 million).

It was less than the United States was offering in CCC credits, but Clark hastened to explain that the British money would have fewer strings attached. It was not tied to food or agricultural purchases but could and should be used to buy British manufactured and industrial goods. Britain was about to get involved in building the Iraqi war machine.

The credit package was delivered despite an official trade embargo barring British firms from supplying Baghdad with arms, ammunition, or anything else that might "exacerbate or prolong" the six-year-old Iran–Iraq war. That policy, quietly determined at the start of the war, was reiterated with force by Foreign Minister Sir Geoffrey Howe before the House of Commons on October 29, 1985. But the official position, which specified that Her Majesty's Government "should maintain our consistent refusal to supply lethal equipment to either side," contained a loophole. It did not determine what "lethal" meant and failed to rule out weapons-manufacturing machinery. Like the Department of Commerce, DTI refused to publish a list of export licenses awarded to British manufacturers selling to Iraq and, like Commerce, this refusal was motivated by the very high number of licenses for equipment that directly fed the Iraqi war machine. Over the next four years, Britain would supply more than $1.5 billion worth of high-technology goods to Iraq according to the official trade figures it supplied the OECD.[13]

Shortly after Clark's visit, the Iranians launched a series of intensive, well-planned offensives against Basra, Fish Lake, and areas to the north, which took the Iraqis by surprise. The Karbala offensives of December 1986 and January 1987 revealed a strikingly more powerful Iranian military machine than most Western analysts believed still could exist. The key to the Iranian comeback was a secret military resupply effort orchestrated initially by the staff of President Reagan's National Security Council. The "Iran initiative" was revealed on November 4, 1986, following the release by pro-

Iranian terrorists in Beirut of American hostage David Jacobson. As the story unraveled, it became apparent that the U.S. government had violated its own embargo on arms sales to Iran in an effort to win the release of the hostages. The "private policy," which totally contradicted the U.S. public policy, had begun to undercut the efforts of Ambassador Richard Fairbanks, who had resigned as the head of Operation Staunch in September 1985 just as the NSC-sponsored arms deals began. It soon opened the floodgates to arms dealers all over the globe, hoping to make a buck in Iran.

By conservative estimates, the arsenal of American weapons sold to Iran in 1986 as part of the "initiative" topped $650 million and included:

- 10,000 to 12,000 TOW antitank missiles at the black market price of $10,000 each
- 200 Phoenix antiradar missiles at $1.8 million each
- spare parts, engines, and avionics for F-4 and F-14s, worth upwards of $150 million
- 246 Hawk missiles and radar sets worth $20 million, some of which were delivered by former National Security Advisor Robert C. McFarlane in May 1986.[14]

When this vast resupply operation was completed in late 1986, it tipped the military balance momentarily in Iran's favor. The Iraqis noticed the difference on the battlefield and in the air. Thanks to the Hawks (and to Swedish-supplied RBS-70 laser-guided missiles), Iraq lost between forty-five and forty-eight Soviet MiGs and Sukhois during the Karbala offensives, Iraqi military sources said. The Phoenix was responsible for the destruction of many of the new French Mirages, and Iranian TOWs checked Iraq's armored divisions in counterattacks to the east of Basra. For the moment the military situation had radically changed.

The U.S. deliveries revived the Iranian air force to a level it had not reached since 1982, increasing its capability by 80 percent, to 110 combat aircraft. In January 1987 U.S. satellite photos began detecting whole squadrons of Iranian F-14s in the air — up to twelve F-14s at once — whereas two years earlier Iran could barely keep two or three F-14s in the air at any time. "The Iranians have a far greater military capability than they did a year ago," a former high-ranking State Department official said ruefully in January 1987. "That is because of direct U.S. action, and because of the general discrediting of the public policy."

Sounding the alarm on the renewed vigor of the Iranian armed forces with Richard Murphy's former deputy, James Placke, who was now working with Fairbanks as a professional lobbyist on behalf of the Iraqi Embassy. The pro-Iraq lobby in Washington took the Iran-contra caper as the perfect justification of what they had been arguing all along. The United States needed to swing fully behind Iraq, with all the might of trade and aid and technology sales, to prevent the Iranian brand of radical Islam from sweeping across the Mediterranean. With the Iran-contra scandal, the last restraints on the flow of U.S. technology to Iraqi weapons projects disappeared. From then on, anything could go.

FOURTEEN

The Missiles Begin to Fly

The Iran-contra affair and the Iranian offensives at the end of 1986 convinced Saddam Hussein to accelerate his missile programs. Iraq needed a weapon capable of "bringing the war to the people of Persia," as Amer Rashid put it. "Only ballistic missiles offered us this opportunity."

In December 1986 American spy satellites picked up intense activity in southern Iraq. American diplomats and intelligence sources said that covered trucks arriving in Baghdad from the Red Sea port of Aqaba were ferrying in the largest bulk delivery of SCUD-B missiles the Soviet Union had ever made outside of Eastern Europe. The sale, which they said included as many as 300 SCUDs, came in response to a personal request by Saddam during his trip to Moscow earlier that year. But Saddam was not entirely happy with the SCUDs. He had asked for the longer-range (900 kilometer) SS-12 missiles, which would have allowed him to hit Tehran; the SCUD-B could fly only one-third the distance. To placate Iran, where the KGB had made dramatic gains over the past six years, the Soviets had refused to deliver the SS-12. They saw no reason to jeopardize their new and fruitful relationship with Tehran by allowing Saddam to win what they considered his "personal" war.

If Iraq had truly been threatened by the Iranian advances during the Karbala offensives, Saddam would not have hesitated to use his new SCUDs. He could have loaded them with nerve gas and launched them against Iranian border cities such as Dezful, as he had in 1982. The Iraqi troops managed to contain the Iranian thrusts, however. They took a beating, but they held the line around Basra by hitting back repeatedly with mustard and nerve gas agents manufactured at Samarra, al-Fallujah, and Akashat, and by dropping hundreds of U.S.-Chilean cluster bombs.

As the Soviet SCUD-Bs were being trucked from Aqaba, an Iraqi military delegation flew into São José dos Campos to watch the first successful test launch of a new Brazilian surface-to-surface missile, the SS-300. This missile, made by Avibras, was one of the many projects Brigadier Hugo de Oliveira Piva had discussed with the Iraqis two years earlier. Now the Brazilian missile could fly, but it was scarcely better adapted to Iraq's need to hit Tehran than the SCUD-B. Like the SCUD, the SS-300 had a range of just under 300 kilometers. Iraqi technicians and Brazilian industry sources say that instead of purchasing these experimental solid-fuel missiles, the Iraqis struck a deal with Piva and the Aerospace Technology Center (CTA). Half a dozen SCUD-Bs were shipped to São José dos Campos, where the Brazilians, with a little help from French and West German engineers, would reverse-engineer them.

For years the French had been helping Brazil build ballistic missiles through private firms such as Sagem, which specialized in missile guidance systems, and through state-owned companies and research labs. One of the most important of these was Intespace, based in Toulouse, the aerospace capital of France. Intespace was a joint venture owned by the French National Space Agency, Aérospatiale, Matra, and Alcatel-Espace. Intespace had trained the Brazilians in advanced ballistics and missile design and had built the CTA's entire research complex in São José dos Campos, where the Iraqis sent their engineers for training beginning in 1984.[1]

The SCUDs reached CTA's research center in early 1987, Western intelligence officials say. In special hangars off the military airstrip at São José dos Campos, Iraqi and Brazilian engineers took them apart piece by piece under the watchful eyes of a team of French missile experts. They were trying to figure out how to enlarge the SCUD's fuel tanks so they could double its range. They found that by cutting up and rewelding the fuel tanks from three SCUDs they could make longer fuel tanks for two missiles, increasing fuel capacity from four to five tons. Three hundred SCUD-Bs could thus be transformed into two hundred longer-range missiles. A bit of additional tinkering was needed on the missile warhead to reduce it from 800 kilograms to around 190 kilograms. The actual production work on the missiles was to be done in Iraq at the al-Fallujah weapons complex, at Taji, and at Saad 16.

The missile engineering agreement with Brazil was only one of a long list of military programs that swung into high gear in early 1987. The Russian refusal to provide the SS-12, combined with Iraq's worsening financial situation, gave added weight to Saddam's decision to develop an indigenous arms industry. Foreign weapons suppliers had grown leery of entering into new contracts while older deals still remained to be repaid. Even Saddam's old friend Jacques Chirac threw up his hands when confronted by the Iraqi debt. Chirac was forced by his powerful finance minister, Eduard Balladur, to put a cap on major new military sales to Iraq, despite the fact that French weapons manufacturers had earned $16 billion on Iraqi sales over the previous ten years. Balladur even blocked delivery of the last batch of Mirage fighter-bombers until the Iraqis made payments on a debt now estimated to exceed $6 billion. "What else could we have done?" a high-ranking Finance Ministry official said when asked about the de facto embargo. "Not delivering these aircraft was the only means of pressure we had if we wanted to settle the financial dispute with Baghdad once and for all. Remember: it wasn't we who were refusing to deliver, but the Iraqis who refused to pay."

Private firms continued to make a few new deals with Iraq, but they could no longer turn for loan guarantees to the Finance Ministry's export insurance and credit agency, COFAS. Whatever they exported to Iraq from December 1986 on was their own affair. Many would lose heavily because of their imprudence. The effect of Chirac's decision, one arms exporter said, "was to make Iraq's military debt a political affair. For us, this was a disaster." Dassault continued to build Mirages for Iraq, and Chirac even authorized one last sale of sixteen planes toward the end of the year, discreetly announced as a "replacement of war losses." But industry and government sources in Paris say none of these planes was delivered for as long as Iraq was at war with Iran. When they rolled off the Dassault assembly line near Bordeaux, they were wrapped in airtight cocoons to prevent deterioration and stored in hangars off the tarmac at the Bordeaux-Merignac airport. Some of them remained there for three years, while Dassault kept paying interest to the banks. It was one of the best-kept secrets of the Iran–Iraq war.

The French refusal to deliver the fighters may have been the straw that broke the Iraqi camel's back. Amer al-Saadi, the father of Iraq's ballistic missile program, offered a cool, self-confident appraisal of this difficult period during an interview in Baghdad. "The real lesson we have learned is to rely on ourselves. When we wanted things that we could not obtain from the outside for one reason or another, we made them ourselves. I am personally grateful to many of the no's we received from our arms suppliers. This made us insist, and concentrate our efforts. This was certainly the case with ballistic missiles."

Just about every military program that had been under way in Iraq was dramatically accelerated in 1987. Funding for the Sakr-80 in Egypt, a joint program to develop a solid-fuel artillery rocket based on a French design, was increased. The Iraqis told the German and Austrian contractors building Saad 16 to expedite their work. They placed large orders with German companies to complete the poison gas complex at Al-Fallujah and to expand the gas works at Samarra. Carlos Cardoen of Chile was hired to build a factory for his cluster bombs, designated Saad 38. An American company — GTE Valenite, of Royal Oak, Michigan — supplied $4.5 million worth of carbide-tipped machine tools for this plant, listing the end-user on their Department of Commerce license application (which was granted) as the Huteen State Establishment. Cardoen also contracted to build a $60 million production line code-named April 7, to build pyrotechnic fuzes for the cluster bombs and perhaps for fuel-air explosive warheads.[2]

Rush orders for the Iraqi military industries were flying around the world. Perhaps no one came under more pressure than Ekkehard Schrotz, the new director of the Consen group. Schrotz and his colleagues were told to step up acquisition of critical solid-fuel missile technology from Argentina, West Germany, the United States — wherever and however they could find it. The United States and its allies were going to close the door on sales of sensitive missile technology by ratifying the Missile Technology Control Regime, and the Iraqis were determined to get the horse out of the barn before that door closed.

Saddam's determination did not go unnoticed, and the United States' claims of ignorance about Iraq's missile and chemical weapons programs have a disingenuous ring. In late 1986, for instance, the Israelis were so worried about developments at Saad 16, the military research center outside Mosul, that they sent RF-4 reconnaissance aircraft over the site, one of which the Iraqis claimed to shoot down.[3] Israeli intelligence officials repeatedly warned the United States about the buildup of Iraq's military industries. But in some cases they were passing on information already known to the CIA, the State Department, and the White House.

Jonathan Pollard, a satellite photography analyst for the Naval Intelligence Service, was arrested and condemned to life imprisonment for having passed to Israel KH-11 satellite photographs of Iraqi military factories. For providing Israel with an "early warning" of Iraq's chemical and ballistic missile research, he was tried for treason in 1987. "The problem," he wrote in a letter subsequently published by the *Wall Street Journal*, "lay in the fact that many of the photos I turned over to the Israelis were of a number of Iraqi chemical weapons manufacturing plants which the Reagan administration did not want to admit existed. . . . The photos I gave Israel," Pollard wrote, "would have jeopardized the administration's policy of callous indifference towards this issue, in that they constituted hard, irrefutable proof that Iraq was indeed engaged in the production and widescale use of chemical weapons. What the administration was really concerned about was being placed in a position where it would have to admit that it had tacitly condoned the creation of an Iraqi chemical weapons manufacturing capability."[4] In fact, as careful analysis of the export licenses awarded U.S. companies selling high-tech goods to Iraq would show, the Department of Commerce, the State Department, and the White House knew exactly what the Iraqis were up to. And they decided to let them steam ahead.

Within the close-knit German community in Baghdad, once word got out that more weapons plants were to be built to upgrade Iraq's SCUD missiles, German manufacturers tripped over each other to snatch up the contracts. Trade figures supplied to the OECD in Paris show a dramatic rise in German exports to Iraq from 1987 to 1988, now that Saddam's ire over West German business with Iran had subsided. In four key areas — chemicals, manufactured goods, heavy machinery, and machine-tool controllers and scientific instruments — West Germany more than doubled its sales to Iraq in twelve months. Sales of iron, steel, and heavy manufactured goods rose from $104.9 million to $302 million, while sales of metal-working equipment, machine tools, and electronic switchgear to power them rose from $207 million to more than $432 million. Total West German high-tech exports to Iraq rose from $374.8 million in 1987 to $826.8 million in 1988. The West German technological powerhouse was directly feeding Iraq's heavy industrial plants. And these were almost exclusively devoted to manufacturing what Saddam wanted most: arms.

One engineering company vying for its piece of the action was run by Gerhard J. Paul, a former employee of the German state steel company Salzgitter. Company documents show that on December 13, 1986, and again on June 24, 1987, Paul signed commission agreements with an American-born Iraqi agent, in an effort to get his foot in the door. The agent, Samir A. Vincent, ran a consulting company called Torrington Investment, officially domiciled at the Geneva headquarters of the Union Bank of Switzerland. This was a common practice for arms brokers and intermediaries of all sorts to prevent investigators from discovering the true nature of their business. Although Torrington was registered in Panama on November 8, 1985, Vincent was actually based in Annandale, Virginia, and worked closely with Texas oilman Oscar Wyatt. (For his oil dealings, Vincent set up another firm, called Phoenix International, in McLean, Virginia.) Vincent had gone to school with Iraq's powerful ambassador to the United States, Nizar Hamdoon, and was a close friend of the rising star in the Baath party firmament, Colonel Hussein Kamil Hasan al-Majid, who was put in charge of SOTI in January 1987.

Connections like that commanded top dollar, and Gerhard Paul's company, Havert Industrie Handel GmbH, agreed to pay Vincent a hefty commission for access to clients at the Iraqi Ministry of Defense, contract documents show. More important, Vincent suggested he could open doors at SOTI, which was now in charge of centralizing all Iraqi purchases of weapons-manufacturing technology abroad.

The SCUD-upgrade program was the most urgent but the least ambitious of the many ballistic missile projects started in early 1987. Project 1728, as it was called, grew in scope from the cannibalization of existing Soviet-built missiles to the manufacture in Iraq of major components, including the missile cases. More and more Western companies became involved; most of them were West German, and some may have been Iraqi fronts operated in coordination with Barzan al-Tikriti's clandestine procurement network. A 1990 German Customs search of the Havert offices in Neu-Isenburg, near Frankfurt, turned up 250 file folders believed to be connected to Iraqi business. "When we opened them," said one German Customs investigator, "we discovered lots of drawings for missiles." Gerhard Paul admitted that his company received "individual drawings of stabilizers" for the missiles, but he insists his company was innocent of wrongdoing. "We are being accused of something that we did not do and about which we did not know anything," he told reporters. "Do you think that a trading company each time asks the client what the material supplied can be used for?" Nevertheless, *Stern* alleged that Paul was working on orders to ship mixing stations and a filling plant for rocket fuel.[5]

Besides Havert Consult, a number of companies were singled out in German press accounts for their contributions to the SCUD upgrade program from 1987 on.

• Tramac GmbH, owned by Eberhardt Hesse-Camozzi, a former business partner of Gerhard Paul. After ten years in Baghdad as Paul's representative, he married an Iraqi woman. His company served as a cover for Iraqi purchases of European technology intended for Project 1728.

• Leifeld & Co. (Leico). This firm supplied rocket nozzles for the missile engine.

• Graeser Technology Transfer GmbH, owned by Gert-Uwe Graeser and Ramzi al-Khatib, who claimed to be a cousin of Hussein Kamil. European intelligence sources say that al-Khatib channeled commissions on huge industrial deals into numbered bank accounts controlled by Hussein Kamil. Graeser came under investigation for having negotiated the contract for the main Taji complex for Ferrostaal, a subsidiary of the MAN group. Graeser admitted to having sold equipment to the 1728 missile project — "steel plates, for example." German Customs officials said the steel plates in question were used to reinforce the missile's jerry-rigged fuel tanks so they wouldn't fall apart during launch. Graeser also claims he knew nothing about the "content of the project" when his firm first got involved.

• Anlagen Bau Contor GmbH, of Stutensee. Created by a well-known West German nuclear specialist, Dr. Holger Beaujean, to service Project 1728 contracts, this company acknowledges having provided $4.4 million worth of valve-testing stands and laboratory equipment for the Iraqi missile program, believed to be a complete testing plant for missile propulsion systems. Beaujean later came under investigation for having supplied a plant for making liquid rocket fuel, including inhibited red fuming nitric acid, kerosene, and UDMH (unsymmetric dimethylhydrazine), which gives the fuel an extra kick. Beaujean allegedly disguised this deal as a "complete mixing station" for the "petrochemical industry." In addition to Anlagen Bau, which sometimes used the services of a mailbox company in Liechtenstein known as Transmerkur, Beaujean used his own Beaujean Consulting Engineers for 1728 deals. A search of company premises by a German court turned up blueprints for the rocket fuel plant, although Beaujean continued to proclaim his innocence. All this equipment, he told *Stern,* was for "measuring pressure, temperature, strength, and flow rates," while the test stand was intended for "destructive crushing strength tests." It was sold to an Iraqi technical school or workshop, he said, and had nothing to do with missiles.

• Mercedes-Benz. An investigation by the West German counterespionage service, the BND, showed that the German vehicle manufacturer sold SOTI twenty-eight tractor-trailer trucks, which were thought to have been converted into missile launchers. The launcher hydraulics were said to have been supplied by the French manufacturer Bennes Marrel, which had helped build the Ariane launch pad in French Guiana. Mercedes acknowledged the sale of the twenty-eight trucks but denied that it had produced or delivered missile launchers to Iraq.

• Saab-Scania. The Swedish auto maker set up a truck assembly plant in Iraq in the 1970s, but production quality was so poor that most of Iraq's heavy-duty Saab trucks were actually manufactured in Sweden. "All the Iraqis assembled locally was the nameplate," one salesman admitted sheepishly. But when Iraq finally put its new missiles on display in Baghdad, it showed them on a Saab-Scania launch vehicle. In fact, the truck cabs for the missile launchers were manufactured in the Saab plant in Brazil. Saab-Brazil filled an order for 1,000 heavy-duty cabs in 1988.

• Thyssen Industries. This industrial conglomerate had its finger in many Iraqi pies. Company officials acknowledged a delivery of thirty-five turbo pumps for Project 1728, to drive the missile's fuel system.

• Inwako GmbH, run by Friedrich-Simon Heiner, and Weihe GmbH of Kiel served as intermediaries for larger West German companies, such as MBB. Heiner and Klaus Weihe were long-standing business associates who got involved in a wide variety of shady deals, including exports of gas-centrifuge technology for enriching uranium. One of their deliveries for 1728 involved German-built gyroscopes for the guidance system.

These West German firms all claimed in their export license applications that they were selling equipment to a civilian project. To prove it, they provided certificates to the Federal Economics Agency signed by the Iraqi director of Project 1728, Dr. Modher Sadiq Saba. Written on letterhead stationery from the Nassr State Enterprise for Mechanical Industries at Taji, the certificates were nothing more than Dr. Modher's pledge that his organization would "not make re-export to third countries without approval of the Bundesamt fuer Wirtschaft." The documents made no mention of the project's nature, but for the Eschborn "controllers," that was not a problem. Missile launchers, rocket fuel, test stands, whatever — all were suitable for export to Iraq.

Iraq's most ambitious missile program came to be known as Project 395. Led by Amer al-Saadi, Project 395 was the logical synthesis of the Condor II project with Egypt and Argentina and of Iraq's collaboration on missiles with Brazil. It combined the sophisticated technology of the Condor II with the rustic do-ability of the upgraded SCUD. In early 1987, al-Saadi was given the go-ahead to transform the project into a $400 million industrial expansion program grouping four major sites:

• Saad 16, the missile R&D bureau in Mosul
• a solid-fuel manufacturing plant dubbed Project 96 run by the al-Qaqaa State Establishment, to be located some forty miles south of Baghdad near the industrial city of al-Hillah
• a missile body plant, Project 124, already under construction by German and Austrian companies within the al-Fallujah chemical weapons complex
• the an-Anbar Space Research Center, a launch site in the desert

near the Shiite holy city of Karbala, where an exact replica of Brazil's French-built aerospace research labs was to be constructed. Missile parts were also planned to be manufactured here.[6]

Project 395 tapped into the existing procurement networks set up in Europe and the United States by Consen and the Egyptian Defense Ministry. But instead of focusing on the Condor II, which would have meant at least some sharing with Argentina and Egypt, the Iraqis now concentrated on building their own missile. A new organization was set up in Baghdad to centralize purchasing. Ultimately supervised by Hussein Kamil but operating on daily guidance from Amer al-Saadi, it was called the Technical Corps for Special Projects, Techcorps, or the even shorter Teco. The Germans referred to Project 395 as DOT.

Research on missile guidance, trajectory plotting, and warheads was conducted at Saad 16. A sophisticated wind tunnel, supplied by the West German firm Aviatest, a subsidiary of Rheinmetall, allowed Iraqi and West German ballistics engineers to test potential designs to achieve the best aerodynamic properties. Computers supplied by a host of American companies, including Electronic Associates, Inc., Gould, Tektronics, Hewlett-Packard, Digital Equipment Corp., and International Imaging, allowed the Iraqis and their helpers to simulate missile flights and to make subtle design changes as they discovered flaws. Other specialized laboratories researched new cryogenic fuel mixtures, with technology obtained from China via Brazil. MBB, which continued its deliveries to Saad 16 despite urging from the West German government that it stop, pointed out that its equipment was reaching Iraq through former employees and intermediaries. "One shouldn't make links between the company and people who have worked in our company and who are now delivering to Iraq," a spokesman said. "Those people are simply buying on the open market."

Project 96, or the al-Qaqaa propellant plant at al-Hillah, was a major achievement. Amer Al-Saadi had been envious of his colleagues in Egypt for many years. In 1979, the Egyptians had purchased a turnkey chemicals plant from PEPCON in the United States, to make ammonium perchlorate, a controlled substance that was the principal ingredient in most solid-fuel propellants for rockets and missiles. The plant, built at the Abu Zaabal Company for Specialty Chemicals, was known as Factory 18 and was out in the desert beyond the Cairo suburb of Heliopolis. In March 1980 the Egyptians approached PEPCON to build a second ammonium perchlorate line, but they were apparently turned down.

In December 1980, however, according to documents obtained by CNN, PEPCON received another request for an ammonium perchlorate plant, this time from a firm in Salzburg called In-duplan-Chemie. Induplan said that they wanted to build an AP plant "for a client in the western hemisphere" whose name would be revealed once a cooperation contract had been signed. The client was Argentina. Induplan-Chemie belonged to the BOWAS group, which was partially owned by the von Bohlen und Halbach family, the heirs to the Krupp fortune. Their principal company, Bohlen Industries of Essen, had spawned Consen in the early 1980s. The ammonium perchlorate plant was intended to fuel Condor II.

Amer al-Saadi, who had followed these developments with great interest, was determined to do what the Egyptians had done, and better. With Consen's help he set up an entire AP plant at al-Hillah. Here the propellant was manufactured, mixed with an aluminum stabilizer and a binder, then poured into the missile bodies. On cooling, it hardened into a solid cake. X-ray equipment checked the missile bodies for faults before filling. The operation was so successful, al-Saadi said in an interview in May 1989, that Iraq began selling stabilizer compounds for solid fuel propellants to Egypt. "All this talk you read in the international press about Argentina is pure nonsense," he scoffed. "Look at Argentina: do they have a missile? No. But we in Iraq do. So why should we be funding Argentina? Our missile has been proven, everyone could see it and what it could do: and it is purely Iraqi."

While Amer al-Saadi was the technical genius behind the Iraqi missile programs, he owed his success to one man: Hussein Kamil al-Majid, who was on his way to becoming the second most powerful figure in the Baathist regime after Saddam. His rise to power had been so rapid and so complete that many Iraq-watchers believed he could be the next on Saddam's hit list. In January 1987, Saddam put Hussein Kamil in charge of SOTI and gave him orders to throw all of Iraq's resources into the building up of the military industries. Hussein Kamil was Saddam's son-in-law as well as his cousin.

Hussein Kamil had joined the army in 1968 shortly after the Baath party seized power. After being promoted to lieutenant, he caught Saddam's eye and was detailed to presidential security. He soon became a trusted bodyguard and accompanied Saddam's wife and daughters on shopping trips to London in the late 1970s and early 1980s. "He was little more than a package bearer," Iraqi exiles who crossed him at the time say. "Like someone carrying a basket of fruit." But because he was Saddam's cousin, he was "family" and could converse with the women, whereas men outside the family could not.

Saddam's official biographer, Amir Iskander, says Hussein Kamil personally prevented an assassin from killing Saddam in 1982 or 1983. Whether or not this is true, in 1983 he asked to marry Saddam's oldest daughter, Ragha. This led to a quarrel between Saddam and his half-brother, Barzan, who had his eye on Ragha as a future wife for his own son. Hussein Kamil got the girl. Barzan was sent off to Switzerland and was stripped of his post as head of the Mukhabarat, although he kept control over the family billions.

With a propitious marriage under his belt, Hussein Kamil was promoted to colonel. In 1984 and 1985 he frequently accompanied Saddam on tours of the front lines, and he appears next to the Iraqi president in many photographs of that time. By 1986 Saddam decided he wanted a family member to supervise SOTI, so he shifted Hussein Kamil over to serve as an aide to Amer Rashid al-Ubeidi to learn the ropes. Within a year, Hussein Kamil was promoted to brigadier and became Amer Rashid's boss. In addition to running SOTI, he was put in charge of the newly created National Security Council within the Amn-al-Khass (Presidential Security Bureau), where he was supposed to supervise Iraq's efforts to procure Western military technology.

At thirty-one, Hussein Kamil looked like a younger version of Saddam. Swarthy, thick-jawed, with a full black mustache and a decided swagger, he wasted no time in exerting the authority Saddam had invested in him. Within months he transformed SOTI from a technical appendage of the Ministry of Defense into a full-fledged industrial ministry and procurement agency under his sole command. At first it was called the Military Production Authority. Later it became known as the Ministry of Industry and Military Industrialization, or MIMI for short.

Hussein Kamil was told by Saddam to exploit the vast clandestine procurement networks in Europe and the United States to the fullest. Every arms seller in the world soon claimed to know Hussein Kamil al-Majid; those who didn't wished they did. The State Department's Richard Murphy, who met the Iraqi after leaving U.S. government service, described him as "glib, smart. He was a quick study, and immediately grasped the essentials. This was somebody who was used to exerting his authority. He was a carbon copy of Saddam."

Even at this stage, however, he was giving Saddam trouble. His taste for luxury made him the butt of jokes in Baghdad, and his greed was well known to foreign contractors. He was said to demand a 10 percent commission on all major weapons purchases, which he placed in a numbered account in Switzerland. In one meeting in Baghdad, Chinese officials from the state marketing agency, Norinco, presented Hussein Kamil with a mahogany box containing a solid gold .38-caliber pistol chased with purple and ivory enamel. After examining the pistol, Kamil turned the box upside down, looking for an envelope. Finding nothing, he handed it indifferently to an aide.[7]

Hussein Kamil's former boss, Amer Rashid al-Ubeidi, vividly recalled the dramatic changes that occurred at this time: "When our present minister, Hussein Kamil, took over this job in early 1987, he started out with a plan to make better use of existing resources, without adding anything new. As a result, we saw jumps — not just increases — in production rates at existing establishments. Then he launched an extensive program of research and development in 1987. The results were unbelievable even to those of us who took part in this effort. The secret? New, highly motivated management and intensive support from the government, which made developing our military industries a top priority. All this was thanks to our minister, and his especially close ties to our president. It has meant a revolution in our military establishment. Every step along the way has been like a high mountain. If you had asked me two or three years ago if we could do such things, I would have told you you were out of your mind."[8]

Christopher Drogoul was frantic. His friend and business contact at the Central Bank of Iraq, Sadiq Taha, had made an unusual request, and neither Drogoul nor his associates at the Atlanta branch of BNL were certain they would be able to fulfill it in time. Drogoul had gone to Washington to meet with Taha and a trade delegation on January 10, 1987. Taha spent the next few days at the Johns Hopkins University Medical Center, undergoing tests for a chronic heart problem. While he was there, he asked Drogoul for a favor. Could the banker pick up a few hand-held television sets for the Iraqis to take home with them? Drogoul agreed immediately. It wasn't until he phoned to Atlanta that he realized he had a problem. American televisions don't use the same video standards as the French-built SECAM system in Iraq, and Von Wedel spent three days scouring every video store in Atlanta before he came up with some Panasonics that were adaptable to the French standard. But Drogoul's orders were firm: Von Wedel was to do anything to please their best client, even if that meant dropping legitimate bank business to run personal errands.

By the time Von Wedel arrived in Washington on the fourteenth, Drogoul had already agreed in principle to advance the Iraqis $650 million in agricultural loans for the year, and Von Wedel was carrying all the necessary papers for the signing the next day. When the two men got together in the Jefferson Hotel that evening, Drogoul told Von Wedel about the shopping spree he had offered Taha and his colleague from the Rafidain Bank, Dr. Abdul Munim Rasheed. After purchasing a year's supply of heart medicine for Taha, Drogoul trooped them through a Washington shopping mall, where the two Iraqis took a liking to some casual shirts. Drogoul was only too happy to settle the bill, but when they got back to the hotel, Drogoul said, hardly able to keep a straight face, Taha and Rashid had sheepishly cut out the "Made in Israel" labels. They really had liked those shirts, Drogoul explained. It would have been a pity not to take them back to Iraq.

Court records in Atlanta show that Drogoul and Von Wedel signed three agreements with the Iraqis the next evening during a reception at the Vista Hotel sponsored by the U.S. Wheat Board. The agreements committed BNL Atlanta to providing $562 million in short-term CCC loans, $25 million in freight financing, and another $57 million in midterm GSM-103 credits, a new program under the CCC umbrella. As Von Wedel recalls, the Iraqis were overjoyed at the signing until it was time for them to present their own gifts to the Atlanta bankers. Von Wedel, with a few whiskeys under his belt, found the occasion hilarious. When he opened the jeweler's box and saw a watch, he shouted in glee. "This is great, my kids will love it. A G.I. Joe watch!" Drogoul's face fell, and Sadiq Taha was visibly annoyed. It wasn't a G.I. Joe watch but a Swiss timepiece bearing the face of Saddam Hussein. Many an arms dealer would have sold his wife into slavery to receive a similar expression of esteem.[9]

On the other side of the Atlantic, Roy Ricks was about to make the deal of his lifetime. A British businessman from Essex, Ricks had recently lost his job as managing director of Modern Fire Alarms International. He was looking around for another job when he stumbled across Anees Mansour Wadi, an acquaintance from Baghdad who had worked for Ricks years before as a fire alarm salesman. Now Wadi told Ricks that he had hooked up with a powerful official from Baghdad named Kassim Abbas, who had been sent to Europe on an industrial shopping spree.

Kassim Abbas drove a big Mercedes and wore expensive ties and elegant suits. To his neighbors at 5, Via Ampere in the Italian industrial town of Monza, he was "reserved and nice." Like his brother, Abdul Hussein, an engineer with whom he shared the house near Milan, he spoke fluent Italian. No one would have guessed that he was working for Barzan Ibrahim al-Tikriti, the former head of Iraqi intelligence, or that he was involved in the search for new weapons technology in Europe. The Abbas brothers ran a small company in Monza called European Manufacturer Center, or Euromac, which exported industrial machinery. Kassim Abbas never hesitated to tell his suppliers that "almost all of our clients are in Iraq." Their specialty was air conditioning equipment, they said. The business was so lucrative that Abdul Hussein soon purchased a big BMW to rival his brother's Mercedes.[10] The "air conditioning equipment," "household appliances," and "furniture" they were shipping to Baghdad were intended for government buildings — not offices, but military plants.

Abbas wanted Wadi to set up a similar company in Great Britain. So with Ricks, Wadi formed Meed International Ltd., based at 13 Duke Street, in London's Mayfair district. Like Kassim Abbas,

Wadi now called himself an engineer who "specialized in air conditioning equipment."

Using introductions from the commercial attaché at the Iraqi embassy in London, Wadi and Ricks contacted British machine tool companies to find out what was available for export to the Iraqi market (other than air conditioning equipment, which it appears they never sold). Iraq was planning to expand its industrial complex at Taji, Wadi said, and wanted British companies to get their fair share of the cake. There was no reason why Iraq should privilege the West German tool-making industry, especially now that the Germans were cozying up to Iran.

That was enough to open the doors. In Coventry, where many British tool makers are based, Wadi and Ricks made the rounds. By spring 1987 they had made enough contacts to set up a whirlwind tour for a top-level Iraqi delegation headed by Dr. Safa Haboby. At the time, Haboby was still in charge of the Taji weapons complex, and doubled as managing director of its purchasing arm, the Nassr State Enterprise for Mechanical Industries. In addition to his qualifications as an engineer and an efficient plant manager, Safa Haboby was now serving as Hussein Kamil's bagman, signing contracts and distributing commissions.

The first deal Wadi and Ricks put together was worth some $10.2 million (£6.4 million), and it only paved the way for more. Wickman Bennett, a machine-tool company that belonged to the Berisford group, could not have had any doubts as to the real use of the machines the Iraqis had ordered. According to a report in the *Sunday Times* of London, the contract between Wickman Bennett and Meed stated that the machines were programmed to produce mortar shells of calibers ranging from 60 to 120 mm. There could be no doubt that Taji was a weapons plant.

Dr. Haboby invited four British machine-tool makers to meet with the Iraqi commercial attaché in Bonn, Dr. Ali Muttalib Ali, to discuss money. To their surprise, the four Brits were not alone. Rival companies had sent their own delegations for the circus, and the tool makers jostled each other on their way into the Iraqi embassy. The Iraqis "were changing the goalposts all the time," said one engineer who attended these negotiating sessions. "The order they'd discussed with us in Britain was doubled on the spot."[11]

One British company eager to jump on the Iraqi bandwagon was TI Machine Tools, of Coventry. Discussions reached an advanced stage on two contracts for Iraqi weapons plants worth $31.5 million (£19 million), to supply equipment for making cluster bombs at Carlos Cardoen's Huteen factory and artillery shells at Taji. Other deals were signed by BSA Machine Tools of Birmingham, to equip the April 7 artillery fuze factory, and by Colchester Lathes. This company won two separate contracts to supply machine tools for the al-Qaqaa explosives and propellant factory in al-Hillah, and for the Badr General Establishment at al-Yusufiyah. The corporate director responsible for Colchester, Lathes, Hugh Ashton, said later that his company had no idea that al-Qaqaa was a munitions plant; they had been led to believe that the Badr plant made consumer goods. Colchester soon opened an office in Baghdad with a staff of about twenty.

The sudden boom in Iraqi business worked wonders for the British tool-making industry. According to the Machine Tool Technologies Association (MTAA), sales from British tool makers to Iraq jumped from £2.9 million in 1987 to more than £31.5 million in 1988. The MTAA would become a powerful addition to the pro-Iraq lobby. Like other trade lobbies in West Germany and the United States, it threw its full weight behind the Iraqi ventures. And none of them could pretend they didn't know what it was all about.

Hussein Kamil's "new, motivated management" began to reorganize Iraqi procurement networks in Europe and the United States with a flourish. Mansour Wadi was promoted and given a license to sign on new suppliers. One of his finest discoveries was a West German technology concern called H+H Metalform, located in Drensteinfurt, near Münster. This small company, run by two engineers, Dietrich Hinze and Peter Hütten, was about to expand into almost every corner of the Iraqi technology shopping basket.

Documents show that Mansour Wadi sent a fax message on June 22, 1987, from Meed in London to Peter Hütten in Drensteinfurt. The subject was listed as "122, 130, 152, 155 mm," and the message began: "In reference to our telephone conversation, we thank you for sending prices for our request." Three days later, H+H sent a fax to the Nassr State Enterprise at Taji, referring to yet another "request" that had been received through Meed, this one for "drop tanks" believed to be intended for the dispersal of chemical weapons agents from aircraft.

On a list drawn up by the Iraqi Embassy in Bonn of forty European companies that had proved willing to supply equipment for Iraq's weapons industry, H+H figured in first place.[12] H+H and a grab bag of other small German technology specialists soon got to work on Techcorp's most advanced project: a uranium enrichment plant.

Moshe Tal was not the type of person you would have imagined to swallow the Iraqi hook. An Israeli citizen who had fought in the Israel Defense Forces, he emigrated to the United States in 1972, drawn by promises of a more prosperous life. He started off with nothing, working as a cab driver. But by 1980 he had saved enough to start his own company in Arizona. As business picked up he expanded, moving to Las Vegas and then to Oklahoma City. Tal, a genius when it came to chemistry, specialized in formulating mixtures that could be added to ordinary fuels to give them extra punch. Tal's most promising product, RPV, was developed with military markets in mind. It boosted the power of jet fuel, gasoline, and, especially, liquid rocket fuel.

In March 1987, Tal was contacted by a Texan named Art Valentz, who eventually identified himself as the Houston agent for the Iraqi-born tycoon Ihsan Barbouti. Barbouti had made a fortune in Libya and Iraq, supplying industrial complexes through an international network called IBI Industries. Without going into details about Barbouti's true business, Valentz told Moshe Tal that IBI was interested in buying his company, TK-7 Corp. The letters stood for Tal and Keiden, the two investors. "I guess the 7 was thrown in because they thought it was lucky," says Tal's Oklahoma City lawyer, Mike Johnston.

Court documents show that Barbouti himself went to Oklahoma City to meet with Tal in April 1987. He mentioned in passing that he had recently purchased the Atlantic City, New Jersey, version of the Sands casino in Las Vegas. Barbouti also described his extensive oil and gas industry holdings in Houston. But the real subject of discussion, Tal realized later, was the purchase of TK-7, so that Tal's expertise could help fuel Iraqi missiles on their way to targets in Tel Aviv and Tehran. At the time, of course, Barbouti never mentioned Iraq. He told Tal that IBI was based in New York City.

But that was not all. When Tal questioned him about IBI companies in West Germany, Hong Kong, Belgium, Austria, Switzerland, Great Britain, and Italy, Barbouti replied that they were all "paper companies" owned and controlled by the Barbouti family. "He told me that IBI stood for Ihsan Barbouti International and that he generally modeled his logo after IBM," Tal recalls. "Dr. Barbouti also said that he had created numerous companies that were merely to hold ostensible ownership of individual investment properties (in the United States and elsewhere), but that the real ownership of the investment property always went into the Barbouti family trust."[13]

Negotiations advanced quickly, and Barbouti expounded on his ambitions for the new and improved version of TK-7. He and Tal would set up companies in Europe called TK-7 International and Petchad (Liechtenstein). A financial front called Mesca was to be set up in Panama. In the United States, they would establish IBI Chemical Company International, which would ship raw chemicals to Europe to blend to European specifications. This struck Tal as "feasible, since TK-7 fuel additives would not necessarily be blended in the same way," depending on the fuel with which they were combined.

In May, Barbouti returned to Oklahoma City and convinced Tal to interrupt a planned public offering of company stock so that IBI could buy out the entire operation. "Although I thought Dr. Barbouti was eccentric and inconsistent," Tal says, "I did not suspect any ulterior motives at that time."

Those suspicions would only come later.

On April 16, 1987, in Rome, six Western countries and Japan announced their intention to stop the spread of ballistic missiles to the Third World. After years of haggling, the Missile Technology Control Regime was formally adopted by the United States, Britain, Canada, France, Italy, Japan, and West Germany. The MTCR was a potentially useful tool for controlling exports of equipment and technology that could be used for designing and building ballistic missiles. Some of its measures had been crafted to stop the Iraqi and Libyan missile programs before they got off the ground. But for Frank Gaffney, who worked on the MTCR during the

Reagan administration and later resigned from the Pentagon in protest, the control regime offered too little too late. "It was like closing the barn door after the horse has already left," he said.

Government controls on exports are always a touchy subject. Industry opposes them, because they put a damper on sales; the White House usually opposes them, since they limit the president's flexibility in executing foreign policy; and America's allies abroad scream in protest about U.S. protectionism, since (they argue disingenuously) American export controls tend to favor sales by American industries while restricting sales by Europe and Japan. Missile technology controls were even more sensitive than most, because Europe's missile industry thrived on exports to the Third World. This was the main reason that it had taken so long to get the G-7 allies to adopt the MTCR, long after the United States had informally (and ineffectively) started enforcing it in 1985.

The export control "czar" during the Reagan administration was Assistant Secretary of Defense Richard Perle, who led the U.S. effort to stem the flow of high-technology goods to the USSR and to limit the spread of missile technologies to the Third World. As Perle discovered, resistance to the idea of controlling missile technology was not limited to America's allies abroad or even to the missile industry; it was strongest within certain departments of the United States government. Eighteen months after the United States began informally adhering to the MTCR, Perle wrote to senators John Glenn, Sam Nunn, and Barry Goldwater to protest the lack of cooperation he had received from the Department of Commerce and the State Department. The only way for the Defense Department to obtain information on proliferation cases transmitted from U.S. embassies through State Department channels, Perle said, was "to crash the party."

Senator Glenn was so incensed by this state of affairs that he held hearings on the MTCR in February 1987, just two months before the control regime was officially ratified. Glenn read the riot act to the State Department's Ambassador Richard T. Kennedy, who was in charge of nonproliferation policy, for his failure to cooperate with the Pentagon on missile technology controls. State had increasingly shifted diplomatic cables on proliferation issues "out of the normal channels available to all agencies with a need to know and into special channels such as STADIS, State Department

Dissemination only, and NODIS, no dissemination without the approval of Ambassador at Large [Richard] Kennedy," Glenn said, reading from a Defense Department report. "Out of about 1,000 NODIS and STADIS cables, DoD has received approximately two percent. At the same time, the State Department has virtually eliminated DoD clearances of outgoing nonproliferation cables."

Unperturbed, Kennedy replied: "Senator, let me just say that it has been a long time since I have been in the government when I have heard such poppycock. . . . One of the problems is that there are some people who do not have enough to do. We would love to see them have worthwhile work to do, rather than perhaps playing with preparing fact sheets on their desks or throwing darts at dart boards in their offices."[14]

The dart throwers Kennedy was referring to were Richard Perle and Stephen Bryen, the head of the Defense Technology Security Administration, whose job was to screen high-technology exports for potential threats to U.S. and allied security. Kennedy's testimony made it clear that Perle and Bryen were encountering extraordinary resistance inside the Reagan administration in their attempt to prevent Iraq from building a ballistic missile. But Glenn's hearings had little practical effect. Kennedy remained at his post, the Commerce Department continued to brush off attempts to limit U.S. high-technology exports to Iraq, and the MTCR soon became, in the words of Senator John McCain, "a pious fraud."[15] If the U.S. government was so divided on a critical issue such as ballistic missile proliferation, it was no wonder that West Germany and France failed to take Pentagon and CIA protests about their missile exports seriously. As Perle ruefully put it, the demarches just bounced off the allies like marshmallows.

On August 5, 1987, Saddam Hussein made a dramatic announcement that was greeted with universal indifference in the West. Two days earlier, Iraq had successfully test-fired a new ballistic missile, the president said. The missile, dubbed al-Hossein, had been designed by an Iraqi team headed by Dr. Amer Hamoudi al-Saadi. The design team reported directly to the secretary general of the president's office, Dr. Hamid Hammadi, not to the Defense Ministry, which was still controlled by Adnan Khairallah. The missile had flown 615 kilometers, just short of its planned maximum range of 650 kilometers, and had landed in the designated target area. That was more than double the distance of the SCUD-B, the most powerful missile then known to be in Iraqi inventory. Nobody believed that what Saddam claimed was possible, except for a handful of hard-liners within the Reagan administration and the intelligence community. As one U.S. intelligence analyst put it, "We suddenly realized we had a missile problem in Iraq." The al-Hossein launch provided the first real clue that Iraq had another missile program in addition to its participation in Condor II.

Two months later, a pair of senior American officials arrived at Roissy–Charles de Gaulle Airport to deliver a top-secret message to the French government. The two officials, who described their visit later in background interviews on condition they remain anonymous, told the French they had discovered a clandestine Iraqi procurement network that was operating on French soil. Two French trading companies were serving as intermediaries for Iraqi weapons and technology purchases, they said. One was at 99, Champs-Élysées, while the other was just around the corner at 43, avenue Marceau. What concerned the Americans most, however, were sales of ballistic missile technology directly to Iraq and through Argentina, Brazil, and Egypt. "The company that really bothered us was Sagem," the officials said; Sagem was one of the largest defense electronics contractors in France, specializing in gyroscopes and inertial guidance systems.

In documents the Americans said had been taken from the offices of Consen SA in Zug, Switzerland, in June 1987, Sagem was listed as one of the companies Consen turned to for special assistance on its missile projects. Sagem was working on every missile project in France, including the Ariane space rocket, and it had cooperation agreements with Argentina, Egypt, and Brazil. The American officials presented details to the French of Sagem's contribution to Condor II and to Project 1728. When they had finished talking, the French politely ushered them out and assured them they would take care of the matter.

One of the French officials who received the American demarche on Sagem gave his own account in an interview two years later. "Of course we were aware of what Sagem was doing," the official said. "We had to be: we had given them official approval! We explained to our American friends that we had different notions of how best to enforce the MTCR. Our view was that we could be more effective in keeping an eye on worrisome missile programs as they were developing if we showed some cooperation and understanding to the countries involved."

Sagem does appear to have acted more prudently, after the American protest. Later sales of gyroscopes and guidance kits to Iraq were earmarked for the Vulcan Project, the artillery deal negotiated by Sarkis Soghenalian. French officials and defense industry sources confirmed that at least 200 additional NSM 20 guidance kits were shipped to Iraq in this way, in three separate follow-on contracts. They were ostensibly used on AMX-10 light-armor reconnaissance vehicles, to enable Iraqi gunners to aim their 155 GCT guns with pinpoint precision. But the Iraqis themselves, starting with Amer Rashid, acknowledged that some of these systems had been adapted for use on ballistic missiles.

France was not the only European country to receive a barrage of "demarche-mallows." A similar note was delivered by the minister-counselor of the U.S. Embassy in Rome to the Italian government, protesting sales to the Condor II project of solid-fuel propellant technology by Snia Bpd. Like Snia Techint, which delivered nuclear hot cells to Iraq in the early 1980s, Snia BpD belonged to the Fiat group, one of Italy's largest industrial conglomerates. The Italians immediately launched an official investigation, and a few weeks later delivered their official whitewash to the Americans, according to a *Financial Times* correspondent, Alan Friedman. In the top-secret telegram they sent on to Washington, the Italians noted that "only a small part of the activity of Snia BpD is not in complete harmony with the Missile Technology Control Regime," and these activities "have already been stopped," Friedman wrote. Snia Bpd was much more interested in participating in the lucrative SDI program in the United States than in contributing to an Iraqi ballistic missile, the Italians said.

In the meantime, however, Representative Howard Berman and others on Capitol Hill disbarred Snia for six months from all defense contracts with the Pentagon. A high-level team from Snia's Rome headquarters went to Washington in the fall of 1987, imploring Berman and the Pentagon to take Snia off the embargo list. What had concerned the Americans most was a contract to deliver to Iraq the secrets of a new solid-fuel propellant that Snia had jointly developed with the French state-owned explosives manufacturer SNPE (Société Nationale des Poudres et Explosifs). The new propellant, called propergol, was to be used in the solid-fuel boosters strapped onto the Ariane V rocket. A compromise was finally reached a few months later, and in April 1988 Snia was taken off the black list.

Business was so good for Mansour Wadi and Roy Ricks that they needed help; Meed International was swamped. On August 12, 1987, Mansour Wadi sent a fax message to the Iraqi commercial attaché in Bonn, Ali M. Ali, listing potential European suppliers for an Iraqi industrial project. He told Ali that he had arranged meetings for Thursday, August 20, and Friday, August 21, with a series of companies from Finland, Switzerland, and France. One of the companies, La Physique Appliqué Industries (LPAI) of France, was then under investigation by DTSA and U.S. Customs for illegally exporting American computer-chip-manufacturing equipment to the USSR. "The rest of the companies are British," Wadi wrote, "and I will arrange for meetings to be held in London, week beginning Monday 24 August 1987."

These small high-tech firms specialized in equipment needed to shape nuclear warheads and to manufacture carbon-carbon fiber, which the Iraqis were seeking to build ballistic missile nose cones. The equipment Wadi mentioned in his fax — hot isostatic presses and annealing furnaces — would figure in other procurement schemes in the United States and the United Kingdom. Pentagon intelligence analysts who viewed this list said the equipment was "clearly intended for ballistic missile and possibly nuclear weapons applications."

At the same time, Wadi made another call to H+H Metalform and arranged to buy centrifuge-manufacturing equipment for uranium enrichment. Iraq was in the process of setting up a top-secret enrichment plant near the site of the bombed-out French reactor in Thuwaitha.

Weapons factories, machine tools, ballistic missiles, uranium enrichment: it was too much for Wadi and his partners, Kassim and Abdul Hussein Abbas. So in September 1987, they requested that the Iraqi government play a more direct role in the procurement schemes. In October, Wadi located a small British firm called Echo-save Ltd., which he arranged for the Iraqis to buy out for a song, giving them a foothold in the European Community. To make sure that the purchase could not be traced back to the Iraqi government, it was worked through a front company in Baghdad called Al-Araby Trading.

Al-Araby bought Echosave and renamed it the Technology and Development Group, or TDG, which was entered on the commercial registry in London on October 13, 1987 (registry number 2150590). Offices were established at 2 Stratford Place. The head of the new company, chosen from the board of Al-Araby Trading in Baghdad, was no stranger to Iraq's British and German suppliers. It was Hussein Kamil's bagman, Dr. Safa Jawad al-Haboby.

Also on the Al-Araby board was another Iraqi from the clandestine network, who would play a major role in coming events. Fadel Jawad Kadhum had received his law degree from the University of Montpellier in France. Like his former roommate, Christopher Drogoul, who now ran the BNL agency in Atlanta, Kadhum was energetic, enthusiastic, and pushing forty. But Kadhum did not have to skirt the law in his country to make his fortune; he had the full and open support of the Iraqi leadership. "Fadel Kadhum was our privileged point of entry when we needed to speak to Hussein Kamil," executives at one French aerospace company said. He spoke fluent French in addition to his good English, and he had an excellent eye for business. But more than anything else, Fadel Kadhum was a top clandestine operator, who knew how to disguise a money trail so thoroughly that it would stump the best investigators.

At Kadhum's prompting, TDG immediately set up a second front company in Great Britain to create yet another screen between its procurement activities and the government of Iraq. The new company was called TMG Engineering. Its first official act was to buy out TI Machine Tools of Coventry, for some $9 million. Before the Iraqi purchase, the company was already on the auction block. But within weeks, TI Machine Tools was given a new name — Matrix Churchill Ltd. — and plenty of new business.

Owning a machine tool company gave the Iraqis unlimited access to sophisticated manufacturing equipment with only minimal controls. Within days of taking charge of the new company, TDG placed its first order, a $31.5 million deal for 150 computer-driven lathes, enough to equip a very large armaments factory. And indeed, that was where the machine tools were headed. By Matrix Churchill's admission, the lathes were shipped to the Huteen State Establishment, where Carlos Cardoen was making his cluster bombs. Other machines from this order were sent to Taji. Thirteen others, according to documents obtained by the BBC, went to Saad 16.[16] Nobody cared where the machines were headed. The business was good and sorely needed. Instead of laying employees off, Matrix Churchill expanded its work force to 470.

To get financing for these and other deals to equip Iraqi weapons plants, Fadel Kadhum turned to his old schoolmate, Chris Drogoul, at the BNL. He also arranged for a 15 percent "commission" on all Matrix Churchill and other BNL-sponsored loans, to be paid into account number 706655 at the Paris headquarters of the Union de Banques Arabes et Françaises (UBAF).[17] This account, controlled by Kadhum and Al-Araby directors, was used to distribute kickbacks into secret Iraqi accounts at the Bank of Credit and Commerce International (BCCI) in Grand Cayman, Luxembourg, and Switzerland, where the money could be recycled into the weapons business or stashed away for the benefit of Saddam's Tikriti clan. It was all borrowed money anyway.

Moshe Tal, the rocket fuel specialist, became suspicious when Ihsan Barbouti showed up late for their meeting in Zurich in September 1987. Barbouti had asked Tal to meet with him and an associate who ran the Belgian shipping company Cross Link. They were to confirm plans for Tal to purchase chemicals for Barbouti in the United States and ship them to the Cross Link warehouses in Antwerp, where they would be blended to meet "European specifications." Where they went after that was anybody's guess. Josef Gedopt, Barbouti's associate, was supposed to do the rest.

When Barbouti failed to arrive on time, Moshe Tal called his London office to find out where he was, since the two were supposed to fly on together to Britain. After a quick check, the secretary told him that Barbouti's flight into Zurich had been delayed. He should check the arrival time with the Libyan Arab Airways counter; Barbouti was flying in from Tripoli.

When Barbouti finally arrived at the Zurich airport, Tal ushered him into the lounge and offered him a drink. By the time the next flight to London was ready for boarding, the Iraqi was thoroughly intoxicated. Taking advantage of Barbouti's state, Tal began plying him with questions about the true nature of his business. "Dr. Barbouti told me that he had several projects going in Libya," Tal recalls, "including an industrial park and a water purification plant. When I asked him about the water purification plant, Dr. Barbouti told me that Colonel Qaddafi wanted a plant to produce heavy water in order to be able to construct an atom bomb. He said that Qaddafi was considering a scheme whereby Qaddafi would smuggle an atomic device into United States waters aboard a commercial shipping vessel and blow up an American port city with a nuclear blast, in retaliation for the United States' raid on Tripoli."

Until these drunken revelations, Tal says he had had no idea that Barbouti was working on Libya's heavy-water plant at Homs, nor that he had helped put together the Rabta chemical weapons plant with Dr. Jürgen Hippenstiel-Imhausen of West Germany. But now he became suspicious. When they separated in London, Tal went to see an old friend in Israeli intelligence. After an initial check, the Israeli told him that Mossad had never heard of Barbouti but would take a closer look.

In meetings the next month in Zurich and London, Tal says he became convinced that Barbouti's real intent was to purchase his company so he could lay hands on the TK-7 rocket-fuel formula. Barbouti urged Tal to give his formula to a Liechtenstein trust company for "safekeeping," to prevent unscrupulous individuals from stealing it. At one meeting, Barbouti offered Tal a significant amount of cash if he would liquidate his company and get rid of the other stockholders. Barbouti said he and his family would purchase all the assets of TK-7.

Tal's suspicions peaked when he discovered that one of his chemists was delivering chemical formulas and information on company activities to Barbouti. Later he learned that among the men present at the London meetings in the fall of 1987 was Sabbowi Ibrahim al-Tikriti, a half-brother of Saddam Hussein, who played a key role in clandestine procurement. In the end, Tal severed relations with the Iraqi and took the information to a friend, Bob Corbin, who was then serving as the Arizona state attorney general. Corbin informed Arizona Senator Dennis De-

Concini, who was deeply concerned about the proliferation aspects of the case. DeConcini turned the matter over to the new CIA director, William Webster, who had just replaced the ailing William Casey. Only later did Tal's Mossad friends get back to him with overwhelming evidence that Barbouti was involved in strategic weapons projects for both Libya and Iraq. Tal's misadventure may have tipped off the CIA and the intelligence community that Project Iraq was about to blow.[18]

FIFTEEN

The Race for Armageddon

The leadership change in Iraq's defense industries sent ripples throughout the entire military establishment. Most concerned over the ascendancy of Saddam's son-in-law, Hussein Kamil, was another prominent family member, Defense Minister Adnan Khairallah. Since 1978 he had ruled over everything military, making sure that the professional soldiers adhered to the Baath party line. With the advent of Hussein Kamil and his autonomous Military Production Authority, Khairallah's fiefdom was shrinking daily.

Iraq's foreign cooperation partners also felt the change. French technicians working in a huge Iraqi army complex known as Base West World (BWW), 200 kilometers south of Baghdad in the industrial city of As Samawah, noted the shift in late 1987. Iraqi engineers now insisted on doing the repair work themselves, rebuilding engines on French, German, and Brazilian tanks. Other teams of Iraqis upgraded older Soviet tanks with night-vision devices obtained from a Dutch company called Delft Instruments NV (Delft had imported them illegally from Hughes in the United States, claiming they were to be used by the Dutch army). Base West World had been built according to plans for a "vehicle assembly plant" drawn up by a West German consortium led by Weidleplan, Integral, and Kohlbecker.

In late 1987, French technicians say, control over BWW operations was taken away from the Ministry of Defense and handed over to Hussein Kamil's Military Production Authority. "They began to work a ten-hour shift, and planned to work around the clock to step up production. The Iraqis began wearing overalls for the first time in ten years — even the colonel who ran the base."

Defense production had become a most serious business. Iraq was determined to sever the umbilical cord with its Western suppliers.

Dr. Bruno Stemmler was one of the world's foremost experts in the centrifuge technology needed for uranium enrichment. In the 1970s he had pioneered a new type of gas centrifuge for his West German employer, MAN Technologie, which was used widely in uranium enrichment plants in West Germany, Britain, Holland, and Brazil. In the autumn of 1987 Stemmler traveled to Baghdad at the invitation of the Iraqi government. He told his company that it was just a routine consulting job, to service a solar energy and irrigation project.

In an account provided later to London's *Sunday Times*, however, Stemmler gave a different version of events.[1] When he arrived at Saddam International Airport, Stemmler was welcomed as if he were a visiting hero. He was taken to a luxurious suite at the Rashid Hotel, just across the street from Hussein Kamil's new offices. The next day his Iraqi hosts ushered him over to the Military Production Authority complex, where a set of blueprints was spread in front of him. In the account he gave the *Times*, Stemmler says he was amazed. The designs before him were "almost identical" to those he had used at MAN laboratories in West Germany to build uranium gas centrifuges. He presumed the plans had been stolen, for they were clearly labeled in both English and Arabic.

The Iraqis then explained that they were having a problem. The blueprints showed them how to build the centrifuges, but they needed fine-tuning that only a scientist of his experience could provide. They took Stemmler out to a squat concrete building on the outskirts of the city, and once they had gone through the security fence and cleared the guards, they led him into a buried building protected by a thick concrete shield that housed a top-secret nuclear laboratory. Stemmler was about to become an unwitting participant in Iraq's latest attempt to acquire the bomb.

After the Israelis destroyed the bomb plant at Thuwaitha in 1981, Iraq had begun looking for another solution to the problem of nuclear weapons fuel. In January 1983, Tarek Aziz had secured a promise from the foreign minister, Claude Cheysson, that France would rebuild the Osirak nuclear reactor. St. Gobain Nucléaire, a semiprivate export office set up to handle tricky nuclear deals, sent teams of technicians to Iraq to inspect the damage, but President Mitterrand eventually killed the deal.

In July 1984, a former colonel in the Italian secret service, Massimo Pugliese, offered to procure some 34 kilograms of bomb-grade plutonium through intelligence contacts in France. Pugliese, who arranged the deal through a complex web of front companies based in Geneva, appears to have benefited from high-level contacts in the French nuclear establishment. Pugliese was arrested later that year, before any nuclear material was shipped. Most proliferation experts have concluded that this deal was a fraud and that Pugliese had lied to the Iraqis about the plutonium. But the Italian investigating judge who reviewed all the documentary evidence of the case, Carlo Palermo, remains convinced that it was a true case of black marketeering and that it came dramatically close to success. Palermo said in an interview that unreleased prosecution documents show that the conspirators had negotiated to purchase the plutonium from a semiofficial nuclear export emporium in France and had made complex arrangements for shipping it to Iraq.

The Pugliese case was the last documented attempt by Iraq to acquire plutonium or plutonium-based technology on the international market. From then on the Iraqis sought technology to enrich uranium using gas ultracentrifuges. Centrifuge enrichment was quiet, small, and could easily be hidden from prying eyes. It was the other route to the clandestine bomb.

What Bruno Stemmler saw in late 1987 was the last step in the complex process of uranium enrichment. The pilot plant buried in the vicinity of the Thuwaitha nuclear center housed Iraq's first working gas centrifuge. "I was astonished," Stemmler says. "It seemed perfect."

In the laboratory the Iraqis had gathered together the best equipment then available in the West. They had succeeded in purchasing several prototype centrifuges from Brazil, which the Brazilians had acquired from West Germany under the terms of the nuclear cooperation agreement signed in 1975. Stemmler saw vacuum pumps and bellows made by Veeco, a high-tech firm in the United States that had been implicated in illicit sales to the USSR through LPAI and a French middleman, Aimé Richardt. Stemmler saw valves, high-temperature furnaces, and other equipment made by VAT of Liechtenstein and by the West German companies Leybold AG and Heraus. To acquire this and other equipment he had not yet seen, Stemmler later learned that the Iraqis had set up a procurement organization called the Industrial Projects Company (IPC), that worked hand in hand with SOTI. Both were now controlled by Hussein Kamil. For their most secret purchases, they went through Mansour Wadi's front company in London, Meed International.

Enriching uranium by centrifuge is a bit like making bootleg whiskey. But instead of being heated and distilled, the uranium is transformed into a gas, then supercooled and spun in a centrifuge. Each time the gas is spun, the heavier U-238 atoms, which are of no use for making bombs, are projected against the walls of the centrifuge. The lighter bomb-grade material collects at the bottom, then is recycled through the process again and again — sort of like pouring coffee through a filter over and over until it becomes black. Uranium has to pass through the centrifuge a thousand times to become weapons-grade fuel. So in most gas enrichment plants, thousands of centrifuges are connected together to form what nuclear experts call a "cascade."

Iraq had large supplies of uranium yellowcake, which it had purchased legally from Brazil and on the black market from Portugal and Niger. (The Portuguese government finally admitted in October 1990 that they had supplied Iraq with 252 tons of yellowcake between 1980 and 1983.) In addition to these supplies, well in excess of 500 tons, Iraq had its own uranium deposits. Uranium had been extracted from phosphate ore at Al Qaim since late 1980, plant engineers say. And a Soyuz satellite photograph commissioned for a Canadian television broadcast showed that in 1987 Iraq was building a uranium mine and yellowcake processing plant in the Qarachoq mountains south of Mosul. The Sovfoto showed a series of covered warehouses arranged in an H in a mountainous surrounding, with telltale milling equipment. This plant was believed to have been built by the Brazilian firm Constructora Mendes Junior. Brazilian geologists continued to prospect for uranium deposits in Iraq, Somalia, Libya, and Mauritania.

But the transformation of raw uranium into uranium hexafluoride gas involved a relatively sophisticated process known as "fluorification," which in the prelude to the Gulf war allied intelligence agencies were saying Iraq had not mastered. In fact, however, the Iraqis had purchased an entire fluorification production line from the Swiss company Alesa Alusuisse Engineering AG, which was set up in a separate facility just outside the Al Qaim phosphates mill. The $15.6 million contract was signed in March 1977. Belgian and French engineers who worked at Al Qaim say they first noticed "something funny" in 1980, when the Swiss began to arrive. They were heavily protected by Iraqi soldiers, and they built their plant at a distance from the rest of the complex. "They were very secretive about what they were doing," one engineer recalls. "All we knew was that it had something to do with uranium. But you just didn't talk about this kind of thing when you were in Iraq."

When the Iraqis told Stemmler they were having a problem with the vacuum system, he was not surprised. Regulating the vacuum pumps, tubing, and valves to function properly as a coherent unit had been one of his greatest challenges at MAN. A vacuum had to be created inside the centrifuge to eliminate air resistance, allowing the finely tuned rotor to spin at hypersonic speed. This is where Stemmler came in.

"When I had solved their problem," Stemmler told the *Sunday Times,* "they said thank you very much. It was only the vacuum that was a problem. They didn't want to know anything about the rotor. I got the impression they knew it all already."

American officials say Iraq turned to China for help with the first centrifuges. Iraqi scientists also used the experience they had gained by working in Brazil on a similar project, and they may have received as many as twenty centrifuges from Brazil for the pilot enrichment plant. But Brigadier Hugo de Oliveira Piva, who managed their contacts in Brazil, kept telling them to go back to the source if they wanted to build a full-scale uranium enrichment plant, since Brazil would arouse suspicion in the West if it started bulk exports of finished centrifuges to Iraq. The only source willing to sell the top-secret centrifuge technology was West Germany — despite the international agreements signed by successive West German governments to limit the spread of nuclear weapons and technology.

Once again the Iraqis decided it was more prudent to build their own than to depend on foreign suppliers. So instead of purchasing additional centrifuges from the Germans, they sought German, Swiss, and French suppliers of the machine tools and special steels needed to manufacture them.

On April 24, 1987, Mansour Wadi had good news for Safa Haboby, who was supervising procurement of the machines. In a telex sent from his London office to Baghdad, he told Haboby about the West German company H+H Metalform. "They have delivered similar machines to Brazil for the same purpose," Wadi wrote in his message. "They have under construction a machine that will be delivered in July. They can supply the machines in less than 6 months time and it seems they are more competitive than Boko," a British lathe maker Wadi had contacted that spring.

When the special spinning lathes to build the centrifuges arrived from H+H, they were set up in a top-secret production unit called Factory 10, within the Taji weapons complex. Safa Haboby was so happy with the supplies from H+H Metalform that he and Fadel Kadhum made arrangements to buy out the company, just as they had done with Matrix Churchill. From then on, whenever the Iraqis sought equipment for uranium enrichment or other particularly sensitive deliveries, they merely turned to Hütten and Hinze. With a German company as their procurement front, they had nothing to worry about.

Over the next few months they placed large orders with companies all over Europe to meet their uranium enrichment needs. From Usinor-Sacilor in France and from Saarstahl in West Germany, they purchased corrosion-resistant steels for the rotors and piping (uranium hexafluoride gas is highly corrosive and difficult to handle). From Kavo in West Germany they ordered electrical components to control the speed of the centrifuge motors (Kavo says it thought it was supplying switches to a dental laboratory). From Gachot in France they bought vacuum pumps and valves. Meanwhile the three spinning machines purchased from H+H Metalform went into production at Taji. Each one could turn out one hundred rotors a week. By a conservative estimate, it was enough to equip three complete production cascades in a year, each capable of enriching enough uranium for one — and perhaps several — atomic bombs per year.

In total secrecy, Iraq was making giant strides toward the bomb.

According to Stemmler, the experimental enrichment cascade was only a few steps away from the Thuwaitha nuclear center, which the International Atomic Energy Agency visited twice yearly. If the inspectors stumbled on the centrifuges, Iraq would be exposed to international sanctions for having violated the Nuclear Non-Proliferation Treaty. Pulling it all off under the noses of the inspectors gave Saddam Hussein and Hussein Kamil a special pleasure. It made them feel virtually invincible.

Iraq's new interest in manufacturing technology was not lost on its traditional foreign partners. When Lieutenant General Abdel Jabbar Shenshall returned to Cairo in November 1987 to attend Egypt's second International Defense Equipment Show, European weapons makers fell over each other to sell him machine tools for weapons plants. (Interestingly, Iraq chose not to exhibit as it had three years earlier, perhaps concerned with maintaining secrecy now that its weapons industry had become a reality.)

Most remarkable for its presence in Cairo was the West German BOWAS group, which had bought out Induplan Chemie, the apparent supplier of an entire factory to make ammonium perchlorate rocket fuel for the Condor II missile. Also present were Catton and Company, Ltd., a British steel-casting company, and three of Iraq's best West German suppliers: Hertel, Klöckner Industrie, and Thyssen, which made no bones about linking the machine-tool trade to the arms business. In the show directory, which was exclusively devoted to defense, Thyssen advertised its ability to provide "complete solutions for large-scale projects. Package deals comprising the entire range of machinery and equipment. . . . industrial plants on a turnkey basis." If that was not enough to get the Iraqis' attention, Thyssen boasted that it could "operate a multifaceted trading organization" to procure other equipment and services "in more than 60 countries all over the world."

For the Iraqis, it was not a question of finding a partner willing to bend the rules; it was one of choosing among the hundreds of companies eager for their business. The death lobby was no longer an elite club. It was a public eating house, and West European companies were stampeding through its wide-open doors.

*   *   *

On January 20, 1988, Britain's junior minister of trade and industry, Alan Clark, met with representatives of the Machine Tool Trades Association, in his top-floor suite at the DTI building in Victoria. According to London's *Sunday Times*, it was a key meeting for the pro-Iraq lobbyists. Present were John Nosworthy, the MTTA director-general, and the managing directors of three of Iraq's most important suppliers: Paul Henderson of Matrix Churchill, Keith Bailey of BSA Machine Tools, and Brian Carter of Colchester Lathes. The three, with contracts to ship machine tools to Iraqi weapons plants, were worried about a Foreign Office attempt to restrict exports to Iraq and had come to solicit Clark's support.

Minutes of this meeting made available to the *Sunday Times* show that the lobbyists needn't have worried. Clark applauded their success in obtaining lucrative contracts in what he called "a difficult market" and reassured them that nothing would happen to block their contracts as long as rival firms in Germany and France were also selling to Iraq.

Then Clark gave them some unusual advice: he showed them ways to fill in their export license applications so not to arouse the suspicions of DTI inspectors. On this issue Clark was at odds with Foreign Minister Geoffrey Howe, who had insisted in Parliament that licenses for Iraq be subjected to "the most careful scrutiny." According to the confidential minutes of the meeting, Clark told the lobbyists that "the intended use of the machines should be couched in such a manner as to emphasize the peaceful aspect to which they will be put. Applications should stress the record of 'general engineering' usage of machine tools." In case any doubts remained, Clark told the industrialists that he would support their case "strenuously, up to cabinet committee" level.

This was no ordinary conspiracy. Clark, who would become minister for defense procurement one year later, was well aware of the sensitivity of this business. He specifically advised the machine-tool companies to "make every effort" to avoid press attention. According to one of the managing directors who attended this meeting, "Everybody knew the machines could make shells." Said another, "People in Iraq weren't buying machine tools halfway through a war for producing motor cars."[2] The lobbyists had come to get official approval from the British government to help build the Iraqi arms industry. And that approval was given them by Alan Clark.

Clark's support soon paid off. A review of trade statistics made available by the OECD shows that 1988 was a boom year. Iraqi machine-tool purchases for the year topped $1.2 billion, up from $800 million the year before. Matrix Churchill, now under Iraqi ownership and selling almost exclusively to Iraqi weapons establishments, would show a profit for the first time in a decade.

Dr. Gerald Bull had known Amer al-Saadi for several years. His first contact with the Iraqis went back to 1982, when the Iraqi army was having problems with the GHN-45 guns it had purchased from Noricum/Voest-Alpine in Austria. That was when Sarkis Soghenalian brought him to Baghdad for the first time. Later, with an introduction from Bull and help from James Guerin of ISC in the United States, al-Saadi went to South Africa to purchase a better version of Bull's howitzer. In January 1988, he invited Gerald Bull to Baghdad, certain they could make a deal.

When Bull met with al-Saadi's boss, Hussein Kamil, he was like a man possessed. Bull was convinced that he could build a "super-gun" like nothing the world had ever seen, if only an enlightened leader such as President Saddam Hussein would finance the project and leave him alone. Thirty years ago, Bull explained, he had acquired, from the daughter of one of the German engineers who designed it, a complete set of blueprints for the most extraordinary artillery piece ever built, generally known as the "Paris Gun." The Germans had stationed it outside Paris during the final year of World War I and had lobbed huge shells onto the French capital from more than sixty miles away. The Paris Gun was the masterpiece of the masters of German artillery, the Krupp family. In 1959, Bull explained, he had decided to pick up where the German design team had left off forty years earlier.

Bull began work on his super-gun at McGill University in Canada. He called it the High-Altitude Research Program, or HARP. The idea was to use a huge but inexpensive gun to launch satellites into space. As a top-secret analysis of Bull's project by the Canadian Security Intelligence Services explained, HARP "became Bull's dream and obsession." Before long, the Canadian ballistics engineer had attracted the attention of the U.S. Department of

Defense. In 1963, he moved down to a secret military installation on the island of Barbados, where he set up a prototype of his "super-gun" and began work on a rocket-powered projectile capable of carrying a satellite into orbit.

But Bull's association with the Pentagon on HARP did not last for long. When the U.S. Air Force got wind of the ballistics tests on Barbados, they brought the program to a halt on June 30, 1967. Why? Because the air force had been given mountains of money to build expensive rockets to launch satellites for NASA and the National Security Agency and did not want to see its budget slashed in favor of some outsider's gun that could do the job for only a fraction of the cost.

For just $10 million, Bull told Hussein Kamil, the gun could be built right in his own country. The idea immediately appealed to the Iraqi. Indeed, what was $10 million? It would buy scarcely a dozen Soviet tanks! And the project would give a dramatic boost to the Iraqi weapons industry. So Hussein Kamil signed a contract with Gerald Bull and his Brussels-based Space Research Corporation on the spot. Together they would build four super-guns. The first, a prototype, would be a direct copy of the original HARP gun in Barbados, which was already the biggest gun in the world. The barrel measured 56 meters in length and had a smooth bore of 350 mm. The production guns were three times that size and simply defied imagination. The 1,000-mm barrel was so big and the tube so long (over 107 meters) that the gun required 10 tons of specially prepared explosives to fire off a single round. Bull told Kamil he would deliver the drawings and the gun barrels and assemble them in Iraq.

The Babylon Project was born.

To finance this and other industrial projects, the Iraqis needed fresh funds. Only weeks after the Iraqis signed with Gerald Bull, Christopher Drogoul and Paul Von Wedel arrived in Baghdad via Amman, Jordan. They were met at the airport gate at 1:30 A.M. by Sadiq Taha of the Central Bank of Iraq and a security officer, who took their passports and whisked them through Customs without the usual formalities. It was Von Wedel's first trip to Baghdad, but not Drogoul's. As they were heading out to the hotel, Taha asked

Drogoul if he had brought the agreements. "What agreements?" Von Wedel asked. Drogoul's assistant claims to this day that he had no idea his boss was about to embark on a series of illegal deals that would cost him his job — and cost the U.S. taxpayer hundreds of millions of dollars.

Later that evening Taha acknowledged that the real purpose of their trip was to sign a five-year loan agreement worth $200 million to finance "reconstruction" projects and a hydroelectric dam along the Tigris at Badush, near Mosul. In fact, internal BNL documents and court records show, Drogoul had pledged in writing to extend his unsecured medium-term loan during a visit by Taha to Washington and Atlanta in October 1987, so the Baghdad trip was merely a formality. It was the first time Drogoul had stepped outside the careful cover of the CCC program, which guaranteed agricultural exports only.

On the evening of February 22, 1988, Drogoul and Von Wedel were picked up at their hotel by the Iraqi security man and taken to the Ministry of Trade for the signing ceremony. As Von Wedel recalls, Taha was overjoyed. All the anxiety he had been suffering over the past six months seemed to vanish from his face. He was so happy he gave the Atlantans his worry beads. But when they arrived at the ministry building, Taha's face fell. The copy of the agreement they were given was riddled with errors. Drogoul offered to sign a blank last page and retype the agreement once they got back to Atlanta. Taha said he would clear it with the minister.

When they were escorted to meet Trade Minister Mohammad al-Rahwi a bit later, Von Wedel and Drogoul got the surprise of their lives. "It was like a cocktail party at a terrorists' convention," Von Wedel says. "Camouflage uniforms, guns, mustaches. I was scared stiff."[3] In fact, the Iraqis were celebrating the new loan. The minister was so pleased with the agreement that he made no bones about signing only the last page.

The agreement itself is a remarkable document. Its generosity would have made an American businessman drool. Although it was called a medium-term loan, the first two years of the five-year term were really a grace period during which no money was due. Furthermore, the five-year clock only began "at the end of third year after last shipment," the document specified. In other words, the Iraqis could keep on spending BNL's money in the United States for years to come and only begin to worry about repayment eight years after the last shipment. "These were virtually indefinite loans," said Dennis Kane, an investigator for Congressman Henry Gonzales of Texas, who chaired the House Banking Committee's investigation of BNL.

The Iraqis were so pleased with the free money that they asked Drogoul and Von Wedel on the spot to handle contracts guaranteed by the Export-Import Bank (Exim bank) as well. "Without hesitation," Von Wedel recalls, "we both said yes at the same time."

While they were in Baghdad, the two Atlantans crossed paths with one of their superiors from BNL's head office in Rome, Teodoro Monaco, who saw them as they returned to the hotel one afternoon. Monaco asked Drogoul what he was doing in Baghdad. According to Von Wedel, Drogoul said they were following up on the food credits guaranteed by the U.S. Department of Agriculture. But Drogoul says he told Monaco exactly what he was doing and that Monaco approved the unsecured loans. The Italian was accompanied by a technical expert named De Niezio from the Italian Commerce Department. No one knows what these two were doing in Baghdad. In the coming months, Drogoul faxed Monaco numerous letters, later seized by prosecutors, concerning his projects in Iraq.

Safa Haboby worked very hard to spend the BNL money. When the Technology and Development Group — TDG — in London bought Matrix Churchill, it also purchased the company's subsidiary in the United States. Safa Haboby became the chairman of Matrix Churchill Corporation of Cleveland, Ohio, in addition to his other responsibilities. His first act was to set up a procurement unit at the company, staffed by Iraqis, to seek out American suppliers of high tech.

But he was also seeking a means of channeling some of the BNL money back into his own pocket and into the Baath party slush fund. Early in 1988, court documents show, Haboby began a grand tour of the United States, meeting representatives of high-tech companies and promising them juicy contracts in Iraq. On February 26, 1988, he sent a letter to SerVaas, Inc., of Indianapolis, Indiana, directing them to pay Matrix Churchill Corporation a 5 percent fee on every purchase they made in connection with a $40 million brass smelting and casting plant SerVaas was going to build in Iraq, financed with BNL money. It amounted to a $2 million kickback. But SerVaas didn't blink. The Iraqi business was too good to quibble over.

Haboby sent a similar letter — this time demanding a 10 percent commission — to the head of XYZ Options, of Tuscaloosa, Alabama, which had won a $14 million contract to build a carbide-tipped machine-tool factory in Iraq, financed with BNL money. On April 27, Haboby demanded a 10 percent commission from a British manufacturer, CCM (HK) Ltd. CCM had contracted to build a $27.3 million plant to manufacture ductile iron pipe in Iraq, financed with BNL money, through its American branch, Centrifugal Casting Machine Corporation of Tulsa, Oklahoma. On May 2, Haboby demanded 10 percent from a SerVaas subsidiary named Bridgeport Brass Corporation, which was also spending BNL money to build an artillery-shell plant in Iraq.

It was a great setup Haboby had contrived, borrowing money with one hand, paying the suppliers with the other, and pocketing 10 percent for himself in between.

The final phase of the Iran–Iraq war began on February 29, 1988, when Iraq launched its first attacks against Tehran using ground-based ballistic missiles. Almost immediately the missile attacks became known as the "War of the Cities." On the first day, Iraq fired nine missiles at the Iranian capital, which is 550 kilometers from the closest point of the Iraqi border, or more than double the range of the SCUD-Bs Iraq had purchased from the USSR. By the time the attacks were over, Iraqi forces launched 189 ballistic missiles against Tehran and five other Iranian cities. Ballistic missiles that Iraq supposedly did not possess.

The Iraqi attacks puzzled military observers. Initial press accounts speculated that the missiles were Soviet SS-12s, which Iraq had allegedly received in 1985. But deliveries of the SS-12 were soon denied by Moscow — and even by Washington. As the weeks wore on and the missiles kept crashing into Tehran, it became clear that Iraq had developed its own missile capability, just as Saddam had announced six months earlier to a deaf world.

The first concrete evidence of how the Iraqis had done it came from Tehran. One of the missiles failed to explode, and Iranian television broadcast video images of hydraulic pumps, fuel tanks, and other hardware that had come crashing down on the city. One picture showed Cyrillic letters on a fuel pump, indicating the part and lot numbers.

U.S. intelligence analysts who examined the photographic evidence from Tehran positively identified the parts as belonging to Soviet-built SCUD-B missiles. But even the most modern version, the SCUD-C (which Iraq had never received), could fly no more than 400 kilometers. The conundrum had the analysts tied in knots. If the missiles were SCUDs, they could not have reached Tehran. Since the missiles had reached Tehran, they could not be SCUDs. But the photographs showed parts used on the SCUD. The confusion was total.

When the fog of war cleared, it became apparent that Iraq had upgraded the SCUDs by trading extended range for decreased payload. A close examination of undetonated missiles in Tehran led Iranian missile technicians (who were working with the North Koreans on their own ballistic missile projects) to announce that the Iraqi SCUDs had been significantly modified. They estimated that the Iraqis had cannibalized three SCUDs to produce two al-Hosseins, as the new Iraqi missiles had been dubbed. Welding marks on the fuel and oxidizer tanks led the Iranians to conclude that the Iraqis had taken original parts from three missiles, cut them in half, then welded them back together to make two new missiles. To compensate for the change in the center of gravity, air tanks were moved from the missile's tail to the nose.[4]

As a reward for the successful missile program, Hussein Kamil was promoted yet again in February 1988, when the Revolutionary Command Council issued a decree merging the Ministry of Industry, the Ministry of Heavy Industry, what was left of SOTI, and the Military Production Authority. The new entity was called the Ministry of Industry and Military Industrialization — MIMI, for short — and it controlled everything from oil refineries to missile shops. It ran chicken farms and chemicals plants, phosphates mines and gun factories. It was responsible for obtaining computers from foreign suppliers to track ballistic missile trajectories and for selling Iraqi-made televisions to Jordan. Hussein Kamil was now officially the second most powerful man in the country, with personal control over Iraq's entire industrial apparatus. His father-in-law had given him a mission, and he intended to make good on it. Break the

Western technology embargo, Saddam told him. Develop everything we need here in Iraq.

To help him, Hussein Kamil promoted the two experts, Amer al-Saadi and Amer Rashid. As his top deputies, they were given power they had never known before. New weapons were developed on the basis of a single phone call between military commanders and MIMI engineers. "Because of the war," Amer Rashid recalls, "all of us were in a hurry." The red tape, the controls, the feasibility studies, the reports — anything that would have slowed the process — were abolished. After all, the new minister was Saddam's personal representative. He either approved a project or turned it down. "We have had no paralysis by analysis," said Amer Rashid.

The diversion of civilian equipment to military ends was now completely institutionalized. MIMI purchased equipment for steel mills and car factories, saying they were to be used by the Ministry of Industry, when in fact they were destined for military plants. Western suppliers conveniently dropped the last part of Hussein Kamil's title, referring to him simply as the minister of industry. "Our experience in the war taught us that you can't have separate factories for civil and military products," Amer al-Saadi said in an interview. "You have to have both types of production in a single factory." It made sense from a purely industrial point of view and even greater sense from the procurement angle. Whenever the military were stymied in procuring high technology in the West, they simply detailed a civilian establishment to fill out the forms.

A host of new projects were begun at once. With a Yugoslav partner, MIMI developed a long-range multiple-rocket launch system similar to the Brazilian-made Astros-II. With the help of French engineers, they took in-flight refueling probe kits purchased from Dassault and adapted them to their Russian-built MiG-23s. From the Poles they bought a license to manufacture the T-72 tank. Progress had already been so rapid, Amer al-Saadi said, that by the end of 1987 Iraq was "self-sufficient in ammunition, artillery ammunition, aircraft bombs, mortar bombs, RPGs, rockets, tube-launched rockets, and mortars. From then on, we could concentrate on other areas." The top priority was to develop an even longer-range missile, capable of reaching Tel Aviv as well as Tehran.

On April 25, 1988, just before the War of the Cities came to a close, Hussein Kamil reported the successful test launch of the al-Abbas missile. This new engine of death flew 860 kilometers from the launch site near Mosul to an unspecified target. In fact, it was one of the last Iraqi missiles to hit Tehran.

Unlike the al-Hossein, the al-Abbas was not just an upgraded SCUD-B. It used some of the same design specifications as the SCUD and may have used Soviet-built parts, but it was an Iraqi missile and it had rolled off Iraqi assembly lines, the first of a long series that brought life to Saddam's dream. Still, even as the missile campaign against Tehran was drawing to a close, Western intelligence analysts were insisting that the Iraqi weapons industry was virtually nonexistent. They just didn't want to know.

The Iraqi missile program was so lucrative for Brazil that the aerospace companies Embraer and Engesa decided early in 1987 to set up a new unit called Orbita Space Systems, to pool their ballistic missile design and development resources. The head of Orbita, Ozilio Silva, was a former head of Embraer. Together with his senior executive, Sergio Prado, and officials from Engesa's foreign marketing bureau, Engexco, Silva set out to design an even better missile for Iraq than the jerry-rigged al-Hossein. That was how the al-Abbas came into being. The place to start, Silva knew, was in the fuel.

Brazil's CTA had made dramatic progress in the field of solid-fuel propellants using American and Italian technology. But CTA lacked expertise in liquid-fuel propellants. According to a report on ballistic missile research prepared by the Congressional Research Service, CTA solved that problem in late 1986, when it signed a comprehensive space research agreement with the People's Republic of China, swapping the secret of Brazil's solid-fuel propellant for Chinese assistance in missile guidance and liquid fuel mixtures.[5] Supercooled, or "cryogenic," liquid propellants had been around since the 1950s, but they were tricky to use and even more difficult to store. To launch a ballistic missile the size of the al-Abbas required five tons of liquid oxygen cooled to temperatures approaching absolute zero. But this appears to be the direction the Iraqis and their Brazilian and German helpers took.

Asked in Baghdad about the secret of the long range of the al-Abbas, Iraqi engineers pointed to the oversized refrigeration tanks on the launcher. "Think cryogenic," one said. "We have packed more punch into the fuel."[6]

Iraq had abundant supplies of liquid oxygen and liquid nitrogen, thanks to European petrochemicals companies such as Italy's TPL. This company, formerly known as Technipetrole, worked extensively in Iraq over the past fifteen years. Among TPL's handiwork was an oxygen production unit at the Baiji refinery, known as Project 1545, and a nitrogen production and liquefaction unit in gas fields near Kirkuk.

It was but one more example of Amer al-Saadi's credo of fulfilling military needs at ostensibly civilian establishments.

Meanwhile Abdelkader Helmy, the Egyptian-American rocket specialist who worked at the U.S. government's Jet Propulsion Laboratory, was scouring the United States in search of materials for Iraq's solid-fuel missiles. From the Advanced Composite Materials Corporation of Greer, South Carolina, he purchased samples of a ceramic-ceramic composite, and from Kaiser Aerotech, of San Leandro, California, he purchased blocks of a carbon-carbon composite called K-Karb. The Iraqis and their Egyptian partners wanted to determine which of the materials worked best for missile nose cones and rocket nozzles. The samples were smuggled out to Egypt in late 1987 by the head of the Egyptian Condor II procurement team, Colonel Fuad al-Gamal.

Tests in Egypt showed that K-Karb could be machined locally, so Helmy ordered five blocks of it from Kaiser Aerotech. On March 8, 1988, Helmy delivered the K-Karb to Egyptian officials at the embassy in Washington, who smuggled it out of the United States. The ceramic material was more tricky, so the Egyptians returned it to Helmy, who then found a U.S. company willing to machine it into nose cones.

Composites were crucial for ballistic missile nose cones, not merely to save weight but also to improve accuracy. Warheads made of ordinary metal burned up as the missile reentered the earth's atmosphere, making it wobble and sending it off course, whereas carbon-carbon did not burn. Helmy prepared a special report for the Condor II team, explaining how carbon-carbon technology could be used for "atmospheric re-entry applications" and for rocket nozzles. Court documents later showed that Helmy obtained most of his information from a top-secret NASA document entitled "Evaluation of Carbon-Carbon Composites for Space Engine Nozzles." With his top-secret security clearance, obtaining such documents was a snatch.

The Brazilians had provided a shopping list of solid fuel propellant ingredients, which Colonel Ahmed Khairat and the Condor II team turned over to Helmy. But Helmy was no specialist in clandestine operations. On his shopping list were a number of controlled substances, such as military-grade aluminum powder (a stabilizer), Cyanox, and HTPB, a special type of synthetic rubber. The aluminum and Cyanox didn't require export licenses for sale to Egypt and were shipped legally in March 1988. But the HTPB did. When Helmy tried to buy it from the Integrated Research Corporation, of Los Angeles, he said he wanted to use it to manufacture plastic bottles, shoes, and glue. The company still insisted that it required an export license, so he let the matter drop.

Jim Huffman wasn't going to be put off in the same way. When Helmy told him his problem, he just picked up the phone and called the Chemical Systems Division of United Technologies Corporation. He said the product was intended for "commercial applications in our area" in the United States, and UTC agreed to ship it. To make this and other procurement operations for the Iraqi missile program appear more legitimate, Huffman used his U.S. company, Mesa Associates. He had the chemicals shipped in drums to a warehouse in Shelby, Ohio, where Huffman and his son stripped off the identifying labels and sent them on to a freight forwarder in Maryland. The chemicals were then smuggled out on a military C-130 by Egyptian officials.

Huffman had imagination, at least. When he tried to buy another controlled rocket fuel additive, called HMDI, the sales representative at Mobay Chemicals objected that hexamethylene diisocyanate was used primarily in rocket fuels, and what did he need it for anyway? Huffman was not taken aback. He said he wanted to use it as a paint additive for redoing the floor of a local gym. The company didn't buy that line and declined the sale. In a telephone conversation intercepted by law enforcement officials, Huffman then told Helmy to hold off before contacting other chemical companies. "I don't want to make anybody nervous and make them suspicious so they start sending somebody around to investigate," he said. "We have to be very careful about that."

In March 1988, Helmy traveled to Washington for talks with Colonel Fuad al-Gamal, his "control" at the Egyptian embassy. Gamal was nervous and told him that the Condor II procurement effort had to be speeded up. Saddam's entire strategic plan depended on developing the new missiles.

The Iraqi missile attacks against Tehran emptied the Iranian capital of its population. Public schools went on recess, businesses closed. Anybody who could afford to take a vacation at the seaside resorts along the Caspian Sea did so. But the missile attacks did not end the war; two other events did.

The first occurred in northern Iraq, following a successful Iranian attack against the Kurdish town of Halabja, some 16 kilometers inside Iraq. Furious over what he considered to be the "collaboration" of Iraqi Kurds with the Iranian enemy, Saddam Hussein condemned this entire small city to death. Like his distant ancestor Nebuchadnezzar, Saddam believed that collective punishment was the only way to bring a rebellious population to heel.

For two entire days, March 17 and 18, the rugged hills surrounding the town of Halabja echoed with the sounds of shelling. Iranian reporters in the area covering Iran's Val Fajr 10 offensive cocked an ear. The explosions had an eerie quality. They were muted, distant, not nearly as loud as ordinary bombings. And yet they were persistent. Finally, a group of reporters set out in the direction of Halabja, which Iranian troops had evacuated a few days earlier. What they found chilled them to the bone.

There was not a soldier in sight, nor was there any trace of bombing. But the streets of Halabja, which in normal times counted 70,000 inhabitants, were strewn with the bodies of ordinary citizens — women and children and old people caught as they tried to flee from some terrible scourge.

They had been gassed with a hydrogen cyanide compound the Iraqis had developed with the help of a German company. The new death agent, made in the Samarra gas works, was similar to the poison gas the Nazis used to exterminate the Jews more than forty years before.

As word got out to the international press, the Iranian Revolutionary Guards Corps sent in its own video crew to capture this latest example of the murderous cynicism of the Iraqi dictator. In minute detail, they filmed dead mothers clutching their babies, children lying alone without a trace of assault (hydrogen cyanide leaves no blisters or burns, as other military poisons do). They captured the horror of whole families desperately trying to keep the fumes from reaching them by wrapping themselves in blankets out on the streets. More than 5,000 civilians were killed, and another 7,000 maimed for life. Saddam Hussein didn't even try to hide his culpability. He announced that he had decided to punish the Kurdish town for "the crime of collaboration."

The Revolutionary Guards video team thought to capture for posterity these "dark pages" of human history as a record of Saddam's barbarity. But their film, shown in training schools throughout Iran, also demoralized the Iranian army. Instead of inciting young recruits to hate Saddam, it instilled in them a fear from which they never recovered. This was the awesome power of the Iraqi dictator, the pictures said. Confront him ye who dare.

The second event that ended the war was the battle to recapture Fao. That city was considered so vital to the survival of the Baathist regime that in the days following the Iranian victory in 1986 Saddam put General Saadi Tuma al-Jaboori Abbas in charge of the counteroffensive. Saadi Tuma, who went on to become defense minister in December 1990, was a longtime Baathist and was fiercely loyal to Saddam. Foreign observers in Baghdad called him the "political general." Parachuting him down to Fao from his staff job in Baghdad was a sure sign of Saddam's anxiety. And yet, both Saadi Tuma and the elite Republican Guards who were put under his command (three armored divisions normally under direct presidential orders, considered Iraq's best combat units) bloodied their noses in Fao and failed.

So in early 1988 Saddam switched generals and put Lieutenant General Maher Rashid in charge of preparing the counterstrike. Rashid, arguably Iraq's best military mind, had been waiting for this command. He bore an old grudge against Saddam for the assassination of his uncle from Tikrit many years before. Like Saddam, he was a man of cunning and patience. In March 1982, while Saddam was near the border, inspecting troops fleeing from an Iranian offensive, his convoy got caught in the crossfire. Fearing capture, Saddam called on nearby units for help, and it was Rashid who eventually delivered him — but only after Saddam promised to rehabilitate the memory of Rashid's dead uncle. To ensure his continued loyalty, Saddam married his second son, Koussay, to one of Rashid's daughters. General Rashid saw the Fao command as his chance to win the war. And he was right.

Rashid devised an ingenious strategy aimed at convincing the Iranians he was about to launch an attack more than 200 kilometers to the north. In early April he moved most of his armor from the Fao swamplands up to the desert near Al Amarah. The Iranians concluded that the much-awaited offensive would occur there, with Iraqi troops sweeping southward after an initial thrust across the border. In response to General Rashid's feint, they moved their heavy equipment north, away from Fao, and relieved the seasoned Revolutionary Guards stationed at Fao with young recruits and old men.

On the night of April 17–18, Rashid struck. He loaded some two hundred tanks of an entire armored division onto Faun transporters, purchased from West Germany, and headed down the road to Fao. Before dawn, his tanks had overrun the Iranian front lines, while the Iraqi air force created panic with its new nine-ton Nassr bomb. Captured Iranians later said they thought an atomic bomb had gone off, so powerful was the explosion. Rashid's "secret weapon" had been built at Taji with British machine tools, in a plant engineered by the West German company Ferrostaal.

As night was falling, Saddam's Republican Guards belatedly joined the fray, pounding the Iranians with chemical artillery shells and slaughtering the few stragglers who had not already fled. But by that time Rashid's Seventh Army was sweeping into Fao. This total rout of the Revolutionary Guards was devastating to Iranian morale. From then until the final victory in July, General Rashid had the Iranians on the run.

Louis Champon was not the type of person you would have suspected to be working on Saddam Hussein's death projects. He ran a small company in Boca Raton, Florida, that specialized in natural flavorings for food. His greatest ambition in life was to become the Emperor of Ice Cream. But by a series of coincidences, Champon became involved with the Iraqi procurement agent Ihsan Barbouti in 1988. His brush with the Iraqis would cost him dearly.

Champon had developed a new process for making bitter almond oil from apricot, peach, plum, or cherry pits. Bitter almond oil is the ingredient that gives the cherry flavor to cherry vanilla ice cream, and is normally made from benzaldehyde. Champon says his formula was the only one that could be called a "natural" flavoring.

Patent in hand, Champon began looking for backers and stumbled on Barbouti in February 1988. The Iraqi agreed to provide $5.3 million in seed money. In May he and Champon set up a new company called Product Ingredient Technology, or PIT, in Boca Raton, Florida. Barbouti said he expected the new company would eventually produce 100 tons of cherry flavoring per year — half the world market — and generate $100 million annually in sales of the flavoring and its byproducts.

But one of the byproducts of Champon's new process was ferric ferrocynanide, which can be transformed into hydrogen cyanide, the gas used to kill Kurdish civilians in Halabja. "Dr. Barbouti kept insisting that we take the byproduct and ship it to West Germany," Champon told the *Florida Sun-Sentinel*. "I kept refusing, and then the money stopped," and the company went broke.

According to Peter Kawaja, a private electronics expert who installed a $1 million security system in the PIT plant, the cyanide compound was taken during "night trips" to another site in Florida run by Barbouti's agents, who repacked it before sending it on to Iraq. "Shipments have left the U.S. and technology has left the U.S.," Kawaja alleged. "We're talking about the research and development of chemical weapons in the United States."[7]

So far, little evidence has surfaced to document deliveries of hydrogen cyanide precursors to West Germany or Iraq, although Florida investigators are actively pursuing a lead that cyanide compounds may have been shipped to Iraq via Carlos Cardoen in Chile. But the cherry-vanilla saga shows just how far the Iraqis were willing to go to acquire ever-better instruments of death.

Ekkehard Schrotz considered himself a lucky man. As he told the French police when they questioned him later, if he had taken his car to work in Monaco as he normally did, he would have been dead. By a fluke he left the Peugeot outside his villa in the neighboring town of Grasse, and heard about the explosion on the morning of May 27, 1988, when his wife called him at work.

Schrotz's work took him around the world. As a director of the German-owned Consen group, he procured missile technology from France, Italy, West Germany, and the United States and supervised its transfer to Iraq. Only three weeks before the car bomb went off, Schrotz told the police, he had been in Iraq to discuss a purchase of propergol solid fuel for Iraq from the Franco-Italian consortium led by Snia BpD and SNPE.

Within minutes of the mysterious car bombing, the local office of Agence France Presse received an anonymous phone call claiming responsibility for the attack. The caller identified his group as the "Protectors of Islam" and said that Schrotz had been "condemned to death because of his crimes in the service of Saddam Hussein. He built rockets for Saddam Hussein." But the German businessman was not the only one. "All collaborators in this crime" would be punished, the caller warned. Not long after going to the police, Schrotz disappeared.

A few days later, unidentified intruders broke into the Consen head office in Zug, Switzerland, and rifled the files, taking lists of scientists and businessmen who had played a role in building the Iraqi missiles. They also took company documents that showed just how the international procurement network operated. Some of these documents later surfaced in the press and helped expose the activities of the Consen group and its ties to the West German missile maker MBB.

At first it was assumed that Schrotz's attackers were Iranian. Later suspicions turned to the Israeli Mossad. In February the Iraqis claimed to have shot down a second Israeli surveillance aircraft flying over a military factory. This time the intruder was not an F-4 but a remotely piloted drone. The Iraqis claimed they shot it down as it was escaping back across the border with Saudi Arabia and Kuwait, along civil aviation route R-19.[8]

Within days of the Zug break-in, Titus Habian presided over a tense meeting in an office building on Palestine Street in Baghdad. The date was June 8, 1988. Habian and his co-workers had just lived through three harrowing months of Iranian missile attacks (the Iraqi capital was close enough to the border for the Iranians to hit it with SCUD-Bs purchased from China and North Korea). But they were more afraid of Mossad than they were of the Iranian SCUDs.

Habian, who hailed from Linz, Austria, was the chief engineer in

Iraq for the Consen group. According to minutes of the meeting prepared later, he informed the twelve-man crisis committee of "current company problems." Then he warned them "of their duty to maintain the strictest secrecy" even when talking with sub-contractors, given the recent events in Europe. The situation was so tense that "vacation trips to Europe should be avoided whenever possible" until new security measures had been put in place. If Mossad's arm was too short to reach them in Baghdad, Habian warned, in Europe each of them was in danger of losing his life.

Some of those present worked for Feneberg, an Austrian engineering firm involved in Project 395, or DOT, the Iraqi program to build a long-range solid-fuel missile like Condor II. Others worked for Delta Consult, a subsidiary of Consen based in Salzburg. These men knew precisely what they were doing. As one engineer who helped build the three missile plants at Fallujah, Al Hillah, and Karbala said, "Whoever was on the DOT construction sites had to realize that an arms factory was under construction." Not only were the missile plants filled with all types of special equipment, but key facilities were buried below ground and connected by a series of reinforced concrete tunnels. It was not the type of place where cars were made.[9]

Gerald Bull returned to Baghdad at the beginning of June to report back to Hussein Kamil and Amer al-Saadi on the Babylon Project. The Canadian ballistics expert brought good news. His initial efforts to procure materials in Europe had been wildly successful. But then, Bull's long experience in South Africa had taught him how to operate a clandestine arms procurement and supply network. If there was one thing he understood in addition to ballistics, it was how to get around the law.

The trick, he explained to the Iraqis, was making sure there were enough screens between him and the companies actually supplying the goods. To start with, Bull set up branches of his own company, Space Research Corporation, in Brussels, Geneva, and Montreal. Next, through a holding company called Paragon Ltd. (named after Paragon House in Barbados, where he had stayed when working on the HARP project), Bull set up a shell company called the Advanced Technology Institute, or ATI, with offices in Athens and Brussels. ATI would serve as the procurement front, working with European suppliers, while the SRC companies did the engineering.

In addition to his network, Bull explained, he had a special deal going with one of Europe's largest manufacturers of military explosives, Poudreries Réunis de Belgique. When he moved to Brussels in the late 1970s, Bull had convinced PRB to take a 45 percent stake in SRC International. Through PRB, Bull explained, the Iraqis could get all the explosives they needed to operate the super-gun. Belgian arms makers were so heavily involved in clandestine arms deals that the black market brokers called them the "dogs that do not bark."

Bull put a British engineer named Christopher Cowley in charge of ATI. On April 17, 1988, documents later seized by British Customs show, Dr. Cowley met with representatives of Walter Summers and the Sheffield Forgemasters in Great Britain to inquire about building the 350-mm prototype of the super-gun. Cowley explained that he was purchasing pipeline sections for a new petrochemicals complex in Iraq and gave the specifications to company engineers. As Bull had explained to the Iraqis, one of the most brilliant features of his design was the smooth-bore barrel. Because the super-gun used a rocket-assisted projectile, pressures inside the barrel were kept to a minimum, so it could be made of fairly ordinary pipe sections, bolted together on the outside. The design made it easier to purchase the pipe on the open market and lowered the cost. "Characteristically," Bull wrote, "one meter diameter launch tubes of lengths up to 300 calibres could be built for well under ten million dollars . . ."[10]

Still, the Walter Summers representatives responded cautiously to Dr. Cowley's request. Anxious not to get involved in an illicit deal with Iraq, the company sent a telex message to Rex Bailiss at the Department of Trade and Industry licensing bureau, to inquire whether export of the pipe sections to Iraq needed special approval. In a return telex dated the next day, which was made available by sources close to SRC, DTI signed off on the deal. "For the information requested, there is no need for an export license." Gerry Bull could build his gun in Iraq without a care.

One thing Bull never told Hussein Kamil was that he had offered his super-gun to another country in the Middle East in 1983. After conducting a feasibility test, they decided the project was "unworkable" and turned it down. The country was an old customer of his: Israel.

* * *

Hussein Kamil was so pleased by Bull's report that he suggested they work together on other projects. For several years the South Africans had been trying to sell Iraq a huge self-propelled gun called the G-6. With its huge wheels and tiny cab, the G-6 looked like a cross between a brontosaurus and a wrecking crane. The Iraqis liked the gun because of its long range (40 kilometers) and its ability to maneuver in the desert. What they didn't like was the price, and they wanted to know if Bull could build them a similar gun for less.

The Canadian told Hussein Kamil that the G-6 used his own 155 mm gun. It would be child's play to redesign the vehicle and build the whole thing in Iraq. On June 6, SRC and Kamil signed a contract to design and build prototypes of two self-propelled howitzers with 155 mm and 210 mm guns and enhanced ammunition (the Iraqis later called the guns al-Majnoon and al-Fao). SRC also contracted to run ballistics training courses for Iraqi army personnel at SRC headquarters in Brussels.

To build the new guns, Bull turned to contacts in the international arms market. Creusot-Loire of France agreed, in a contract worth $3,361,124, to build three gun barrel prototypes. In Spain, Bull got in touch with Trebelan SA, which had supplied rocket casings that the Iraqis filled with chemical warfare agents. For $400,000, Trebelan agreed to build vehicles for the guns, with six giant wheels on each side, while Mercedes supplied a low-slung diesel cab. To pay for it all, the Iraqis told the companies to contact Christopher Drogoul at BNL Atlanta. The gun barrels, the special trucks, and the Mercedes cabs all fell within the category of "reconstruction projects," Drogoul agreed. As soon as each was delivered to Iraq, BNL paid the bills.[11]

Michel Bull, who was deeply involved in his father's companies, told Mike Wallace of "60 Minutes" that he made a special trip to Washington in 1988 to advise the State Department's Office of Munitions Control about his father's plans to help Iraq. They were not selling guns, he pointed out. "We sold engineering . . . and yes, the OMC was made aware of what we were doing."

"And what did they say?" Wallace asked.

"Fine."[12]

*   *   *

Saddam Hussein's best friend in France, Jacques Chirac, was roundly trounced in a bid for the French presidency in May 1988, and one month later was replaced as prime minister by the Socialist Michel Rocard. The Iraqi lobby lost one of its most powerful supporters, but it gained a new one in the exchange.

Jean-Pierre Chevènement, the black sheep of the French Socialist party, headed its most extreme left-wing faction. He had resigned once from an earlier government over disagreements with President François Mitterrand. But Mitterrand preferred to have Chevènement nearby, where he could keep an eye on him. So when the new government was announced in June, Chevènement became defense minister.

Chevènement was an old friend of the dictator of Baghdad. In 1985 he founded the Franco-Iraqi Friendship Society, along with an apologist for the ultra-right National Front party in France. As defense minister, Chevènement did his best to reopen the arms pipeline to Baghdad, which had slowed to a trickle during the previous year because of Iraq's mounting financial difficulties. Chevènement played a key role in convincing the reluctant finance minister, Pierre Bérégovoy, to approve financing for the Tulip and Jacinthe helicopter contracts that had been signed but left hanging by the Chirac government — and that was only the beginning.

Dassault's Hugues de l'Estoile, Thomson-CSF's René Anastaze, Matra's Jean-Luc Lagadère, and Aérospatiale's Henri Martre needed no one to explain to them the importance of Chevènement's arrival at the crucial defense position. The pro-Iraq lobby had a firm friend in a high place, someone who had the president's ear.

A C-130 military transport plane left Washington, D.C., on June 10, 1988, on its way to Egypt. On board were nine drums of embargoed chemicals, purchased by Abdelkader Helmy and Jim Huffman from companies around the United States. Huffman had changed the labels on the containers and made sure the airway bills disguised the true nature of the shipment. Helmy had provided fraudulent invoices to cover the goods, so they could pay the shipping agent his commission.

Unknown to either of them, a U.S. Customs officer had tracked the cargo to a warehouse in Maryland, where it was stored before the final leg of the journey to Egypt. He took samples of the chemicals contained in the nine drums. When the results came in a few days later, all doubts were off. Helmy, Huffman, and officials at the Egyptian embassy in Washington were conspiring to smuggle U.S. technology to an Arab ballistic missile project, as wire taps and earlier surveillance operations by Customs had suggested. To keep them from succeeding, Customs launched Operation Ali Baba, using undercover agents in Maryland, Ohio, and California.

The Iraqis were pressing the Egyptians to deliver the missile nose cones, so the Egyptians put the squeeze on Helmy, who became nervous. In one conversation intercepted by U.S. Customs agents, he berated Abdel Rahin al-Gohary at the Egyptian embassy in Washington for failing to understand the sensitivity of the embargoed rocket technology that Helmy had been asked to ship. Al-Gohary, whose job was to procure U.S. weapons for the Egyptian armed forces, asked Helmy whether he had secured the proper export permits and invoices — a perfectly normal request coming from an officer who had daily dealings with the Pentagon on U.S.–approved arms sales. Then he told Helmy that it could take one or two years to get the "full fifteen tons" of his strange materials and equipment to Egypt. A complete transcript of the exchange was submitted by the prosecution at Helmy's trial.

Helmy: Sir, the minister, he wants these items to get there by all means, and this is what I was informed about. And then they told us that you, Sir, can place these items on board the plane that leaves to Egypt every day, always.
al-Gohary: Every day??!!!
Helmy: Maybe every week.
al-Gohary: Every month. Once every month.

Helmy then picked up the phone and complained to Egyptian Defense Minister Abu Ghazaleh's office about al-Gohary's attitude. In a call to Colonel Ahmed Khairat, who supervised the missile technology procurement team for Abu Ghazaleh, Helmy explained the dangers he was incurring by contributing to the scheme. "I told [al-Gohary] those items are not easy to buy normally. We were able to acquire [them] through our own personal ways which require us to store it in two separate warehouses en route, so that no one could tell where it is going. So if this matter becomes known I shall be in great trouble. You should understand that in one single minute I could be thrown in jail here and my children will never see me again! . . . He should realize that very sensitive things are involved, especially things like antennas."

Helmy and Huffman had ordered telemetry antennas from an American company, Vega Precision Laboratories, to transmit flight information from the missile back to its base during flight. They had also ordered large quantities of maraging steel, a corrosion-resistant nickel-steel alloy used in making gas centrifuges for uranium enrichment as well as rocket motor parts.

Another sensitive commodity needed for the missile project was carbon phenolic fabric, which the Iraqis were seeking to manufacture flexible rocket nozzles, which could improve the missile's accuracy. Huffman ordered 426 pounds of the fabric, called MX-4926, from a company called Fiberite in California. When Fiberite shipped the fabric to Huffman's warehouse in Ohio on June 9, 1988, the four cardboard containers were all clearly stamped with notices stating that the contents were subject to U.S. export controls. After several discussions with the Egyptians in Washington, Huffman called Helmy and told him they would pack the special fabric in one wooden crate and mark it "Air Force Club" before shipping it on to the Egyptian Embassy's freight forwarder in Maryland, hoping in this way to get it through Customs without attracting attention. "Wish us luck. Haven't gone to jail yet," Huffman said.

But he and Helmy were close. Fiberite had gotten suspicious, and before shipping the material to Huffman's warehouse had called the U.S. Customs office in Cleveland, which agreed to deliver the goods to Huffman as part of a sting operation. In the following days, Customs agents looked on as Huffman and his son loaded the fabric into the wooden crate, changed the labels, and effaced the export control notices. Before the crate left the warehouse in Shelby, Ohio, Customs knew exactly where it was headed, and why.

The next Egyptian military C-130 was to leave Washington on June 25. At the insistence of Abu Ghazaleh, room was made on the plane for the carbon phenolic fabric and rocket fuel ingredients that Huffman and Helmy had managed to acquire. But when Huffman and Helmy arrived at the airport to make sure their cargo was safely placed on board, Customs agents arrested them on the spot.

For his efforts to aid the Iraqi missile program, Egyptian Defense Minister Abu Ghazaleh lost his job. Helmy and Huffman were sentenced to four years in jail — nothing compared to the life sentence imposed on Jonathan Pollard for warning Israel of the menace the Iraqi weapons programs posed.

The Iranian collapse at Fao that April led to a string of defeats in June and July. The Iraqis' extensive use of chemical weapons totally demoralized the Iranians. The Iraqis recaptured Majnoon and Fish Lake, then pushed the Iranians out of parts of Iraqi Kurdistan they had seized in fighting the year before. In early July Iraqi troops stormed across the border, capturing 1,000 square kilometers of Iranian territory. The Iranians were so terrified of the advancing shock troops and their chemical weapons that they simply abandoned their equipment without a fight and fled. The Iraqis seized 570 artillery pieces and 1,478 armored vehicles, including more than 150 tanks. The booty was so extensive it took them weeks just to haul it back across the border.

As the Iraqis plundered Iran's heavy equipment, Ayatollah Khomeini called his closest advisors for a council of war. They argued that it was time to throw in the towel, before the Iraqis seized major cities in the west of the country. For the aging ayatollah, making peace with Saddam Hussein was as bitter as drinking "a cup of poison." But he had no choice. On July 20, Khomeini gave in. One month later a UN ceasefire put a tentative end to eight years of war.

The day the ceasefire went into effect, Saddam wheeled around and unleashed his forces in the biggest attack he had ever launched against Iraq's Kurdish population. Some 60,000 troops, including three crack Republican Guard divisions, were given orders to devastate Kurdish towns and villages in the north. Their aim was to drive as many Kurds as possible out of the country, finishing off the work begun the year before. Dozens of villages were bulldozed into the ground.

The August 1988 offensive against the Kurds also marked Saddam's most extensive use of chemical weapons against his own population. Eyewitness reports, collected by UN observers and a team of Senate Foreign Relations Committee staffers, who interviewed Kurdish refugees in early September, provided unequivocal evidence of gas attacks. Saddam's air force dropped chemical bombs from Soviet-built fighters. Iraqi army aviation used Swiss-built Pilatus PC-7 and PC-9 trainers equipped with hard points for carrying chemical bombs. On August 28, one group of 300 Kurdish and Christian refugees was gassed as they attempted to flee across the border into Turkey. In this attack, eyewitnesses say the Iraqis used a new type of helicopter. The descriptions they gave matched that of the BO-105, which MBB in West Germany continued to sell to Iraq through various fronts, ostensibly for "civilian" purposes. Indeed, the Kurds were civilians, and the helicopters were just spraying them with insecticide.[13]

Not long afterward, MBB officially requested a license to export an additional twenty helicopters to the Iraqi police, but was turned down by the West German authorities. Eager to make the sale nevertheless, MBB delivered the choppers via a front company in London. The deal remained a secret until a West German peace group, the Society for Threatened Peoples, broke into an MBB warehouse near Munich in September 1990. The peace activists photographed documents on a large shipment of helicopter spares, which they had been tipped was on its way to Iraq. The equipment included advanced avionics gear made by a German defense electronics contractor, Becker Aviation.

As Saddam was gassing the Kurds, business went on as usual. In May, only two months after the massacre at Halabja, the U.S.–Iraq Business Forum held a symposium for business leaders interested in investing in Iraq; they were warmly encouraged to intensify their cooperation with Baghdad by A. Peter Burleigh, the assistant secretary of state in charge of northern Gulf affairs. Meanwhile, the Commerce Department continued to approve high-tech exports to Iraqi weapons plants and establishments. A review of licenses approved in the eight months following Halabja shows deliveries of virus cultures, fungi, and protozoa to the Iraqi Atomic Energy Agency, and deliveries of dual-use electronics gear and machine tools to the Saad 16 missile design center, the Badr bomb plant, the Saddam missile factory, the Salahuddin and Mansour defense electronics factories, and the Taji weapons complex.

In July, Bechtel won a consulting contract potentially worth $1 billion with Hussein Kamil's Ministry of Industry to design and eventually build a new petrochemicals complex near Al Musayib, south of Baghdad. Hussein Kamil and Amer al-Saadi planned to use the complex, called PC-2, to produce mustard gas precursors and ethylene oxide, the latter for fuel-air explosives and rocket propellants. Later that year the Commerce Department sponsored an exhibit of U.S. high-tech equipment at the Baghdad Trade Fair, proclaiming that Iraq was wide open to U.S. business now that the war with Iran was over.

For once, it was the State Department — or at least, some officials at State — that expressed reservations about Saddam's activities. In an interview in Washington only days before the news of Saddam's latest Kurdish campaign broke, Peter Burleigh's top assistant, Lawrence Pope, predicted that Saddam would use his victory against Iran as a pretext to turn against the Kurds. "We can anticipate some fireworks soon in remote areas, far from public eyes," he said. "It's going to be a mess, and we are concerned. We will have to criticize Saddam's behavior toward the Kurds. Saddam's human rights record is the biggest damper on better U.S.-Iraqi relations."

When the brutality of Saddam's August campaign became apparent, however, the State Department did nothing. Instead, senators Jesse Helms and Claiborne Pell sent a team from the Senate Foreign Relations Committee to investigate. Larry Pope quietly agreed to cooperate and set the staffers up with the head of the Political Section at the U.S. Embassy in Baghdad, Haywood Rankin.

Rankin, a career Foreign Service officer, had just spent four years in Syria. He spoke Arabic and knew many Iraqi Kurdish leaders personally. Working in total secrecy, he managed to ferry the Senate investigators into Iraqi Kurdistan without arousing the suspicion of the Baghdad government. Peter Galbraith, who led the Senate team, did not mention Rankin's help in the published version of their report. Instead, he thanked some State Department officials based in Turkey, who helped conduct interviews on the Turkish side of the border.

The Senate report, published in October 1988, provided a grisly account of Saddam's use of poison gas against his own people. It also raised the question why the United States government, which knew what Saddam was doing in great detail, did nothing whatsoever to qualify its support for the Iraqi despot. Iraq had won the war with Iran, and U.S. allies in the region no longer ran the risk of being overrun by a radical Islamic regime. And yet the United States' backing of Saddam not only continued, it intensified, with active aid from the Commerce Department and political support from the State Department.

"The lack of international response has encouraged Iraq to make more extensive use of chemical weapons," the Senate report argued. If Saddam Hussein cared little about global public opinion, "the Iraqis do understand more direct forms of pressure. As it seeks to rebuild after eight years of warfare, Iraq will be looking to Western loans, to Western commercial credits, and to Western technology. Sanctions that affected Iraq's ability to borrow or to import Western goods, including technology, could make the price of continued chemical weapons use and of continuing the slaughter in Iraqi Kurdistan unacceptably high. This is particularly true since Iraq's most recent use of chemical weapons is totally unrelated to the struggle for national survival against Iran."

Following the staff report, the Senate passed the Prevention of Genocide Act of 1988, which it tacked onto more comprehensive legislation intended to impose sanctions on Iraq. Predictably, the Reagan administration reacted by stating that the proposed legislation was "premature."

The very threat of sanctions, however, was enough to get the pro-Iraq lobby up in arms. In October 1988, Marshall Wiley of the U.S.–Iraq Business Forum picked up his pen to lobby President Reagan against the Senate bill. He chose to write his letter on Forum stationery, which listed the organization's impressive roster of Fortune 500 members. It was a none-too-subtle hint of whose interests he was defending. "We fully understand and agree with your desire to limit the use of chemical weapons," Wiley wrote. However, he urged the president to oppose sanctions against Iraq because they "would have the opposite effect." As Wiley explained in a subsequent interview, "We didn't like the idea of sanctions because they were unilateral. They only affected the United States. Sanctions would have had no effect on Iraqi behavior. But they would have shifted business away from the U.S. to other exporters."

Neither the sanctions bill nor the Prevention of Genocide Act ever became law. On the contrary, the United States did even more business with Iraq. In November the Iraqis found out about Haywood Rankin's contacts with the Kurds. If he hadn't been a diplomat, they would have arrested him for spying and executed him. As it was, they declared him *persona non grata* and expelled him from the country, along with three British diplomats who had been caught looking a bit too closely at Iraqi weapons plants. As for Lawrence Pope, the only senior State Department official who had ever expressed public concern for the Kurds, he lost his job not long afterward. His boss, Peter Burleigh, was too busy forging closer ties with Iraq to be bothered by the country's abysmal human rights record. In this he was supported by Richard Murphy, Undersecretary of State John Whitehead, and the White House, which had been in total disarray since the Iran-contra scandal.

But the pro-Iraq policy was getting its most vigorous support from the American business community. Saddam's Iraq was a great untapped market for American exporters. With expert guidance from the U.S.–Iraq Business Forum, they let their congressmen know it.

SIXTEEN

The Gang's All Here

With the end of the Iran–Iraq war, businessmen around the world expected to cash in. Both countries had been heavily damaged by the war and needed extensive infrastructure repairs. Estimates of the damage ranged from $200 billion to as high as $500 billion. But on one thing the experts agreed: the war had hit Iran much harder than it had Iraq. By the end of 1988 it was apparent that the Iranian economy was in shambles, and the Islamic regime's record of supporting international terrorism did not make the Western powers eager to finance reconstruction. Iraq, on the other hand, was making all the right noises — if one could ignore the mute agony of massacred Kurds. To open the economy to foreign investment, the Iraqis hastened to announce a myriad of gigantic "reconstruction" projects, such as the $1 billion PC-2 petrochemicals complex in Al Musayyid. Businessmen from France, West Germany, Italy, Japan, Britain and the United States flocked to Baghdad to stake their claim to the next gold rush.

Problems soon became apparent. Iraq was deeply in debt, perhaps by as much as $70 billion, if one counted the $35 billion in protection money and borrowed oil Saddam Hussein had extorted from his Arab neighbors to save them from Islamic Iran. The finance ministries of West Germany, France, Britain, and Italy sounded quiet notes of alarm. They argued that a "London Club" of Iraq's creditors should convene to reschedule the entire Iraqi debt so that new contracts could be signed on a sounder footing.

Global rescheduling was what Saddam feared the most, because it would put a damper on his mounting ambitions. One by one, he let his suppliers know that Iraq intended to reward those countries and companies that had kept the faith during the dark days of the war. Juicy new contracts would be sent their way — *if* they shied away from any London Club arrangement, which would have put his economy under international surveillance, with Iraq's creditors tapping directly into its oil revenues in a kind of international withholding tax. The business lobbies and the arms salesmen got the point and pressured their governments to find "creative" solutions to Iraq's debt.

The West German government was one of the first to react. Export credits for Iraq were reinstated in 1988, after a July 1 meeting in Bonn between Chancellor Kohl and Iraqi Foreign Minister Tarek Aziz. A further meeting, between Kohl's deputy for intelligence affairs, Wolfgang Schauble, and Iraqi Vice President Taha Moheddin Marouf, in Bonn on November 23, focused specifically on expanding trade. The West German government pledged to maintain its easygoing attitude toward industrial exports to Iraq. As Lorenz Schomerus, who was in charge of export policy at the West German Economics Ministry, explained, "Nobody saw any interest in maintaining strict controls."[1]

When the figures for the end of the year came in, Germany's understanding of Iraq's special needs shone through clearly. The Federal Republic sold $826 million worth of high-technology products to Iraq in 1988, more than double the sales of the year before. In 1989, West German high-tech exports would roar past the $1 billion mark. The vast majority of these Iraqi purchases were going into known weapons plants, such as Taji, Badr, Saad 16, the Al Fallujah and Karbala missile works, and the al-Hillah rocket fuel and explosives plant. It was a great victory for Schomerus, who never lost an occasion to explain that his employer, after all, was the Ministry *for* Economic Affairs, not against them.[2]

Now that the war was over, American exporters were not going to take a back seat to the Germans. U.S. exports to Iraq took a giant leap forward in 1988, breaching the $1 billion mark for the first time. However, the bulk of the exports consisted of food. Iraq was now the biggest foreign market for companies like Comet Rice, which figured prominently in the U.S.–Iraq Business Forum. High-technology goods shipped from the United States tended to be specialized items unavailable on other markets. But if their dollar value was less, their military value was high.

The United States shifted its commercial policy toward Iraq.

Industrial exporters were openly encouraged by the State Department, the Commerce Department, and the Business Forum to seek Iraqi contracts, and before the year was out, the United States became the largest single buyer of Iraqi oil. From 1988 on, companies such as Coastal Oil, Chevron, Conoco, and Occidental purchased one out of every four barrels of oil the Iraqis exported.

The U.S.–Iraqi relationship had all the trappings of a solid partnership. President Reagan was not going to see all that good business go down the drain just because of a few Kurds. Neither was George Bush. Senate hearings on Iraq in January 1989, after Bush's inauguration, led to a bill calling for trade sanctions to punish Iraq for using chemical weapons against its own citizens. The Senate bill, the Chemical and Biological Control Act of 1989, which passed on January 25, instructed the government to block export licenses to Iraq of sensitive technology and to cut off government-supported loans, including the CCC guarantees and credits from Eximbank. Worse, in the eyes of the U.S.–Iraq Business Forum, it stipulated that "the United States shall not import any good, commodity, or service" from Iraq. It amounted to a trade embargo as complete as the one imposed by the United Nations following Iraq's invasion of Kuwait.

One of President Bush's first official acts was to veto the Iraq sanctions. The new administration meant not merely to continue business as usual with Iraq but to ensure that business got better. In the early months of the Bush administration, the White House issued a National Security Decision Directive calling for improved relations and more business activity in Iraq, to be implemented by all government agencies. With open encouragement from the administration, U.S. trade with Iraq climbed past the $3 billion mark in 1989 and was set to go higher in 1990 — until Saddam Hussein burst the bubble by his invasion of Kuwait.

Bill Muscarella ran a small outfit in Tuscaloosa, Alabama, XYZ Options, which had just won a $14 million contract with Iraq's Ministry of Industry (and Military Industrialization) to build a tungsten-carbide machine-tool bit plant for the Badr State Establishment in Al Yusufiah, just south of Baghdad. After signing the deal with Safa Haboby, the ministry's principal buyer, Muscarella was told he could pick up his money at BNL.

In an affidavit submitted to federal court in Atlanta, XYZ's vice president, Richard W. Kendrick, explained that the June 12, 1988, contract with Iraq's Machinery Trade Company was "to furnish the architectural services to construct three interconnected factory buildings, and to furnish the machinery, equipment, and machine tools to be installed within those buildings, all of which will comprise the factory for manufacturing carbide tools." In a subsequent interview, Kendrick explained that the Iraqis expected to slash between $14 and $16 million per year from their import bill by making the tungsten-carbide cutting bits themselves. "These were generic tools," he said. "They could be used for just about everything, including weapons."

Despite initial reluctance at BNL to deal with an unknown firm such as XYZ, the Atlanta bankers confirmed the Central Bank of Iraq credit number 88/3/2407 and made an initial payment of $6,154,534 in August 1988. Odd details about the Alabama company and this contract emerged later. One document filed by BNL lawyers in Atlanta alleged that XYZ "was a start-up company with absolutely no prior experience in international commerce or finance; that XYZ was somehow introduced to the possibility of participating in a major construction project in Iraq through an unsolicited telecopy from a company — Matrix Churchill Corp. — it had allegedly never heard of, which was managed and controlled by Iraqi Nationals; that XYZ agreed to pay Matrix Churchill a 'finder's fee' of $1.4 million if XYZ secured the contract . . . and that the United States Department of Commerce has refused to date to issue an export license for one of the pieces of machinery that XYZ wishes to export because of the potential for use of the equipment in manufacturing arms and the inability of the Department to confirm the bona fide nature of the alleged importer."

Unwittingly or not, XYZ Options had become an Iraqi front company. Orders for specific pieces of equipment for the weapons plants were transmitted to Safa Haboby in London, who sent them on to Matrix Churchill in Ohio. But even these screens were not enough to satisfy the Iraqis. Matrix Churchill then hired XYZ Options to sign contracts on its behalf with thirty other suppliers from a list provided by Safa Haboby and another Iraqi, Abdul Qaddumi, a "project manager" at Matrix. Banking documents and telexes show that suppliers included the aircraft engine manufacturer Pratt & Whitney, General Industrial Diamond of New Jersey,

Waida of Japan, EWAG in Switzerland, and other machine-tool companies in Brazil and Europe. Nowhere is Safa Haboby's TDG mentioned. Haboby's concern was to hide his involvement as much as possible from American authorities; he did not want to appear as the final purchaser.

He had excellent reasons for such caution. One consignment of computer-controlled machine tools ordered by XYZ was intercepted by U.S. Customs officers on its way to Iraq from GTE Valenite in Royal Oak, Michigan. Shipping documents showed the destination as the Huteen State Establishment in Al Iskandariyah, which was part of the industrial belt south of Baghdad. Huteen was one of the largest weapons complexes in Iraq, a fact even the Department of Commerce was having difficulty avoiding.

Because of Commerce's doubts, Moore Special Tool of Bridgeport, Connecticut, had trouble getting a computer-controlled jig grinder worth $380,564 cleared for export to Iraq. The Commerce Department, suspecting the tool could be used for military ends, requested additional information from the company. Jig grinders are essential for manufacturing nuclear weapons and for producing high-precision components such as gyroscopes for ballistic missile guidance systems. The Department of Energy, identifying Moore Special Tool as the sole American source of jig grinders for U.S. nuclear weapons programs, blocked a takeover attempt by Fanuc of Japan.

Richard Kendrick of XYZ Options had been in the machine-tool business for thirty years and fully understood the strategic nature of the Moore jig grinder, but he said he was convinced that the Iraqis were serious about building a legitimate machine-tool industry, since they had sent thirty-three technicians to Alabama for training and intended to send more. Once while in Baghdad to supervise deliveries, he offered to take U.S. Embassy officials around the Badr and Huteen plants, to reassure them about Iraqi intentions to manufacture only commercial parts such as truck engines and transmissions.

Moore was not the only company having difficulties with its export licenses. A subsequent request, in February 1989, to ship metal-working machines worth $5,669,977 to Huteen shows that the Department of Commerce understood the true nature of the weapons complex. It also shows that Commerce understood in detail the involvement of BNL Atlanta, yet it sounded no alarms. In the file accompanying DoC case number D006442, investigators noted that they called Christopher Drogoul at BNL Atlanta, who was financing the deal, "in an attempt to get end-user information" about Huteen. Drogoul shrugged them off with the excuse that the "letter of credit in question was received by the bank in the same batch as a number of other letters of credit relating to the Badoush [sic] Dam project," a released version of the file shows. Incredible as that explanation appeared, Commerce let the matter drop. A later attempt to purchase $185,000 worth of computers, which was eventually turned down, said the equipment was needed at Huteen "to handle its huge workload."

The Huteen complex included several different production lines, to manufacture everything from explosives and propellants to Cardoen cluster bombs. But why did the Iraqis need the specially hardened machine-tool bits? According to former Deputy Undersecretary of Defense Steve Bryen, they may have been intended for cutting and shaping depleted uranium to manufacture artillery rounds similar to those used by the U.S. Army's latest tank, the Abrams M1A2. "The theory, and so far, it's only a theory," Bryen said, "is that they received large quantities of depleted uranium from Eastern Europe, and especially East Germany, which produces tons of the stuff every year as nuclear waste." Depleted uranium is extremely hard, and shaping it eats up numerous bits. Hence the need to have the bits made in Iraq, so they wouldn't have to bother with export licenses. Kendrick didn't blink when questioned about the possibility that Iraq was manufacturing uranium penetrators. "Sure, these machines could do it, and we sold them other machine tools which we use here in the U.S. to make uranium fuel pellets for nuclear power plants," he said in an interview. "But the Iraqis got them without all the radiation protection, which would make it pretty hairy if they ever wanted to use them for that purpose. I mean, their operators would have a very short life span if they did that."

Sadiq Taha journeyed to Atlanta on October 4, 1988, to work out a new $300 million loan agreement with Drogoul. Taha, who was still being treated in the United States for a heart ailment, was accompanied by a man who gradually replaced him as the principal Iraqi negotiator, Raja Hassan Ali. Besides working for the Central Bank, Ali said he was director general of the Ministry of Industry and had been put in charge of financing Iraq's industrialization projects. Like so many other Iraqi purchasers in those days, he conveniently forgot to identify his ministry by its full name.

This second unsecured loan agreement was signed on October 6. The document specifies that the money was intended to finance "the construction of industrial projects and/or the purchase of equipments, materials and services from the U.S.A. and/or other countries." It was a long way from the CCC grain credits. Now BNL was doing business directly with the Ministry of Industry and Military Industrialization, providing the money Iraq needed to build its weapons plants. For Drogoul's sake, the Iraqis spoke only about a project to build a hydroelectric dam across the Tigris at Badush, not far from Saad 16. The head of the Badush Dam project, Abdul Muneim Rashid, came to Washington to meet with Drogoul and government officials in August 1988. Rashid was later indicted in the United States for his participation in the BNL blunder.

In a letter attached to the second loan agreement, Drogoul can almost be heard counting his profits. "We are pleased to refer to the signature today of the new Medium Term Loan Agreement," he writes, "and to confirm to undertake to provide additional USA dollar 500 million loan to be utilized by the Ministry of Industry of the Republic of Iraq during 1989." In return, the Iraqis promised to give Drogoul the lion's share of the lucrative CCC business for 1989, as well as Eximbank credits, which export bankers considered a cash cow.

A few weeks later Drogoul traveled to London to visit Taha in the hospital, where he was awaiting a donor heart. But the Iraqi banker was not so ill that he didn't seize the occasion to introduce Drogoul to the men in charge of spending the BNL money: Dr. Safa Jawad Haboby and Fadel Kadhum.

Drogoul signed the third protocol on December 3, 1988, in Washington, apparently without telling anyone at BNL Atlanta. This time Sadiq Taha was replaced by Raja Hassan Ali from MIMI and a new man from the Central Bank, Abdulwahad Toma. Court documents in Atlanta say it was in Washington that Raja Hassan

Ali first suggested to Drogoul that they work out a more discreet formula, which they called "Option B," for handling industrial financing projects.

Instead of processing the money in the normal way, Option B used "front" accounts to pay for Iraqi purchases, in the same way that Safa Haboby used front companies to order the equipment. Whenever the Iraqis had bills to pay, they simply sent notice to BNL of the amount, and the money was paid into a series of clearing accounts. According to the indictment handed down by the U.S. attorney in Atlanta, on February 28, 1991, this procedure "effectively concealed not only BNL-Atlanta as the source of the funds generated, but also the identities of ultimate recipients of the funds and the purposes for which they were used."

By this time, it was clear that BNL's principal business in Iraq was not grain.

In the summer of 1988, Bruno Stemmler returned to Iraq. At the request of his Iraqi hosts, the German nuclear engineer brought along a former colleague from MAN Technologies, Walter Busse. The seventy-six-year-old German was an old Middle East hand. In the 1950s and 1960s he had worked in Egypt for President Gamal Abdel Nasser, helping to design ballistic missiles and military jet engines. Before retiring, Busse had been in charge of centrifuge production at MAN, which was why he was in Baghdad; the Iraqis had a production problem they wanted to solve. A West German intelligence report shows that Stemmler and Busse stayed for several months in 1988 and 1989, helping the Iraqis iron the kinks out of the centrifuge program.

When the two Germans arrived, they were taken immediately to the MIMI offices, just across the road from the Rashid Hotel. Once again they were shown the blueprints of the gas ultracentrifuge, a duplicate of the MAN design. Then the two were taken by car on the road to Samarra, to visit the top-secret centrifuge production unit at Taji, Factory 10.

"It looked like a very modern factory," Stemmler told the *Sunday Times*. "The buildings were low and spread out over an enormous area, so that it could not be easily destroyed by aircraft."

Stemmler says the Iraqis told him that the Taji plant had been built during the Iran–Iraq war to manufacture artillery barrels.

Now it was also making gas centrifuges for uranium enrichment. "They were producing lots of them (outer casings)," Stemmler recalled. "That is why Mr. Busse was called to be there."

The problem was in one of the milling machines that spun the outer casings. "They asked me real production questions," Busse told a reporter from the *Sunday Times* Insight team. "For example, on the end caps for centrifuges. I told them you can produce them by forging or by lathe or by cutting from steel sheet."

Despite these details, both Germans insisted they had no idea the Iraqis were building the centrifuges for uranium enrichment. "If you are producing parts, you don't know what they are parts for," Busse said. "I was only there to do consultancy work on production." But the parts they discussed — centrifuge casings, end caps made of specially hardened maraging steel, and ring magnets made of samarium cobalt — were so particular and so rare that their combination in one place could mean only one thing.

In a confidential briefing to the West German Bundestag on August 21, 1990, Economics Minister Helmut Haussmann admitted that federal intelligence agencies had extensive knowledge of West German involvement in Iraqi weapons programs, but did nothing about it. After naming dozens of West German companies, he singled out Busse and Stemmler for their efforts to assist the Iraqi nuclear weapons program. "Components and system parts of the Iraqi gas ultracentrifuge show the engineering characteristics of various types of German gas ultracentrifuge," Haussmann said. "The assumption is being made that an important role in this was played by two former employees of the MAN Technologien GmbH Company in Munich. . . . After they left the company, both of them were in Iraq for extended periods in 1988 and 1989. They also attempted, without success, to obtain other centrifuge experts for Iraq." Haussmann hastened to add that a criminal investigation of Busse and Stemmler "yielded no evidence to confirm suspicions of illegal technology transfer." Of course not. Advising the Iraqis on the most efficient techniques for enriching uranium into weapons-grade fuel was perfectly legal under German law.[3]

With full-scale production of centrifuges beginning at Taji and with the experimental cascade up and running in Thuwaitha, it was a matter of only two or three more years before Iraq would have enough highly enriched uranium to make a bomb. Over the next eighteen months, Iraqi procurement agents (including TDG, Techcorps, Industrial Projects Company, H+H Metalform) purchased large quantities of maraging steel on the open market, which was shipped to Taji to be cut into end caps and other centrifuge parts. They also attempted to buy finished end caps and ring magnets, which suggests there were snags in local production (maraging steel in extremely hard, brittle, and difficult to machine). Having taken the clandestine route to the bomb, the Iraqis had to expect problems. What was extraordinary was just how quickly they resolved them. "Iraq's progress was directly proportional to the amount of money they threw at the problem," one Defense Department analyst explained. "And they threw lots of it into the centrifuge program. Much more than a country like Pakistan, or even Brazil."

Meanwhile, unknown to anyone in the West, Iraqi scientists had embarked on a parallel program to enrich uranium, using a technique called magnetic isotope separation. This technique, perfected by physicists of the Manhattan Project during World War II, required large amounts of energy and bulky equipment; because of its inefficiency, magnetic isotope separation was abandoned by the United States in the late 1940s, after it had yielded enough weapons-grade fuel for the bombs that devastated Hiroshima and Nagasaki.

Unlike the centrifuge program, which required controlled technologies that were difficult to purchase and even harder to master, magnetic isotope separation relied on a device called the California cyclotron, or calutron, whose design could be found in a university-level textbook. "This was all basic stuff," a Defense Department analyst explained. "The technology had been decontrolled for years and was widely available, so it was a bit like K Mart shopping: pick up a magnet on aisle A, a transformer on aisle B, and you're all set."

Because the equipment needed to build the calutron required no export licenses, Iraqi purchases in the United States and Europe left few traces, if any. "No one gave this a thought back in 1988 or 1989," the DoD analyst said. "There are four major processes for obtaining weapons-grade fuel. Now we know that Saddam was spending billions of dollars to pursue them all, simultaneously."

To operate the calutrons, Iraq's Army Corps of Engineers built two large-scale facilities (which no Westerner had ever seen before UN inspectors demanded entrance in July 1991) in Tarmiyah, 20 kilometers north of Taji, and at Ash Sharqat, roughly midway between Mosul and Tikrit. Each plant was equipped with its own 100-megawatt power station, making it independent of the national power grid and further enhancing secrecy. Hussein Kamil's Ministry of Industry purchased switchgear, transformers, and power substations from Hyundai in South Korea, Merlin Guerin in France, and ASEA in Sweden — an unusual step, since purchases of power-generating equipment were generally made by the State Organization for Electricity.

An Iraqi electrical engineer who had been working at the buried Ash Sharqat site defected to U.S. Marines positioned in northern Iraq in June 1991; he was the first to reveal the existence of the calutron program, which he said had produced some 90 pounds of bomb-grade fuel by the time he defected. He also told intelligence officers that the Ash Sharqat plant had never been bombed during the allied air campaign against Iraq and that four other undiscovered nuclear plants had survived the war without a scar.[4]

With his nuclear physicists so close to their ultimate goal, Hussein Kamil decided it was time to begin the final push to get the bomb. In September 1988, he ordered his procurement networks to launch an all-out effort to purchase nuclear triggering devices called krytrons. These miniaturized electronic switches were the key to detonating a nuclear explosion, but they were available only from a handful of companies in the United States and Britain. Their sale was tightly controlled.

Hussein Kamil never believed he would have any difficulty obtaining his precious switches in the United States, given his success everywhere else. Indeed, on February 10, 1988, one of his network's best suppliers, Leybold AG of West Germany, had obtained an export license from the U.S. Department of Commerce to purchase vacuum pumps and numerical controllers worth $888,000 for the Taji ultracentrifuge project, and an initial batch of 184 capacitors similar to krytrons had been acquired legally from a San Diego company called Maxwell Laboratories. But the capacitors had not been up to nuclear specifications, and the Iraqis needed more.[5]

Jack Kelly headed the Strategic Investigations Unit at the U.S. Customs Service in Washington. His job was to bring technobandits of all stripes to justice. In an interview in Washington, he expressed admiration for the professionalism of the Iraqi procurement network. "The Iraqis were much more sophisticated than the Iranians had ever been. They knew what they wanted, where to find it, and had a well-established purchasing structure in the U.S. and in Europe. They activated this network in 1987, when their need was the greatest. We only got onto them on the tail end of the curve. Before then, we just don't know how much stuff got through."[6]

When the school year ended in June 1988, Abdul Hussein Abbas pulled his two sons out of school in Monza, Italy, and decided to resettle in West Germany. He had recently been indicted by a judge in Rimini for selling arms to Iraq. Although the charges were dismissed, his brush with the law convinced him that it was time to seek a milder climate.

His brother, Kassim Abbas, stayed on in Italy, and in mid-1988 set up a branch of his European Manufacturing Center in Great Britain with another Iraqi, Ali Ashour Daghir. The new company, Euromac (London), located in the suburb of Thames Ditton, was conveniently close to Heathrow Airport. It was officially in the business of exporting food products and air conditioning systems. In fact, Kassim Abbas and Ali Daghir took orders from Safa Haboby. Anxious as ever to disguise his activities, Haboby decided to use Euromac as a front for purchasing the krytrons.

In September 1988, Abbas and Daghir made contact with a Massachusetts company, EG&G, whose name had been given to them by Pakistani friends (Pakistan had done business with EG&G in 1984). But EG&G became suspicious and refused to quote a price on the krytrons.

The next call the Iraqis made met with more success. They located a high-tech firm in California called CSI Technologies. The president of the company, Jerold Kowalsky, said sure he'd take a look at the capacitors they needed. He asked them to fax over the specifications, and he'd get back to them.

When Kowalsky got the fax, his first call was not to Kassim Abbas but to the local office of the U.S. Customs Service. He explained the request he had just received from the two Iraqis. It was clear to him that the only equipment corresponding to the Iraqi specifications was a type of krytron that could be used only for nuclear detonation. In fact, his company made them to equip the Midgetman ballistic missile. What should he do?

Stay on it, the customs officer told him. String them along.

Customs assigned Special Agent Daniel Supnick to the case, and Kowalsky agreed to let him pose as a CSI employee. They code-named the proposed sting Operation Argus. It would take nearly eighteen months to come off, but when it did, it would explode with a bang heard round the world.

Gerald Bull's Babylon Project was moving ahead faster than any-one could have foreseen. His procurement network in Europe, long prepared for this momentous undertaking, was just waiting for the word go.

In November 1988, Space Research Corporation contracted with its part-owner, PRB of Belgium, to purchase 235 tons of double-base extruded powder for the giant rocket-powered projec-tiles of the Babylon gun. The contract was worth $17.86 million. To play it safe, PRB listed Jordan as the destination of the ship-ments in all documents submitted to the Belgian government. An end-user certificate was even provided by the Royal Jordanian Armed Forces, stating that the special propellants (25 tons of small-grain and 210 tons of large-grain powder) were for use by the Jordanian army and would not be reexported to a third country.

Meanwhile, Christopher Cowley of ATI had made arrangements with Sheffield Forgemasters and Walter Summers to cast pipe seg-ments for the 350 mm "Baby Babylon" gun. On February 25, 1989, a special Iraqi air force Ilyushin-76 cargo plane arrived at Manchester airport to take on a precious cargo: three giant steel tubes, each ten meters long and weighing several tons. When they were strapped into the cargo plane's hold, flight IA 14707 took off. On the flight plan logged with the airport authorities, its destina-tion was clearly marked: Mosul, Iraq.

In early March a Belgian air force C-130 cargo plane took off from a military airport and headed for Amman, carrying the first twelve tons of small-grain powder ordered by Bull's agents. Later that month the prototype super-gun was placed on a specially built rail for testing high-speed projectiles near Saad 16, and the first horizontal firing trials were held.

Back in Britain, Bull was hard at work with Safa Haboby trying to find a sure source of advanced composites and carbon-fiber materials of the kind Abdelkader Helmy had tried to purchase in the United States. He wanted them in order to make a rocket-assisted projectile that would be able to reach Israel when fired from the super-gun. In Belfast, Northern Ireland, Bull spotted a company that make exactly the materials they wanted. Learfan had been up on the auction block since 1985, when it had failed in a venture to make business aircraft out of composite materials. When Bull discovered LearFan, the premises had been rented out for storage, but all the manufacturing equipment was intact.

Haboby and his legal advisor, Fadel Kadhum, proposed the next steps. Rather than buying the company directly, they set up a front called the Canira Technical Corporation Ltd. and registered it in Northern Ireland. Canira was owned on a fifty-fifty basis by SRC and TDG; the name stood for CANada–IRAq. To make sure the ownership could not be traced, Canira set up another front company called SRC Composites Ltd., which bought the Learfan factory in Belfast. Soon afterward, the new management applied to the North Ireland Industrial Development Board for a $3.6 million development grant to put the company back on its feet. After all, they argued, it would mean new jobs.

Only fourteen months after beginning the Babylon Project, Gerald Bull was seeing his dream finally take flesh. But instead of a satellite launcher, it had become a full-fledged weapons system.

After the horizontal trials in March 1989, Saddam Hussein ordered Bull's technicians to dismantle the gun so it could be hauled to a specially prepared site for permanent installation. The site, dug out of the Jebel Makhoul, a ridge of mountains just to the east of the Baiji oil refinery, was so well protected that only the tip of the 56-meter-long barrel would ever stick out above ground. Each super-gun shell, made at Taji of high-strength maraging steel, would carry approximately 500 kilograms of high explosives a distance of 1,000 kilometers. It was as good as the Condor II, and it certainly put less of a dent in the Iraqi budget.

* * *

Each of Iraq's successes in transforming or adapting an existing weapon system created additional demands and new ambitions, and Saddam wanted to realize them all. He wanted to equal the exploit of South Africa, which in braving the UN arms embargo imposed in 1977 had succeeded in creating its own armaments industry "from the earth to the sky." Although Iraq did not possess the same wealth of minerals as did South Africa, it had enough oil to buy what it needed on the open market. Like the South Africans, Saddam wanted total control over the entire weapons manufacturing process, from pouring the steel and bending it into shape to the final line of computer code that guided a missile to its target.

The Taji weapons complex was one key to Saddam's ambition. The steel plant, built by Thyssen Rheinstahl, was churning out the basic materials for a wide variety of weapons. Since 1986 Ferrostaal and dozens of West German subcontractors had been building a "universal forge" at Taji with the full knowledge and approval of the Bonn government. According to documents quoted by Hans Leyendecker and Richard Rickelmann of *Der Spiegel* and interviews with German customs officials, the plan was to build 1,000 artillery pieces per year at Taji, in calibers ranging from 105 millimeters to 203 millimeters.

And in a separate production unit built by Klöckner Industrie, Iraqi tanks were being rebuilt. In addition to retrofitting older T-54 and T-62 tanks, Iraqi officials say they began to assemble the newer T-72 at Taji in early 1989, in a license agreement signed with Buman-Labedy of Poland. They called the new tank the Asad Babil, or Lion of Babylon. But Iraqi armaments engineers were not content with assembling the tanks from knock-down kits. They argued that once you factored in the cost of building the plant, kit assembly did not lead to any appreciable savings in the overall unit cost. Amer Rashid and his colleagues at MIMI wanted Taji to become a steel manufacturing center for all applications, including tank bodies and tank armor. Taji was Iraq's attempt to build tanks and artillery pieces "from the earth to the sky," just like South Africa. To finance it, they turned to BNL-Atlanta. BNL shelled out hundreds of millions of dollars to manufacturers in Italy, West Germany, Great Britain, and the United States to turn Taji into one of the most modern, complete weapons facilities in the world.

On January 24, 1989, Danieli SpA, of Udine, Italy, signed a

contract worth $89.7 million to build a steel rolling mill at Taji for special steels. Contract documents precisely list Iraqi requirements: "Engineering steel, spring steel, bearing steel, free cutting steel, high tensile steel, steel for welding electrodes, tool steel, and stainless steel," in thicknesses ranging from 5.5 millimeters to 7 centimeters. "That's the size of most armor plate," noted Steve Bryen.

Cecelia Danieli, who doubles as managing director and chief executive officer, said in interviews that her company was not building a weapons plant. "This was a rolling mill intended for purely civilian products," she insisted. "It was for the construction industry." In a subsequent interview after Operation Desert Storm began, she insisted that her company "did nothing wrong, since we never delivered a thing. The contract was suspended because of the UN embargo before we could ever get past the foundation work."

German prosecutors seized 750 cases of documents at Ferrostaal headquarters, including complete blueprints of the artillery pieces to be manufactured at Taji; but at Danieli the Italian government discovered no smoking gun. And U.S. intelligence experts readily acknowledged that Taji included both civilian and military production areas, separated by a road. But the steel to be produced at the Danieli plant was no ordinary product; it was to consist of six highly sophisticated alloys with clear military applications. The Taji deal was only the prelude to a far bigger contract, worth $377.2 million, to build a second turnkey steel mill at the Khor al-Zubair industrial complex near Basra. This deal, code-named the Ashtar Project, was signed on March 4, 1989; the factory was to produce two million tons per year of hot rolled strip steel from scrap iron and sponge iron. It was one way of recycling the older tanks: put them into the smelter and forge new ones.

To celebrate his "victory" over Iran, Saddam decided to build a triumphal arch at the entry to Baghdad. The monumental arch, towering 140 feet above the highway, was formed by a pair of crossed swords held aloft by gigantic bronze hands. From the scabbard of each sword was strung a net bag full of Iranian helmets, supposed to have been taken from actual battlefield casualties. The German company that built the monument says it was given a photograph of Saddam's own forearms to use as a model. The triumphal arch may have been the builders' only completely legitimate contract with Iraq. They were H+H Metalform, the same company that had built another monument to Saddam by supplying him with equipment for the uranium enrichment project.

Christopher Drogoul was having second thoughts. On the one hand he was eager for Iraqi business. The Atlanta branch of BNL was turning a good profit and his superiors were happy. He was getting only the most positive feedback from U.S. officials in Washington and Baghdad, where he now traveled often. BNL had become an instrument of U.S. foreign policy; the idea, as Richard Murphy and others at the State Department liked to explain, was to "bring Iraq back into the community of nations" by trade and by aid. On the other hand, Drogoul didn't like the fact that BNL Atlanta was the only bank in the world issuing new credits for Iraq. Like most businessmen, bankers dread working alone. Drogoul, beginning to fear he had ventured too far out into left field, tried to scale back the size of the Iraqi loans. In a lengthy telex sent to Sadiq Taha only days after the signing of the third medium-term-loan protocol in December 1988, Drogoul laid his doubts on the table.

> I would like to express my appreciation to you and to all your staff who have worked diligently in the furtherance of our relations. . . . As you may be aware, our involvement in providing finance on a large scale was initiated in 1986 . . . during a period when many institutions were reticent to provide financial support to Iraq in view of the general drop in oil prices, in view of the weakness of the U.S. dollar, and given the conflict between your country and Iran.
> At that time, we extended CCC guaranteed facilities and related unguaranteed facilities in order to ensure the success of your foodstuffs import program. This support was extended even though we put aside a generally accepted banking practice of maintaining a diversified portfolio so as not to be too dependent on a particular source of loan income. I will add that we were only too happy to provide support. . . . .
> Lately, the world economic indicators have improved. The price of oil has risen from its lows of 1986, and most importantly the conflagaration [sic] which has torn your country appears to be ended. . . . The process of rebuilding and industrializing will be an expensive and time-consuming process. Here too, we are pleased to be of assistance, as evidenced by our recent commitments.
> . . . You will certainly agree that neither of our institutions should

be too dependent upon each other, especially now that the trials of the past years are behind your country and you need to diversify your sources of finance.

In view of all the above, we wish to take this opportunity to request that we begin to scale back our level of activity to normal and prudent banking levels. . . . We would like to request that we begin the process of reducing your overall dependence on us, and to do so we propose not to provide any further facilities in favor of Iraq for the time being, except for short term trade lines.[7]

But almost as soon as he had begun, Drogoul dropped his attempt to limit the Iraqi loans. Instead, on January 11, 1989, he faxed Raja Hassan Ali at the Ministry of Industry and Military Industrialization to "keep our name out of the picture until we have agreed to handle transaction" through Option A or Option B. "If Option B is selected, it is not necessary for supplier even to know our name." For Drogoul and his colleagues at the bank, secrecy soon replaced prudence.

From then on, demands for payments flowed in. SerVaas Inc. of Indiana came to collect $8.3 million to start work on a plant in Ameriya, to separate copper from brass. The idea was to use the millions of spent artillery shell casings the Iraqis had fired during the war to make copper wire and new artillery shells. Ameriya was conveniently located near the Al Fallujah missile and poison gas works. Centrifugal Casting Machine came to collect on its contract to install machines for manufacturing "water and sewage pipe" at the Badr General Establishment in Al Yusufiah, a plant that also made bombs and artillery shells. Dozens of other letters of credit were issued by BNL in the first two months of 1989 alone. On February 10, Yavuz Tezeller, of the Turkish grain trader Entrade, submitted documents prepared by the Compagnie Européene du Sud in Luxembourg relating to a $4.5 million shipment of rolled steel to Iraq. On February 15, Raja Hassan Ali informed Drogoul of a new $96 million project he wanted to split up into several smaller letters of credit. Two days later, Ali came back and asked for a $30.7 million facility, to fund purchases from the Bulgarian state arms trading organization, CE Kintex.

Almost all of these deals involved deliveries to Iraqi weapons plants. Many required export licenses from the U.S. Department of Commerce. Yet Drogoul, Von Wedel, and their colleagues never seemed to bat an eye.

On February 22, Drogoul and Von Wedel went to London to meet with Safa Haboby, Fadel Kadhum, and Abdul Qaddumi of TDG and Matrix Churchill. They were escorted to the Matrix plant in Coventry to get their first look at the business they were financing. It had nothing to do with grain. When they returned to the TDG offices, Haboby asked the bankers if they could fund the Danieli steel projects, which would swallow up $468 million of the BNL credit line for Iraq. Drogoul said he could see no objection.

Meanwhile, U.S. Customs blocked a February 1989 shipment of vacuum pumps, bound for Iraq from a Rochester, New York, manufacturer. The pumps were designed for use in a gas ultra-centrifuge cascade for uranium enrichment.

Also on February 22, Rear Admiral Thomas A Brooks, the director of U.S. naval intelligence, shocked a congressional sub-committee by declaring that Iraq was "actively pursuing" a nuclear weapons program. According to nuclear proliferation expert Leonard Spector, this was the first time a high-ranking American intelligence official had gone on record to warn about Iraq's nuclear activities since the destruction of the Osirak reactor in June 1981.[8]

An Iraqi delegation headed by one of Hussein Kamil's top deputies arrived in Rome on March 2, 1989, for an extended negotiating session with the Italian government. Now that the war with Iran was over, the Iraqis wanted the four Lupo-class frigates and six Assad-class corvettes ordered in 1981 that had been embargoed by the Italian parliament since 1986.

The Italians agreed that the embargo no longer applied. But officials from the Fincantieri Navali Riuniti shipyards of Genoa and from the munitions firm Oto Melara claimed that Iraq had only paid $441 million out of the total contract value of $2.646 billion. Before they released the frigates, they wanted their money.

Without blinking behind his austere steel glasses, the head of the Iraqi delegation, the wily Amer Rashid, told the Italians that Iraq was willing to pay its debt — if Italy was prepared to make fresh loans available. Before the Italians had time to object, he came back with his second shot: Iraq was at any rate obliged to withhold some $400 million, because the munitions it had ordered back in 1981 were by now too old.

"What do you mean, old? They are brand new!" the Italians objected.

"And so they were — five years ago," General Amer replied. "We ordered new weapons and paid good money for them," he scolded. "We intend to get new weapons or nothing at all."

The Italians were aghast. The munitions in question — a large number of Otomat surface-to-surface missiles (an Italian equivalent of the Exocet) and a wide assortment of naval ordnance — had been manufactured for delivery in 1986. But for three years they had been stored in warehouses and would need extensive maintenance to ensure that their sophisticated electronics systems were still functioning.

General Amer had the Italians over a barrel, and they knew it. Rather than break off negotiations (BNL Rome stood to lose $228.7 million in performance bonds, according to a report prepared by the Central Bank of Italy), they agreed to manufacture a new complement of munitions. The "fabulously lucrative" Lupo deal was on the way to becoming a net loss. The little detail of the munitions cost the Italian taxpayer $400 million.

The Lupo deal may have cost much more besides. A secret parliamentary commission in Rome had been investigating Iraq's payment record since 1987. What concerned them were Iraqi claims that they had advanced $1.824 billion for the ships in June 1982, not just $441 million. The Iraqis presented deposit slips showing that the money had been paid into two numbered accounts at the SBS Bank in Zurich — (account numbers P4 632.367-0 and P4 632.367-2). But Fincantieri and Oto Melara stuck to their guns: they had not seen a penny more than the $441 million advance and were willing to open their ledgers to prove it.

As the Italians pursued the matter, they discovered that the Swiss bank accounts the Iraqis claimed to have used were controlled by an investment company called Kapital Beratung AG. Discreet requests for information were made to the Swiss authorities, intelligence sources say, to discover what had become of the company and its accounts at SBS. After checking the commercial registry, the Swiss reported that Kapital Beratung was liquidated on September 14, 1982, and declared bankruptcy on February 4, 1983. The registry also showed that Kapital Beratung belonged to a Zurich holding company called Trans-KB, whose vice-president, Hans W. Kopp, was the husband of the Swiss justice minister. After that the trail went cold. Kopp's alleged involvement in a billion-dollar drug-money-laundering operation run by the Lebanese Sarcachi brothers had forced his wife's resignation from the Swiss government in January 1989.

The finances of Iraq Inc., were getting murkier all the time.

Drogoul went off the deep end on April 8, 1989, when he agreed to a fourth Iraqi loan request from Raja Hassan Ali during a visit to TDG in London. This open-ended loan, worth an incredible $1.155 billion, was enough to cover 25 percent of Iraq's industrial purchases for 1989. Drogoul made no attempt to control how the Iraqis spent the money. They could purchase machinery, whole companies, or even arms, and BNL would front for the bills. During Saddam's reign, Iraq went from self-sufficiency in food products to near total dependence on imports while building up a huge arms industry to become self-sufficient in defense. From Iraq's ploughshares, Saddam proposed to forge swords. And BNL was there to pay for the conversion.

Drogoul may not have understood why the Iraqis wanted so much money, but Hugues de l'Estoile of Dassault Aviation certainly did. As soon as Amer Rashid won his $400 million door prize in Rome, he headed for Paris, where he was joined by Amer al-Saadi, to work out an entirely different type of agreement with the French.

It was the first time the two Amers had come to France together. The Iraqis had reserved an entire floor of the Hotel Crillon, just across the street from the U.S. Embassy and the Place de la Concorde. They were accompanied by a host of technical experts and by Fadel Kadhum. The delegation made the rounds of all that was powerful and influential in France: the Finance Ministry, the Chamber of Commerce, and the French Employers Union, the CNPF. The grand tour, as one participant put it, was intended to "send a clear message" that the Iraqis appreciated what the French had done for them during the war and understood how difficult it had been. "They were saying: 'Believe in us again.'"

The Iraqis attended their last, but most important, meeting on March 21, 1989, at Dassault's luxurious Mirage 2000 chalet in the posh suburb of Vaucresson. Minutes of the meeting and subsequent interviews with most of the participants show in detail what the Iraqis' message was.

De l'Estoile was accompanied by top officials from Snecma and Thomson-CSF, the two indispensable partners in any French military aircraft program. After years of trying to overcome their hesitation, de l'Estoile had finally convinced them that the time had come to relax restrictions on technology transfer. Marcel Dassault had always said that production under license in a country like Iraq posed a threat to direct sales of military equipment in the future. But with his death, de l'Estoile had won the argument. It was time to cash in. By the end of the afternoon the three French companies and the Iraqis had signed a $6.5 billion protocol that set out Iraq's goals for the next ten years and established guidelines for how the French would help. They called it the Fao Project. It involved building an entire aerospace industry in Iraq in three interlocking phases:

Phase I: construction of depot-level maintenance facilities to service the Mirage F1 fleet. Instead of sending the planes back to France for their midlife overhaul, scheduled to begin in 1991, the Iraqis wanted to rebuild the engines and airframes themselves.

Phase II: construction of an aircraft factory, called Saad 25, with tooling, training, and complete technology transfer, to manufacture 134 Alphajet trainers, a joint product of Dassault and Dornier of West Germany.

Phase III: delivery, with some assembly during the final stages at Saad 25, of 54 Mirage 2000-S "strike" aircraft. This newest version of the Mirage 2000 was equipped as a low-level penetration bomber with an advanced terrain-following radar, which would allow these planes to sneak in under enemy air defenses.

Financing remained the sticking point. Participants in the negotiations say that Fadel Kadhum tried to convince Dassault to use the BNL credit line, but the French aircraft maker refused. Instead, the Fao protocol signed on March 21 stipulated payment in cash, oil, and other energy goods, on condition that the French government provided export financing and insurance. The contract was to be executed over nine to fourteen years.

The intention behind the Fao Project was double. On the one hand, the Iraqis wanted to lay the framework for an indigenous aerospace industry. On the other, they wanted to ensure that no one

— not even the French — could interfere in their military programs in the future. If they needed to overhaul their planes, or build new ones, they could do it themselves.

In Iraq, Saddam Hussein's birthday is a national holiday. School-children are encouraged to sing songs for their president. Hotels bake birthday cakes; cars and buses are festooned with flowers. Baghdad itself becomes a festival of colored lights. But April 28, 1989, was a birthday unlike all the others. Saddam had decided to prepare an additional surprise for his subjects, his arms suppliers, his bankers, and his technology brokers. He called it the First Baghdad International Exhibition for Military Production. Its symbol was an Iraqi flag shaped in the form of a dove. Its slogan was "Defense equipment for peace and prosperity." To Saddam it was not a joke.

The theme song for the arms fair was "The Gang's All Here." One hundred forty-eight companies from twenty-eight countries paid hefty prices to exhibit their equipment. In addition to the arms salesmen, many machine-tool companies were present — an unusual occurrence at arms fairs. The Bulgarians, Poles, Hungarians, and Romanians were out in force, showing 1960s-era machine tools driven by Fanuc controllers bought from Japan. The Germans and the Austrians were there, proposing equipment and turnkey military factories, just as they had in Egypt two years before. The Chinese set up their own pavilion, where they showed an artillery spotter used to direct counter-battery fire, based on a Hewlett-Packard computer.

A Franco-Lebanese middleman, Hussein Zeineddine, greeted visitors to the French pavilion as if he held the keys to all that was inside. Zeineddine was barely thirty, but his International Trading Group had mailbox offices on the Champs-Élysées in Paris, in Geneva, and in Liechtenstein and had already earned the ire of many legitimate arms exporters. A former employee of the French government export agency Sofma, Zeineddine had apparently been fired for questionable business practices. But the Iraqis loved him and set him up in the entry hall to the French pavilion. Christopher Drogoul also loved him, it seems. ITG was awarded four BNL loans in 1989, worth a total of $3,744,988. Zeineddine boasted of his access "to a large network of manufacturers in the high-tech markets," for products as varied as tantalum capacitors, microwave antennas, spectrum analyzers, and discrete semiconductors. His specialty was technology transfer.

Gerald Bull was also on hand, along with Chris Cowley of ATI, showing a 1/35 scale model of the super-gun to anyone who cared to look. Bull was the proud father of two dramatic new Iraqi weapons systems on display: the gigantic Majnoon and al-Fao self-propelled howitzers, which married a French gun, a Spanish truck, and a Swedish cab. He and Cowley had set up shop at the stand of Astra Holdings, a British financial group that had recently bought out PRB in Belgium on promises of a $1 billion contract with Iraq. Soon both groups would go bankrupt.

But stealing the show was Matrix Churchill, which had been rebaptized "Nasser" for the occasion by its Iraqi owners. In fact, the Iraqis had taken Matrix Churchill brochures and pasted on a sticker bearing the Nasser name and an address in Taji. They didn't even bother to change the company logo. If you peeled the sticker away, you could still read the Churchill name underneath. Iraqi officials openly acknowledged that they had bought out the company in an effort to duck Western export controls. "We are now making three-axis machine tools here in Iraq," they said at the arms fair. "Soon we will be making five-axis machines, with computerized numerical control." With few exceptions, these machines were going into the weapons factories.

Normally, sophisticated machine tools like these were barred from export to most Third World countries and to the Soviet bloc, because of their importance for weapons manufacturing, but by purchasing Matrix Churchill the Iraqis simply skirted the embargo. It was brilliant.

The only major Iraqi supplier not officially present at the Baghdad arms fair was the United States, which had withdrawn a few days before the show began, apparently anxious not to arouse speculation that the U.S. government was prepared to authorize arms sales to Iraq. Instead of setting up a pavilion displaying U.S. weaponry manufactured by members of the U.S.–Iraq Business Forum, American companies arranged for private delegations to attend the show. Some, such as General Motors, even got to meet with Hussein Kamil. The U.S. military attaché in Baghdad received orders from Washington not to wear his uniform when he toured the show. He and other embassy officials took photographs of every Iraqi weapon they could see.

The arms show opened on a note of tragedy, when an Egyptian pilot flying an Alphajet trainer that had been assembled in Helwan, Egypt, overshot the runway at Baghdad's al-Muthena airport, and mistakenly turned toward the presidential palace. The war with Iran might be over, but Saddam's Republican Guard was ever alert. Before the Egyptian could maneuver out of forbidden airspace, his Alphajet was torn to shreds by Soviet-built antiaircraft guns on the palace roof; it crashed into a residential area of Baghdad, killing twenty people. The pilot and his navigator were seriously injured when they ejected.

The arms fair was intended to show the world what the Iraqis could do and to convince foreign partners that Iraq was still the best game in town. "All over the world you can hear people bragging about how much they will do," Amer Rashid pointed out, "and at the end of the day they have nothing. We have chosen to keep silent all these years, even as others mocked us. Today we have something to show that no one can deny." Although it was not, strictly speaking, the first time Iraqis had shown locally made weapons, it was the first time Iraq had opened its doors to foreign manufacturers, military delegations, and the press (few journalists deigned to come) to take a detailed, firsthand look at the Iraqi arsenal. For many, including some of Iraq's oldest friends, what they saw was a shock.

One poignant scene took place beneath the wing of a French-built Mirage F1 fighter-bomber at al-Muthena airport. General Maurice Schmidt, the French chief of staff, had come to Baghdad as the personal representative of Defense Minister Jean-Pierre Chev-ènement, an ardent admirer of Saddam Hussein. Schmidt, too, admired the independence and hard work the Iraqis displayed. But when he saw what the Iraqis had done with the Mirage he could hardly contain himself.

"What the hell is that?" he shouted at Hugues de l'Estoile, pointing to an unfamiliar missile hanging beneath the wing of the French fighter on display.

"Well, General, if you ask me, it looks like a Soviet-built AS-14." The AS-14 was a laser-guided missile that the Iraqis had bought in large quantities. The AS-14, believed to incorporate stolen French technology, presented two distinct advantages over the French-built AS-30L: it had a slightly longer range and was much less expensive.

Schmidt looked de l'Estoile in the eye: "What have you people been up to over here, anyway?"

"Don't look at me. We had nothing to do with this. The Iraqis have been working all by themselves."

De l'Estoile then took the general in his white kepi and summer dress uniform over to another plane, a Soviet-built MiG-23. "See that refueling probe?" De l'Estoile pointed to the nose of the fighter. "That's one of ours."

Schmidt was not amused, even though de l'Estoile hastened to explain that the Iraqis had adapted the probe to the Soviet fighter without asking Dassault. In an interview later, after Iraq's invasion of Kuwait, General Schmidt said it was here, at the Baghdad arms fair, that he first "began to wonder whether we hadn't gone a bit too far" with Iraq. "I realized we had better begin paying closer attention to what the Iraqis were developing in the way of armament."

The arms fair was not only Saddam's birthday present to himself, it was Hussein Kamil's coming-out party. He was the host, flanked by his two deputies, Amer al-Saadi and Amer Rashid. The three greeted their guests at the entrance of a pavilion designed to resemble a large desert tent. Serge Dassault, who had taken over the company in 1985 upon his father's death, and Hugues de l'Estoile were met with Arabic-style kisses. So were the bankers from BNL, Drogoul and Von Wedel, who showed up for the event. Von Wedel watched the planes cavorting in the sky and cursed himself for having run out of film.

The bankers had been to the Badush Dam near Mosul, to see what their money had wrought.[9] Their Iraqi guide, Fadel Kadhum, had planned the trip to reassure them. But in the end, he sowed more doubts than he resolved. Von Wedel says he learned with surprise that Hussein Kamil had decreed that all future contracts for Iraq had to go through TDG, which was authorized to charge suppliers a 10–15 percent consulting fee for its services. "A consulting fee is a sophisticated term for kickback," Von Wedel commented.[10] The Iraqi minister was on the take.

Later it became apparent that Hussein Kamil was taking direct kickbacks from the Iraqi government as well. Just before the arms fair he purchased $120 million worth of state-owned manufacturing establishments as part of a widely publicized drive to privatize Iraqi industry after the war. But when Kamil said he couldn't pay, the Revolutionary Command Council (run by his father-in-law) passed a decree waiving payment for the factories, "in appreciation of Hussein Kamil's services to military industrialization."[11] Saddam liked to keep the family jewels close to home.

To anyone interested in putting it all together (and few cared to at the time), the Iraqis displayed weapons that had been manufactured at no fewer than nineteen identifiable manufacturing plants, most of which had completely escaped the notice of the West. European arms salesmen at the Baghdad fair acknowledged that they had heard of as many as "eighty separate Saad projects, run by the State Organization for Technical Industries." (The numbered Saad factories had recently been renamed after famous battles and heros.) Yarmuk, Tabuk, and Al Qods made Kalashnikov rifles and ammunition. Tarek make 9 mm pistols under license from Beretta in Italy. Al Nassira made RPG-7 antitank rockets. Al Jaleel made mortars of all calibers, from the 60 mm commando variety, to the 160 mm giant that had to be towed behind a truck. The Saddam factory made 122 mm howitzers under a Yugoslav license. Sawary was making a wide variety of commando patrol boats based on fiberglass Chris-Craft boats imported legally from the United States. The Salah al-Din electronics plant, built by Thomson-CSF of France, was making proximity fuzes and other control mechanisms for the al-Hossein and al-Abbas ballistic missiles and assembling ground-based surveillance radars (Thomson-CSF models 2215 and 2230), for a meshed air defense network intended to cover all of Iraq. Many of these and other arms factories were financed with loans provided by Drogoul and Von Wedel.[12]

One French engineer who specialized in munitions ran his finger over the rough welding joints of an Iraqi bomb. "They don't lose any sleep over quality control, do they? And you know something? In the end, they're right. We spend a fortune trying to smooth out those rough edges. We make three-star bombs, polished as a mirror and as expensive as jewels. But in the end, they're all the same. They only get used once, and the guy who's on the receiving end of one of these is never going to complain because of a few manufacturing defects."

Iraqi engineers were proud of their creations. In the pavilion where they displayed the al-Hossein and al-Abbas missiles, one Iraqi ballistics expert claimed he had waited five days just to meet an American journalist who had written extensively about the Iraqi defense establishment in the past. He addressed the American by his last name, then his first name, then his middle name. Then he proceeded to tell him exactly how Iraqi engineers from the Military Production Authority had solved the problem of increasing the range of the SCUD-B missile so it would hit Tehran. Without mentioning the help from Brazil, he said that Iraq had improved the fuel. "Think cryogenic," he said, winking.

In his opening speech at the fair, Hussein Kamil announced that Iraq was now manufacturing "three different types" of fuel-air explosives. He didn't say how Iraq had come to master this sophisticated technology, nor did he mention extensive Iraqi contacts with Honeywell and MBB.

Amer Rashid stood in front of a huge Soviet jet cargo plane, an Ilyushin-76, that his engineers had converted into a crude sort of airborne warning and control aircraft, to detect approaching enemy fighters and guide interceptors to shoot them down. A careful examination of the plane, which they had dubbed the Baghdad I, showed that Western companies had provided the technology that made it work. It used a Rockwell-Collins IFF pod slung underneath and incorporated electronic countermeasures from Thomson-CSF in France, Selenia in Italy, and Marconi in England. But the principal foreign partner was Thomson-CSF, which was responsible for overall systems integration and had built the fiberglass and composite radome that replaced the Ilyushin's belly doors. (It was a cheaper and easier solution than using a roof-top radar disk that turned, as on the American AWACS.) Elements of the plane's avionics suite — in particular, the main radar system, a Tiger-G — were built at Thomson's Saad 13 plant in ad-Dawr. An initial contract, financed by BNL, had covered the delivery of six radar kits for assembly in Iraq. The program worked so well that the Iraqis bought a license to manufacture the Tiger-G themselves, which they called the Salahuddin G, using the new name of the Saad 13 plant.

The Tiger-G radar, a sophisticated 2-D ground-based radar, had never been designed for use in an AWACS plane. Perhaps this is why Thomson-CSF and the French government agreed to the deal. No one could have imagined that the Iraqis would hang it upside down inside the Ilyushin to detect incoming planes, thus transforming it from a defensive device into the major component of a powerful offensive weapon system. It was sort of like stripping down a Volkswagen beetle to make a dune buggy. "I don't believe in it for an instant," one French aerospace executive said after taking a close look at the design. "The Tiger-G gives out so much heat when it turns, the people manning it in the back of that plane are going to fry after half an hour."

But Amer Rashid was not deterred by criticism. "See that plane?" he said, all admiration for the efforts of his workers. "We built that entire system in just three months. Our men worked day and night to perfect it. Some of our engineers actually slept on that plane, to be able to work late and get started again early the next morning. Because of the war, all of us were in a hurry. And this allowed us to cut red tape. You know what they say: necessity is the mother of all inventions."

Pride was an easy trickle-down in Iraq. But sometimes it manifested itself dangerously. Serge Dassault and General Maurice Schmidt still recall how they were forced to hit the deck on the VIP reviewing stand at al-Muthena when an Iraqi pilot flew loops in his MiG-29 only fifty feet above the ground, then headed straight for them, afterburners lit. Lieutenant Colonel Khalid Khalil won applause from Hussein Kamil when he taxied up to the reviewing stand after landing. That type of flying was usually forbidden at air shows because it was dangerous, but it impressed the hell out of Hussein Kamil and not a few of his foreign partners. Iraq was the new frontier, the Wild West of the complex East.

"Not as many of us would have come," said de l'Estoile, who kept his elegant French cuffs buttoned despite the heat, "if we didn't believe in Iraq." Pressed about Iraq's growing financial difficulties, the debonair arms salesman swept them away with the back of his hand. "Don't confuse a poor country with one that has a budgetary problem. Iraq has oil resources almost equal to those of Saudi Arabia. This is a rich nation, even though it has temporary problems paying its bills."

De l'Estoile wore his watch bearing the portrait of Saddam Hussein like a trophy of glory. It was said that his right hand — the one he signed contracts with — was worth more than $50 billion. If all went well during the negotiations then under way in Baghdad, that right hand would be worth another $6.5 billion.

"Iraq's main goal today is to create an industrial base," de l'Estoile explained. "Military production is important, but it is not all. In ten to fifteen years, fifty percent of Iraq exports will probably be products other than oil. I believe the days of outright arms purchases by Iraq are over. Today, we have to sell the technology needed to build the arms, if we want to sell anything at all. We at Dassault are ready to play the game. As far as I'm concerned, it is an ineluctable step. There's simply no getting around it."

De l'Estoile acknowledged that he was discussing the first stage of a long program and referred specifically to the Fao Project. "You begin by rebuilding existing systems, modifying them, upgrading them, modernizing them. The more you rebuild the old, the more you begin to build the new." The core of the Fao Project, he explained, was to teach the Iraqis the complex art of aircraft manufacturing, until they were capable of going it alone. "Iraq has a driving ambition to become an industrial power," he concluded, "and it has the means to accomplish this goal. No banker can seriously say that Iraq does not have a future."

The French were not alone in seeking to build the Iraqi aeronautics industry. Strong competition was coming from Spain, Italy, and Czechoslovakia, all of which had jet trainers less sophisticated than the Alphajet to offer for export. Spain's state-owned Construcciónes Aeronáuticas SA had their entry, the CASA C101, flown in from Jordan, where it was in service with the Royal Jordanian Air Force. The Spaniards were counting on the Jordanian card to help sell their plane. Within three days of arriving in Baghdad, they had Iraqi pilots flying their aircraft and had convinced Hussein Kamil to send a MIMI delegation to corporate headquarters in Madrid for talks on setting up an aircraft factory.

"What we have to offer is ten years of experience in technology transfer and local production," a company officer said. "Coproduction is a priority market for us." Competition for the Fao Project was hot and heavy. Everyone wanted to help Iraq build its military aircraft industry, and they offered substantial government credits to back their proposals. But the strongest competitor to the Alphajet was without a doubt British Aerospace's Hawk. Far superior to the Spanish or Italian planes, it could also be configured as a single-seat ground-support fighter. And the British were dead serious about breaking into the Iraqi military market. Alan Clark, now minister for defense procurement, dispatched his top aide, David Hastie, to Baghdad to make the British case. Assistant Secretary of Defense David Hastie was a sophisticated player and was better known to the men at British Aerospace as a former director of the company. "I don't know what hat he's wearing today," said one of the BAe team in Baghdad. "But I can tell you this: he is pretty bloody senior."

The subject of British–Iraqi relations was a sensitive one, but David Hastie was better prepared than most to take advantage of the slippery terrain. He had a keen understanding of the Iraqi military. Better yet, he had an in-depth knowledge of recent events, having played a role in shaping them. He understood one thing about Iraq that many others overlooked: you could not prepare for the future without knowing the past — a past he described in detail during discussions at the Baghdad arms fair.

Saddam Hussein was fascinated by Britain and attracted by British efficiency and discretion, while loathing what he termed Britain's "hegemonistic intentions" toward Iraq. In 1979 the Iraqi air force tried to convince Saddam to sign a billion-dollar deal with British Aerospace to purchase Hawk jet trainers in knock-down kits for local assembly, but the outbreak of the Iran–Iraq war and Saddam's suspicion of the British had put the deal on ice.

During the early years of the war, Britain had maintained discreet contacts in Baghdad. "We did our best to keep the bed warm," Hastie admitted. Some thirty to forty Iraqi pilots were trained every year on British air bases and by private contractors such as CSE Aviation. "We weren't going to let the French get every contract, now, were we?"

There were other contacts as well. When Iran was under an international arms embargo, the Iranian government set up a buying office on London's Victoria Street, just a stone's throw away from Scotland Yard. Most of Iran's attempts to procure tanks, aircraft, missiles, and electronics on the black market went through London until the end of the war, despite increasingly strained relations between Britain and Iran. It now appears that Britain's MI5 monitored its activities around the clock and passed on some of the intelligence gleaned on Iranian arms purchases in Europe to Saddam's intelligence chief, Barzan Ibrahim al-Tikriti.

British intelligence also put Barzan in contact with former Special Air Service (SAS) commandos, who were available on "private contract" to help train Iraqi Special Forces units at a top-secret base on an island in the Tigris River. A British firm, Racal Electronics, built the base's security perimeter using sophisticated electronic sensors, "but no member of the firm was ever allowed onto the island itself during the whole construction project," wrote one of the British trainers. "It is probably the most sensitive military installation in the country." The "jungle ears" Racal installed for the Iraqi Special Forces were similar to devices that were first used by the Green Berets in Vietnam to detect intrusions by Vietcong guerrillas.[13]

If the British couldn't get the billion-dollar Hawk deal, they would fight their competitors on the terrain where they were at their best: intelligence. In 1985 the French had lost two large contracts to British electronics companies. Marconi signed a contract to supply "troposcatter" microwave transmitters that Thomson-CSF thought it had won. The transmitters allowed Iraqi forces to dispatch orders from Baghdad to the southern front without relying on telephone lines (and they confounded allied intelligence during Operation Desert Storm). Racal stole the second deal from Thomson, this time to build a factory for its Jaguar frequency-hopping radios, the most advanced military radio then on the market anywhere in the world. But that was nothing compared to the business now in the offing. David Hastie had been dispatched to Iraq to snatch the Fao contract out of the hands of the French.

David Hastie and Hugues de l'Estoile knew and respected each other, but it was the type of respect one reserves for an old and brilliant enemy. "Did you notice the reception the Iraqis gave Serge Dassault?" Hastie commented one afternoon during a conversation in the British Aerospace trailer at al-Muthena. "They all stood up when he approached the reviewing stand and gave him an ovation. He was treated like a visiting hero." The diminutive Hastie could afford to be generous. After a fight lasting nearly ten years, he figured he had won.

De l'Estoile was less elegant when it came to British Aerospace. "The Brits should have gotten the Saudis to bring in a Tornado," he sniped. De l'Estoile had suffered the biggest defeat of his career when David Hastie convinced the Royal Saudi Air Force to select the Tornado over a twin-engine version of the Mirage 2000 in 1987. "They didn't dare, because then everybody would have seen that all the Saudi pilots were British."

Hastie was a smooth operator, but he also came with some powerful ammunition to convince the Iraqis that Great Britain would be the best cooperation partner for the aerospace project. For one thing, Iraq could purchase many of the machine tools from British companies they already owned, such as Matrix Churchill. In addition, Her Majesty's Government was prepared to offer a generous financing package of "soft loans" totaling $628 million in addition to long-term oil purchases. The French were notoriously weak when it came to project financing. De l'Estoile had never succeeded in convincing the barons at the Finance Ministry, Philippe Raymond and Jacques Desponts, who continued to veto his projects for Iraq.

After meeting with Hussein Kamil, Hastie knew that victory was within reach. The Iraqi minister led him to believe that he had chosen the Hawk, not because of its performance or because it was slightly cheaper than the Alphajet. "What Saddam really wants," Hastie revealed, "are American fighter planes. I guess he figures that buying British is the next best thing, a way of getting his foot in the door." Hussein Kamil was particularly impressed to learn that British Aerospace had been selected by the U.S. Navy to train pilots for the Hawk. "This is what the Iraqis want," Hastie said. "They want American-style training, American-style tactics, American-standard aircraft. If they can't get them from the United States, then they will get them from us." Hastie played his strong suits and spoke much less about the aircraft factory, although it was an integral part of the deal.

By May 1989, Iraq owed French arms suppliers approximately $2 billion in arrears. They owed civilian contractors another $4 billion, most of it from contracts at least five years old. It was a miracle the sum was not higher.

Serge Dassault and Jacques Deville of Aérospatiale threw a gala reception for their Iraqi clients in the palm-shaded gardens of the Hotel Rashid. All evening Dassault stood in a corner by the steps leading down into the garden, just in case Hussein Kamil showed up. Dassault was so eager to make his first real export sale after taking over the company (de l'Estoile had negotiated the sale of all 133 Mirages to Iraq) that he could scarcely concentrate. Friends he had known for years he brushed off with an absent sigh.

When the French ambassador to Iraq, Maurice Courage, showed up, he tried to reassure Dassault of his support. "You know I have always done everything I could," Courage whispered, "to help further French arms sales to Iraq."[14]

"The Iraqis are shopping hard," said one French arms salesman at the reception. "I don't expect Hussein Kamil to show up for one minute. All this cinema is just an attempt to get Dassault to lower his price."

Another longtime Baghdad hand ridiculed the stance of the French Finance Ministry, which he believed was going to sabotage the Mirage 2000 and Alphajet deal. "Iraq's military debt to France today only amounts to six percent of our total military sales to Iraq since the Gulf war began. We could afford to simply wipe the slate clean, if that were the price of getting these new contracts."

At the height of the party, as white-jacketed waiters carried silver platters of shish kebab, fruit juice, and Iraqi sweets, Dassault's co-host was called out to an urgent meeting at the ministry. Hussein Kamil greeted him in his private office suite with good news. Iraq would make down payments to Aérospatiale on the Tulip and Jacinthe helicopter contracts so production could begin. In return, Kamil wanted Deville to submit plans to build a helicopter assembly line in Iraq for Aérospatiale's latest antitank machine, the Panther. Aircraft manufacturing was not enough. To have a complete aerospace industry, Kamil argued, you needed to build helicopters as well.

One person who failed to show up at the Baghdad arms fair was Defense Minister Adnan Khairallah. Asked about his absence, Raja Hassan Ali, who had donned his brigadier's uniform for the show, confided that Minister Khairallah was not even expected. "You know, he is in quite poor health." But the poor health of Saddam's brother-in-law had little to do with his age or physical condition.

He wasn't even lucky enough to have a "diplomatic" cold. He was simply out of favor, and worse was on the way.

If Saddam had managed to sell the Iran–Iraq war to ordinary Iraqis as his "Qaddisiya," or crusade, against the hereditary Persian enemy, he was less successful in convincing the professional officers' corps of his prowess as a military commander. It was Khairallah who softened the rocky relationship between the Baath party and the army. Without Khairallah, the army would have balked at Saddam's orders on numerous occasions. Even with his help, the officers' discontent nearly erupted into insubordination on at least two occasions, in 1982 and in 1986. Both times the officers criticized Saddam's handling of the war and blamed him for major Iraqi losses.

Khairallah commanded the respect of the professional officers because he was not just another of Saddam's yes-men, a mere vehicle of presidential whim. He intervened on their behalf with Saddam. In 1985, for instance, he convinced Saddam to relinquish control over the choice of bombing targets, allowing the air force commander, Lieutenant General Saad Shaaban, to plan his missions according to strictly military criteria. Before this shift, Saddam had insisted on being consulted before every bombing campaign, and he tended to choose highly visible "political" targets, while ignoring targets of military significance. The decision to grant more independence to military planners gave a dramatic boost to their effectiveness.

Another morale booster engineered by Khairallah was the decision to allow the Iraqi press to mention the names of field commanders. Until then they had remained anonymous, whether victorious or defeated. Khairallah argued that they would perform better if given the public recognition (or criticism) they deserved. The new ruling made him immensely popular with the top officers, who could now play to a captive audience at the rear.

One of the first commanders to distinguish himself in this way was Lieutenant General Maher Abdul Rashid. In July 1984, not long after Iraq's first acknowledged use of poison gas, General Rashid was interviewed by *Washington Post* correspondent Rod Norland. It is not known whether Rashid's comments angered Saddam, but they were repeated around the world. "When you are faced with insects," Rashid said, "you use insecticide."

When the war ground to a halt after a string of Iraqi victories in April 1988, Khairallah's popularity with the professional officers' corps soared to unprecedented heights. Much of the credit for the final "victory" was directed Khairallah's way. Saddam had almost taken a back seat to his brother-in-law, who was becoming a public figure in his own right. Once again there loomed the specter of a challenge to Saddam's rule from the army.

The first hint that resentment against Saddam was brewing just under the surface occurred in June 1988, when Maher Rashid took public issue with Saddam over a question of medals. Rashid had led the successful battle to retake Fao, but when the time came to distribute medals Saddam heaped honors on General Saadi Tuma, the "political general" who headed the Republican Guards, passing over Rashid completely. Backed by Khairallah, Rashid stood firm. If his men of the seventh Army were not rewarded as well, he threatened to resign and let people know why. Saddam's response was not long to come. General Rashid was arrested and has not been heard of since. Some sources believe Saddam arranged an "accident" for him a few months later, although this has never been confirmed. Meanwhile, Saddam had his son Kusay divorce Rashid's daughter. Rashid had become an outcast, a pariah.

The arrest of General Rashid came as a shock to Adnan Khairallah and to many top army officers. Although it is not known whether Khairallah was actually plotting a coup, or whether other Tikritis joined in his disenchantment over the president's megalomania, Saddam now saw him as a threat and sought an excuse to get rid of him. In the weeks following General Rashid's demise, more than one hundred top Iraqi officers were executed.

In the end, it was a family feud that got the better of Khairallah. Through the intercession of his food taster and personal valet, Kamal Hana Gegeo, Saddam had begun to taste the joys of extramarital sex. He became so enamored of one mistress, the daughter of a prominent Baghdad merchant, that Saddam proposed taking her as a second wife. The love affair soon blossomed into a family scandal. Saddam's eldest son, Uday, feared he would lose his position as heir apparent if his father repudiated his mother and remarried. In a drunken fury one evening in October 1988, he burst into a high-society reception in Baghdad, stormed past Suzy Mubarak, the visiting wife of the Egyptian president, insulted Saddam's vice president, Taha Moheddin Marouf, then sought out Kamal Gegeo and beat him to death with a club.

Later that evening Saddam called his son into his private office on the second floor of the presidential palace. "With which hand did you strike Kamal Gegeo?" he asked. Uday held up a hand, and his father shot a hole through it with his revolver. Meanwhile Uday's mother, Sajida, heard the shouting and called on her brother for help. When Khairallah came running into Saddam's study a few minutes later, it was all he could do to keep the president from pistol-whipping his own son to death. Uday was admitted to the hospital later that night. His wounds were explained away to the Iraqi press as a suicide attempt. Something broke between Saddam and Adnan Khairallah that night. Their relationship would never recover.

In a panic, Khairallah phoned King Hussein, who flew in shortly before dawn at the controls of his private jet to console Saddam over his son's behavior. The Jordanian monarch was probably the only confidant Saddam had. "This kind of thing happens with boys," he said. "You mustn't get carried away by your emotions." It was all he could do to keep Saddam from hopping on board his plane and flying to Cairo to apologize to Hosni Mubarak. If he couldn't kill his son, Saddam intended to disown him and his lineage (including his wife and Khairallah) for good.

Rumors that Khairallah was in danger spread like wildfire across the Gulf in the coming months. Khairallah himself told the Kuwaiti defense minister, Nawaf al-Ahmad al-Sabah, that he felt his life was in danger and that dire things were about to happen in Iraq. By spring 1989, people like Raja Hassan Ali were admitting that Khairallah was "in bad health."

On May 6, just days after the Baghdad arms fair closed, Saddam announced that Khairallah had been killed while flying a helicopter in Kurdistan the day before. It had been a "crazy storm," Saddam said. Indeed, of the three helicopters flying in formation over the mountains, only Khairallah's had gone down. French apologists for Saddam would later come to his defense. "There really *was* a sandstorm," one said. "I was there, and you could hardly see a thing."

Iraqi exiles say Saddam killed Khairallah with his own hand during a drinking bout at his mountain hideout in Sarsang, near

Mosul, the night before the supposed crash. "Adnan was family," they argue, "and you don't let other people kill members of your family. If there is killing to do, you do it yourself."

Khairallah was given a state funeral in Tikrit and was said to have left behind a fortune estimated at $3 billion — not bad for a country boy. Saddam decreed that the Iraqi AWACS plane be renamed the Adnan-1 in his honor, and he publicly wept over his "loss." But he was careful to return Adnan's body to his family in a nailed coffin, telling them not to open it because the corpse had been horribly disfigured in the fire that followed the helicopter crash. It is more likely that the corpse would have revealed the true circumstances of Khairallah's death.

SEVENTEEN

An Explosion at al-Hillah

April Glaspie, the new American ambassador to Baghdad, saw herself as a friend of the Arab world, but she was not a great hit on the social circuit. In the early days of the Bush administration, after several years in Damascus as the deputy chief of mission (not an easy assignment), Glaspie took up residence in Baghdad with her mother and her dog. She had been appointed by the new assistant secretary of state for Near Eastern affairs, John Kelly, a former ambassador to Lebanon.

April Glaspie was a fervent supporter of U.S.–Iraq trade. And she became involved in two of Amer al-Saadi's largest civilian-military projects from the start of her short term as ambassador: the PC-2 complex built by Bechtel and Lummus Crest of Bloomfield, New Jersey, and a $1 billion deal to build military cargo trucks that was championed by the soul of America itself, General Motors. Glaspie fired numerous cables back to Washington detailing the Iraqis' eagerness to purchase American high-technology goods. She said the Iraqis complained, however, that the U.S. government was blocking good business opportunities by holding up export licenses and by failing to provide sufficient financing. If the United States wanted to secure its place in postwar Iraq, she urged, both of these problem areas needed to be addressed.

In May 1989 the National Security Council took her advice and spread the word throughout the executive branch of government. Dennis Kloske, the Bush administration's nominee to head the Bureau of Export Administration at the Department of Commerce, eagerly put the new sell-all policy into effect. Angered that the Pentagon continued to object to the sale of advanced computers and electronics to Iraq, Kloske fired off a memorandum to the acting head of the Defense Technology Security Administration, "informing" him that the Commerce Department would no longer refer Iraqi licenses to DoD for review. "The development of biological and chemical weapons, as well as the missile technology regime, are part of the foreign policy controls and are beyond the preview [*sic*] of the Department of Defense," Kloske wrote.

The memo showed not only Kloske's determination to stake out his bureaucratic turf, but also his abject failure to comprehend what was going on in Iraq. "As someone who had just spent the past six years at DoD," a former colleague said, "Dennis Kloske of all people should have known better. He knew in great detail how U.S. high-tech goods were serving the Iraqi defense industry. He just chose to ignore it."

Instead, Department of Commerce publications distributed to American companies interested in doing business with Iraq encouraged them to sell "oil field and refinery equipment, computers, and other high-technology goods and services."

Marshall Wiley, of the U.S.–Iraq Business Forum, took the ball and ran with it. The time for the payoff had come.

Wiley arrived in Baghdad on June 4, 1989, at the head of a twenty-three-member blue-chip delegation. Capitalizing on a personal invitation from Saddam Hussein, Wiley brought representatives from Fortune 500 companies that were eager to expand their business in Iraq. As Wiley boasted later in the *U.S.–Iraq Business Forum Bulletin*, "In order to keep the delegation at the size requested by the Government of Iraq, only senior executives from Forum member companies with annual sales in excess of $500 million were invited to participate."

The highlight of the trip was an unprecedented two-hour meeting with Saddam Hussein and his chief economic advisor, First Deputy Prime Minister Saddoun Hammadi. "Of course I was pleased," Wiley said later. "This was the first time Saddam Hussein had ever met with a commercial delegation."

Among the chosen were chief executives or senior directors of Amoco, Mobil, and Occidental Petroleum, which were largely responsible for expanding American purchases of Iraqi crude to nearly $1.6 billion in 1988. Westinghouse, General Motors, Xerox, and Bell Textron also came along for the ride, as did former Senator Charles Percy, whose consulting company was doing a booming business in the Middle East, and who was a prominent member of the Forum. The delegation wouldn't have been complete without the Forum's chairman, A. Robert Abboud, who was chairman and CEO of First City Bancorporation of Texas. Abboud, an old hand at the influence game, had retained Richard Murphy, the newly retired head of the State Department's Near East Division, as his lawyer-lobbyist in Washington.

"Saddam was very relaxed during the meeting," Wiley recalled. "All the others were wearing Baathist uniforms, but Saddam was in a civilian suit. He told us he wanted to expand economic ties to the United States but was having trouble with the banks. We said he needed to reschedule his debt all across the board, so Iraq stopped defaulting on its loan obligations." That, of course was the one thing Saddam didn't want to do. Global rescheduling of Iraq's debt meant handing the country over to its creditors.

The most controversial member of the delegation that met Saddam was Alan Stoga, who was a senior associate of Henry Kissinger's consulting firm in New York. Stoga specialized in the tricky economics of debt restructuring. "The Iraqis specifically invited Stoga to come," Wiley said, "because their biggest problem at this time was obtaining credit to finance their reconstruction programs." They had invited him as a representative of Kissinger Associates, undoubtedly hoping to enlist the former secretary of state as a member of the pro-Iraqi lobby. "Kissinger later tried to claim that Alan only went as an observer," Wiley says, "but he got into the nitty-gritty of debt rescheduling and trade financing with Saddoun Hammadi and Saddam." Some of Kissinger's best clients were doing good business in Iraq, including Fiat (whose subsidiaries were hard at work on Iraqi missile programs), Volvo, Coca-Cola, Hunt Oil, and Britain's Midland Bank, which had financed some of Saddam's earliest weapons purchases in the West. And two former members of Kissinger Associates had moved on to become top players in the Bush administration: Brent Scowcroft, the national security advisor, and Lawrence Eagleburger, number two at the Department of State.

With friends like that, Saddam figured he couldn't go wrong.

The first to seize the initiative were Volvo and GM, which had both been involved in Iraq for some time. Now they were hoping to build an assembly line for "heavy-duty cargo trucks" for the Iraqi Ministry of Industry and Military Industrialization. General Motors had sent an exploratory team to Baghdad for the May 1989 arms fair. To disguise their presence, they rented a stand under the aegis of GM Canada. GM's real business was conducted during a series of meetings with al-Saadi and his boss, Hussein Kamil. Heading their delegation was Ken Passmore of GM Canada and two representatives from Detroit.

By this time General Motors had developed a good working relationship with Iraq. An initial deal to sell 5,125 Chevrolet Celebrities to the Iraqi State Enterprise for Automotive Industry had brought in $77 million in 1988. A second deal was signed during the arms fair, for 10,000 Oldsmobile Cieras worth $154 million, which BNL's Christopher Drogoul agreed to finance. The next step was the assembly plant. The GM plan called for a yearly output of 5,000 trucks. But every time GM representatives met with the Iraqis the project got bigger and bigger.

The Iraqis had initially intended to buy the trucks outright. On March 12, 1986, they had submitted a proposal through a Washington consultant called Gateway International to purchase $491 million worth of military trucks, built by the defense contractor LTV. The State Department recommended that the deal be approved, and a license was issued six weeks later. But at that time Iraq was short of funds, and the deal never materialized. Two years later, when the BNL loans came through, the Iraqis resubmitted the proposal as a direct purchase by the Ministry of Defense. Although the military nature of the deal was hardly disguised, once again the State Department lobbied heavily within the administration, and the deal was approved. Despite the fact that this was a military sale, Congress was never told a word.

With the end of the war, Iraq no longer had such an urgent need for the trucks and began to consider the more attractive alternative of building a truck factory. This would further develop Iraq's industrial base and bring in export earnings. They turned to an international consortium based in the United States, the Volvo GM Heavy Truck Corporation. GM was a member of the U.S.–Iraq Business Forum and Volvo was a client of Kissinger Associates.

Only days after the Forum delegation left Baghdad, documents show that a proposal was presented to Hussein Kamil that had been prepared by the president of Volvo GM, Thage Berggren, concerning a joint venture involving Volvo, General Motors, the Eaton Corporation, Cummins Engines, and Rockwell.

When the Iraqis looked at the proposal on June 25, they just laughed. "Immediately they realized our misconception of the Iraqi technical infrastructure," an internal Volvo GM account of the Baghdad trip shows. "The Iraqi infrastructure is very advanced" and did not need to be built from scratch, as the American-Swedish group had believed. They agreed to withdraw their proposal while reevaluating Iraqi needs.

The Iraqis took a group of engineering consultants from the Eaton Corporation, headed by Cesar Cerri, on a tour of fourteen heavy manufacturing plants in three separate locations in the Baghdad–Babylon area. During the five-day tour they were chauffeured around by Brigadier Nazar Kassim, the former head of the Saad 13 electronics plant. An internal report on this tour, dated July 18, 1989, shows that without a doubt the consultants were shown some of Iraq's most sophisticated weapons facilities, at Taji, Al Iskandariyah, and Al Yusufiyah. "Our group was brought to a number of plants where everything was unveiled," the report reads, "even what would be considered top secret defense operations in any country."

The Iraqis' aim was to show how advanced their industrial infrastructure was so that the new truck plant could capitalize on equipment already functioning in Iraq. Whereas the Volvo GM team had thought the initial goal of building 50 percent of the trucks locally was optimistic, by the end of the tour they had changed their tune. "It is fully possible to meet the Iraqi requirement for local integration," the Eaton report states. "Iraq demands 75 percent of the finished product value to be Iraqi." It was a significant change.

The inspection team's report then presented a confidential summary of the fourteen facilities they had toured, a document that gives rare insight into just how far the Iraqis had come in their fifteen-year quest to build a self-sufficient weapons industry. The American and Swedish engineers were taken by surprise; even though some of them had worked in Iraq at times during that period, the Iraqis' sudden openness and their willingness to unveil the weapons plants, "caused great astonishment between [sic] the delegation members."

> All in all it is evident that the technological degree and production capacity achieved by Iraq is much higher and perhaps better than many other Middle East countries.
>
> The professionalism and technical level of employees and managers, in parallel with their discipline, makes a good impression and is very promising for the future manufacture of automotive parts and components in Iraq.

The plants they visited included computerized precision casting facilities and large foundries for special steels. Two complete factories were devoted to making production tools and dies for a wide variety of weaponry, and another one to the assembly of Matrix Churchill machine tools. Already the Iraqis were making some of the machine-tool parts themselves in their large steel foundries and casting plants. Soon they intended to start building sophisticated numerical controllers and very large scale machining centers, each a factory in itself. The engineers visited plants for turning, milling, grinding, and vacuum heat treatment; they saw plastic injection molding lines and hot forging dies. Throughout this remarkable description, the words "huge," "high capacity," and "enormous" appear frequently.

They had seen the fruit of fifteen years of labor conducted in near-total secrecy, and the results were simply astonishing. The Iraqis had concentrated all their efforts on purchasing machine tools and manufacturing equipment, the basic building blocks of the weapons industry. And as the Eaton engineers noted, the machine tools were "of the best makes possible to find," supplied exclusively by Western firms.

The extraordinary industrial buildup had cost Iraq $14.2 billion in hard currency since 1984, in high-tech imports from Britain, France, Germany, Italy, and the United States. And it was devoted entirely to making guns, missiles, tanks, and bombs — whatever was needed to keep Saddam in power, to circumvent international embargoes, and to give him the means to achieve his goal of regional domination.

* * *

When he got back to Atlanta after the Baghdad arms fair, Christopher Drogoul was worried. His superior in New York, Pietro Lombardi, wanted to send a BNL auditor to go over the Atlanta books. Drogoul was sure that Rome had figured out what he was doing and intended to curb his activities.

Louis Messere was the BNL vice president in charge of internal auditing. He knew Drogoul and the Atlanta branch well. It wasn't his first trip from New York to go through the books. He had half a dozen BNL branches to audit in the continental United States, but he always spent extra time in Atlanta because he knew that Drogoul was careless about accounting. According to Messere's written conclusion after a September 2, 1988, audit of BNL Atlanta, there was "need of improvements in most areas. . . . Several accounting procedures were either not being followed or were not being properly handled, particularly with regard to the booking of Letters of Credit." Drogoul was sloppy, Messere felt, but neither he nor Drogoul's superiors in the United States seems to have discovered the secret Iraqi loans.

When he returned to Atlanta on June 14, 1989, Messere again saw evidence of Drogoul's sloppiness. He pored over the books, requesting specific documentation for letters of credit, proof of deposits, and more. While he was glued to BNL Atlanta's perfectly licit export trade business, dozens of urgent telexes were coming in each day from the Rafidain Bank in Baghdad, asking Drogoul to pay out large sums that had been promised to this or that American exporter. To meet the Iraqi requests, Drogoul was borrowing money on the day-to-day money market and selling it off the same evening in an effort to gain a fraction of a percentage point to cover the Iraqi loans. But Messere noticed none of this frenetic activity going on right beneath his nose. Not once did he request information that might have led him to the gray books on Iraq, which by this point contained more than $2 billion worth of questionable business and were being shuffled from office to office in a series of cardboard boxes to keep them out of the auditor's way.

When Drogoul received Messere's report, filed on July 26, he was so relieved that he decided to head off to France on vacation. Either BNL Rome knew and approved of what he was doing, or else the jerks up in New York were so blind they didn't deserve to be enlightened. Messere had seen nothing.

*   *   *

Drogoul's undoing did not come about through the actions of either New York or Rome. It was the result of unrequited love. While Drogoul was visiting his father in France, a frustrated co-worker in Atlanta ratted on him to the FBI. Billions of dollars had been paid out in unauthorized loans, she whispered excitedly in a phone call to the FBI. All the records were kept in a set of gray books stored in Drogoul's garage and in the trunk of another co-worker's car. It was a huge scandal, and the FBI had better come quickly if it wanted to seize the books.

After putting out feelers to the Treasury Department, the local Customs office, the Federal Reserve, and the U.S. attorney in Atlanta, the FBI raided the plush BNL office on the twentieth floor of the Gas & Light Tower a few minutes before closing time on Friday, August 4, 1989. Guided by Assistant U.S. Attorney Gail McKenzie, who was legally in charge, they dumped all the BNL files onto the floor and began shuffling the loose paper into plastic trash bags. McKenzie, who had never conducted a major financial investigation and scarcely knew where Iraq was located on a world map, was worried that her prey would get away.

While she and other investigators grilled the sixteen bank employees then on the premises, another team quietly rang the doorbell of a suburban residence several miles away. The house belonged to Paul Von Wedel, who was fixing up an office in the basement of his home in preparation for leaving his job at the bank. In the ensuing weeks the U.S. attorney's office offered Von Wedel a deal, which he reluctantly accepted: they would not pursue criminal charges against him in exchange for his full cooperation with the investigation.

That evening, Drogoul's friend and co-worker, Therese Bardan, who was indicted with him on February 28, 1991, phoned Drogoul in Paris to tell him about the raid. Drogoul was so confident that his Iraqi loans had not only been covered by Rome but were in total accord with U.S. government policy that he returned to the United States on Monday morning. Drogoul met with his superiors at BNL in New York, caught a plane to Atlanta, and turned himself in. His lawyer, Theodore H. Lackland of Arnall Golden & Gregory in Atlanta, would later point to Drogoul's prompt return as a proof of his innocence. "If Drogoul had been out to defraud the bank, or had taken windfall profits, he would have stayed out of the country."

Drogoul gave a candid account of his activities when he met with Gail McKenzie and FBI agent Joe Hardy on August 10 in McKenzie's office in the federal court house at 75 Spring Street. According to an official memo recording this interview, Drogoul admitted to the gray books, to the four medium-term loans totaling $2.1 billion, to nearly $2 billion more in CCC loans, and to virtually every other accusation he was later charged with, including the fact that one of his customers — the Turkish grain emporium Entrade — was paying his travel expenses out of its corporate account.

Despite Drogoul's apparent cooperation, it took Gail McKenzie more than eighteen months to gather evidence for an indictment. In the meantime, top Customs officials say she shut them out of the case. (Customs was the only investigative agency with extensive experience in cases of international financial fraud and money laundering.) Fourteen months after interrogating Drogoul, McKenzie was still asking newsmen for the full name of the MIMI, and she had never seen a photograph of Hussein Kamil, although it frequently appeared in the press. "Gail's problem was that she insisted on doing all the investigative work herself," intelligence sources in Washington said.

Staff investigators for Henry Gonzales, the chairman of the House Banking Committee, were less accommodating. "Gail McKenzie refused to supply documents, she refused to appear before our committee, she refused to cooperate in any manner whatsoever," one staffer said. When Gonzales insisted on convening hearings on BNL's activities nevertheless, he was immediately assailed by the U.S. attorney general, Richard L. Thornburgh, who had final authority over all U.S. Attorney's offices. In a letter dated September 26, 1990, Thornburgh warned the congressman away from "a sensitive case with national security concerns." When that failed to deter Gonzales, FBI Director William Sessions pitched in, arguing that congressional hearings could cause "serious damage to a very sensitive and important case."

The BNL blunder had all the trappings of a major coverup. BNL's $4 billion loans to Iraq had nothing to do with national security. They were a national embarrassment.[1]

It was midafternoon on August 17, 1989, when the al-Hillah plant went up in smoke. The explosion was so loud that it could be heard all the way to Baghdad, nearly 80 kilometers to the north. No one had seen or heard anything like it during all eight years of the Iran–Iraq war. The explosion momentarily blinded the NSA's KH-11 Keyhole satellite when it passed over Iraq several hours later. Al-Hillah was the site of the top-secret al-Qaqaa State Establishment, which made solid-fuel propellants for a wide variety of Iraqi missiles, including the Condor II.

The casualty reports started to come in the next day — not from Baghdad, which did not acknowledge the disaster, but from Cairo, where the Al Mazaa air force base had been sealed off to accommodate the wounded. Three Egyptian military transport aircraft had been sent to Baghdad to ferry back the dead and wounded, since most of the factory workers were Egyptian. By the time the fire was put out, the Egyptians counted 700 of their own dead and another 800 wounded, some of them severely disfigured by the fire. Iraq subsequently put the death toll at 19.

To this day, no one knows for sure who built the ammonium perchlorate plant at al-Hillah. Initial suspicions pointed to partners of the Consen group, which Iraq had retained as overall project manager for its solid-fuel ballistic missile programs. But Aaron Karp, a missile proliferation specialist at the Stockholm International Peace Research Institute believes that a French company built the plant. "Only the French had the expertise and the political structure to build this type of plant secretly," he said.

The Société Nationale des Poudres et Explosifs was one of Europe's largest manufacturers of military explosives. It was also a major exporter of turnkey manufacturing facilities. In the 1970s it built one of Iran's largest powder plants at Parchin. In 1986, it contracted to build a solid-fuel plant in Egypt to power the Sakr rockets, which Egypt exported heavily to Iraq. The Sakr series, which came in ranges from 30 to 120 kilometers, were fired from the back of a truck, just like the Soviet-built katyusha.[2] SNPE denies they ever built a rocket fuel plant in Iraq and claims that the Sakr deal never went through. In April 1988, however, they had been deep in negotiations with Consen's Ekkehard Schrotz to sell Iraq the secrets of propergol, their solid rocket fuel.

The origin of the al-Hillah explosion remains a mystery. Fuel specialists at SNPE speculated that it was poor plant design. "It looks like a Soviet-built factory if you ask me," one said. Much later, Adel Darwish wrote in the *Independent* that the plant blew up because of "a fault in the wiring of the fuel clusters."

When they finally acknowledged that an accident had occurred, the Iraqis tried to minimize the damage. They said a fire had broken out in a storehouse for highly inflammable petroleum products, when "by coincidence" a truck carrying industrial explosives was passing by on its way to a dam construction site. Most of those killed, the Iraqis said, were firemen. In private, the Iraqis were convinced that the explosion was military sabotage. They blamed Mossad, the CIA, and MI6 for the blast.

It took a good two weeks for the news to reach the West. British reporters began flocking to Baghdad by early September, ostensibly to cover the first government-sponsored elections in Iraqi Kurdistan. Among the journalists was an Iranian-born freelancer named Farzod Bazoft, on assignment for the *Observer* newspaper, who arrived on September 6. Bazoft was no stranger to Iraq. He had traveled to Baghdad six times over the past year using his British passport, each time with the proper Iraqi authorizations. As a freelancer, he was always out for a scoop, something that would show his editors that they had been right to place their confidence in a man who only a few years earlier had been serving time in a British jail on robbery charges.

He made friends with a fifty-two-year-old British nurse named Daphne Parish. While other reporters were hanging around Baghdad trying to glean bits of information from laconic Iraqi officials, Bazoft put his instincts to work. He convinced Parish that the Iraqis had been making chemical weapons at the al-Hillah plant (the initial press reports from Egypt had spoken of "horrible burns," similar to those caused by CW agents). As a nurse with a special permit, she was authorized to travel freely throughout Iraq without an official minder. Bazoft convinced her to take him to al-Hillah.

Three weeks after the explosion, the plant was still in an uproar. Bazoft donned a long white smock and posed as an Indian doctor. When they drove up to the gates of the military plant in a Range Rover with a red cross on the side, Daphne Parish showed her pass and they were let in without a search. After all, they were doctors. Bazoft snapped photographs and took soil samples from around the damaged building. The plant was so huge that no one seemed to have noticed them as they drove around the compound. Bazoft was so intoxicated by their success that he convinced Parish to return to the devastated plant the next day. Again he posed as an Indian doctor, and they got in and out of the plant without a hitch.

The problems came only later. Like many reporters, Bazoft was driven to boast of his exploits. At the hotel bar he told British, American, and Egyptian journalists what he had done. "I've got the proof right here in my camera," he told one television reporter. "This is the biggest scoop of the year."[3]

Bazoft thought he had made it when he and Parish drove out through the gates of the al-Qaqaa plant the second time, but as he was preparing to leave for the airport to return to London, the Iraqi security police whisked him away. He was arrested on charges of spying for Israel. Under torture, he even confessed — much to the delight of Saddam's men. Apparently led to believe that the Iraqis would release him if he told a wild story about his life as a spy, Bazoft allowed himself to be filmed while he responded to an unnamed interviewer's questions:

> When were you recruited for spying and for whom?
>
> In 1987 I was recruited by some Israeli intelligence elements in the UK, who are working in Britain under known covers. . . . After I got the job with the British newspaper *The Observer* in 1987, they started to exploit me and my work to serve their purposes as intelligence officers. They then trained me in writing reports, gathering information, and obtaining information from people, directly or indirectly, in a way which would not raise suspicions about me.
>
> Did the British authorities know about your work against Iraq and for Israeli intelligence?
>
> Yes, the British knew. . . . Israeli influence in Britain is strong and has a great effect on British political decision-making.[4]

In the Iraqi script of Bazoft's "confession," Britain and Israel were one — it was a way of killing two birds with one stone. Bazoft's main target in Iraq was to spy on military installations, he said.

The BNL bust didn't make headlines in the United States, but it soon became a matter of grave concern in Iraq. The goose that laid the golden eggs was dead. Iraq urgently needed to find another source of export financing.

Iraq's American partners did their best to come up with a solution. Marshall Wiley began lobbying the Bush administration heavily to open up direct government loans for industrial contracts in Iraq through Eximbank. In the *U.S.–Iraq Business Forum Bulletin*, Wiley lamented the $200 million limit that had been placed on Eximbank loans. "Business Forum members who are aware of potential business opportunities in Iraq which would require medium or long-term credit guarantees from the Eximbank are encouraged to write Acting Chairman William F. Ryan," Wiley wrote, "informing him of the existence of these opportunities and asking for an expansion of the Eximbank credit guarantee program." To help out, Wiley supplied Eximbank's address in Washington. He also encouraged members to write to Secretary of State James Baker and Secretary of Commerce Robert A. Mosbacher, "to call to the attention of the administration the great need by the American business community for an expansion of U.S. government credit guarantees for trade with Iraq." What Wiley neglected to explain was that Eximbank had suspended Iraq several times from its list of countries eligible for loans because of its long history of nonpayment.[5]

Marshall Wiley's lobbying effort had an electric effect, according to the chairman of the House Banking Committee, Henry Gonzales. "Because of its tough stance against loaning billions to Iraq, the Eximbank was repeatedly chastised by the staff of the State and Commerce departments," Gonzales told a public hearing on BNL. "During 1989, criticism from State and Commerce Department staff was severe enough to cause the Eximbank board of directors to reconsider its negative conclusion regarding Iraq's credit-worthiness. Even April Glaspie . . . visited the Eximbank to lobby on behalf of U.S. businesses in Iraq."

On August 18, 1989, General Motors took its case to Eximbank directly. GM's vice president for international exports, John E. Rhame, and their chief Washington lobbyist, Carolyn L. Brehm, met with Eximbank officials to discuss the vehicle assembly plant Volvo GM proposed to build for Hussein Kamil's Ministry of Industry and Military Industrialization. They argued that they faced tough competition from Toyota in Japan and Volkswagen in Germany. "Without Exim[bank] support," the GM brief reads, "General Motors is concerned that sales of assembled vehicles, sales of machinery and equipment for assembly and manufactur-

ing, as well as component sales, could be lost to the competition."
The deal — which had been expanded to include car assembly as
well — could be worth as much as $800 million a year to the
Detroit car maker, they said, and half of the deal could be sourced
from the United States.

Bechtel applied similar pressure to win Eximbank credits to
finance the PC-2 project in al-Musayyib, not far from al-Hillah. In
letters to Eximbank officials, Bechtel acknowledged that their contract covered supply of a turnkey plant to manufacture ethylene
oxide and ethylene glycol, more useful to Hussein Kamil as ingredients for fuel-air explosives and thiodyglycol, a mustard gas
precursor, than as materials for plastic bags and antifreeze. In an
interview with the *Financial Times,* former Secretary of State
George Shultz said the plant specifications so worried him that in
the end he told Bechtel to get out of the deal.

As the importance of the BNL cutoff became clear, the lobbying
effort intensified and became intensely personal. At one U.S.–Iraq
Business Forum reception, the Eximbank case officer for Iraq, Luis
Echeverria, was introduced to Forum Chairman Abboud as "the
person at Eximbank responsible for holding up business with
Iraq." Nevertheless, Echeverria stuck to his guns. "Today," said
Congressman Gonzales, "the taxpayer is better off because of the
Eximbank's diligence."

On a single day just before the meeting with General Motors,
Echeverria received no fewer than twelve letters from Congressman
James V. Hansen of Utah, a Republican, and Senator Terry Sanford
of North Carolina, a Democratic, and a delegation of congressmen
from North Carolina, urging Eximbank to support the truck assembly plant in Iraq. According to Echeverria's files, which were
subpoenaed by the House Banking Committee, the North Caro-
linian lobbyists were Democrats Walter B. Jones, William G. Hef-
ner, Tim Valentine, David E. Price, Charles Rose, Howard Coble,
Stephen L. Neal, and H. Martin Lancaster, and Republicans Cass
Ballenger and J. Alex McMillan. When Eximbank didn't budge,
Echeverria received more letters on September 13 and September
15, from Utah Governor Norman H. Bangerter and Senator Jake
Garn, both Republicans, and from Utah's Democratic congressman, Wayne Owens.

The pressure was intense, and it was coming not only from

industry and its congressional allies but also from within the Bush administration itself. "During the latter half of the 1980s," Henry Gonzales told members of the House Banking Committee in a memo dated April 15, 1991, "Eximbank was pressured by Iraq, the State Department, and U.S. exporters to increase its exposure to Iraq despite Eximbank analyses that concluded Iraq would not be able to repay such extensions of credit."

The organization within the administration responsible for approval of CCC credits and Eximbank loans was called the National Advisory Council, an interagency body that included representatives from the National Security Council, the State Department, and the CIA. From 1983 to 1989, despite repeated warnings from Eximbank, Gonzales wrote, "the NAC provided approximately $4 billion in Commodity Credit Corporation guarantees to support the export U.S. agricultural goods to Iraq," in addition to a total of $267 million that escaped the bureaucratic stamina of Eximbank. "At present, the U.S. government owes various U.S. and foreign companies over $2 billion because of Iraqi default under various CCC and Eximbank programs."

On September 9, 1989, Euromac (London) faxed an order to Jerry Kowalsky's CSI Technologies in California to purchase ninety-five "capacitors." The total transaction was worth a mere $10,500, but it had immense strategic potential. Forty of the devices were similar to the krytron switches needed to detonate a nuclear warhead; the others were slightly less sophisticated but also had military uses.

Two days later, U.S. Customs agent Daniel Supnick, posing as a CSI employee, arrived in London, where he met with Ali Daghir of Euromac and two engineers who had flown in from Baghdad to discuss how to ship the krytrons to Iraq. When the Iraqis reiterated their specifications for the capacitors, Supnick remarked that it sounded like krytrons. "They didn't say yes or no," Kowalsky reported later. In court depositions the Iraqis maintained that the capacitors were "intended to be used for an 'aerospace' application."

The Iraqis suggested they label the cases as "air conditioning parts," since that was Euromac's favorite front. Supnick agreed, and the contract was signed. The Iraqis became so buoyant that evening, Supnick recalled later, they even invited him to go to Iraq to meet the head of Iraq's nuclear weapons program. "I could see he was tempted," says Jack Kelly, Supnick's boss at Customs. "But I told him don't go."

On September 18, Supnick was glad that Kelly had held him off. The U.S. Customs attaché in Rome faxed him in London an article that had appeared in that evening's *Corriere della Sera,* describing an ongoing Italian counterespionage investigation that involved black-market arms deals with Iraq. Italy's Guardia di Finanza had just searched the Monza headquarters of a virtually unknown company called Euromac, which had disguised its arms shipments to Baghdad as "air conditioning parts." They had also prepared a list of companies that had received funding from BNL Atlanta and were believed to be working on Iraqi weapons projects. Both Euromac and Gerald Bull's Space Research Corporation figured prominently on the list.

Supnick was convinced that the Iraqis would pull back and regroup their clandestine networks, but he was wrong. Instead, they ordered Euromac to plunge ahead even faster. Saddam wanted his nuclear triggers.

The exposure of the BNL loans, coming on the heels of the Abdelkader Helmy case involving carbon-carbon exports for the Iraqi missile program, led the press ineluctably to other scandals. It wasn't long before a spate of articles appeared detailing Iraq's solid-fuel missile programs and the missile research center, Saad 16.

In West Germany, Gildemeister AG was headed for trouble. Since 1985 it had benefited from its role as the prime contractor for Saad 16. Only months after the initial contract was signed, Gildemeister had sold 15 percent of its shares to Litton Industries in the United States. Just before things soured in 1989, Litton got out, selling its Gypro shares for roughly four times their original cost.

But the Bush administration was not so prudent. Just as details of Iraq's strategic weapons programs began to emerge, Secretary of Commerce Mosbacher staged a gala event for American exporters. He invited them all to Baghdad for yet another trade fair, from November 1–15. In the pamphlet handed out at the entry to the U.S. pavilion, Mosbacher encouraged American and Iraqi companies to do business together. "Greater trade between our countries brings increased profits for mutually stronger economies," he wrote. "I encourage you to seize this moment and pursue business ventures with the firms represented here."

Not to be outdone, April Glaspie got in her word as well. A record number of companies had signed up for the fair, she noted, "representing a wide range of America's most advanced technologies and demonstrating American confidence in Iraq's bright future. The American embassy places the highest priority on promoting commerce and friendship" between the United States and Iraq. As part of that promotional effort, during the fair Glaspie arranged for Deputy Assistant Secretary of Trade Donald D. Maurino to meet with Minister of Industry (and Military Industrialization) Hussein Kamil al-Majid.

George Bush welcomed the Iraqis and Americans in a written message "on behalf of the people of the United States" and expressed a firm commitment to "an open, mutually beneficial world system of trade." Trade without barriers, technology transfer without license. In ordinary circumstances, as West and East left the Cold War behind, it would have been a perfectly normal aspiration.

Documents obtained from arms traders in Geneva, court records, and other sources detail the curious story of one Iraqi procurement agent, desperately looking for someone to give him a loan now that BNL had cut off funds for Iraq.

Hassan Ibrahim, born in Egypt in 1928, had been in the commodities business for years. He claimed he had run a construction business in Egypt, before moving to Western Europe and then the United States. To facilitate his type of international trade, he set up a series of import-export offices around the world, which he called Sitico or Sitico International. Government investigators have found traces of Sitico companies in West Germany, Italy, the Bahamas, Belgium, and Minneapolis. But each time they closed in on Hassan Ibrahim, the elusive Egyptian disappeared.

After the fall of BNL, the Iraqis turned one of their projects over to Hassan Ibrahim. He got in touch with Werner Erhard, a well-known West German arms dealer who headed an outfit called Prometheus Explorations GmbH, or Promex. Ibrahim told Erhard that he had a $100 million letter of credit issued by the Central Bank of Iraq and authorization to purchase on Iraq's behalf a long list of earth-moving equipment and other supplies. All he needed was a bank willing to confirm the letter of credit. But in the wake of the BNL blunder, the banks wanted no part of Iraqi business.

On October 25, 1989, Erhard faxed the letter of credit and a brief description to a friend in Geneva with whom he had worked many deals in the past. Heinz Pollman's company was called Verwaltungs und Finanzierungs AG, or VUFAG for short. Its offices, on the third floor of an office building at 32, rue Malatrex, had the appearance of a perfectly legitimate business, from the bronze nameplates to the Carrera marble entryway. "Dear Heinz," Erhard's fax began. "For obvious reasons central bank will not issue an official request. But they will cooperate when details for financial transaction will be available and agreed mutually and also a bank has been nominated by the financing group."

Erhard knew he was dealing with an old pro, who needed no further explanations to get the point. Heinz Pollman had gotten his start in the arms business during the Algerian revolution, when he shipped Swedish bazookas to the FLN. He could claim credit for having helped along a half-dozen fledgling Third World governments in the decades since then. With the help of a Swiss businessman named Raymond Sueur-Cantamesa, he shopped the Iraqi letter of credit around with little success. One Geneva bank was willing to confirm it — for a fee of $25 million. On November 5, Werner Erhard faxed VFAG again to inform them of a second deal worth £75 million for "pharmaceuticals." Ibrahim told them the Iraqis also wanted "cats and steel."

In the United States, Hassan Ibrahim contacted Mack Trucks, Caterpillar, and a variety of other suppliers of earth-moving equipment to organize the purchases while the Geneva group put the financial package together. In fact, Ibrahim was shopping a list identical to one put together earlier by Christopher Drogoul and BNL Atlanta; that list had named Terrex, Rotec, Dresser Industries, Goodyear, Snap-On Tools, and other major U.S. firms as suppliers.

Fate was catching up with the aging Egyptian. His financial difficulties from other deals were dragging him into ruin — and this Iraqi deal was proving to be far more difficult than he had thought. Soon he was forced to close down the Minneapolis branch of Sitico and move to Chicago, where he continued to wave the Iraqi letter of credit around as if it were hard currency. He was being sued by his former valet for unpaid wages, by his former mistress for unpaid rent, by his lawyer and even by his dry cleaner for money owed. As his woes mounted, Ibrahim kept calling Erhard to push the Geneva group harder. When they still failed to come up with the money, he asked Erhard on November 14 to look elsewhere.

Erhard sent the credit documents to a group called Intec Consult GmbH, which was then under investigation in West Germany for having helped Libya fit its Mirage F1 fleet with in-flight refueling probes. Intec sent the documents on to the Commerzbank in Hamburg, where the director of the foreign department agreed to open accounts when he received the funds, "to buy equipment and steel bars for Iraq Establishment." In the end, however, the deal fell through. No one was willing to advance funds to purchase the equipment without additional guarantees from the Central Bank of Iraq. Doing business with Baghdad was not for amateurs or for the old-style black marketeers. It was an affair of state. With the proper backing, the profits were huge. Without backing, it was not worth getting involved.

U.S. intelligence experts began to lose sleep over Iraq on December 7, 1989, when they had analyzed the data from the satellite photographs taken two days earlier. Iraq was about to graduate from the status of a major Third World military power to that of First-Class Threat.

Gerald Bull was back in Iraq. Amer al-Saadi had invited him to the an-Anbar Space Research Center out in the desert near Karbala for the event, which he would not have missed for the world. What they had planned would remind him of the good old days at Paragon House in Barbados. On December 5 Iraq launched its first long-range missile from the an-Anbar range under the authority of the Minister of Industry (and Military Industrialization) and not the Ministry of Defense, as would be the case anywhere else. Hussein Kamil called the new missile al-Abid, the Worshiper. The three-stage, 48-ton rocket stood 25 meters high and was capable of hurling a military warhead at a target some 2,000 kilometers away, Kamil said. Film footage of the launch showed Iraqi technicians shouting "Allah Akbar" — God is Great — when the missile disappeared into the upper atmosphere without incident. When he announced the missile launch in a December 7 message to the Iraqi president, Hussein Kamil revealed for the first time in public the name of the scientist who headed Iraq's ballistic missile programs: Lieutenant General Dr. Amer al-Saadi.

Saddam Hussein said that Iraq had developed not one, but two surface-to-surface missiles, each capable of striking targets in a 2,000-kilometer range. The second one he called Tammuz, the Arabic word for July, the month of the revolution, and the name of the nuclear "research" reactor destroyed by Israel in 1981. The missile's name was a clear indication of Saddam's intentions. By December 8, U.S. officials were telling reporters in Washington that Iraq's missile programs had become "a subject of major concern" to the Bush administration.

EIGHTEEN

Pride Before the Fall

In hindsight, the events of 1990 that led up to Iraq's invasion of Kuwait seem to follow an extraordinary logic. The wide variety of weapons procurement and development programs Saddam Hussein had launched were all coming to a head, bringing the Middle East closer to a new era, the era of Iraqi domination. At the same time, however, the past was catching up with Iraq. Mountains of debt had made creditors wary, while Saddam Hussein's blatant use of chemical weapons against his own population was causing some congressional leaders in the United States to seek strong sanctions against Iraq. The next eight months would become a race to see which force would dominate, Saddam's will or the West, slowly awakening to the knowledge of what it had done. At the outset it looked as if Saddam would win.

Jean-Pierre Chevènement, the French minister of defense, viewed the American commercial invasion of Iraq with concern. If France did not do something fast, she would lose her privileged position in Iraq. Fighting "imperialism" had always been high on Chevènement's list of priorities. Coupling that with another favorite theme — the adoration of Saddam Hussein — provided an opportunity too good to pass up. Not long after the New Year, Chevènement picked up his pilgrim's baton and went to woo the Iraqi dictator, as so many Frenchmen had before him. His arrival on January 25, 1990, marked the first trip to Baghdad by a French defense minister in more than ten years. French officials said it was intended to "raise our bilateral relations to a higher level," which meant reopening the arms pipeline between Paris and Baghdad.

As soon as Chevènement arrived, he paid obeisance to the lord of the land. In a long interview with a Baath party paper, he bubbled over in praise. "President Saddam Hussein has a clear and interesting outlook," Chevènement began, "which he qualifies by leading his people toward peace and the construction of his country, in spite of the challenges and difficulties with which he was confronted during the war with Iran." To make sure he got the point across, he added, "President Saddam has the respect and esteem of French leaders."

Chevènement held highly visible talks with Saddam and his minister of industry and military industrialization, Hussein Kamil. On the menu was a broad range of new military industrialization projects for Iraq, as well as direct arms sales. These had been made possible by a generous settlement of the Iraqi debt on September 14, 1989, which Chevènement had managed to shove down the throats of the French Finance Ministry.

The first to benefit was Thomson-CSF. Only days before the Chevènement trip, the company signed its first new arms contract with Iraq in more than two years, to supply sophisticated avionics for Iraqi fighters. The retrofit package, worth $161 million, was believed to include ground-attack radar for the Sukhoi-25 Frogfoot delivered by the USSR and an upgraded weapons system for the MiG-23/27 fleet, to transform these aircraft into precision fighter-bombers capable of launching laser-guided missiles and bombs. Unlike previous sales, this time the Iraqis paid cash up front. That had been Thomson's sole condition for closing the deal. After accepting two BNL letters of credit worth $5.7 million, to pay for radar kits for the Iraqi AWACS plane, Thomson wanted no more of the flaky Atlanta bank, especially since the French government still refused to guarantee export sales to Iraq. Either the Iraqis would pay cash, or there would be no deal.

Another sale involved side-scan aerial surveillance cameras to equip Iraqi Mirage F1 and MiG-25 spy planes. A squadron of Iraqi Mirages based in Jordan had been flying missions high over the Jordan River since August 1989, looking deep into Israel using an earlier version of the sophisticated French reconnaissance cameras to update Iraq's operational targeting maps. Ze'ev Schiff reported in *Ha'aretz* that the new cameras gave the Iraqis the capability of spotting targets 65 kilometers inside Israel, as opposed to the 40-kilometer maximum range of Jordan's F-5E reconnaissance planes.

The Iraqis could now accurately map the area from the Jordanian border to the Tel Aviv suburb of Ramat Gan, where key defense manufacturing plants and a major Israeli air force base were located.

These deals were of little consequence compared to what the Iraqis really wanted from Chevènement. They were seeking French government financing for the Fao Project, to build their own aeronautics industry. But here even such a powerful ally as Jean-Pierre Chevènement was unable to deliver. The French Finance Ministry just said no. "We note that an enormous share of Iraq's GNP is currently being devoted to military industrialization projects," a key advisor to Finance Minister Pierre Bérégovoy said in private while Chevènement was discoursing with Saddam. "We do not want to finance regional destabilization. Nor will we issue any more export credit guarantees until the Iraqis make good on the debt rescheduling deal we worked out. If defense companies like Thomson-CSF want to sell to Iraq, they will have to take that risk on their own." The advisor went on to reveal that the Finance Ministry was still blocking the delivery of the last eight Mirage F1s left over from the fourth contract signed by Jacques Chirac. "When the Iraqis pay, they will get their planes," he said.

The Iraqis had another iron in the fire in case Chevènement wasn't able to deliver what they wanted. Two months earlier, on December 1, 1989, the French president's brother, Jacques Mitterrand had flown to Baghdad with a delegation of senior French aerospace executives to discuss details of the Fao Project with Hussein Kamil. General Mitterrand headed the government export agency devoted to military aircraft sales, the Office Général de l'Air (OGA). On December 2, he met with Saddoun Hammadi, who was in charge of Iraq's debt negotiations. Three days later he choppered up to Saddam Hussein's snowbound mountain retreat in Sarseng, near Mosul, to deliver a "personal message" to the Iraqi president from his brother. Sources said President Mitterrand's message extended "political support" for Saddam's reconstruction plans, but gave no promise of financial aid. In the meantime, the French president made it clear he was leaving the details of Franco-Iraqi military cooperation to his brother and Chevènement to straighten out — with the French Finance Ministry.

*   *   *

The Babylon Project was advancing rapidly. Gerald Bull returned to Iraq in February 1990 to supervise the final firing trials of the Baby Babylon gun. Unlike the earlier tests, company documents show that the plan this time was to calculate range and accuracy with the gun inclined at a 45-degree angle. It was a useless position for launching satellites, the pretext Bull used when discussing the project with his son; but it was ideal for a ballistic trajectory. With Bull's rocket-assisted projectiles, Baby Babylon could reach targets 700 kilometers away, such as Kuwait. But its big brother, the S-1000, could do better than that; from the permanent base in the Makhoul Mountains near Baiji, it could hit Israel — at least that's what Gerald Bull told the Iraqis.

On February 7, Lieutenant General Amer Hamoudi al-Saadi announced that Iraq was ready to launch two versions of a domestically produced satellite, which he said would serve "nonmilitary purposes." Al-Saadi told the United Arab Emirates' *Air Force* magazine that the satellites had been "produced and designed solely by Iraqis" — indeed, like every other weapon Iraq had designed and produced . . . with help from Germany, Argentina, France, and Brazil. The satellite project, if indeed it really existed, appears to have resulted from a cooperation agreement with the Brazilian government's CTA and the private Brazilian space venture Orbita. Al-Saadi's real purpose in announcing the launch, however, seems to have been to forestall a reaction from Israel during the super-gun firing trials. Israel could not fail to detect the ballistic trajectory of the Babylon rockets, whose 500-kilogram warhead was twice as large as Iraq's upgraded SCUDs.

More of PRB's special propellant mixture was arriving from Belgium via Jordan every day. PRB's new owner, Astra Defense Systems Ltd., of Britain, had reviewed the Belgian company's deals with Gerald Bull and Iraq, and in a November 2, 1989, internal memo, had approved them. "You are hereby instructed to proceed with this contract," Astra board members told PRB, "subject to provision to extend the Letter of Credit." A top-secret report dated September 17, 1989, by Italy's military intelligence bureau, SISMI, shows that some of the cash needed to fund the Babylon Project was fronted by BNL Atlanta.

A subsidiary of PRB in Canada, Technologies Belcan, was put in charge of the firing program in Iraq, according to Radio Canada journalist Norman Lester, who published a book on Gerald Bull called *Les Canons de l'Apocalypse*. Belcan, well known in the arms business for its expertise in ballistics trials, did consulting work for the Pentagon, Canada, and for other NATO defense ministries. The gun captain for the February 1991 trials was a Belcan employee named Bruce Smith, who had known Bull for nearly twenty years. Documents seized by British Customs show that Smith had been hired for the occasion by one of Bull's front companies, Advanced Technology Institute.

An internal memo drafted in preparation for the trials by engineers at Bull's Space Research Corporation shows the real purpose of the Babylon guns. All pretense that they would provide a cheap means of launching civilian satellites had been dropped. "The lack of a suitable radar means that the range of these projectiles will be determined by spotting the fail or shot, rather than by tracking the early part of the trajectory and extrapolating," the document reads. "To assist in spotting the impact point, it is proposed that the nose of the projectiles be filled with powder paint, which will be dispersed on impact."

When the guns were up and ready, they could fire conventional warheads or chemical rounds at a maximum rate of two shots per minute. If Iraq succeeded in obtaining the krytron switches needed to detonate nuclear warheads, the Babylon guns could vitrify Israel before the Israeli air force even got off the ground.

John Kelly arrived in Baghdad on February 12, 1990, for talks with Saddam Hussein. It was his first trip to Baghdad as the State Department's top Middle East hand, a position he had inherited from Richard Murphy the year before. He was received that same afternoon by Saddam in the presidential palace, accompanied by Ambassador Glaspie. In the year that she had been posted to Baghdad, Glaspie had yet to meet the Iraqi leader one on one.

Kelly had decided to flatter Saddam by calling him a "force of moderation" in the region. He also reassured the Iraqi that the Bush administration was determined to strengthen ties to Baghdad, despite continued efforts on Capitol Hill to impose sanctions on Iraq. Concerned senators had recently succeeded in getting the $1 billion CCC credits to Iraq cut in half for 1990, and they threatened to take more severe measures if Iraq's human rights record didn't improve. Kelly assured the Iraqi leader that the Bush administration would continue to oppose these efforts, whatever the cost.

The next day Richard Murphy was in town as a private "consultant," a nuance lost on the Iraqis. He said he was representing the First City Bancorporation of Texas, whose chairman, Robert Abboud, also headed the U.S.–Iraq Business Forum. Murphy didn't meet with Saddam, although he did compare notes with John Kelly later on. The purpose of Murphy's visit was to discuss "development projects" with Hussein Kamil. "Hussein Kamil gave me the same speech almost word for word that Saddam Hussein had given Kelly the day before," Murphy said. "The Iraqis were worried that Israel was planning an attack against them, and Hussein Kamil said they had solid evidence to back up their suspicions. What evidence? I asked. Never mind, he said. It's just a given. Israel is going to repeat its 1981 attack on us, and soon."

Disaster for the death lobby and for Saddam's plans struck on February 15, in the form of an editorial broadcast on the Arabic service of the Voice of America, which purported to represent the views of the U.S. government. The writer castigated Saddam Hussein's record of human rights violations, calling him one of the worst dictators to have ever darkened the face of the planet. The editorial made Saddam furious, and when he linked it to the halving of agricultural credits and to all the fuss about an Iranian journalist arrested for spying, to Saddam's way of thinking it amounted to a full-blown conspiracy. Washington was plotting against him behind his back and orchestrating a vicious "campaign" against him in the Western press. He and other Iraqi officials would return obsessively to this theme in public statements over the next few months.

Two days later, just as Baby Babylon was firing its successful first shots, Jordan officially announced the formation of an "All Arab Air Squadron" based in the desert near Israel, composed of Jordanian and Iraqi Mirage fighters — thus revealing what the Israeli's had known for some time. Editorialists in Amman called it "a first step down the path of establishing Arab military unity . . . to confront the Zionist ambitions supported by U.S. aid." Like Saddam, the Jordanians deeply feared the influx of Soviet Jewish immigrants to Israel. But so far, neither they nor Saddam Hussein had succeeded in rallying other Arab leaders (except Yasser Arafat of the PLO) behind their condemnation of this dramatic new development in the Middle East.

The new air force squadron stepped up its reconnaissance flights along the Israeli border. For the second time in six months, Israel relayed a message to the Jordanian government through Washington, saying that it took a "grave view" of Jordan's plans to build a joint military power with Iraq. On February 19, Israeli defense planners told the newspaper *Hadashot* in Tel Aviv that this type of operational cooperation between the Jordanian and Iraqi air forces was "merely the first stage in a more comprehensive military growth plan." On February 20, Defense Minister Yitzhak Rabin told the Knesset's Foreign Affairs and Defense Committee that Israel "would not be able to sit idly by if Iraqi military forces are deployed in Jordan where they were only a four-minute flight from Tel Aviv."

Saddam Hussein flew to Amman on February 23, 1990, for a meeting with King Hussein, Hosni Mubarak of Egypt, and President Ali Salem of Yemen. They had just celebrated the first anniversary of a regional coalition, the Arab Cooperation Council, with festivities in Baghdad the week before. Now it was time for Saddam to unveil his vision of the new political order that should result from the end of the Cold War. When it came to the Arab world, his way of thinking contained only enough room for one leader — himself — and one major military power, Iraq. "There is no place among the ranks of good Arabs for the fainthearted," who believed they had "no choice but to submit" to the will of the United States, he sneered. The message was not to the liking of Hosni Mubarak, who was gobbling up $3 billion a year in U.S. aid for signing the Camp David peace agreements with Israel. Mubarak walked out of the conference hall with his entire delegation. He was already furious with Saddam for having gotten Egypt involved in an international smuggling ring in the United States, which was exposed when Abdelkader Helmy was arrested for trying to obtain missile technologies on Iraq's behalf. Calling him a boot-licker was an irreparable insult.[1]

For the remainder of his speech, Saddam Hussein lashed out repeatedly at the United States for pursuing "suspect policies" that were driving down the price of oil and depriving Iraq of the means to accomplish its "destiny." America "must respect the Arabs and respect their rights, and should not interfere in their internal affairs under any cover." As he had often done in the past, he projected his own fears onto others, turning them into conspiracies. Because American strategy "needs an aggressive Israel, not a peaceful one," he said, there was a "real possibility that Israel might embark on new stupidities" within the next five years. By this he meant a repeat of Israel's 1981 attack on Osirak, but this time directed against Iraqi military plants.

It was the most extreme public presentation Saddam Hussein had made in years, blowing to shreds the whole fiction so carefully constructed by the State Department's Richard Murphy, and now John Kelly, that Iraq was moving toward a more moderate and constructive role in the Middle East, thanks to trade and aid from the United States. In his tirade, Saddam called on the United States to pull out its "occupying naval forces" from the Gulf (glossing over the fact that he had welcomed the U.S. reinforcement in 1987, when Iraq was suffering from the Iranian naval blockade). He accused the Americans of trying to control Arab oil and warned the Arabs that if they were not careful, "the Arab Gulf region will be governed by the U.S. will."

What Saddam was really worried about was the sorry state of the Iraqi treasury. Kuwait and Saudi Arabia were in no mood to forgive the $35 billion Iraqi war debt, and the price of oil had plummeted to a historic low; even BNL, which had saved his military industrial program for the past three years, had been "sabotaged" by the U.S. government. Saddam was so broke that he had mortgaged Iraq's future for two generations by selling long-term oil contracts in order to buy weapons and build an arms industry today. Rather than face facts, he preferred to invent an international conspiracy.

"We should have taken his words a lot more literally," Richard Murphy realized in hindsight. "But as Arab specialists, we have been trained to disregard the rhetoric and seek the underlying substance. In Saddam's case, however, the rhetoric was as close as you could get to his real thinking." This is what Hussein Kamil had meant when he told Murphy that Iraq "had proofs" that Israel was planning to launch a preemptive strike. In fact, Iraq was making those war preparations itself, to stave off its creditors and bankruptcy. The "proofs" were its own aggressive plans.

"Saddam's ambitions were beyond imagination," an Egyptian diplomat said, referring to Saddam's attempts to transform the Arab Cooperation Council into a council of war. "He is the most bloodthirsty leader the Arab world has ever known. We had hoped we could temper his appetites, control his excesses. But we were wrong. How could you temper such an appetite?"

When Richard Fairbanks read the Amman speech a few days later, he "filed for divorce" as a paid lobbyist for the Iraqi embassy in Washington, D.C. "I sort of fired them as a client," he said.

The first unmistakable sign that Saddam had flipped out was the execution of Farzod Bazoft. If Bazoft was a spy, as Saddam reasserted the day before his execution, then he was one of the clumsiest spies ever to have practiced the world's second oldest profession. Interviews with three reporters who spoke with him just before his arrest in Baghdad show that he had one strong trait: the total inability to keep a secret. Bazoft was so thrilled to have discovered the truth about the explosion at the al-Hillah weapons plant that he broadcast it from the rooftops. Or rather, from the hotel bar counter.

Had Saddam and his inner circle been in full possession of their faculties, they would have released Bazoft after sentencing him to death, life imprisonment, or whatever. Even the Afghan leader, General Najibullah, had had the presence of mind to release a French journalist captured in even worse circumstances than Bazoft a few years earlier. Making the press understand that there were limits not to cross was less difficult than it sometimes appeared. But Saddam wanted to show off his strength. He wasn't going to be pushed around by somebody's media campaign.

At the last minute the British government sensed the hardening of Saddam's position and publicly called on the Iraqi leader to exercise his presidential pardon. Prime Minister Thatcher became so appalled by the grotesqueness of the accusations against Bazoft that she asked the secretary general of the United Nations, Javier Pérez de Cuéllar, to intervene. But the appeals for clemency came to nothing, and on the morning of March 15, 1990, the thirty-one-year-old reporter was hung. Only minutes before his execution, Bazoft insisted once again that he had been only a journalist "going after a scoop." His last words were recorded for posterity by the British consul-general in Baghdad, Robin Kealy, who was summoned by the Iraqi authorities to Bazoft's prison to watch the show.

"Thatcher wanted him alive," gloated the Iraqi information minister, Latif Nussayyif Jassim, once the corpse was dispatched to the British Embassy later that day. "We sent him home in a box."[2]

Monique Jamine sensed no particular anxiety in her companion as she drove him home on the evening of March 22 to the posh apartment block in Uccle, Belgium. Jamine was Gerald Bull's personal assistant at the Brussels headquarters of Space Research Corporation, which shared offices with another Bull company, ATI Belgique. She let him off downstairs and went to park the white Volkswagen Golf (license plate number ANB 399) around the corner. Investigators have not determined whether she knew he had rented the sixth-floor apartment under a pseudonym in order to avoid publicity. But one thing was sure: when she went back upstairs to bring him some papers he had forgotten, Bull was dead. An unknown assailant had fired two bullets into the back of his neck and pumped three more into his body, using an automatic Colt pistol equipped with a silencer. When they examined the body later on, the Belgian police found $20,000 in cash in Bull's wallet that had not been touched. The dead engineer was still holding the keys to his apartment in one hand. It was a professional job.

The cold-blooded assassination sent ripples through the arms community, where Gerald Bull was well known, if not always well liked. "Whoever assassinated Gerald Bull knew one thing," said Amazia Bar-Am of the University of Haifa, an expert on Saddam's Iraq. "With one bullet, you eliminate a whole big project, and a very threatening one. So I suppose it was effective."

Did the Israelis really assassinate Gerald Bull? That was certainly the impression Mike Wallace, of "60 Minutes," chose to leave with his viewers. He believed the Israelis had sufficient motivation to do the job. Their goal was to set an example for other scientists around the world who were collaborating with Iraqi weapons programs. "Work with Iraq and somebody will put a bullet in the back of your head," as one of Bull's former colleagues put it.

But another theory, first spread by Mossad and later picked up by French and other European intelligence agencies, said that the assassins had been paid by Iraq. French writer Gerard de Villiers made it the theme of a political thriller called *Les Canons de Baghdad* published a few months after the crime. The idea was elegant, and it fit perfectly with the conspiratorial thinking of people like Saddam. Long before signing the super-gun project with Iraq, according to this theory, Gerald Bull had gone to work for Tel Aviv. While he was supplying advanced technology to Iraq, he was keeping the Israelis abreast of his activities and providing them with vital details on Iraqi weapons programs gathered during his trips to Baghdad. When the Iraqis discovered the double cross, the theory went, they did him in. After all, they had all the blueprints for the gun. They didn't need Bull anymore. They could make the doomsday cannon themselves.

In yet a third theory, Michel Bull told reporters that his father and others working for him had received letters of warning before the murder, postmarked Brazil. "Bull had Iraq's traditional arms suppliers on the run," a French intelligence source said. "They were worried he would squeeze them out of a very lucrative market. They were not at all happy about Iraq's success in expanding its arms industry, since this cut deeply into their sales." Proponents of this theory say that one, or perhaps several, of the world's largest arms manufacturers hired a professional killer to do the job. Their message to Iraq was buy guns, not the technology to make them.

Bull's assassination was only one of a string of disasters to hit Saddam Hussein that spring. It was as if the house of cards called Iraq was falling down all around him.

The West was slowly waking up.

For more than a week, British Customs agents had been tailing the movements of forty-nine-year-old Ali Daghir. Arriving in unmarked cars, they posed as surveyors on the village green of Thames Ditton, where Euromac and Daghir's Atlas Equipment Corporation had their offices. The nuclear triggers Daghir had ordered from CSI Technologies in California had arrived on TWA flight 760 at Heathrow Airport earlier. There they had been intercepted by U.S. and British Customs agents. The wooden crate labeled "air conditioning parts" had been carefully pried open, and the forty-one krytrons replaced with convincing fakes, which had been built to order by krytron manufacturer EG&G of Salem, Massachusetts.

After baiting their trap, Customs settled down to wait. On the morning of March 28, they saw Daghir hurriedly leave the premises and drive away, headed for Heathrow, nearby. When he arrived, he met with an Iraqi Airways employee named Omar Latif, and the two went to the freight office where the krytrons were stored, to sign the necessary papers to get the crate loaded onto Iraqi Airways flight 238, bound for Baghdad. As soon as the two Iraqis had signed the papers, they were arrested by British Customs officers.

Meanwhile detectives from Scotland Yard raided the Euromac/ Atlas offices in Thames Ditton, seizing boxes full of documents and computer files, which described the clandestine procurement ring in detail. Besides Latif, who was expelled after the Home Office accused him of heading Iraqi intelligence in London, and Daghir, three other Iraqi agents were arrested in Britain, including a French citizen, Jeannine Specman. An indictment unsealed a few days later in San Diego named three more Iraqis said to be engineers from the al-Qaqaa State Establishment who had master-minded the nuclear smuggling operation. The indictment specified that al-Qaqaa was controlled by Iraq's Ministry of Industry and Military Industrialization, run by the powerful nephew of the Iraqi president, Hussein Kamil al-Majid.

When she announced the arrests later that day in Washington, Customs Commissioner Carol Hallett said that Euromac "has purchased millions of dollars' worth of equipment for this government during the Iran–Iraq conflict. . . . I think it's fair to say that we have stopped some very serious business from going forward."

The Iraqis immediately cried foul. An official statement from Hussein Kamil's office declared that the nuclear triggers had been purchased "in abidance with the export measures in the country of origin" and that Iraq "has the full right to transfer technology" to further its national development. Iraqi ambassadors abroad hastened to deny that there was any connection between the krytrons and a nuclear weapons program. Iraq had survived eight years of war without nuclear weapons, they said, and would continue to survive the peace without them.

No one was quicker to deny that Iraq was pursuing nuclear weapons than Abdulrazzak al-Hashimi, the Iraqi ambassador to France. All the fuss over the krytrons, he told a Radio Monte Carlo interviewer, "is a continuation of the campaign that started with the Bazoft case. . . . Everybody knows that the Iraqi nuclear program is for peaceful purposes." The media attention was a plot by Great Britain, the United States, and "the Zionist entity . . . to find the necessary justifications or atmosphere for a new Israeli military aggression against Iraq similar to the one it carried out on the Tammuz reactor in 1981."

Al-Hashimi knew exactly what he was saying. A nuclear physicist by training, he had been on the team of Iraqi negotiators who closed the Tammuz deal with French Premier Jacques Chirac in 1976 and must have known in detail about the clandestine procurement scheme. But Saddam dropped all pretense not long afterward. During a televised speech, he ridiculed the Customs sting and said that Iraq was now capable of making krytrons in its own weapons factories. To prove his point, he held up an American-made krytron in one hand and a pair of Iraqi krytrons in the other. "Can this detonate a nuclear bomb?" he asked with a smirk. He had never seen a nuclear bomb, he added, "but this is one of the capacitors they talked about." It had probably been manufactured in the Salah al-Din electronics plant north of Baghdad, built by Thomson-CSF in France.

Saddam gave a fiery speech on April 2 that was reprinted all over the world. Castigating the "psychological, media, and political" campaign against Iraq, he threatened to "burn half of Israel" if his country was attacked. Iraq now possessed "the binary chemical weapon," Saddam announced. If true, Saddam could thank his German collaborators for having developed it for him. In binary weapons, two inoffensive chemical agents combine to make a deadly poison gas. They have an advantage over ordinary poisons in being easier and safer to stockpile.

War fever was gripping the region, and Saddam Hussein was presenting himself increasingly as the new Nebuchadnezzar, the biblical leader of Babylon who carried the Jews into captivity. PLO leader Yasser Arafat seized on Saddam's extraordinary self-infatuation. "We say to the brother and leader Saddam Hussein — go forward with God's blessing," he declaimed on April 3. "The heart of the Arab nation is with you and around you until Arab victory soars with the flags of the Arab victory march." In another comment Arafat addressed Saddam as "al-Faris," the Arab knight. "We will enter Jerusalem victoriously and raise our flag on its walls. You will enter with me on your white horse," he said. Addressing Israeli leaders, Arafat continued: "We will fight you with stones, rifles, and al-Abid." This was a reference to the three-stage ballistic missile the Iraqis had launched in December 1989. If Saddam needed any encouragement, Arafat was ready and willing to provide it.

On April 11, Gerald Bull's network began to come apart at the seams. British Customs agents stormed into the dockyards at the port of Middlesbrough and seized eight huge, cylindrical wooden crates about to be loaded onto the MV *Gur Mariner,* a Bahamas-registered cargo ship on its way to Iraq. The Customs action was dubbed Operation Big Bertha in memory of the giant German gun that had shelled Paris during World War I. Customs officials claimed the crates contained sections of a giant gun barrel which, when assembled end to end, would measure 40 meters and weigh 140 tons. The Iraqis and their British suppliers, Walter Summers and the Sheffield Forgemasters, claimed the crates contained pipe intended for a petrochemicals complex and that they had cleared the deal with Britain's Department of Trade and Industry. This was in fact true, but the shipping documents showed that the pipes had been purchased by the "Ministry of Industry and Mines, Petrochemical Project, Baghdad, Iraq." Such a ministry did not exist.

Artillery experts were incredulous when confronted with the idea that the 39-inch-diameter pipes could be assembled into a gun that would lob shells at targets 700 or 1,000 kilometers away. But as the name of Gerald Bull became associated with the gun, and the involvement of his Space Research Corporation became known, the experts changed their tune. Iraq had launched a doomsday project to annihilate its neighbors, they grudgingly admitted, which had been foiled as if by chance at the last minute.

The pro-Iraq lobby in the United States was slow to react to the new events in the Middle East. The axiom of this half-baked mixture of farmers, high-tech vendors, car makers, and their congressmen could have been drawn from Shakespeare's *Othello:* Put money in thy purse.

Senators Robert Dole of Kansas and Alan Simpson of Wyoming, both representing states with a vested interest in expanding trade with Iraq, led a delegation of senators to meet with Saddam Hussein at his Mosul hideout on April 12, 1990. Their object was to plead with the Iraqi leader not to jeopardize the foundations of a sound business relationship. The complete transcript of this meeting, read by an announcer on Baghdad Radio as a show of American support, was published by the *Foreign Broadcast Information Service* daily bulletin for the Middle East, dated April 17, 1990.

Senator Dole led off by telling Saddam that their goal was to improve U.S.–Iraqi relations. President Bush had encouraged Dole and his delegation to go to Iraq and had just phoned them to reaffirm his support. But Dole was worried because just the night before, NBC News had reported that Iraq was developing bacteriological weapons. How can we improve our relations, he asked, when we see a report like this?

Saddam brushed the question aside. Instead of worrying about Iraq's strategic weapons programs, the senators would do better to worry about what Israel was hatching behind Iraq's back. The way the international media had reacted to the execution of Farzod Bazoft, the krytron case, and Saddam's comments about burning half of Israel showed that a "large-scale" media campaign had been launched against him by Israel, Europe, and the United States.

"Not from President Bush," Senator Dole cut in. "Yesterday he told us he does not support this." The person responsible for the Voice of America editorial that had offended Saddam "has been fired," Dole declared. (In fact, as William Safire told readers of his column a few weeks later, this was not true.)

Saddam repeatedly returned to the issue of a campaign against him, and finally Senator Simpson thought he had the answer. "I believe your problem is with the Western media, not with the U.S. government," he said. "The press is spoiled and conceited. All the journalists consider themselves brilliant political scientists. They do not want to see anything succeeding or achieving its objectives. My advice is that you allow those bastards to come here and see things for themselves." Saddam was not so sure this was the answer, especially when Dole suggested he allow Western reporters to inspect the Salman Pak chemical plant, which had been built by Thyssen Rheinstahl of West Germany. The Western press was like "a spoiled child," Saddam agreed. But "if this child is given a sweet in response to his desires and cries, he will continue to cry all the time, wanting more."

For all the banter, Saddam remained intractable. He told the senators that he had given orders to Iraqi air force commanders to load chemical weapons and fire them against Israel in the event he or the High Command was knocked out. And he made no bones about his true intentions. The Arab world, led by Iraq, was duty-bound to become the military equal of Israel, equipped with modern missiles, chemical weapons, and even nuclear bombs. "A just peace is possible when, if Israel possesses one missile, the Arabs possess one missile, so neither can use it."

Hearing Saddam's fiery threats to Israel, the Commerce Department's Dennis Kloske finally understood that it was time to limit the flow of high-technology equipment to Iraq — if only to keep the Israeli lobby and the "ankle-biters" at the Pentagon from tripping up his career.

In April he brought up the subject of imposing new controls on licenses for exports to Iraq at an interagency meeting, aides said. Kloske's timid attempt (after years of urging by the Pentagon) was criticized by Robert Gates, deputy director of the National Security Council. It was shot down in flames by Robert Kimmitt, the undersecretary of state for political affairs. The United States' policy was to support Iraq, Kimmitt said — repeating what his predecessor Michael Armacost, had been saying for years — not to hinder it. If the United States didn't sell high technology products to Iraq, then France, Britain, and Germany would.

Others in the Bush administration began to worry that their actions in favor of Iraq would become known to the public. In an internal memo at the U.S. Department of Agriculture, the head of the CCC Program, F. Paul Dickerson, weighed the pros and cons of bucking the congressional cutback on CCC credits to Iraq. His agency wanted to restore Iraq's $1 billion credit line. Iraq was America's "largest market for rice," he argued, and a good customer for feed grains, wheat, protein concentrates, wood products, and sugar. "U.S. suppliers of these commodities would suffer the most" from a lower level of CCC guarantees. Furthermore, Dickerson feared that the Iraqis "might stop paying on their GSM obligations" if the program were scaled back.

This was the same argument Christopher Drogoul liked to use to justify new BNL loans to Baghdad. If you didn't give the Iraqis new money, they wouldn't repay the old.

But Dickerson's biggest worry was possible indictments resulting from the BNL scandal. "If this occurred there would be considerable adverse Congressional reaction and press coverage," he wrote in the February 23, 1990, memo. "In the worst-case scenario, investigators would find a direct link to financing Iraqi military expenditures, particularly the Condor missile." His statement shows that the U.S. government could not pretend any longer that it did not know exactly and in great detail where the BNL money had gone.

Dickerson sent a team of USDA investigators to Baghdad in April to examine the Iraqi books on the agricultural credits. What they discovered was a pattern of surcharges, averaging 15 percent on every transaction, that could not be explained by freight or other costs. It looked as if Saddam was taking a hefty kickback from the U.S. taxpayer as a reward for purchasing American grain.

Despite these mounting reservations about the wisdom of doing business with Saddam, a motion to scale back the Iraqi loan guarantees through an amendment to the farm bill was defeated on Capitol Hill. Leading the charge to maintain trade and aid to Iraq was Kansas Senator Robert Dole.

Other bits and pieces of Gerald Bull's super-gun had been put on board trucks before the Customs seizure at Middlesbrough, and Iraqi agents and Customs officials all over Europe now began a mad dash to see who could get them first. On April 23, Turkey announced that it had intercepted a Hungarian tractor-trailer truck as it was heading for the Haydarpasa Customs station on the Asian side of Istanbul. It was carrying a 10-meter-long steel tube believed to be part of the Babylon gun. The same day, Greek officials seized a British truck convoy carrying other parts of the giant artillery system.

On April 25 the British authorities arrested Dr. Christopher Cowley, an engineer working for ATI Belgique. They accused him of having placed purchase orders for the super-gun with companies throughout Europe. On May 12, seventy-five tons of super-gun parts turned up in the Italian port of Naples. They had been made by the Società delle Fucine of Terni, a subsidiary of the Italian conglomerate IRI. Like the earlier shipments, they were labeled as parts for a petrochemicals plant. Another fifteen tons of forged steel components were seized at the Fucine steelworks near Rome, while a half ton of specially designed metal parts was impounded in a warehouse in Brescia, to the north. Press reports said these parts had been forged of "titanium steel" and were intended for the breech block of the giant gun.

On May 15, Customs in Frankfurt, West Germany, seized seventeen containers addressed to a Mr. Aktari at the Ministry of Industry (and Military Industrialization) in Baghdad. Markings on these crates showed that some of the equipment had been manufactured by Mannesmann AG and a subsidiary company, Brueninghaus Hydraulik GmbH. They were also identified as parts for the Babylon gun.

Everything was falling apart. To Saddam's mind, there had to be reason, a conspiracy; on May 15, he thought he had pieced it together. Iraqi exiles say this is when Saddam called former intelligence chief Fadil Barrak back to Baghdad and arrested him. He also tracked down and arrested Khalil Shaker, one of Barrak's top aides. Shaker had made a name for himself for having executed Iraqi opposition leaders abroad using a KGB poison, thalium.

Saddam accused Shaker and Barrak of having aided British intelligence in cracking the clandestine procurement rings. Barrak had been in London off and on since 1989, when he had left the Mukhabarat to take over the Presidential Affairs Department (Amn al-Khass). His job was to supervise the most critical technology procurement networks in the West and to provide them with funds from Saddam's secret bank accounts. In late 1989 Barrak is believed to have made the decision to maintain the krytron negotiations despite the exposure of Euromac in Italy in September. Barrak's failure and the arrests in London led Saddam to suspect that Barrak had blown the whistle on the Iraqi spy ring in exchange for help from British intelligence in mounting a coup against him.[3]

Saddam's first deputy premier, Taha Yassin Ramadan, explained Iraqi paranoia about Britain in an interview with an Arab journalist. It all went back to Iraq's colonial past. British politicians "do not believe, nor do they want to believe, that history has changed," he said. "Iraq is not like the Iraq they left behind." Britain had never accepted Iraq's independence, Ramadan believed. In this light, the Bazoft case, the seizure of the krytrons, and the super-gun affair were all of a piece. It was a British, American, and Zionist plot against Saddam Hussein, against Iraq, and against the Arab world. They wanted to weaken the Iraqi leader because he had proven to the world that an Arab nation could stand on its own feet. They wanted to bring him down because he was proud.[4]

As tensions mounted, Saddam gave the order to accelerate the nuclear weapons program. Iraqi engineers were taken off other weapons projects and reassigned to the uranium dioxide mill near Baiji and the hexafluoride plant at Al Qaim, to keep the raw materials flowing into the enrichment units. Work at the two calutron enrichment plants, Tarmiyah and Ash Sharqat, was given priority over industrial projects such as PC-2. Saddam was emboldened by the latest inspection of the bombed-out Osirak reactor by the IAEA in April. The international "watchdog" agency asserted that Iraq had not diverted any nuclear material to an undeclared weapons program. Once again, the inspectors had seen nothing. As watchdogs, they were a thief's best friend.

One enrichment cascade was now operating around the clock. To keep it running, Iraqi engineers needed more end caps, maraging steel, and other raw materials. Purchases of the necessary equipment were stepped up on the European market. Then in June 1990, Safa Haboby of TDG came up with a better idea. Why not buy into a company that made the hard-to-get maraging steel alloy? That way Iraq would be guaranteed a steady supply. For strategic projects such as this, Saddam always had cash, accumulated over the years in secret Swiss accounts, thanks to his 5 percent personal tax on oil sales. It was only the Iraqi people who were broke.

Haboby and Fadel Kadhum settled on a company called Schmiedemeccanica (SMB). Not only did it make maraging steel, it could provide the machine tools needed to shape it as well. Better yet, it was located in the paradise of all arms dealers, dope peddlers, dictators, and money launderers: Switzerland.

Haboby proceeded in much the same way he and Gerald Bull had organized the buyout of the Learfan factory in Northern Ireland. TDG worked through a pair of trading companies called Durand Properties Ltd., and Fartrade Holding SA. For added protection, Haboby stayed in the background, sending an accountant, Robert Kashoba, to negotiate the purchase. Kashoba traveled to Lugano, Switzerland, on June 7, 1990, to settle the final details that would give Iraq control over 18 percent of SMB shares. In a few weeks' time, Kashoba told SMB President Gianni Martinelli, his partners would buy an additional 12 percent of the company. Meanwhile they needed some parts made of maraging steel. Kashoba claimed that the specially forged parts were to be used as gears. He took advantage of the occasion to order ten specialized machine tools as well.

In July the shipment of maraging steel was blocked at the Frankfurt airport. When contacted by the press, Martinelli said he had no idea that companies controlled by the government of Iraq had bought into his firm, nor that he had sold the Iraqis equipment for their nuclear weapons program. He was not an arms dealer, he said; he had been tricked. He believed he had sold "gears," not end caps for uranium enrichment centrifuges.

Far away in Rancocas, New Jersey, the Iraqis were assembling one of the final pieces of their nuclear puzzle. Thanks to the diligence of Undersecretary of Commerce Dennis Kloske "and his mindless minions," as William Safire described them, Iraqi procurement agents didn't always have to resort to clandestine means.[5] They made this purchase openly. Commerce not only okayed it, they actively promoted it.

When the manufacturer cabled the Commerce Department representative at the U.S. Embassy in Baghdad about the prospective sale, he received an enthusiastic response. "Hooray for you," the DoC's Russell Smith cabled back. "Look forward to your coming. Please do not hesitate to ask us for any service."

The sale involved four very large vacuum furnaces for melting titanium, zirconium, plutonium, and other heavy metals. "Used together, the four furnaces would have formed a powerful production line," said Gary Milhollin, who heads the Wisconsin Project on Nuclear Arms Control. "Iraq would have had a 'Cadillac' production line for atomic bomb and ballistic missile parts, even better than the facilities at American nuclear weapons labs."

Incredible as it may seem, it was the company, not the Commerce Department, that had doubts about supplying this equipment to Iraq. In a conversation the year before with Commerce Department engineer Jeff Tripp, Consarc President Raymond J. Roberts had raised the possibility that the "skull" furnaces (so called because of their appearance) could be used in Iraq's nuclear weapons program, the *Washington Post* reported. "I told him . . . there is nothing to stop them from melting zirconium, the main use of which is a cladding material for nuclear fuel rods," Roberts wrote in a memo dated February 15, 1989.[6]

One week later, Consarc tried to impress on a second Commerce Department engineer, Alan C. Stoddard, the fact that the furnaces could be used "without modification" for nuclear applications. To Stoddard's relief, Iraq provided a letter stating that the furnaces would be used to make prostheses for handicapped war veterans. But Roberts was not happy with the government's attitude. "We were being encouraged by the Commerce Department in Washington and by the U.S. Embassy in Baghdad to go get this order," the head of Consarc said. "The feeling we got from our government is that this is business we should be going after."

It wasn't until June 1990 that the Defense Department first learned about the prospective sale to Iraq of skull furnaces to shape their nuclear weapons. And it wasn't Dennis Kloske who offered the information. It was the former deputy undersecretary of defense for trade security policy, Dr. Stephen Bryen. "I first learned about the furnaces from a reporter in Philadelphia, Mark Fazollah," Bryen testified before a congressional committee later. The reporter had called "to tell me that he had some information about this pending transaction and needed some help with it. . . . What I did was arrange a meeting in my office between the reporter and staff people from my old agency at the Defense Department to do a preliminary scrub on this proposed export."[7]

That first meeting occurred in June. Within days, DoD understood the real purpose behind the Iraqi purchase. Bryen's successor at the Defense Trade Security Administration, William N. Rudman, was incredulous: "Saddam is so caring of his own people that they're all going to be walking around with hi-tech wooden legs." In fact, he said, it was clear that the "end-use was nuclear. The Iraqis were lying."

Rudman's deputy in charge of technology security operations, Michael Malouf, asked Customs to issue a twenty-day restraining order to keep the furnaces from leaving the United States while they figured out how best to proceed. Malouf's action was not to the liking of Dennis Kloske. He dispatched a trade specialist from the Commerce Department's International Trade Administration, Michael Manning, to argue with Customs that they had got it all wrong. On July 11, Manning telephoned Customs from Consarc's head office to warn them that DoC and the State Department had approved the sale. Malouf and his "ankle-biters" over at the Pentagon were "running around . . . stirring things up when there really is no issue," a Customs Service memo describing Manning's intervention states.

All the "running around" had gotten the attention of the *Philadelphia Inquirer*, which mentioned the restraining order blocking the Consarc furnaces. When they saw the *Inquirer* article, senators Jesse Helms, Connie Mack, Jeff Bingaman, and five others wrote to President Bush, protesting that the furnaces could be used to shape fissile material and cladding for nuclear weapons and that the Commerce Department was actively backing the sale.

In the end the case was brought to the National Security Council, where General Scowcroft's top Middle East advisor, Richard Haas, ordered the Commerce Department to revoke its own export license. "The goods were due to be shipped out of the country on July 20," Steve Bryen told Congress. "The decision from the White House to block them came on July 19, just at the very last minute as an Iraqi freighter was heading for Baltimore harbor."

Dennis Kloske refused to testify in person to explain how this incredible series of events could have occurred, but in his written reply to questions put by Congressman Doug Barnard, Jr., he stated that "the furnaces in question were not listed on any control list. As such, Commerce had no authority to control" them or to prevent their export to Iraq. Asked how well he thought the present export control process was working, Kloske gave an answer that left Barnard and his staff breathless. "The process works well. Commerce enjoys a good working relationship with all agencies involved in the export control arena."

*　*　*

Right up until the invasion of Kuwait, companies in Germany, Italy, Brazil, the United States, Britain, and France continued to work hand in hand with Iraq. They were not going to get involved in the quagmire of Middle Eastern intrigues. Saddam's excited statements about Israel would pass, but the contracts would remain, they believed.

In July the French reached a final settlement on the thorny problem of the Iraqi debt. After a three-year wait, Dassault received authorization to deliver the eight remaining Mirage F1 fighters that had been sitting in cocoons at the Bordeaux airport since 1987. The debt protocol was scheduled to be signed in Paris on August 4 by Iraq's first deputy prime minister, Saddoun Hammadi, but the curtain came crashing down on the night of August 1–2, when Saddam Hussein sent 100,000 troops across the border into Kuwait.

The invasion of Kuwait was a desperate attempt by Saddam to fill up an empty state treasury. Without fresh revenues, Iraq would have to declare bankruptcy in a matter of months, which would have meant relinquishing control over whole sectors of its economy to foreign banks. As he had done in 1974–75, when he launched his war against the Kurds, and again in September 1980, when he invaded Iran, however, Saddam Hussein miscalculated in giving the order to storm Kuwait. He failed to understand that the USSR could not come to his aid, given its new dependence on Western financial support, and he grossly underestimated the resolve of President Bush to punish him for his aggression.

"If Saddam had only invaded Kuwait a few days later," one French arms salesman sighed, referring to the debt payment scheduled for August 4, "we would have been free and clear." Even so, the French government hesitated for more than a week before responding to the Iraqi invasion, hoping that Iraq would leave Kuwait before the crisis got out of hand. Saddam's chief apologist in the French cabinet, Defense Minister Chevènement, refused his president's summons to return to Paris from his vacation in Tuscany. "They don't need me to carry out Bush's policies," he told reporters. While Mitterrand dispatched French warships to the region, Chevènement prolonged his Tuscan idyll until August 17.

In Germany, more than fifty companies disregarded the UN trade embargo on Iraq altogether. They kept supplying Saddam with missile parts, chemical agents, heavy engineering equipment, and even arms, right up through Operation Desert Storm. The Kohl government shrugged off repeated requests from Washington to investigate the embargo busters. After all, a mark was a mark.

In Italy the Banca Nazionale del Lavoro renegotiated the fourth protocol signed by Christopher Drogoul early in the year. The new agreement provided Iraq with nearly $1 billion in fresh credit, as long as the money was spent on purchases from Italian companies. Steel heiress Cecelia Danieli put her lawyers to work to determine whether she could fulfill her $500 million contracts to build two new steel plants in Iraq. They told her to file for reimbursement from the Italian state export credit insurance agency, SACE, a process that took four months. "You understand," she said in an interview, "if the Gulf crisis had ended before December 8, then of course we would have fulfilled our contracts."

In Washington, Defense Intelligence Agency analysts were furiously assembling new estimates on the Iraqi nuclear weapons program. The conventional wisdom only six months before the invasion of Kuwait was that Iraq was easily five to ten years away from obtaining the bomb. The attempt to smuggle nuclear triggers to Iraq forced a drastic downward revision, since these are usually acquired toward the end of the clandestine nuclear race. By June, Pentagon analysts conceded Iraq was somewhere between two and five years from having nuclear weapons.

By the end of September, the DIA had received new information from satellite photographs and other sources showing that Iraq was far more advanced than had been previously believed. Huge stockpiles of uranium yellowcake had been purchased clandestinely, uranium mines and processing facilities had been built, and a full-scale centrifuge enrichment plant was now believed to be operational. "All of a sudden," Pentagon analysts said, "we realized that Saddam was only six months to a year from the bomb. That's when we really started sounding the alarm."

Brigadier Hugo de Oliveira Piva had returned to Iraq in late 1989 with twenty-one rocket scientists in tow. Before retiring from the Aerospace Technology Institute (CTA) in São José dos Campos, he had been put in charge of Brazil's clandestine uranium enrichment program. Now he was just a private businessman, struggling to make ends meet with his own company, HOP Consultants; but Washington believed he was helping Iraq perfect an atomic bomb.

Piva laughs at the accusation. "I am no superman," he told a Brazilian interviewer. "There is no truth in that. . . . That is like saying that if a person is able to manufacture a truck, he can then manufacture . . . a precision-loading gun. Our team has nothing to do with an atomic bomb or large rockets. . . . Our team simply gives technical assistance to the [name indistinct] missile project, which is a defensive, tactical missile."[8]

Like Gerald Bull and how many hundreds of others, Piva had no scruples about making his very special knowledge available to Saddam Hussein — for a price. "My conscience is at peace," the sixty-three-year-old former soldier said.

Saddam Hussein's extraordinary buildup of conventional weapons and weapons manufacturing facilities could never have been accomplished without aid from the West. Thanks to the death lobby, Saddam became much more than a two-bit local despot. He became an international threat.

Iraqi diplomats, of course, claimed that such charges were a fabrication, that the real aim of those who sought to block cooperation and hi-tech exports to Iraq was to maintain the Arab world in a state of "permanent underdevelopment." Why should Israel be encouraged to develop its scientific and technological resources, they argued, when the Arabs were branded as warmongers for doing the same thing?

Saddam Hussein put this lie to rest. In a speech celebrating the achievements of twenty-two years of Baathist rule, which he delivered only two weeks before the invasion of Kuwait, he returned obsessively to a single theme: Iraq's "achievements in the field of military industrialization."

From the day the Baath party seized power on July 17, 1968, all of Iraq's "scientific, industrial, and economic progress" had been devoted to this end. Science, progress, development, advancement: all were just catchwords to disguise Saddam's quest for absolute power. Power that came from the end of a gun.

From beginning to end, this was the cause Western companies and Western governments were serving in Iraq. Most argue that they did so unknowingly, and in some cases this may be true. But they all contributed to the making of the Arab world's Dark Knight. For Saddam Hussein there was no such thing as a "civilian" project; there were no such things as civilians. There were only good Baathists, renegades, and . . . flies.

EPILOGUE

How to Prevent Another Iraq

Once the guns fell silent from Operation Desert Storm it became clear that the allies had put a severe check on Saddam's ambitions, but they had not blocked them altogether. Many more tanks, aircraft, and chemical weapons survived the allied onslaught than was first thought. Key Republican Guards units stayed in Baghdad to protect the regime's survival and allow it to fight again another day. When Saddam wheeled around and ruthlessly suppressed Kurdish and Shiite rebellions in the north and south of Iraq, he had more than enough weapons to do the job, including hundreds of tons of the deadly chemicals the allies victoriously claimed they had destroyed on the first day of the war. The chemical agents that the Iraqi helicopters dumped on the rebels had been manufactured at a buried factory near Akashat and stored in secret underground depots, thanks to German companies. The massacre was so ruthless that more than one million Kurdish civilians fled for their lives. They preferred to face uncertainty and hardship in the mountains than face certain death at the hands of Saddam.

One reason the Pentagon and the White House were caught short by Saddam Hussein's success against the rebels was purely technical. Bomb damage assessments and KH-11 satellite photographs showed that the allied bombing campaign had almost totally destroyed Iraq's three major oil refineries, at Baiji, Daura, and Basra. Iraq couldn't turn its tanks and helicopters on the rebels, Joint Chiefs Chairman Colin Powell told President Bush, for one simple reason: they were out of gas.

But Powell was wrong, and President Bush knew it — or he should have known. For many months Pentagon analysts had been tracking the activities of Iraq's Western suppliers of dual-use technology and had compiled an extensive list of the weapons plants and other militarily useful facilities those companies had built in Iraq. They knew, for instance, that Marubeni of Japan had supplied Saddam with hundreds of buried fuel storage tanks that escaped Allied bombardment. They knew that a Franco-Italian petrochemicals consortium had built an entire underground diesel fuel plant just twenty miles away from the heavily damaged Baiji refinery and that the plant was still capable of transforming 31,000 barrels of oil each day into fuel for Iraqi tanks and helicopters. Kurdish refugees and Shiite villagers thank the companies that built these plants — and the Germans who supplied Saddam Hussein's poison gas works — every day.

General Brent Scowcroft, the President's national security advisor, told Jewish leaders in Washington on March 5 that the Pentagon began to realize during the air campaign against Iraq that it was facing a far more sophisticated enemy than had been thought. "We'd knock out a command and control facility, and the next day we'd find that another one had taken its place. We'd hit that one, and he'd have yet another backup," Scowcroft said. "The incredible expense and planning he has put into building up his military capability is awesome."

Iraq was prepared to fight a major war well before it invaded Kuwait, Scowcroft said. It had stockpiled heavy equipment in bombproof shelters deep underground. From French, German, and Japanese companies, Iraq had purchased "civilian" telecommunications gear that the military used with great success. When the allies moved into southern Iraq, they discovered thousands of miles of fiber-optic communications cables buried on both sides of the Euphrates and dozens of automatic switching units. (This state-of-the-art equipment was banned by COCOM for export to Eastern European countries such as Czechoslovakia, but not to Iraq.) Thanks to software provided by a major European defense telecommunications firm, Saddam Hussein could still transmit orders to his commanders in the south despite the heavy allied bombardment. When the allies started to move in on the ground, Saddam told his commanders to move out. The mother of all battles would be fought another day.

Scowcroft took great pains to explain why the allied bombing campaign had lasted so long (forty days and forty nights). "We'd hit an ammunition bunker, or a fixed military facility, and fly back the next day only to discover that it was still operational," he said. "The Iraqis had fitted these sites with special blowout walls, so we'd have to go back and hit the same target again and again." The blowout walls had been shipped in secret to Iraq by an Austrian company to equip a "university" research center. One member of Saddam's Foreign Legion (the term Senator Jesse Helms used to refer to the hundreds of Western companies that helped Saddam build his military industries) called this "linking the special needs of the East to the awesome talents of the West."

The responsibility for building Saddam Hussein's military power must be shared by Iraq's many suppliers and supporters, but the weapons alone would not have transformed Saddam Hussein into an international threat. If any nation must be singled out for this particularly grave responsibility it is Germany, the same Germany that pledged after World War II never to become a threat to world peace again. Without the aid of German companies and the support of the Bonn government, Saddam Hussein would never have been able to build a chemical weapons industry, nor would he have made such strides toward the atomic bomb and toward the development of a new generation of ballistic missiles, capable of delivering nuclear warheads against any capital in the region.

Proliferation policy in the United States and in other Western countries has yet to change in any significant fashion, despite a series of highly publicized "initiatives" intended to calm the political storm raised by the deliveries to Iraq. Once again an American president and his top policy makers are using trade and aid to transform Third World dictators into American friends. Once again a German chancellor has turned his back on the past. Like fairy magicians, they vainly hope to turn the frog into a prince.

Regimes similar to Iraq's exist today in Syria, Iran, China, and elsewhere and have proven track records as proliferation threats. All have devoted immense resources to develop chemical and nuclear weapons and the long-range missiles needed to deliver them to distant targets. These regimes do not need encouragement. Yet Bush administration officials, such as Reginald Bartholomew at the Department of State and Secretary of Commerce Robert Mosbacher, continue to argue that careful coddling by Washington will bring these dictators around, while American allies abroad are using a similar rationale to justify multibillion-dollar sales of industrial plants and machinery to them, as well as arms. This policy failed miserably in Iraq. And it will fail again.

The export control system throughout the Western world is in a shambles. Big-business lobbies systematically overwhelm their opponents. Their policy is a purely economic one: sell anything to any dictator who pays cash (or can get a sympathetic Western government to guarantee a loan). Curb the sales, they say, and Americans (or Germans or Frenchmen) will lose jobs. It's amazing how quickly the big guns are dragged out.

Professor Gary Milhollin and his Wisconsin Project for Nuclear Control have been crusading for years to convince the American government to adopt more effective controls to curb the spread of nuclear weapons technology and other weapons of mass destruction. For Milhollin and other experts, the allied war against Iraq was brought on mainly by the lack of such controls. Preventing another buildup like Iraq's, Milhollin believes, will not condemn entire sectors of the U.S. export economy to death, but it will require selective restrictions targeting critical technologies, and the business lobbies will continue to fight any restrictions.

Milhollin discovered the power of the lobbies in 1990 when he wrote a series of articles in the *Washington Post* and the *New York Times*, arguing that planned sales of supercomputers to Brazil and India were unwise because they would give those nations a ballistic missile capability. No sooner had Milhollin's articles appeared than "platoons of representatives from IBM and Cray have been visiting all of the people involved in this decision and all of the departments on a continuing basis in their offices." Just so the record was clear, Milhollin added: "I don't get a chance to visit any of these people in their offices. The process is totally closed from the public. The people who decide only hear one side of the case, the exporter side. Then after the export is approved, the very record of approving it is confidential." Former Deputy Undersecretary of Defense Steve Bryen agrees. "Corporate lobbying is a very one-sided process. There is not any public interest lobbying that I ever encountered or can recall. Basically, most of the dialogue occurs with companies that want to export their goods."[1]

As it stands now, half a dozen executive agencies around Washington are responsible for examining U.S. exports perceived to pose a proliferation threat. More often than not, they do not coordinate their activities or share their information. The Department of Commerce promotes U.S. exports and regulates U.S. trade — a clear conflict of interest if there ever was one. When the wrong technology gets through to the wrong dictator, such as the Consarc furnaces that were nearly shipped to Iraq, Commerce spends its time sniping at other agencies, trying to shift the blame.

A nine-month investigation by the Commerce, Consumer, and Monetary Affairs Subcommittee of the House Committee on Government Operations, released on July 14, 1991, called for a total overhaul of the export licensing system. Subcommittee chairman Doug Barnard, Jr., stated that the investigation "found that indeed Saddam Hussein's Iraq did receive materials and technologies from the United States which aided that outlaw country in building dangerous weapons which it was ready to use against our troops. This was done in spite of a system of export controls in place which was designed to protect the United States against precisely such a risk. In short, we found that the system was sorely in need of rehabilitation to avoid a repeat of the Iraq situation."[2]

The report criticized the licensing system as "inherently inefficient and ineffective . . . convoluted and confusing." It found that "too many government agencies are involved in the licensing process," that the "agencies' lines of authority are not clear," and that the agencies "do no effectively share information." The secrecy of the system was castigated, including the justification used by many exporters that divulgence of their contracts could be detrimental to them. "This clearly is not sufficient reason to hide export licensing information from the public eye. On the other hand, there is a clear public interest in knowing how much of a particular dual-use commodity was sent to a particular country," the report stated.

The committee recommended creating a single independent agency within the executive branch to handle licensing of all exports, including nuclear-related items, dual-use equipment, and munitions, with the intent of avoiding interagency sniping and ensuring better accountability — both to exporters and to the public — by requiring greater congressional oversight than today exists. In additional views appended to the report, Representative Jon

L. Kyl, a Republican from Arizona, deplored the virtual exclusion of Defense Department experts in export license review cases in recent years and strongly urged that the proposed Agency for Export Administration include Pentagon representatives. "It is absolutely critical that national security be the primary consideration in determining final approval or disapproval of an export license," he said.

But reinforcing strategic export controls in the United States is not enough. Germany and France, to name just two, have shown that American allies abroad have even less concern for preventing the sale of strategic military technology to Third World dictators than the U.S. Department of Commerce. And a House of Commons report published in July 1991 revealed that the British government had approved sales of nuclear materials and of chemical weapons precursors such as thiodiglycol in 1988 and 1989, despite Iraq's repeated use of CW against its own people and its suspected nuclear weapons program. The only way to bring foreign violators of proliferation controls to book is by imposing strict trade sanctions. And yet sanctions legislation passed by Congress has been vetoed again and again by President Bush.

Saddam Hussein's death machine was built almost exclusively by Western companies. The vast majority of the machine tools, computers, and test equipment he needed to build ballistic missiles, bombs, bullets, and guns was provided totally legally by companies who applied for export licenses. A compilation of public sources alone shows that 445 companies cashed in on this macabre bonanza, one third of them in West Germany alone.

Until concrete steps are taken to curb this type of trade, the "new world order" President Bush is so keen on heralding will turn out to be more death as usual.

Notes

1. The Search Is On

1. Elias Farah, *The Arab Homeland after World War II*, Arab Baath Socialist Party [undated, printed in Spain, 1978], pp. 45–46.

2. Michel Aflak, *Choice of Texts from the Baath Party Founder's Thought*, Arab Baath Socialist Party [undated, printed in Italy, 1977; distributed by the Embassy of Iraq, Paris], pp. 114 and 85.

3. Ibid.

4. Judith Miller and Laurie Mylroie, *Saddam Hussein and the Crisis in the Gulf* (New York: Times Books, 1990), p. 31.

5. For a discussion of the Baath during this period, see Helen Chapin Metz et al., *Iraq: A Country Study*, Area Handbook Series (Washington, D.C.: Department of the Army, 1990), p. 53.

6. Metz et al., *Iraq*, p. 54.

7. Fuad Matar, *Saddam Hussein, ou le devenir irakien* (Paris: Editions Sycamore, 1981), pp. 35, 36.

8. On the assassination of al-Nayef, see Samir al-Khalil, *Republic of Fear: The Inside Story of Saddam's Iraq* (Berkeley: University of California Press, 1989), pp. 13, 292.

9. For more on Iraqi intelligence organizations, see al-Khalil, *Republic of Fear*, pp. 12–14. Miller and Mylroie, *Saddam Hussein* (pp. 48–50), draw primarily from al-Khalil's account but add some useful insights.

10. Al-Khalil, *Republic of Fear*, pp. 52 and 50. The Iraqi minister was Salah Umar al-Ali, minister of guidance and a member of the ruling Revolutionary Command Council. His comments were uttered as Iraqi Jews were swinging dead from makeshift gallows set up in Baghdad's Liberation Square. The repeated executions during the early days of the regime earned the spot an ominous nickname: Square of the Hanged.

11. "President Hussein Interviewed by American Senator" (Baghdad: Dar

Al-Mum [government printing office], 1983), pp. 23–24.

12. Saddam Hussein, *Notre Combat et La Politique Internationale,* collected writings of Saddam Hussein (Lausanne, Switzerland, 1977), p. 57.

13. "More than a Madman," *Newsweek International,* Jan. 14, 1991.

14. Saddam Hussein, *Propos sur les Problèmes Actuels,* text of April 8, 1974, press conference, collected writings, pp. 98–99.

15. "Terror arsenal the West ignored; a special correspondent relates how a blind eye was turned on Iraq's build-up of chemical and biological weapons," *The Independent,* Sept. 12, 1990. In a subsequent edition (Oct. 13, 1990), Sabbagh denied the central allegation of this story, which claimed he had advised the Iraqis on chemical and biological weapons programs; *The Independent* apologized for the allegation.

16. The scholar was Jean-François Dubos. Dubos went on to become a top Defense Ministry official under the Socialists in 1981 and was later accused of having authorized clandestine arms sales to Iran in 1984–85. His *Ventes d'Armes: Une Politique* (Paris: Gallimard, 1974) was originally a doctoral thesis. (The quote is from p. 60.) It was the first clear expression of the philosophical underpinning that would distinguish French arms export policy over the next fifteen years.

2. *Saddam's French Lover*

1. "We know very well, my brothers," Saddam continued, "that the sale of arms today, especially sophisticated arms, does not obey commercial considerations. Their delivery depends on the purpose it serves the supplying country. The equipment of our army depends essentially on the Soviet Union. In recent years, when we were fighting the rebel clique in the north, this country offered us sophisticated weapons. By revealing this historical truth, we are not trying to criticize anyone or to seek justifications. We are simply trying to shed light on a historical truth and to put responsibilities in a more general context." Speech of Saddam Hussein, September 17, 1980, announcing the abrogation of the Algiers Accord with Iran (French translation made available by the Embassy of Iraq, Paris). This was the first time that Saddam referred publicly to the 1974–75 Soviet arms embargo.

2. Nita M. Renfrew, "Who Started the War?" *Foreign Policy* 66 (Spring 1987), p. 100.

3. Helen Chapin Metz et al., *Iraq: A Country Study* (Washington, D.C.: Department of the Army, 1990), p. 59.

4. It was not proliferation fears that prompted the French to refuse the Iraqi request. According to Steve Wiesman and Herbert Krosney, in *The*

Islamic Bomb (New York: Times Books, 1981), they refused because by the time of Saddam's visit they had already stopped manufacturing gas-graphite reactors, and so had none to export.

5. "Entente cordiale entre Paris et Baghdad," *Le Monde,* Sept. 9, 1975.

6. Eric Laurent, "Depuis trente ans, l'Irak essaie de fabriquer la bombe A," *Le Figaro,* Sept. 3, 1990.

7. Culotta and Gruver told their story to David Ignatius, "Iraq's 13-Year Search for Deadly Chemicals," *Washington Post,* May 25, 1988. A "Colonel Saddam Hussein" briefly enrolled in a U.S. Army chemical weapons defense training course in the 1960s, Pentagon sources say, although no one knows whether he or the "Hussein" who negotiated with Culotta and Gruver in New York was the future Iraqi president.

3. Bonanza on the Gulf

1. Petrobas had won a 7,900-square-kilometer concession by the terms of an August 4, 1972, agreement with the Iraq National Oil Company, which included three blocks: al-Falluja, Ali al-Gharbi, and Qurnah. The Majnoon find was located in the Qurnah block, which also included the Nahr Umr oil field, according to an internal report on Iraqi oil resources made available by the Compagnie Française des Pétroles.

2. Shahram Chubin, *Soviet Policy Towards Iran and the Gulf* Adelphi Papers 157 (London: International Institute for Strategic Studies, 1984), p. 27.

3. For Montedison, compare *The Observer,* March 11, 1984; "The Secrets of Samarra," BBC Panorama, Oct. 27, 1986; *The Independent,* Sept. 12, 1990. For Technipetrole, see *Libération* (Paris), March 12, 1984. Despite repeated denials by TPL, *Le Canard Enchaîné* repeated the accusations on Feb. 6, 1991.

4. Quoted by *Der Spiegel* journalists Hans Leyendecker and Richard Rickelmann in *Exportateure des Todes* (Göttingen: Steidl Verlag, 1990), pp. 34–35.

5. "The Secrets of Samarra," BBC Panorama.

6. Patrick Sabatier, "Irak, les étranges filières de la guerre chimique," *Libération,* Mar. 12, 1984.

7. Christine Moss Helms, *Iraq: Eastern Flank of the Arab World* (Washington, D.C.: Brookings Institution, 1984), p. 79.

8. Chubin, *Soviet Policy,* p. 27.

4. *Saddam Takes the Helm*

1. I happened to notice the British manuals during a visit to the Iraqi Staff College in 1986. My guide was an Iraqi major general who had been educated at Sandhurst and at Fort Knox armor school in the U.S. "Many of our pilots and tank crews have been educated in the USSR," the general explained, "but all our tactics are based on British military doctrine."

2. Jérome Dumoulin, "L'Irak et la Bombe," *l'Express*, July 19–25, 1980.

3. CIA Director William Webster would mention the Brazil–Iraq nuclear agreement in passing during testimony to the Senate Government Affairs Committee on May 18, 1989. The quote is from Senator John Glenn, Congressional Record, July 30, 1990, S11047.

4. Wilson gave his impressions in "A visit to the bombed nuclear reactor at Tuwaitha, Iraq," *Nature,* March 31, 1983. Leonard S. Spector, in *Nuclear Proliferation Today* (New York: Vintage Books, 1984), pp. 190 and 236, states that the amount of plutonium was enough for one bomb.

5. Lebanese journalist Fouad Matar suggests halfheartedly that Bulgarian and Soviet intelligence may have been behind the 1979 "plot" against Saddam, but most Western analysts discount this. See Fouad Matar, *Saddam Hussein, ou le devenir irakien* (Paris: Editions Sycamore, 1981), pp. 40–52, for a detailed account of this scene.

6. Quoted by Adeed Dawisha, "Iraq: the West's Opportunity," *Foreign Policy* 41 (Winter 1980–81).

7. Portions of this remarkable psychodrama were aired on a BBC "Panorama" program on February 11, 1991, called "The Mind of Saddam." The scene was alluded to by Judith Miller and Laurie Mylroie, *Saddam Hussein and the Crisis in the Gulf* (New York: Times Books, 1990), pp. 43–45.

8. The "tribunal" that pronounced the death sentences was composed of Naim Haddad (who was later executed himself), Sadoun Ghaidan (a Saddam crony who later fell from favor), Tayeh Abdel Karim, Hassan Ali Nassar, Sadoun Shaker (one of Saddam's closest confidants, until he fell from favor following the invasion of Kuwait), Hekmat Ibrahim, and Abdallah Fadel. Those executed, besides al-Mashhadi, included six members of the RCC: Mohammed Mahjoub, who served as minister of education; Adnan Hussein, who was deputy prime minister; Khaled Abed Osman, a Kurd; Mohammed 'Ayeh, minister of industry; Ghanim Abdul Jalil, head of Saddam's personal office; and Muhammed Ayish. For a list of Saddam's political killings and an excellent account of his use of the security apparatus, see Samir al-Khalil, *Republic of Fear: The Inside Story of Saddam's Iraq* (Berkeley: University of California Press, 1989).

9. Official transcript of the speech by President Saddam Hussein on July 17, 1980, to celebrate the twelfth anniversary of the 1968 putsch.

5. The Tilt Begins

1. Spector, *Nuclear Proliferation Today* (New York: Vintage Books, 1989), p. 174. Dr. Ja'afar disappeared from view for a few months in early 1980, after protesting the arrest and trial of one of his colleagues, Dr. Hussein al-Shahristani, a Shiite Moslem. Shahristani was reportedly executed on charges of sedition in April 1980. But Ja'afar was too valuable to Saddam's bomb program to suffer a similar fate. He continues to head the effort today, and met with a UN inspection team in Iraq in June and July 1991.

2. *Sunday Telegraph*, Feb. 10, 1991.

3. Spector, *Nuclear Proliferation Today*, pp. 172–73.

4. Text of 1972 teaming agreement: *Der Spiegel*, Feb. 18, 1991.

5. *Le Monde*, Aug. 8, 1984, reported on the uproar in Germany over the sale; the West German government denied prior knowledge of the sale and claimed that its arms export control laws had been broken. The helicopter sale and the retrofitting were mentioned in the SIPRI yearbooks (all editions from 1981 to 1985) and in the June 1984 *DMS Market Intelligence Report* on Iraq, which gave details of the involvement of Denzel and Transair Swiss. *Defense and Foreign Affairs Weekly*, Feb. 18–24, mentioned that Denzel was to carry out additional retrofitting on these helicopters in Baghdad to equip them with antitank missile launchers.

6. U.S. fears over Saudi stability had been growing since July 1979, when Iranian-backed insurgents seized control of Mecca, Islam's holiest shrine.

7. Eric Rouleau, *Le Monde*, April 18, 1980, interviewing the secretary general of Iran's pro-Soviet Communist (Tudeh) party, Nourridine Kianouri. The Soviets had succeeded in infiltrating a large number of professional intelligence agents into the regime, including one agent who served for years as the personal secretary of Ayatollah Khomeini. For more details, see Kenneth R. Timmerman, *Ol ins Feuer* ([*Fanning the Flames: Guns, Greed, and Geopolitics in the Gulf War*], Zurich: Orell Fusli, 1988).

8. "President Hussein Interviewed by American Senator," transcript of August 25, 1982, talk between Saddam Hussein and Senator Stephen Solarz (Baghdad: Dar Al-Mum, 1983), p. 25.

9. William F. Hickman, *Ravaged and Reborn: The Iranian Army, 1982*

(Washington, D.C.: Brookings Institution, 1982), p. 9.

10. When war broke out on September 22, 1980, this base was one of the first targets of the Iranian air force and was totally destroyed.

11. According to L'Evenement du Jeudi, September 13–19, 1990, Marenches sold the villa in 1977 to a Lebanese intermediary, who resold it two years later to the Iraqi embassy in Paris for exactly the same price. The intermediary held the insurance in his name until 1985, giving rise to speculation that he had been fronting for the Iraqi purchase from the beginning.

12. Alexandre de Marenches and Christine Ockrent, *Dans le Secret des Princes* (Paris: Stock, 1986), p. 234.

13. Geidar Aliev's work in Iran was so successful that when Andropov took over as secretary general of the Soviet Communist party, he promoted Aliev to full membership of the Politburo. In 1986 Aliev was further elevated, this time as the candidate of Mikhail Gorbachev, to the rank of deputy premier of the USSR. For a complete discussion of KGB infiltration in Iran, see Kenneth R. Timmerman, *Fanning the Flames,* chap. 15; Housang Nahavandi, *Le Grand Mensonge* (Paris: Nouvelles Editions Debresse, 1985); and Shahram Chubin, "Leftist Forces in Iran," *Problems of Communism,* July–Aug. 1980.

14. *Le Monde,* July 22, 1980.

15. Each reactor required 12 kilograms of highly enriched uranium (HEU) fuel every four months. This brought Iraq's annual need to around 72 kilograms of HEU.

16. *Le Monde,* December 24, 1980.

6. The Road to Osirak

1. Former Iranian President Bani Sadr has claimed for years that the hostage-release deal he worked out with the Carter administration was sabotaged in October by emissaries acting for presidential candidate Ronald Reagan. Carter's NSC aide for Iran, Navy Commander Gary Sick, renewed allegations of an "October surprise" in a lengthy op-ed piece in the April 19, 1991, edition of the *New York Times.* He alleged that former CIA Director William Casey and perhaps George Bush traveled to Paris for secret negotiations with Iranian emissaries in October 1980 in an attempt to delay the hostage release until after the presidential elections. Congress began investigating the charges in August 1991.

2. At the same time the IAEA dismissed the charges of the two American inspectors who had been to Iraq, it acknowledged that Tammuz I would have been capable of producing around 10 kilograms of plutonium per

year, or enough "for about 1 or 2 significant quantities [weapons] a year," had it ever gone into production. See H. Gruemm, "Safeguards and Tammuz," *IAEA Bulletin* 23, no. 4, Dec. 1981.

3. Interview with officials from the Simon Wiesenthal Center of Los Angeles, who commissioned the report in May 1981. This report, conducted by Georges Amsel, Jean-Pierre Pharabod, and Raymond Sarre of the French National Research Center (CNRS), is also mentioned in Pierre Paen, *Les Deux Bombes* (Paris: Fayard, 1982), p. 172.

4. Amos Perlmutter, Michael Handel, and Uri Bar-Joseph, *Two Minutes over Baghdad* (London: Vallentine Mitchell, 1982), pp. 69–70.

5. Richard Wilson, "A Visit to the Bombed Nuclear Reactor at Tuwaitha, Iraq," *Nature* 302, March 1983; for the use of precision-guided munitions, see "Iraq's Nuclear Programme in Limbo," *Defence* (London), Aug. 1985.

6. The claim that he was working for French intelligence was made in interviews by Captain Paul Barril, former deputy commander of the GIGN commandos (the French equivalent of the Delta Force), and second-in-command of presidential security for Mitterrand.

7. Secrets of Samarra

1. Saddam Hussein, speech before the Council of Ministers, June 23, 1981, denouncing the Israeli attack on Iraq's nuclear reactor. Like many Arab radicals, Saddam Hussein was referring to the Jewish state in Arabic as "the Zionist entity" and "so-called Israel." To convey this attitude, translators usually put the name of Israel in quotes.

2. *Der Spiegel,* Feb. 4, 1991.

3. Rudolf Iambrecht and Gudrun Pott, "Diyala Secret Project," *Stern,* Feb. 7, 1991. Diyala is the Arabic name for the Tigris River, which flows through Salman Pak.

4. Ibid.

5. The Vulcan Project deal for the artillery pieces had been sealed commercially in November 1981. However, French arms exports needed political approval from an interministerial committee, called the CIEMG, and this took slightly longer. CIEMG approval of the package came in early 1982.

6. Samir al-Khalil, *Republic of Fear: The Inside Story of Saddam's Iraq* (Berkeley: University of California Press, 1989), p. 17.

7. Herbert Uniewski, "Saddam's German Shopkeepers," *Stern,* Feb. 28, 1991. Franzl, like the other Kolb officers temporarily detained at the end of 1990 by the German authorities, was released on bail pending trial.

8. The first to reveal the dummy bunkers was Roger Harris, "The

Secrets of Samarra," BBC "Panorama" program, October 27, 1986.

9. Murphy quotes, interview with the author, March 7, 1991.

10. Charles Saint-Prot, *Saddam Hussein: Un gaullisme arabe?* (Paris: Albin Michel, 1987), p. 62.

11. Interview with Soviet diplomat, November 1990.

12. "Interview of President Saddam Hussein with the Kuwaiti Press," Sept. 9, 1982 (Baghdad: Dar Al Mum, 1983), pp. 40–41.

13. Sean Ryan and James Adams, "Has Saddam Gone to Ground?" *Sunday Times* (London), Jan. 20, 1991. See also "L'Irak a été parsemé d'abris et de bunkers souterrains," *Le Monde,* Jan. 25, 1991; and "Saddam Hussein a enterré son nid d'aigle," *Le Figaro,* Jan. 23, 1991.

14. Boswau and Knauer was later bought out by WTB (Walter-Thosti-Boswau), which acknowledged the work on Saddam's bunker.

15. The first report on the Iraqi underground bases appeared in 1985. See Kenneth R. Timmerman, "The Race to Armageddon," *Defense & Armament* 45, Nov. 1985.

16. Shahram Chubin, *Soviet Policy Towards Iran and the Gulf,* Alelphi Papers 157 (London: IISS, 1984), p. 27.

17. As a 1984 Senate Foreign Relations Committee report put it, the Soviets "calculated that their neutrality risked permanently alienating Iraq without compensating gains in Iran."

18. For more on Sarkis, and the attempted deal through Kuwait, see Murray Waas, "What We Gave Saddam for Christmas," *Village Voice,* Dec. 18, 1990.

8. Countering the Ayatollah

1. "War in the Gulf: A Staff Report Prepared for the Committee on Foreign Relations," United States Senate, Aug. 1984.

2. I was interviewing Chamoun in Beirut at the time.

3. Iranian-backed terrorists would launch a series of attacks against U.S. and allied interests throughout the Middle East in the coming months. A double car-bombing near the Beirut airport in October 1983 wiped out 297 U.S. and French Marines. In Kuwait, Iranian-backed terrorists attacked the French and American embassies in December. These and the subsequent seizure of Western hostages in Lebanon reinforced Western hostility toward the Iranian revolution.

4. Interview with Richard Murphy, Mar. 7, 1991.

5. This information is from personal sources. See also Bob Woodward, *Veil* (New York: Simon and Schuster, 1987), p. 480.

6. Herbert Winiewski, "Saddam's German Shopkeepers," *Stern,* Feb. 28, 1991.

7. A preliminary investigation by West German customs, dated November 5, 1987, named seven companies in connection with the Samarra plant: Karl Kolb GmbH, Pilot Plant Engineering & Equipment GmbH, Heberger Bau GmbH, Ludwig Hammer GmbH, Preussag AG, Dipl. Ing. Jacobs Industrietechnik GmbH, and W.E.T. (Water Engineering Trading) GmbH. Well after Samarra had been destroyed by allied bombing raids in January 1991, these individuals and companies were still under investigation in Germany. Twelve individuals were arrested on charges relating to this case in February 1991; eleven were released on bail the next day.

8. The potassium fluoride was blocked in February 1984. Saheeb al-Haddad refused to talk with a BBC "Panorama" interviewer, who presented evidence of these chemicals shipments to Iraq. See "The Secrets of Samarra," Oct. 27, 1986, and Herbert Krosney, "Iraq making deadly form of nerve agent," *Jerusalem Post,* Nov. 26, 1986.

9. Quoted by Robert Harris, "The Secrets of Samarra."

10. Internal brief, dated July 31, 1984, quoted by *Der Spiegel* 24, 1989.

11. François Sergent, "L'Irak veut ses Étendard avant la fin du mois," *Libération,* Oct. 14, 1983.

12. Murray Waas, "What We Gave Saddam for Christmas," *Village Voice,* December 18, 1990.

13. For more details on Operation Staunch, see Kenneth R. Timmerman, "Europe's Arms Pipeline to Iran," *The Nation,* July 17, 1987. My first book on arms sales to Iran and Iraq, *Fanning the Flames,* also treats this subject in depth.

9. *The Condor Takes Off*

1. Jon Swain, "Nerve Gas: The Evidence on Iraqi Battlefield," *Sunday Times* (London), Mar. 11, 1984.

2. Cruz Sierra, "The Thief in Baghdad Is Plundering the Gulf with Spanish Arms," *Cambo* 16 (Madrid), Aug. 27, 1990, and personal sources.

3. Not all chemical weapons experts agreed with Heyndrickx's analysis that the different CW agents had been packed into the same shells. According to Matthew Meselson, co-director of the Harvard–Sussex University Program on CBW Armament and Arms Limitation, mixing cyanide with nerve gases such as Tubun in the same munition was militarily useless because of a chemical reaction known as "flashing." "Cyanide is highly combustible. If combined with other gases in an artillery shell, it will ignite and burn off the nerve agent before it can have any effect." Meselson further doubted that the Iraqis used cyanide because it was "far

less toxic than nerve gas. Cyanide was used once during World War I and never again. To have any military effect, the Iraqis would have had to pour tons of the stuff onto the battlefield." Nevertheless, Heyndrickx says he picked up traces of cyanide during clinical tests of soil, urine, and blood samples after suspected Iraqi gas attacks.

4. See *France Soir,* and wire reports dated Mar. 23, 1984, from the Agence Centrale de Presse. Michel Burton, the owner of this small French press agency, published an aerospace daily on contract to the French avionics manufacturing group GIFAS.

5. *Der Spiegel,* Sept. 10, 1990.

6. Krosney, "Iraq making deadly form of nerve agent." *Jerusalem Post,* Nov. 14, 1986. Krosney helped research the BBC's "The Secrets of Samarra."

7. Kenneth R. Timmerman, "In the Crucible of War: Iraq's Arms Industry," *Mednews,* May 5, 1989. I first met Lieutenant General Amer Rashid in Baghdad in February 1986; an earlier interview I had with him was published in a German defense magazine, *Military Technology,* in July 1986.

8. Footage of Falda del Carmen was shown on NBC News, in a report by Fred Francis and Bob Windrem, Mar. 3, 1989.

9. *Der Spiegel,* Sept. 10, 1990. Daimler-Benz swallowed up MBB in 1989. In July 1990, the group hired Richard Imus as its Washington lobbyist; until June 30 Imus was the economics minister at the U.S. Embassy in Bonn, where his primary responsibilities involved export licensing, regulation, and COCOM affairs.

10. Renzo Rosati, "The Secret Weapon," *Europeo* (Milan), Sept. 29, 1989, pp. 18–21.

11. "We Simply Have an Open Door," *Der Spiegel,* June 12, 1989.

12. Baker-Perkins changed its name to APV International in 1989.

13. Condor I was displayed for the first time at the Paris Air Show in June 1985, designated the Condor C1-A3.

14. Alan Friedman, "The Flight of the Condor," *Financial Times,* Nov. 21, 1989.

15. *Kurier* (Vienna), May 13, 1990.

16. Glenn Frankel, *Washington Post,* Sept. 17, 1990.

17. Al-Khalil, *Republic of Fear,* p. 18.

18. GIPRO has officially acknowledged the $253 million figure (DM 400 million). "Firms Involved in Iraqi Missile Production," *Der Spiegel,* March 27, 1989.

19. "We Are No Helpers of Saddam Hussein," *Die Welt* (Bonn), Feb. 15, 1991.

20. *Der Spiegel,* Mar. 27, 1989.

21. *Profil* (Vienna), May 8, 1989.
22. *Der Spiegel,* Mar. 27, 1989.

10. Corporate High Jinks

1. On the day of the bombing I was being held hostage in the cellar of that building, along with two Frenchmen. Just hours before the Israeli raid, the PLO released us, so I watched the bombing from the terrace of the French ambassador's residence in Baabda. Like everyone else in Beirut, I read the reports about Israel's "vacuum bomb" in the next morning's newspaper. But when I saw the photograph of the demolished building, I realized from the surroundings that I had been held there just hours before.

2. Lavoie was interviewed by NBC News, Nov. 30, 1990, and the *Minneapolis Star Tribune,* Dec. 1, 1990 ("Iraq Bomb Linked to Honeywell"). I have copies of the quoted memos.

3. Thomas L. Flannery, "Iraqi Weapons Have Connection to Guerin," *Lancaster Intelligencer Journal,* Nov. 8, 1990.

4. "Bomblets Away: A Chilean–Iraqi Connection," *Time,* Aug. 27, 1984.

5. Guerin, who was facing trial in a federal court as this book went to press, ordered his lawyers to develop a "CIA defense" to prove that his activities selling weapons to Chile and South Africa had been coordinated in full with U.S. intelligence. See "CIA Allowed Illegal Export of U.S. Missile Secrets," *Financial Times,* May 24, 1991.

6. Thomas L. Flannery, "Probers Finding ISC's South African Ties Were Close," *Lancaster Intelligencer Journal,* Jan. 14, 1991. My interviews at Kentron, Oct. 29, 1985. Flannery reported on the Cardoen connection in the *Lancaster Intelligencer Journal.*

7. The Customs raid was carried out in mid-January 1991. See Tom Hamburger, "Federal Investigators search office linked to weapons supplier for Iraq." *Minneapolis Star Tribune,* Jan. 19, 1991.

8. Personal interviews in November and December 1985 in South Africa. See Kenneth R. Timmerman, "Armscor Comes of Age in Times of Turmoil," *Defense & Armament* (Paris), Jan. 1986. For more on the gunpowder cartel to Iran, in which South Africa participated until 1984, see Timmerman, "Europe's Arms Pipeline to Iran," *The Nation,* July 13, 1987.

9. Kenneth R. Timmerman, "La Tratta Delle Bombe," *L'Espresso,* Aug. 30, 1987, and "Irangate à la Française," *L'Evénement du Jeudi,* July 23, 1987.

10. Murray Waas, "What We Gave Saddam for Christmas," *Village Voice,* Dec. 18, 1990.

11. Interviews with U.S. diplomats in Baghdad, July 1984. See Kenneth R. Timmerman, "Guarantees Considered on Pipeline," *Atlanta Journal-Constitution,* July 29, 1984.

11. *Captains of Industry*

1. On Piva's meeting with Shenshall in 1981, see Faolha de São Paulo, "Piva Offered Nuclear Bomb Project to Iraq in 1981," Feb. 22, 1991. On MBB and the West German Aeronautical Research and Testing Laboratory (DFVLR), see Leonard S. Spector, *The Undeclared Bomb* (Cambridge, Mass.: Ballinger, 1988).

2. Dusko Doder, "Soviet–Iraqi Ties Said to Improve Amid Reports of Credits for Arms," *Washington Post,* Apr. 28, 1984.

3. Lally Weymouth, "Despite Improving Ties, Iraqi Leader Assails United States," *Washington Post,* May 13, 1984.

4. "Global Spread on Chemical and Biological Weapons," hearings before the Committee on Governmental Affairs and its Permanent Subcommittee on Investigations, United States Senate, May 2, 1989, pp. 166–67.

5. Quoted by Roger Harris in "The Secrets of Samarra," BBC "Panorama," Oct. 27, 1986.

6. Janet Wallach, "The Artful Ambassador," *Washington Post Magazine,* Aug. 12, 1985.

12. *The DoC Missile Caper*

1. According to a 1982 agreement, renewed yearly through 1986, Iraq sold France 122,000 barrels/day, of which 80,000 b/day, worth a total of $5.2 billion, went for arms.

2. Charles Villeneuve and Jean-Pierre Péret, *L'Histoire Sécrète du Terrorisme* (Paris: Editions Plon, 1987), pp. 243–45. I have described the French initiative toward Iran, and Audran's assassination, in greater detail in *Fanning the Flames.*

3. I happened to be in Baghdad at the time. When I learned of Carlier's arrival, I contacted him at his room in the Rashid Hotel.

4. "Strengthening the Export Licensing System," a report by the Sub-

committee on Commerce, Consumer, and Monetary Affairs of the House Committee on Government Operations, July 2, 1991.

5. The review agencies were the State Department, the Defense Department, the Department of Energy, and the Subgroup on Nuclear Export Coordination, an interagency group chaired by State that included representatives from Commerce, the Arms Control and Disarmament Agency, DoD, and the intelligence community.

6. Hurtut quotes, interviews in Baghdad in February 1985.

7. Newton quotes, interview in Baghdad in February 1985. See also Kenneth Timmerman, "U.S. Resumption of Ties with Iraq Prompting a Boom in Exchanges," *Atlanta Journal-Constitution,* Feb. 17, 1985.

8. *Minneapolis Star Tribune,* Dec. 15, 1990.

9. The EQ5 was capable of launching the Exocet. The EQ6 could launch the Exocet or the AS30L.

10. Thomson-CSF lost the contract to supply Iraq with frequency-hopping radios, which was won by the British defense electronics firm, Racal, in 1985. Racal agreed to build an assembly plant in Iraq for its Jaguar tactical radios but later claimed that production was never launched because of a contract dispute. However, documents released to the House of Commons in July 1991 show that the company sold hundreds of these radios, assembled and in kits.

11. "Memo Sent to Meese on Iraqi Pipeline Deal refers to hostage swap," *Atlanta Journal-Constitution,* Feb. 28, 1988 (AP story); Jeff Gerth and Stephen Engelberg, "Pipeline Deal: A High-Level Nightmare," *International Herald Tribune,* Feb. 1, 1988.

12. Janet Wallach, "The Artful Ambassador," *Washington Post,* Aug. 12, 1985.

13. Interview with Fairbanks, March 1991.

13. BNL Builds the War Machine

1. Allegation contained in the Feb. 28, 1991, indictment against Drogoul and nine other defendants in the BNL banking scandal, filed by the U.S. attorney in Atlanta; hereafter referred to as BNL Indictment.

2. Iraq made an initial down payment estimated at $441 million when it ordered the ships, but no further payments. See Jacques de Lestapis, *Military Powers Encyclopedia:* vol. 4, 13c, *The Arab League States* (Paris, 1989), p. 45. Some of the corvettes had not left Italy by the time of the UN embargo on all trade with Iraq in August 1990; they are still there.

3. BNL Indictment.

4. Stern, Jan. 10, 1987. *Stern* initially identified the location of the Sarin and Tabun production lines as Samarra, but subsequent accounts agree

that they were set up in Al Fallujah. See also *Der Spiegel* 33, 1990.

5. Interviews with U.S. intelligence officials, Washington, D.C., Mar. 1991; see also *Mednews*, Mar. 18, 1991.

6. Vaughn Forrest and Josef Bodansky, "Iraq's Expanding Chemical Arsenal," Task Force on Terrorism and Unconventional Warfare, House Republican Research Committee, U.S. House of Representatives, May 29, 1990.

7. The Hazelrig report is included in the indictment of Abdelkader Helmy et al. in United States District Court for the Eastern District of California, filed Nov. 8, 1988; hereafter Helmy Indictment.

8. Helmy Indictment.

9. Hashim interview with Ted Koppel on ABC's "Nightline," Mar. 27, 1991.

10. "60 Minutes," Mar. 24, 1991.

11. *Le Monde*, Aug. 28, 1989. For more on the slush fund, see *Financial Times*, Mar. 25, 1991, and *The Economist*, Mar. 30, 1991.

12. Jim Hoagland, "Saddam Hussein Slipped the CIA Hook," *International Herald Tribune*, Feb. 7, 1991.

13. The DTI list was finally released to the House of Commons in August 1991 and proved a political embarrassment for the government. See "British Exports to Iraq," *Mednews*, Sept. 2, 1991.

14. This estimate is based on extensive interviews with black-market arms dealers, Iraqi military officials, Western intelligence sources, Iranian exiles, and sources inside Iran, and includes only equipment that all agree was delivered to Iran. It was reproduced by the *New York Times*, Feb. 2, 1987. Gary Sick, the Iran desk officer at the NSC during the Carter administration, announced in a speech in December 1986 that the United States and Israel had delivered arms to Iran worth between $500 million and $1 billion in nine to twelve separate shipments, and that these deliveries "made a difference" in the Iran–Iraq war (*Washington Post*, Dec. 5, 1986). Other estimates, supplied by arms dealers engaged in selling weapons to Iran, ranged even higher.

14. *The Missiles Begin to Fly*

1. Jean-Michel Caradec'h, "SCUD: Les Français qui ont aidé l'Irak," *L'Express*, Jan. 31, 1991. Intespace and the French National Space Agency would get involved in a scheme to sell Iraq sophisticated infrared cameras for a military observation satellite, that the company hoped to build for Amer Rashid's Scientific Research Council. An earlier report on the satellite project appeared in "Iraq's Spy in the Sky," *Defence* (London), Dec. 1989.

2. Cardoen cluster bomb plant: *Sunday Times* (London), Dec. 2, 1990; April 7 plant: *The Independent* (London), Oct. 14, 1990.

3. *Der Spiegel,* Feb. 4, 1991.

4. Jonathan Pollard, "Appeasement of Iraq Made Me a Spy," *Wall Street Journal,* Feb. 15, 1991.

5. Gerhard Paul, news conference, Hamburg, DPA, Feb. 5, 1991; *Stern* and *Der Spiegel,* Feb. 28, 1991.

6. Seth Carus and Joseph Bermudez, Jr., "Iraq's al-Hossein Missile Program," *Jane's Soviet Intelligence Review* (London), two-part series, May and June 1990. Production facilities: *Mideast Markets* (London), May 15, 1989.

7. I witnessed this particular scene during the Baghdad arms fair in May 1989.

8. Interview with Amer Rashid in Baghdad during the May 1989 arms fair.

9. Paul Von Wedel, "From the Gates of Babylon to the Gates of Hell," unpublished memoirs, p. 21.

10. Personal details about Kassim and Abdul Hussein Abbas: Claudio Gatti, "Armi a Saddam, la trama italiana," *Corriere della Sera,* Feb. 5, 1991.

11. "How Minister Helped British Firms to Arm Saddam's Soldiers," *Sunday Times* (London), Dec. 2, 1990, describes the Bonn meeting in detail; see also *Financial Times,* Sept. 8 and 11, 1990, and *The Observer,* Mar. 18, 1990.

12. *Der Spiegel,* Aug. 20, 1990.

13. Sworn affidavit filed by Moshe Tal in federal court, Oklahoma City, Sept. 5, 1990.

14. "Nuclear Non-Proliferation and U.S. National Security," Hearings before the Committee on Governmental Affairs, United States Senate, Feb. 25, 1987; p. 57.

15. Statement by Senator John McCain, "National Security Implications of Missile Proliferation," Hearings before the Committee on Foreign Relations, United States Senate, Oct. 31, 1989, p. 3.

16. "Saddam's Secret Arms Ring," BBC "Panorama," Sept. 3, 1990. Jane Corbin interviewed Peter Allen of Matrix Churchill, who denied the machines were shipped to Saad 16, claiming that they went to Huteen (another weapons plant) instead.

17. Alan Friedman and Richard Donkin, "Payments by UK Company Linked to Iraqi Arms Network," *Financial Times,* Mar. 25, 1991.

18. Barbouti was the intermediary who arranged for German companies to build Libya's chemical weapons factory in Rabta. Josef Gedopt was arrested by the Belgian authorities in January 1989 for his involvement in the Rabta scheme.

15. The Race for Armageddon

1. "The Trail of Secrets That Gave Saddam Deadly Power," *Sunday Times* (London), Dec. 16, 1990. I have drawn heavily on this "Insight" report and on subsequent German press reports for the Stemmler story.

2. "How Minister Helped British Firms to Arm Saddam's Soldiers," *Sunday Times* (London), Dec. 2, 1990. See the appendix for tables of trade statistics.

3. Kenneth Cline, "Lavoro Bank Scandal: The Inside Story," *Southern Banker,* June 1990.

4. Seth Carus and Joseph Bermudez, "Iraq's al-Hossein Missile Program," *Jane's Soviet Intelligence Review,* May 1990.

5. "Ballistic Missile Proliferation Potential of Non-major Military Powers," Congressional Research Service Report (Washington, D.C., Aug. 6, 1987).

6. *Mednews,* May 8, 1989.

7. *Dallas Morning News,* Sept. 16, 1990. See also Michael Saunders, *Florida Sun-Sentinel,* Sept. 23 and Oct. 3, 1990.

8. *Baghdad Observer,* Feb. 13, 1989.

9. Titus Habian's meeting in Baghdad is discussed in Herbert Langsner and Alan George: "And Tomorrow the Entire World," *Profil* (Vienna), May 8, 1989.

10. Bull explained his project in detail in a book he wrote with an American ballistics expert. Gerald Bull and Charles Murphy, *Paris Kanonen: The Paris Guns and Project HARP* (Bonn: Mittler, 1988), p. 231.

11. BNL's letter of credit number 88/3/3625, was paid to Creusot-Loire on Apr. 25, 1989; the Trebelan payment was finally cleared on June 16, 1989. See also Cruz Sierra, "The Thief of Baghdad Is Plundering the Gulf with Spanish Arms," *Cambo 16* (Madrid), Aug. 27, 1990.

12. "Who Killed Gerald Bull," "60 Minutes," Sept. 17, 1990.

13. Mednews, Nov. 12, 1990. See also "Chemical Weapons Use in Kurdistan: Iraq's Final Offensive," Staff Report to the Committee on Foreign Relations, United States Senate, Oct. 1988.

16. The Gang's All Here

1. Foreign Minister Genscher had not been to Baghdad since November 1987, but this trip was primarily an attempt to win the release of an alleged West German intelligence agent who had been arrested in Iraq. The agent, Iraqi-born businessman Nazar al-Khadhi, had helped negotiate the Samarra poison gas contracts for German companies and was

arrested not for spying but apparently on charges of bribery. Genscher pleaded his case directly with Saddam.

2. Hans Leyendecker and Richard Rickelmann, *Exporteure des Todes* (Göttingen: Steidl Verlag, 1990), p. 43.

3. Minutes of confidential report to an executive session of the German parliament, Aug. 21, 1990.

4. *New York Times,* June 15, July 17, 1991; *Newsweek,* July 8, 1991.

5. *Sunday Times* (London), Dec. 16, 1990.

6. Interview with Jack Kelly, Oct. 19, 1990, Washington, D.C.

7. Telex message dated Dec. 13, 1988, from Christopher Drogoul, BNL Atlanta, to Sadiq Taha and Subhi Frankool, Central Bank of Iraq, and to Raja Hassan Ali, director general, Ministry of Industry, Iraq.

8. Hearings before the Subcommittee on Seapower, Strategic and Critical Materials, Committee on Armed Services, U.S. House of Representatives, Feb. 22, 1989; Leonard S. Spector with Jacqueline R. Smith, *Nuclear Ambitions: The Spread of Nuclear Weapons 1989–1990* (Boulder, Colo.: Westview Press, 1990), pp. 191–92.

9. The Badush Dam was built within a few kilometers of another major dam across the Tigris and was intended solely as a power-generating station, prompting Pentagon analysts to suspect that it was being used for Iraq's clandestine uranium enrichment program.

10. Von Wedel, "From the Gates of Babylon to the Gates of Hell."

11. Times (London), Mar. 29, 1991.

12. A complete list of Iraqi arms factories and their Western suppliers can be found in the appendix.

13. Gayle Rivers, *The Specialist: The Personal Story of an Elite Specialist in Covert Operations* (London: Corgi Books, 1986), p. 280.

14. Sometimes the Iraqis made odd requests of Ambassador Courage. Once they asked him to blacklist a French newspaper reporter who had written "unfavorable" stories about Iraq during the war with Iran. Courage dutifully cabled the message to Foreign Minister Roland Dumas, but was nonplussed when the Iraqis invited the same reporter back to Baghdad a year later. Unwilling to risk offending his patrons, Courage gave orders to the embassy staff not to meet the reporter during his stay.

17. An Explosion at al-Hillah

1. When McKenzie finally handed down her indictment on February 28, 1991, it contained little new information and nothing that would have linked Drogoul to U.S. policy makers. Drogoul, Bardan, and an assistant, Amadeo Decarolis, were charged on 347 counts of conspiracy, mail fraud,

and wire fraud. Also charged were Yavuz Tezeller of Entrade, Sadik Taha, Raja Hassan Ali, Abdul Muneim Rashid, Safa Haboby, and the Rafidain Bank. McKenzie carefully avoided implicating Hussein Kamil and never mentioned the larger question of where the BNL money went.

2. A lightweight eighteen-kilometer version, the Sakr-18, was used by the CIA-supplied guerrillas in Afghanistan.

3. Bazoft's boasting is drawn from press accounts and interviews with three Western journalists who met Bazoft in Iraq after he had ventured down to al-Hillah.

4. Bazoft's "confession" was aired on Iraqi television on Oct. 31, 1989; the transcript is from *Foreign Broadcast Information Service: Near East and South Asia* (hereafter *FBIS*), Nov. 1, 1989.

5. *U.S.–Iraq Business Forum Bulletin*, May 1989, p. 2.

18. Pride Before the Fall

1. Pierre Salinger and Eric Laurent, *Guerre du Golfe: Le Dossier Secret* (Paris: Olivier Orban, 1991), p. 15. The full text of Saddam's speech appeared in *FBIS*, Feb. 27, 1990. Mubarak fired his defense minister, Abdelhalim Abu Ghazaleh, once the Helmy affair became public in the United States, to keep Washington from cutting off military aid to Egypt. Abu Ghazaleh orchestrated the smuggling of U.S. missile technology to Egypt for Condor II.

2. *International Herald Tribune,* Mar. 16, 1989.

3. Barrak was replaced as head of the Mukhabarat in 1989 by another Tikriti, Fadil Solfeej, who was in turn replaced by Saddam's second half-brother, Sabawi Ibrahim al-Tikriti, shortly after the invasion of Kuwait in August 1990.

4. Ramadan interview translated by *FBIS*, May 2, 1990.

5. William Safire, "Calling to Account," *New York Times*, Sept. 17, 1990.

6. R. Jeffrey Smith and Benjamin Weiser, "Commerce Dept. Urged Sale to Iraq," *Washington Post*, Sept. 13, 1990.

7. Testimony of Dr. Stephen Bryen before the Commerce, Consumer, and Monetary Affairs Subcommittee of the Committee on Government Operations, House of Representatives, Sept. 27, 1990.

8. Piva was interviewed on Rio de Janeiro Rede Globo Television, Sept. 6, 1990; the interview was translated by Joint Publications Research Service Report Supplement, *Nuclear Developments, Iraq: Nuclear and Missile Proliferation II* (Washington, D.C.: FBIS, 1990).

Epilogue: How to Prevent Another Iraq

1. Testimony by Gary Milhollin before the Commerce, Consumer, and Monetary Affairs Subcommittee of the Committee on Government Operations, House of Representatives, Sept. 27, 1990, *U.S. Government Controls on Sales to Iraq* (Washington, D.C., 1991), p. 49. Comments by Stephen Bryen are from the same hearing.

2. "Strengthening the Export Licensing System," a report by the Commerce, Consumer, and Monetary Affairs Subcommittee of the House Committee on Government Operations (Washington, D.C., July 1991).

Appendix

Figure 1: High-Technology Exports to Iraq 1984-1989 as Share of Total Exports (in millions of US dollars)

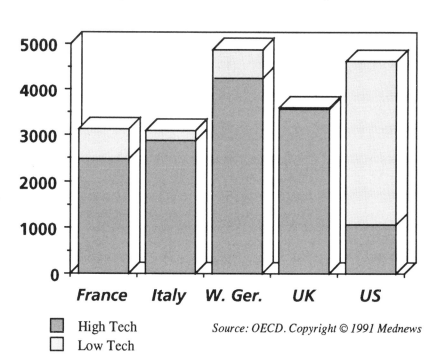

High Tech
Low Tech

Source: OECD. Copyright © 1991 Mednews

Figure 2. High-Tech Exports to Iraq by Category/Year (in millions of US dollars)

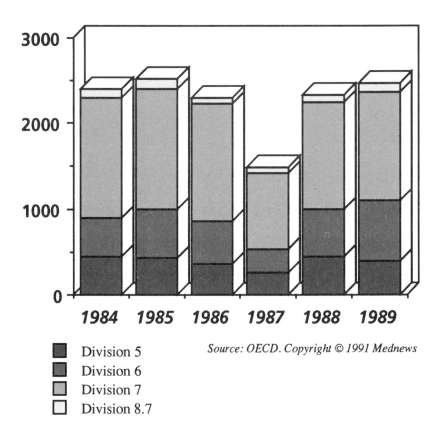

■ Division 5
■ Division 6
□ Division 7
□ Division 8.7

OECD Trade Categories

5	Chemicals and related products (includes most fertilizers and pesticides)
6	Manufactured goods (iron, steel, non-metallic minerals, non-ferrous metals)
7	Machinery and transport equipment (metalworking, telecommunications, electrical apparatus and parts; road vehicles)
8	Miscellaneous manufactured articles (including scientific instruments)
8.7	Controlling instruments

Figure 3. Breakdown of High-Tech Supplies by Country and Category (in millions of US dollars)

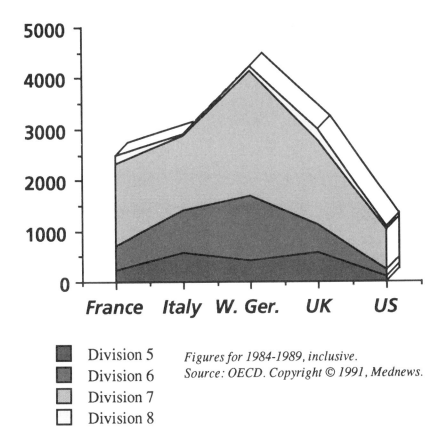

Division 5
Division 6
Division 7
Division 8

Figures for 1984-1989, inclusive.
Source: OECD. Copyright © 1991, Mednews.

Arms Sales to Iraq 1970-1990*

Weapons System	Type	Year	Qty.	Price	Country
AML 60/90	AFV	1970	128	N/A	France
Alouette III SA-316	Helicopter	1971	15	N/A	France
Gazelle SA-342	Helicopter	1974	40	N/A	France
Alouette III SA-316	Helicopter	1974	36	$18.8m	France
EE-9 Cascavel	AFV	1976	600	$250m	Brazil
Panhard M3	AFV	1976	123	N/A	France
Puma SA-330	Helicopter	1976	3	N/A	France
AS 11/AS 12	Missile sys	1976	N/A	$14.7m	France
HOT	Missile sys	1976	160	N/A	Fr./W.Ger.
AMX-10P	AFV	1977	110	N/A	France
Mirage F-1EQ2	Fighter	1977	36	$1.8b	France
Magic I	A/A missile	1977	N/A	Package	France
Sup Frelon SA-321	Helicopter	1977	14	"	France
Exocet AM-39	A/S missile	1977	35	$21m	France
Spare parts	Maintenance	1977	N/A	$400m	France
MiG 23/27	FGA	1978	138	$3b	USSR
SCUD B	S/S launcher	1978	6	Package	USSR
Ilyushin 76 Candid	Transport a/c	1978	16?	N/A	USSR
Mi8	Assault heli	1978	?	N/A	USSR
EE-11 Urutu	AFV	1979	200	$83.2m	Brazil
EE-9 Cascavel	AFV	1979	150	$100m	Brazil
Mirage F-1EQ4	Fighter	1979	24	$3b	France
R550 Magic	A/A missile	1979	N/A	Package	France
ERC-90 Sagaie	AFV	1979	400	"	France
Gazelle SA-342	Helicopter	1979	36	"	France
HOT	Missile sys	1979	360	"	Fr./W. Ger.
HOT	Missile sys	1979	144	"	Fr./W. Ger.
Milan	AT missile sy	1979	850	"	Fr./W. Ger.
AS-202 Bravo	Trainer a/c	1979	N/A	N/A	Switz
SA-6 Gainful	AD launcher	1979	52	$104m	USSR
SA-6 missile	AD missile	1979	520	$209m	USSR
AA-2 Atoll	A/A missile	1979	1,300	$36.3m	USSR
MiG-25	Fighter	1979	55	N/A	USSR
MiG-25R	Recce	1979	8	N/A	USSR
Artillery tubes		1980	600?	$1b	Egypt
MiG 21 spares	Fighter parts	1980	N/A	Package	Egypt
Mortars		1980	1,200	"	Egypt
T-55	Tank	1980	250	"	Egypt
Tank engines		1980	N/A	"	Egypt
Small arms/explosives		1980	N/A	"	Egypt
AT-3 Sagger	AT missile	1980	N/A	"	Egypt
Swingfire	AT missile	1980	N/A	"	Egypt
Shenyang F-6	Trainer	1980	40	"	Egypt/China
Saad 13 factory	Electronics	1980	N/A	$900m	France
Faun	Tank transp	1980	N/A	N/A	W. Ger.
T-59 (T-55E)/T-69	Tank	1980	1,300	$1b	China

* Compiled from public sources (SIPRI, DMS, IISS, Military Powers Encylopedia, etc). *Copyright © 1990-1991, Middle East Defense News/ Mednews.*

Weapons System	Type	Year	Qty.	Price	Country
T-72	Tank	1980	400	$840m	USSR
GHN-45	Howitzer	1981	200	N/A	Austria
Kurassier	Lt tank	1981	100	$230m	Austria
Roland 2	SA system	1981	113	$2.9b	Fr./W.Ger.
HOT	Missile sys	1981	200	Package	Fr./W.Ger.
Martel	A/S missile	1981	N/A	"	France
Magic II	A/A missile	1981	N/A	"	France
Panhard VCR	AFV	1981	100	"	France
Lupo-class	Frigate	1981	4	$2.6b	Italy
Assad-class	Corvette	1981	6	Package	Italy
Otomat	SS missile sys	1981	68	"	Italy
Albatross	SA missile sys	1981	10x4	"	Italy
T-54/55	Tank	1981	400	N/A	Poland
EE-3 Jaraca	AFV	1982	300	$125m	Brazil
EE-11 Urutu	AFV	1982	300	$125m	Brazil
155 mm GCT	SP howitzer	1982	83	$2.6b	France
Super R-530F	A/A missile	1982	N/A	Package	France
Exocet AM-39	A/S missile	1982	342	"	France
R-550 Magic II	A/A missile	1982	N/A	"	France
ERC 90	AFV	1982	200	"	France
M3	AFV	1982	200	"	France
HOT	Missile sys	1982	200	"	Fr./W.Ger.
Proximity fuze		1982	50,000	$15m	France
Type 531	AFV	1982	650	N/A	China
Hughes 500 C/D	Helicopter	1982	60	N/A	US
SA-8 Gecko	AD system	1982	36	$108m	USSR
SA-8 Gecko	AD missile	1982	432	$194m	USSR
SA-9 Gaskin	AD missile	1982	240	$96m	USSR
BRDM-2 Gaskin	AD system	1982	20+	$50.4m	USSR
SU-7 Fitter	FGA	1982	30	$180m	USSR
D-30 122mm	Artillery	1982	504	$146m	USSR
T-62	Tank	1982	300	$300m	USSR
AT-3 Sagger	AT missile	1982	1,000	$25m	USSR
Astros II	MLRS	1983	60	N/A	Brazil
MAS-1	A/A missile	1983	N/A	N/A	Brazil
T-55	Tank	1983	140	$1.5b	Egypt
Grad launchers	MRLS	1983	N/A	Package	Egypt
122mm rockets	Munitions	1983	100,000+	"	Egypt
Shenyang F-7	Fighter	1983	70	"	Egypt
RPG-7	AT rocket	1983	1,190	"	Egypt
EMB-312 Tucano	Trainer a/c	1983	40	$181m	Egy/Brazil
Mirage F-1EQ5	Fighter	1983	29	$1.5b	France
Armat	A/S missile	1983	200	Package	France
AS-30L	A/S missile	1983	20	"	France
Rasit	Ground radar	1983	42	"	France
Roland 2	AD missile	1983	300	"	Fr./W.Ger.
Super Etendard	FGA	1983	5	$500m	France
BO-105	Helicopter	1983	24	N/A	W. Ger.
Faun	Tank transp	1983	N/A	N/A	W. Ger.
G-5	Howitzer	1983	100	$520m	South Africa
PC-7	Trainer	1983	52	N/A	Switz
BM-21 122mm	MLRS	1983	200	$80m	USSR

Weapons System	Type	Year	Qty.	Price	Country
SS-1B SCUD	S/S missile	1983	350	$2b	USSR
Su-20/22 Fitter-C/D	FGA	1983	30	Package	USSR
Mi-24 Hind-C	Att/helicopter	1983	10	"	USSR
Mi-8 Hip	Assault heli	1983	30	"	USSR
MiG 21BIS	Fighter	1983	61	"	USSR
Tank transporters		1983	2,000+	"	USSR
Shenyang F-7	Fighter	1984	20	$500m+	Egypt
BM-21 launcher	MRLS	1984	200	Package	Egypt
Artillery munitions	1984	N/A	$100m	Egypt	
TRC-571 radio	Comm	1984	N/A	N/A	France
AB 212	AS helicopter	1984	8	$164m	Italy/US
PC-9	Trainer	1984	20	N/A	Switz
PC-6	Trainer	1984	2	N/A	Switz
Bell 214 ST	Transport heli	1984	48	N/A	US
T-55	Tank	1984	200	$4.5b	USSR
T-62	Tank	1984	300	Package	USSR
T-72	Tank	1984	600	"	USSR
PT-76	Amph.tank	1984	200	"	USSR
MiG 23BN/277	FGA	1984	50+	"	USSR
MiG 25	Fighter	1984	30	"	USSR
AA-6 Acrid	AA missile	1984	60	"	USSR
AA-7 Apex	AA missile	1984	300	"	USSR
AA-8 Aphid	AA missile	1984	500	"	USSR
AS-4 Kitchen8	A/S missile	1984	24	"	USSR
MiG 23 ML	Fighter	1984	20	"	USSR
MiG 23BN/27	FGA	1984	6?	"	USSR
Il-76	Trans/a/c	1984	19	"	USSR
SS12 Scaleboard??	S/S missile	1984	12?	"	USSR
AS-6 Kingfish	A/S missile	1984	36	"	USSR
EE-11 Urutu	AFV	1985	120	$50m	Brazil
Artillery munitions		1985	50m	$600m	Egypt
122 mm field guns	Artillery	1985	N/A	Package	Egypt
130 mm field guns		1985	N/A	"	Egypt
Mirage F-1 EQ5/6	FGA	1985	24	$1.5b	France
Magic 1	A/A missile	1985	N/A	Package	France
AM-39 Exocet	A/S missile	1985	96	"	France
Gazelle SA-342	AT heli	1985	7	"	France
CORAD	Radar	1985	2+	"	France
SDE-125 Manpack	Radios	1985	N/A	"	France
Thomson 2215/2230	3-D radar	1985		$100m	France
Troposcatter microwave comm sys		1985	N/A	N/A	GB
Jaguar freq. hopping	tactical radios	1985	N/A	N/A	GB
Munitions	Artillery	1986	50 M+	$600+m	Egypt
Sakr-30 (BM-21)	MLRS	1986	80	Package	Egypt
Thomson 2215/2230	3-D radar	1986	6	$100m	France
AM-39 Exocet	A/S missile	1986	260	$416m	France
AS-30L	A/S missile	1986	180	N/A	France
Brandt 120mm	Mortar	1986	N/A	$430m	France
SDE 699 Microwave	Comm	1986	N/A	N/A	France
MiG 29	Fighter	1986	60	$600m	USSR
Su-25 Frogfoot	FGA	1986	60	$1b	USSR
Mi-24 Hind-D	Assault heli	1986	N/A	$3b	USSR

Weapons System	Type	Year	Qty.	Price	Country
AA-8 Aphid	AA missile	1986	304	Package	USSR
AA-7 Apex	AA missile	1986	200	"	USSR
MiG 23 BN	FGA	1986	50	"	USSR
BM-21 122mm	Rocket lncher	1986	240	"	USSR
BTR-80	IFV	1986	800?	"	USSR
M-1974 122mm	Artillery	1986	N/A	"	USSR
T-62	Tank	1986	150	"	USSR
T-72	Tank	1986	150	"	USSR
T-74 (T-74M/T-80)	Tank	1986	?	"	USSR
SS-21 Scarab	SS launcher	1986	12	"	USSR
Su-24	FGA	1986	10	"	USSR
SCUD-B/EE-600	S/S missile	1987	200	N/A	Brazil
Astros II	MLRS	1987	200	N/A	Brazil
SAKR-80	MLRS/R&D	1987	N/A	N/A	Egypt
SA-6	S/A launcher	1987	40	$800m	Egypt
Sakr-30 (BM-21)	MLRS	1987	85	Package	Egypt
Gazelle	AT helicopter	1987	36	N/A	Egypt/France
Mirage F-1 EQ6	FGA	1987	20	$725m	France
AM-39 Exocet	A/S missile	1987	150?	$735m	France
AS-30L	A/S missile	1987	200?	Package	France
Magic II	A/A missile	1987	N/A	"	France
Armat (Bazar)	A/S missile	1987	700	"	France
Apilas	AT missile	1987	N/A	"	France
Tiger-G	AWACS radar	1987	10	"	France
HOT	AT missile	1987	N/A	"	Fr./W.Ger.
BO-105	Helicopter	1987	30	N/A	W. Ger.
Viper MK 22/9	A/c engine	1987	22	$4m	UK
Hawker Hunter	A/c spares	1987	N/A	$2m	UK
Al Hossein	S/S missile	1988	300	N/A	Brazil
Dauphin	Attack heli	1988	6	N/A	France
AS-15TT	Missile	1988	N/A	N/A	France
Super Puma	Helicopter	1988	6	N/A	France
Battlefield computer	Artllery	1988	2,000	$100m	France
Cymbeline mortar locating radar		1988	N/A	$1m	UK
Hovercraft engine	Spares	1988	N/A	$1m	UK
Tank engines	Spares	1988	N/A	$1.5m	UK
Encryption equip	Communication	1988	1,325	$11.5m	UK
Laser rangefinder	Surveillance	1988	N/A	$14m	UK
Transceivers	Communication	1988	N/A	$4.5m	UK
AS-14 Kedge	A/S missile	1988	120	N/A	USSR
Encryption equip	Communication	1989	8	$4m	UK
Multiplexers	Communication	1989	13	$60m	UK
Jaguar freq.hop	Radio	1989	13	$360,000	UK
Jaguar kits	Radio	1989	2,000	$48m	UK
Mapping computer	Surveillance	1989	N/A	N/A	US
Nav equipment	Avionics, spares	1989	N/A	$3m	US
BK-117	Helicopter	1989	12	N/A	W. Ger.
Avionics	Su-25	1990	N/A	$161m	France
Armored vehicle	VIP	1990	2	$3m	UK
Encryption equip	Communication	1990	50	$2m	UK
Cougar radio	Communication	1990	31	$3.4m	UK

UNITED STATES–IRAQ BUSINESS FORUM
MEMBERS, JULY 1990

A.M.E. International, Inc.
American Cast Iron Pipe Co.
American Iraqi Finance & Trade
American Rice, Inc.
Amoco Corporation
Anodyne, Inc.
Arabian National Shipping Corporation
Arthur Andersen & Company
AT&T
Baker Hughes Production Tools, Inc.
The Bank of New York
Bankers Trust Company
Bechtel Group, Inc.
Bell Helicopter-Textron
BMY
British Gas, Exploration & Production Division
British Petroleum
Brown & Root, Inc.
Caltex Petroleum Corporation
Caterpillar Inc.
Charles Percy & Associates
Chevron Corporation
Comet Rice, Inc.
Conoco, Inc.
Continental Grain Company
Crescent Construction Company
Crescent International Petroleum USA
Dantzler Lumber & Export Co., Inc.
Dearborn Financial, Inc.
Dresser Pump Division, Dresser Industries, Inc.
Entrade International Limited
Exxon Company, International
Fairbanks Management Corporation
Fentex International Corporation
First City Bancorporation of Texas, Inc.
Fisher Scientific
General Motors Corporation

The Gronel Company, Ltd.
Gulf Interstate Engineering Co.
Hunt Oil Company
International Resources Trading Corporation
Ionics, Incorporated
J. A. Jones Construction Co.
Jas. I. Miller Tobacco Co.
Lincoln-Kaltek Joint Venture
Lindner and Company
Lockheed Corporation
Luxor California Exports Corp.
Mathey International, Ltd.
Midgulf Industrial Consultants, Inc.
Mobil Oil Corporation
Morrison Knudsen Corporation
M. W. Kellogg Company
Niedermeyer-Martin Company
Norwich Eaton Pharmaceuticals Inc.
Obelisk Corporation
Occidental International Exploration & Production Co.
Ohra Corporation
Pepsicola International
Petrolite Corporation
Philip Morris International
Power Marketing Group, Inc.
Riedel International, Inc.
Servaas, Inc.
SMI/Sneed-McBride International, Inc.
Smith Meter Inc.
Tabikh Interests, Inc.
Teletec Corporation
Telwar International, Inc.
Texaco, Inc.
United Technologies Corporation
Unocal Corporation
Valmont Industries, Inc.
Westinghouse Electric Corporation
Woodhouse, Drake & Carey (Trading)
Xerox

Index